EUROPEAN STUDIES SERIES

Constructing Yugoslavia: A Transnational History

Vesna Drapac

Vesna Drapac provides an insightful survey of the changing nature of the Yugoslav ideal, demonstrating why Yugoslavism was championed at different times and by whom, and how it was constructed in the minds of outside observers. Covering the period from the 1850s to the death of Tito in 1980, Drapac situates Yugoslavia in the broader international context and examines its history within the more familiar story of Europe in the nineteenth and twentieth centuries.

This approachable study also explores key themes and debates, including:

- the place of the nation-state within the worldview of nineteenth-century intellectuals
- the memory of war and commemorative practices in the interwar years
- resistance and collaboration
- the nature of dictatorships
- gender and citizenship
- Yugoslavia's role from the perspective of the 'Superpowers'.

Drawing on a wide range of sources in order to re-create the atmosphere of the period, *Constructing Yugoslavia* traces the formation of popular perceptions of Yugoslavia and their impact on policy toward Yugoslavs. It is essential reading for anyone with an interest in the history of this fascinating nation, and its ultimate demise.

Vesna Drapac is Associate Professor of History at the University of Adelaide. Her previous publications include *War and Religion: Catholics in the Churches of Occupied Paris*.

EUROPEAN STUDIES SERIES

General Editors Colin Jones, Richard Overy, Joe Bergin, John Breuilly and Patricia Clavin

Published

Constructing Yugoslavia
A Transnational History

VESNA DRAPAC

First published 2010 by
PALGRAVE MACMILLAN

Palgrave Macmillan in the UK is an imprint of Macmillan Publishers Limited, registered in England, company number 785998, of Houndmills, Basingstoke, Hampshire RG21 6XS.

Palgrave Macmillan in the US is a division of St Martin's Press LLC, 175 Fifth Avenue, New York, NY 10010.

Palgrave Macmillan is the global academic imprint of the above companies and has companies and representatives throughout the world.

Palgrave® and Macmillan® are registered trademarks in the United States, the United Kingdom, Europe and other countries.

ISBN: 978–0–333–92554–6 hardback
ISBN: 978–0–333–92555–3 paperback

This book is printed on paper suitable for recycling and made from fully managed and sustained forest sources. Logging, pulping and manufacturing processes are expected to conform to the environmental regulations of the country of origin.

A catalogue record for this book is available from the British Library.

A catalog record for this book is available from the Library of Congress.

10 9 8 7 6 5 4 3 2 1
19 18 17 16 15 14 13 12 11 10

Printed and bound in Great Britain by
CPI Antony Rowe, Chippenham and Eastbourne

For my parents

Contents

Acknowledgements

I am grateful to the many people who assisted me with this book. A number of librarians and archivists have been very helpful. Margaret Hosking of the Barr Smith Library at the University of Adelaide enabled me to make the most of the extensive materials available in Adelaide and to access sources held elsewhere. I thank her for sharing her expertise, for her generosity and for her good cheer. When I was a postgraduate student at New College, Oxford working on an entirely different project, I became aware of Robert Seton-Watson's life and work. He had also been a student at New College and left his books and pamphlets to the library. My discovery of the bequest was accidental but I soon became familiar with it. Some years later, I returned to consult the collection and, much to my pleasure, the librarians gave me permission to work once more in the comfortable and familiar surroundings of New College Library. The late Christopher Seton-Watson kindly gave me permission to consult his father's papers in the School of Slavonic and East European Studies at the University of London. The staff of the library of the Museum of Mankind in London assisted me when I was working on (Mary) Edith Durham's papers held by the Royal Anthropological Institute. The library staff at the Croatian Academy of Sciences and Arts (Hrvatska akademija znanosti i umjetnosti) made a number of sources available to me on two visits to Zagreb and also helped me access recent publications on various topics.

A number of years ago I thought of writing a book on the place of the South Slavs in the imagination of nineteenth-century British and Western European travellers to the region. At the time, I was a tutor in History at the Flinders University of South Australia and the University awarded me my first grant to undertake preliminary research overseas on that subject. I have used material from that trip in Chapters 1 and 2. I thank all my friends and colleagues at Flinders University who were receptive to my ideas and so supportive.

On various occasions I presented papers on different aspects of the book and gained a great deal from the interest and response of those present. Mark Cornwall at the University of Southampton, John Horne at Trinity College, Dublin and Steven Welch at the University of Melbourne provided me with a congenial and stimulating environment in which to discuss my ideas. I am especially grateful to them.

Terka Acton was my first editor at Palgrave and she gave me invaluable advice in the early stages of research and writing. After her departure from Palgrave, Sonya Barker took over this project and I would like to thank her for her patience, her positive outlook and her advice, particularly over the past eighteen months. I am grateful to the two anonymous readers who gave incisive comments on a draft of the book. I have tried to incorporate many of their suggestions and I believe the book is better for that. I would also like to thank the series editors, especially John Breuilly and Patricia Clavin, who have given me extremely helpful feedback at different times. Thomas Buchanan, Robert Dare, Danijel Dzino, Christopher Pearson and Julie Thorpe also read and commented on versions of the book. Their insightful observations and their questions helped me to sharpen the book's focus. All errors are, of course, my own.

The Faculty of Humanities and Social Sciences at the University of Adelaide awarded me three grants that helped cover administrative costs and some travel expenses in the early stages of my research for the book. My colleagues in the Discipline of History have been very encouraging throughout. I feel lucky to be working with such a dynamic group of historians. As a student I had inspiring mentors, including Ric Zuckerman, who has shared his love of history with students in Adelaide for over thirty years and with whom I have convened a number of courses. The late Richard Cobb supervised my doctoral thesis. He taught me a great deal about history in general and about the Second World War in particular. He told me to be bold and insisted that I write a book about Yugoslavia; I have finally followed his advice.

Were it not for the unfaltering enthusiasm of my loving husband and intellectual companion, Brendan Moran, I would not have entertained the thought of writing such an ambitious book. He has helped me from beginning to end. He has read (and re-read) drafts of the book and listened patiently to the seemingly endless variations of the story of Yugoslavia's construction. When I thought the book as I had originally conceived it was impossible to write, Brendan encouraged me to continue with the project. I thank him for everything. Our two sons, Thomas and David, watched the writing process from close quarters and all along they have made funny and intelligent observations about the enterprise. Together with Brendan they have offered much needed and much appreciated companionship in the three different studies in which I wrote the book. I will always be grateful to them for that. Other members of my family, my mother and brother, Goran Drapac, in particular, have encouraged me throughout my career and I thank them for their constancy. Finally, I would like to acknowledge my mother and father, to thank them for their example and for awakening within me an enduring interest in Yugoslavia's history. The book is dedicated to them.

VESNA DRAPAC
University of Adelaide

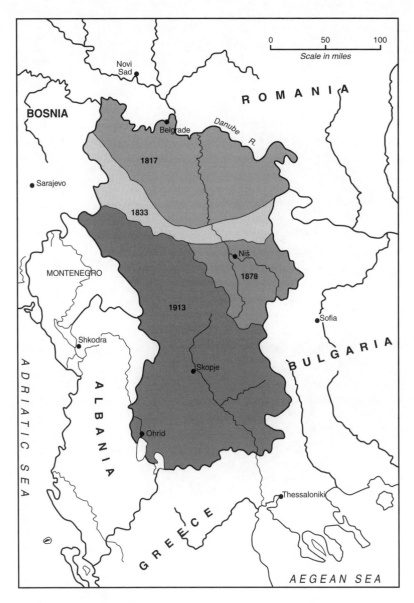

Map 1   The expansion of Serbia, 1817–1913. Adapted from Barbara
Jelavich, *History of the Balkans: The Eighteenth and Nineteenth Centuries*
(Cambridge University Press, 1983)

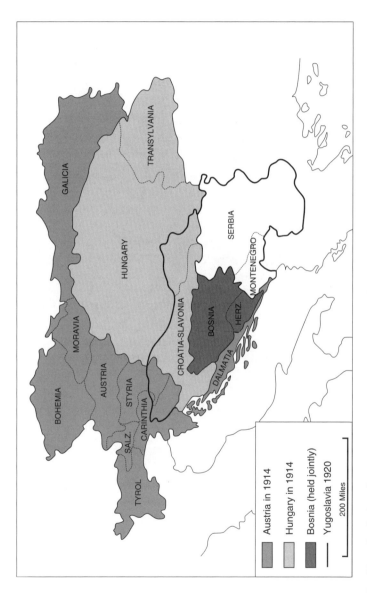

Map 2   Yugoslavia in relation to Austria–Hungary. Adapted from Leslie Benson, Yugoslavia: A Concise History, 2nd edition (Palgrave Macmillan, 2003)

GALICIA

TRANSYLVANIA

HUNGARY

SERBIA

BOHEMIA

MORAVIA

AUSTRIA

STYRIA

CARINTHIA

SALZ

TYROL

CROATIA-SLAVONIA

BOSNIA

HERZ.

MONTENEGRO

DALMATIA

Austria in 1914

Hungary in 1914

Bosnia (held jointly)

Yugoslavia 1920

200 Miles

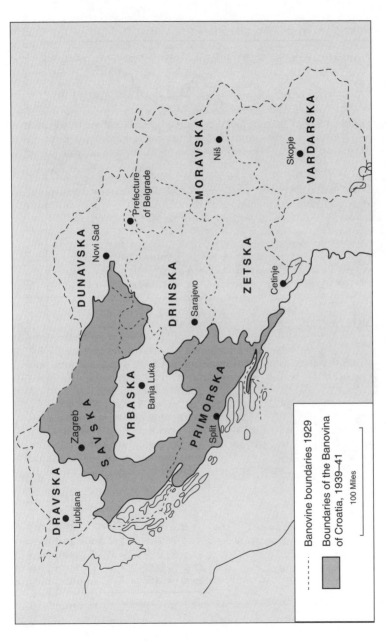

Map 3 The administrative boundaries of Yugoslavia, 1929–41. Adapted from Leslie Benson, Yugoslavia: A Concise History, 2nd edition (Palgrave Macmillan, 2003)

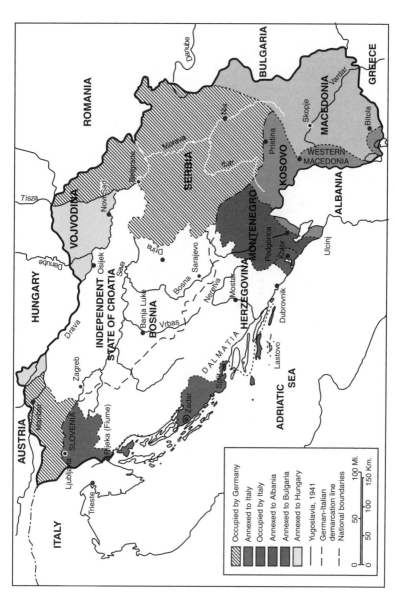

Map 4   The Partition of Yugoslavia, 1941. Adapted from Sabrina Petra Ramet, *The Three Yugoslavias* (Indiana University Press, 2006)

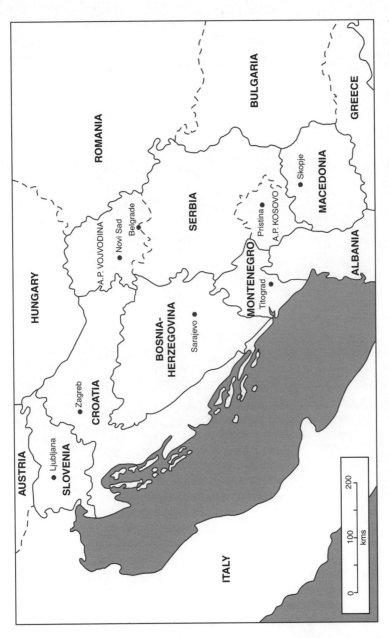

Map 5 Yugoslavia 1945–91: boundaries of the republics and of the autonomous provinces within Serbia. Adapted from Leslie Benson, *Yugoslavia: A Concise History*, 2nd edition (Palgrave Macmillan, 2003)

Introduction

Why This Book?

At the time of Yugoslavia's violent demise in the 1990s there was a considerable degree of bewilderment among many observers. They were shocked by the extent of the disaffection from a regime that they believed was largely benevolent and progressive and that had protected its inhabitants from the worst excesses of Soviet-style communism. Where there was not bewilderment there was recourse to essentialist arguments about the extreme nature of nationalism (or ethno-nationalism) among people on Europe's periphery who had never fully developed and who were driven by atavistic hatreds. These responses to the collapse of Yugoslavia are clearly inadequate and reveal much about the way in which the state had been created, sustained and mythologized throughout its life. A number of general histories of Yugoslavia have appeared since the 1990s and these cover key events, movements and personalities in the formation, development and demise of the state.[1] Almost all of this literature takes the Yugoslav nation-state as the basic unit of analysis and deals with Yugoslavia and Yugoslavs in isolation, historically and historiographically. This book complements and departs from the existing literature in important ways. Its premise is that the history of Yugoslavia is inherently transnational in the sense that it cannot be understood in isolation. It is about the construction of Yugoslavia and its contested nature. Its focus is on outsiders' intense interest in the South Slavs and in the perceived geopolitical significance of the South Slav state from beginning to end. Like other states that emerged from the collapse of empires in 1918, Yugoslavia was

1

a product of particular historical contingencies, but unlike them its actual form was profoundly shaped by what outsiders had imagined it should be from at least the second half of the nineteenth century. Many have suggested that Yugoslavia was an afterthought of the First World War, an artificial and premature creation. However, at the time and subsequently, most outsiders believed the very opposite, in the absolute inevitability, necessity and, eventually, the permanence of the Yugoslav state. They regarded it as the realization of the long-term aspirations of an integrated Yugoslav race and nation and the product of a national revolution. For the historians and writers to whom I refer in the course of this book, and others who exerted influence in international affairs, the nation was modern and, writes Glenda Sluga, the 'most important political form for social progress'. After 1918 new nations, 'built on the ruins of the Habsburg empire owed their form, if not their very existence, to American and British conceptions about the proper composition of a nation'.[2] According to John Allcock, the fact that 'states do not emerge in isolation, but intrinsically ... as components of a system of states', does not mean state-formation occurs 'in accordance with some kind of historical inner necessity'.[3] The nature of Yugoslavism was constructed and contingent but (paradoxically) many of its observers and supporters justified and proclaimed the 'historical inner necessity' of the Yugoslav state in its different guises. The purpose of the book is to explain this paradox and its centrality to the history of Yugoslavia.

Yugoslav studies have been steeped in a scholarly tradition that takes as a given the Yugoslav nation-state, while simultaneously accepting that a history of Yugoslavia constitutes a history of multiple peoples. The book does not attempt either to summarize or compete with this established literature. It is not a general history of key events and personalities. Nor is it a history of the Yugoslav peoples. Broadly, the book covers the period from the 1850s to the death of Tito in 1980. It seeks to identify the changing notions of Yugoslavism and the champions of this ideal over time, notably the outsiders without whom Yugoslavia could not have existed. It focuses on the way in which the country was understood by outsiders and on the influence of this international context on the establishment and development of the South Slav state. I tell the story of the construction of the idea of the state across its various permutations and explain the outsiders' interest and passion channelled into that idea during the period under consideration. Transnational history 'encourages making nations the subject of interrogation',[4] and the book interrogates the Yugoslav state and 'nation' at a fundamental level. Internal or national histories often reify the nation-state, making it the all-embracing unit of analysis and the main vehicle for understanding the lives and identities of the people within it. Often such histories take the nation-state as a preordained, desirable and long-awaited endpoint. They analyse people's political behaviour as either constructive or disruptive without recognizing the role of the state in the ongoing process of nation-building and in the formation of its citizens or, as we will see, its 'uncitizens'. This is especially evident in national and narrowly diplomatic histories of Yugoslavia that tend to generalize from the example and agency of minority political elites. The broader context I evoke in the book enables us to understand more fully why successive governments of the Yugoslav 'nation', said to be centuries old, could not establish a viable and inclusive Yugoslav identity, ethnic or civic.

During the wars of the 1990s and in their immediate aftermath, much of the work on Yugoslavia had, unsurprisingly, the collapse as its centre of focus. Among the specialists responsible for this body of literature were individuals who could not imagine a world in which the Yugoslavia they had studied and nurtured and to which they had attachments, personal and professional, might no longer exist. The disappearance of Yugoslavia would lead to the collapse of a subdiscipline, their very intellectual *raison d'être*, and Yugo-nostalgia often skewed their perspective. The term Yugo-nostalgia has been used variously (and often pejoratively) to describe an inability, or unwillingness, to come to terms with the passing of the communist state and the romanticization of its history. While its use can be loaded and reactions to it strident,[5] I believe the term is helpful. Applied to academic work, it relates to the failure to treat the idea of Yugoslavia and its history dispassionately and in a disinterested fashion. Heavy with regret and hindsight, Yugo-nostalgia has also influenced international policy towards the successor states and has hindered those trying to chart their newly independent countries through the challenging period of political, social and cultural transition.

The book is a lament neither at the country's passing nor for what could have been. More than anything else, it is an attempt to normalize the history of Yugoslavia, to view it not as aberrant but as rooted in the processes and general trends of nineteenth- and twentieth-century history, in particular, the exigencies of *Realpolitik* at a time of social and economic transformation. By normalizing its history I also mean rejecting the exceptionalist approach and instead applying to Yugoslavia terms and historiographical questions routinely applied to other European countries. Exceptionalism, the idea of the singularity or peculiarity of any national history (for example, Germany's apparent *Sonderweg*, or 'special path', leading to the Nazi dictatorship), depends on the problematical notion of the 'implied normality' of other national histories.[6] Any contemporary study of Yugoslavia should place it in a European context and discard dated notions about its 'atypical' development without denying aspects of its distinctiveness. I have tried to avoid some of the tendencies that lead to distortion in assessments of Yugoslavia's history, especially teleological interpretations which account for the country's disappearance as a predictable consequence of 'fatal flaws' evident at birth and resulting from (endemic) extreme nationalisms. While talk of the resurgence of primitive and savage tribal nationalisms in Europe's 'backyard' has subsided in some quarters, there is still a general sense that Yugoslavia's history cannot be treated alongside that of other European countries.[7] The book argues that the story of Yugoslavia is not a story about Europe's backyard but about Europe itself.

Placing Yugoslavia's history in a European context here means breaking down some of the boundaries between East and West and between Central Europe and the Balkans. Accordingly, Russia and the Soviet Union move in and out of view. Russia is important in the nineteenth century and at the time of the rapprochement with France and Britain prior to the First World War. The Soviet Union assumes a significant role as the Second World War draws to a close, in the late 1940s when Tito turns away from the Soviet sphere determined to maintain Yugoslavia's independence, during the Cold War, and as communism collapses. However, Europeanizing Yugoslav history and historiography in this book mostly involves focusing on the view from the West and applying Western historiographical trends and terms to Yugoslavia.

My Approach

Transnational studies involve different disciplines and a range of objectives. Sanjeev Khagram and Peggy Leggit have identified five 'intellectual foundations' of transnationalism: empirical, methodological, theoretical, philosophical and public.[8] As mentioned above,

I accept the 'philosophical' premise that the history of Yugoslavia is best understood as inherently transnational. The book is empirically transnational in that it identifies and describes transnational phenomena as well as 'the mechanics of transmission' of such phenomena. This is particularly important in explaining why certain ideas about Yugoslavia gained popular currency. I draw on some of the methodological and theoretical foundations of transnationalism as outlined by Khagram and Leggit, by taking the long view, by applying existing 'investigative approaches' in 'novel ways' or in unexpected locations and by providing complementary frameworks of analysis without attempting to replace one national master narrative with another. The book thus adds to the literature on Yugoslavia in a number of ways. It focuses on nineteenth-century perceptions of the South Slavs and on the discourse of travel writing which informed the creation of Yugoslavia and perceptions of it in the twentieth century. It takes key terms in the historiography of modern Europe and applies them to Yugoslavia. For example, Western historiography of the memory of war and the nature of collaboration and resistance are especially important in recasting and Europeanizing the history of the interwar period and the history of the Second World War in Yugoslavia. Gender is also a significant variable both in terms of the gendered understanding of the nation-state and the experience women brought to the construction of Yugoslavia. Finally, the disconnect between Yugoslavs' lived experience and the ideology surrounding them is one of the book's connecting strands.

The distinction between process (analysis of events) and policy (ideology or desired outcomes) is often blurred in histories of Yugoslavia. The convergence of process and policy is evident in much of the work under review in the book. According to Patricia Clavin, transnational history does not assume the equal influence of all 'mobile' ideas (nationalism, socialism or fascism, for example) or social and cultural policies and movements. As they cross, seep through or pass over borders these ideas are not of necessity equally transforming or equally transformed by exchanges, encounters and transfers.[9] Sometimes ideas were repelled, and this aspect of transnational history has often been underplayed. For example, globalization or globalizing influences are repeatedly explained teleologically and in a positive and progressive framework of interpretation.[10] This observation is especially pertinent as, directly or indirectly, many of our outsiders were also informing policy on

Yugoslavia. For example, the rejection by Croats of the homogenizing Yugoslav identity politics imposed from above and without
in the interwar years could only be described by partisan observers as reactionary or aberrant. As the preferred endpoint was the
existence of a strong and stable Yugoslav state, any forces construed
to be working against that outcome could not be deemed progressive or acceptable by international standards of the day. Problems
of interpretation arise when historical theories and methodologies
become vehicles for policy, as currently seems to be the case in the
reconstruction of relations among and between the nations once
comprising Yugoslavia and other former communist states. Some
describe the rules for entry to the European Union as 'barriers' to
the 'resumption' of transnational relations here: these rules act as
constraints as the once 'entangled' elements seek to establish new
partnerships with members of the elite Europe club. The attendant plea from contemporary (partial) historians to build on 'good'
and counter 'dark' or 'malign transnational actors' in the Balkans
mirrors almost exactly the stance of earlier generations of liberal
historians who hoped to promote 'good' and extinguish 'malign'
nationalisms in the region.[11] New textbooks, similarly, have as their
goal to present not history, but a worldview that promotes regional
cooperation.[12] As laudable as the latter goal may be, it conflates
process and policy and is not conducive to an open and detached
(academic) attitude towards the subject. Nor, indeed, was the stance
of promoters of Yugoslavia in the early twentieth century who had
argued so fervently that its creation constituted not the unification,
but reunification of a once whole nation.

Yugoslavia, chameleon-like, and more than any other of the successor states, became what outsiders willed it to be, from its foundation up until at least 1945, when they permitted and facilitated
the communist takeover under Tito. Western European outsiders
who were prominent in the construction (imaginary and actual) of
the Balkans made their views clear for the entire period considered. Their voices have determined the most constant themes in
this book. I deliberately privilege the outsider's voice over that of
the South Slavs, notably in the period up to the Second World War,
in order to balance out the very well-known story of the indigenous
'national revolution(s)', which for so long provided the foundation of
the creation narrative of the Yugoslav state. The Yugoslavs may seem
to be obscured and their agency undervalued in this approach, but I
have chosen to pursue this line nonetheless as a way of overcoming

what I perceive to be the impasse in traditional (generally political) national or internal histories of Yugoslavia. By viewing Yugoslavia as outsiders viewed it, and by embracing the Yugoslav cause (or the internal representatives of the cause) as they did, we gain an insight into aspects of the evolution of Yugoslavia that have not so far been woven closely into the fabric of its history. I show that while certain views about the Yugoslav state and nation prevailed, there were dissident voices within and without contesting the established orthodoxy. Right up until (at least) the death of Tito these voices were so discordant with the predominant international mindset about Yugoslavia that they were concealed or distorted. For example, it suited both the liberal historical tradition and, after that, communist historiography, to focus on the theme of national revolution and underplay outside influences in the creation of Yugoslavia because the latter highlights the constructed and contingent nature of its identity and state-formation and fundamentally questions its 'inner historical necessity'.

There is a tendency to treat the emergence of Yugoslavia as the norm for the South Slavs contained within its borders and events predating its establishment as leading to or blocking the path to that desirable and progressive endpoint. Philipp Ther shows that in the quest to establish master narratives, national historians have 'always synthesized and homogenized the multiple histories of one country' and write out of the master narrative (and at times identify as problematic and contentious) what does not fit or what does not support the general proposition or hypothesis of nation-formation as modernizing. He provides the example of historians of German culture of the period predating the emergence of nation-states who routinely ignore Habsburg German culture and that of Germans inhabiting lands in present-day Poland. Effectively their studies are incomplete and flawed.[13] The attendant problem of the national master narrative is that of contending with the fallacy of the ideal nation-state as culturally uniform (or potentially so) and progressive. Historians then have to account for the behaviour of 'anationals', those who do not assume the homogenized identity and contest it, or those who are excluded from the body politic for various reasons. Ther argues that it therefore makes more sense for historians of Central Europe to transcend borders than to choose the nation-state as the primary 'frame of analysis'. The history of Yugoslavia is often depicted as the history of people embracing or failing to embrace a fixed (that is, preferred) Yugoslav identity. In that interpretive framework it is also necessary to explain the failure of the homogenizing (thereby modernizing) process by discussing those who resisted, or even simply questioned it, in value-laden terms.

The book begins in the nineteenth century to present the necessary breadth of view of the ways in which the idea of Yugoslavia evolved transnationally. It takes as a formative premise that Yugoslavia came into existence and survived as long as it did because, as an entity, it fitted into the kind of system of states the international community was prepared to promote and then tolerate and support in Europe at that time. The point of view (especially in the first two chapters) is the place of an imagined South Slav land not merely in the musings, literary and cultural, of the pre-1914 generation, but in the strategic thinking of outsiders. The nineteenth-century intellectual foundation remains relevant throughout and provides continuity across all the chapters. Generally, works on Yugoslavia do not emphasize this early period in any detail other than from the point of view of the small group of South Slav propagandists within the territories of the future Yugoslavia or from the perspective of Serbian state interest.

I draw on the discourse of travel writing and literature elaborated most famously under the umbrella of 'Orientalism' by Edward Said but with particular reference to Maria Todorova's variation on this theme in her 1997 book, *Imagining the Balkans*.[11] Todorova describes how travellers, writers, historians, politicians and diplomats viewed the Balkans. She explains the manner in which these observers constructed the Balkans and how the peninsula, like the Far and Near East before it, came to signify a benchmark against which more highly developed Western and Central European countries might be favourably compared. Additionally, the Great Powers viewed the region and its inhabitants much as they might view any of their colonies, and while noting colourful and quaint local customs and partial or incomplete progress in some instances, overwhelmingly they declared the area backward and savage. However, at the same time, some of these peoples seemed to exhibit a 'manliness' and maturity, suggesting to the outsider that they were on the verge of nationhood and therefore capable of forming states resembling, albeit in a more primitive form, the established and progressive nation-states further west. The South Slavs made up one such 'nation'. On the brink of manhood and deserving attention for that reason, they nonetheless continued to be defined within the Balkanist paradigm.

The book focuses on the impact and memory of war on the foundational tenets of interwar and post-1945 Yugoslavia, but most notably for the period 1918–39. The abuse of the memory and history of the Second World War in populist nationalist propaganda in Serbia in the 1980s is well documented.[15] We know less about the impact of the First World War on state-formation and I attempt to redress the balance.[16] The historiography of the memory of war helps us to understand the failure of nation-building at pivotal moments, that is, in the aftermath of both world wars. This vast historiography, now commonly evoked in works on France, the United Kingdom and Germany, for example, may be usefully applied to Yugoslavia. The memory of war was divisive, and commemorative practices in the interwar period could not unite South Slavs.[17] Apart from the usual problems of post-war reconstruction, Yugoslavia had to contend with its newness as a state and the difficulty of 'coalescing' peoples who had quite different experiences of the war and who had fought on opposite sides. This was also the case in 1945. The effect of the layering of memories of both world wars was cumulative and influenced the way in which outsiders approached the state and its leaders.

In 1918 and 1945 members of the ascendant ruling elites believed their wartime experiences legitimized their position of power. These elites were also cavalier in their attitudes towards individual freedom and democratic processes. Internationally, self-interest and the search for stability and equilibrium were at the root of tolerance for and hypocrisy regarding violations of human and civic rights, violations which were integral to the state-building enterprise in both Yugoslavias. However, rather than concentrating on the internal dynamics of successive governments, parties, individual politicians and various administrations (covered elsewhere in more detail), I emphasize the broader context in which these abuses were able to continue unchecked through to the 1990s. There was a mismatch between the hopes placed in the state and what it became. I suggest that systematic disregard for political rights in the name of a strong overarching (centralist or federal) Yugoslav identity, not national extremism or 'chauvinism', was the main tributary to the collapse of the state in 1941 and in the late 1980s: inequalities were not a by-product of the governing systems of the two Yugoslavias but intrinsic to them. The memory of war impaired the South Slav state's capacity to cater for the multiple needs of all its peoples, especially as outsiders validated the actions of former allies and comrades-in-arms in their quest to retain the monopoly of power.

I have stated that the book departs from most studies in its emphasis on Yugoslavia's 'prehistory' in the transnational context. It is evident from the above that I believe that there is also a need for a reappraisal of the interwar period, which is often observed through the prism of the Second World War. The interwar years are crucial to our understanding of the period 1941–5 and of communist Yugoslavia because the histories of the two Yugoslavias are intertwined. This is clear from the continuities in the construction of Yugoslavia from abroad. For the best-selling author, Dubravka Ugrešić, 1945 was Yugoslavia's Year Zero. Her ahistorical reflections are reminiscent of a socialist primer in which the world begins with the defeat of fascism and with Yugoslav brothers and sisters building cities, roads, bridges and railways for a multinational and multicultural future. Eventually the 'Great Manipulators' destroyed harmony and tranquillity, depriving the 'citizens of Yugoslavia ... of their common fifty-year-long past'.[18] The motives and success of the alleged 'manipulators' make no sense without the broad historical sweep and without an integrated approach to the construction of Yugoslavia.

Considerations of gender also inform my argument. In this sense the book departs from the usual emphasis in Yugoslav studies on high politics, diplomacy, administrative structures, male elites and theoretical discussions of economics, political systems and nationalism. A gendered view of the nation (and by association, the nation-state) emerged in the nineteenth century. In the idealized nation men exhibited courage in the public defence of its borders, notably in war, while women privately sustained it in their role as mothers and nurturers.[19] This conception of the nation was intrinsic to the process of South Slav state-formation. It also underscored the dominant view of Yugoslavia as the Serbs' prize for their heroism and sacrifice in war. At the time of Yugoslavia's formation, historians and the kind of influential men to whom I refer were reaching the apex of their power as legitimizers of nation-building. They had come into their own as professionals at the high point of thinking on the nation-state as the ideal organizational unit.[20] Outsiders, instrumental in bringing to fruition the (minority) South Slavs' ideal of a sovereign state at the crucial moment(s), have been underemphasized in Yugoslav history. Individuals (or representative types) like Robert Seton-Watson (1879–1951) – academic, public intellectual and widely acclaimed expert on the New Europe – and the networks they formed, were the product of the intellectual milieu I describe here. Seton-Watson was the British voice of the Yugoslav cause. I use him as a barometer by which to gauge the popularity or otherwise of various and changing positions on the Yugoslav question in the first half of the book.[21] Just as the idea of Yugoslavia was not static but evolving, so does my approach evolve. By the conclusion of the book we have a transnational 'complementarity' of inside and outside voices, more or less in a state of equilibrium from the point of view of influence exerted.

My outlook has also been shaped by studies of the lived experience of women in the national and transnational setting. This is important, for example, when considering women who travelled (in various guises) to the region primarily for the period up to the publication of Rebecca West's *Black Lamb and Grey Falcon* in 1941. Through their vast endeavours in humanitarian work on the Balkan Front in the First World War British, American and British Dominion women provided transmission belts through which Allied policy and perceptions of the international situation moved easily and freely. In the wartime context these women were primary agents of nation- and state-building in the field, bringing as they did to the (often wretched) situation their own appreciation of civic and multi-ethnic nationhood in a 'united kingdom' or a commonwealth of nations. After the war, they carried home the memory of their extraordinary first-hand experiences and, generalizing from the particular, helped define the context in which war was commemorated internationally, which in turn affected the standing of Yugoslavia after 1918. While at times women's voices were in tune with those of their male co-nationals, at others they were not. The fortunes of one woman, (Mary) Edith Durham (1863–1944), allow for an alternative reading of public intellectual life in the interwar years and of the issues that determined policy towards Yugoslavia at that time. We learn from her example why some transnational forces overrode others. Durham, one of the most intrepid women travellers of her generation, had spent extended periods in the Balkans and recorded her observations in a number of books and articles.[22] Her at times idiosyncratic and unorthodox perceptions of politics in the new South Slav state left her ostracized and with little influence. Durham's career gives us an insight into the machinations in academic and diplomatic circles and the subtle and not so subtle ways in which opinion and policy were formed and applied. She articulated the views of a group of considerable importance numerically and politically within Yugoslavia and yet she counted for nothing. The focus on Durham makes the discussion on the interwar period more nuanced and less dependent on hackneyed debates about the capacity or otherwise of male elites within Yugoslavia to reach some kind of 'compromise' and invest the state with greater legitimacy. Durham also provides a fresh perspective and some respite from the usual emphasis on personality politics and party intrigues. We will see that all the prejudices and assumptions underpinning the writings of men like Seton-Watson, often reflecting the dominant Yugoslav voices from within, were projected onto Durham. Speculating on the reasons Durham's enemies invested so much energy into ostracizing and alienating her sheds light on reasons for the failure of Yugoslavia in the interwar years.

Transnational studies eschew exceptionalism and compare historical phenomena by 'transferring key terms used in one national context to another'.[23] In this regard the book sits squarely within the transnational mode of analysis. For example, the study of the Second World War in Yugoslavia in particular has suffered from historiographical insularity and the exceptionalist approach has dominated since the end of the war. The history of the period 1941–5 benefits from and readily lends itself to transnational analysis given the experience of the war was not quarantined by national borders, not even for the so-called neutrals. The relative isolation of modern Yugoslav historiography of the war and the dichotomous interpretation of resistance and collaboration, combined with historians' obsessive focus on the national question, have been the greatest barriers to our understanding of this period in Yugoslav history. Norman Davies has addressed the general problem of writing an integrated history of the Second World War in Europe, notably that of incorporating the Soviet Union fully into the established Western historiography of the war. His elaboration of the 'Allied Scheme of History' neatly sums up some of the glaring anomalies in studies of the war, especially the double standard involved in the depiction of the conflict as a Manichaean struggle between absolute Good and absolute Evil.[24] In many ways Davies's observations relate to the state of the historiography of the Yugoslavs' war and its impact over time on perceptions of Yugoslavia. This is evident in the treatment of women's wartime experiences in Yugoslavia.

Interestingly, the Second World War witnessed the greater engagement of women in resistance activity of all kinds in 'backward' Yugoslavia as compared to women in 'advanced' France, for example. While it could be argued we should look East to the Soviet women in combat as partisans or regular soldiers for a more appropriate comparison with the Yugoslav women's experience, especially that of the committed communist resisters, the choices were different for the latter, whose country had collapsed and was divided politically and administratively.[25] The narrow perspective of resistance as a primarily military activity has submerged the unique insight the experiences of women can offer social historians of the war. Susan Grayzel, who has worked extensively on women in the First World War, asks: 'What does it mean to fight when the home front becomes the front line?' She invites us to consider this question when defining the nature of total war. In modern wars the 'natural' (gendered) borders are overturned and there are more, and more diverse, active fronts in these conflagrations. Grayzel also identifies the challenge to the progressive-backward dichotomy with regard to women at war between 1914 and 1918: British women assumed support roles as members of the military; French women assumed such roles as civilians; and Russian women alone formed combatant units.[26] This background is important for going beyond the stereotypes of the Yugoslavs' behaviour in the Second World War. Women's experiences, whether in France, Yugoslavia or elsewhere, are important not simply for a study of resistance and dissent but for the insights they afford historians into collaboration and complicity and into all aspects of social life in the war. Overcoming national insularity is essential to the process of normalizing the Yugoslavs' experience of the war and of ending the impasse in the general historiography of the war identified by Davies and perpetuated by the 'Allied Scheme of History'.

My interpretation of Tito's Yugoslavia is in large part an antidote to the tendency to 'democratize' responsibility for the success of totalitarian and dictatorial regimes of the Left and Right. The general acceptance of the idea of 'participatory dictatorships' in communist Europe is linked to the view of ordinary people as the willing agents of the ruling ideologies in Fascist Italy and Nazi Germany. For example, it is common for historians to view women not as victims of National Socialism but as equal agents of Nazi ideology in the home and in their local communities. This is the case even when women had no power and were far from equals in the integrated National Socialist community, or *Volksgemeinschaft*. The findings of general studies of racism in daily life have contributed to this view, as have studies of denunciation. Historians of the instruments and agents of the terror, such as the Gestapo, began to conclude that denouncers and informers did much of the work of these agencies and that the system was therefore all but self-regulating.[27] Susan Pederson, discussing the recent emphasis in histories of gender on the alleged reciprocity in power relations in society, argues that it is a product of the shift from social and political to psychological modes of analysis, from the influence of Marx on historians to that of Freud and Foucault. The essential goal, which has 'haunted the new scholarship', is 'to demonstrate power's multivalent, complex, and even participatory character'.[28] The pendulum has swung too far. The impact of the terror and the power of structures such as the Gestapo and official agents of policy and control in Nazi Germany are now underemphasized. Studies of former communist states have followed a similar pattern. We need to be aware of the power the state had to control and shape citizenship and of its power to determine what political and social choices were available to people. Pedersen's work addresses the place of women as citizens but her concern may be generalized to take account of others, the voiceless and those not fully incorporated into the body politic.[29] This is the background to my critique of the 'consensus school', which posits that life under modern European dictatorships, including Tito's Yugoslavia, more or less went on as long as people's material needs were satisfied. The view that dictators were not challenged or deposed because they ruled with the 'consent' of the vast majority of the population is wanting in many respects. It fails to take account of the limited ethically tolerable options for dissent under a dictatorship and the wider social impact over time of indoctrination, surveillance, arbitrary policing methods and terror. The image of the 'participatory dictatorship' led to complacency on the part of outsiders and their recourse to the superficial assessment of dictatorship as acceptable to most Yugoslavs and as necessary for Yugoslavia's continued existence.

Throughout the period under review comparisons were made between people(s), and this was fundamental to the process of establishing ideal national 'types'. Todorova also discusses comparisons Balkan peoples made between themselves and the Ottomans, the Habsburgs and the West, and among themselves, borrowing the term 'nesting orientalisms' to describe how subgroups moved between the primary classifications she identifies.[30] The interwar construction of a new Croatian identity by outsiders and Yugoslavs attests to the importance of comparisons. Croats came to be categorized as irascible and problematic, first, because of the dissatisfaction of

Croat politicians with the centralist constitution, then because of
the Croats' apparent resilience in the face of the integral Yugoslav
nationalizing campaigns under the royal dictatorship established
in 1929. Their mere persistence as a discrete national unit was
seen as an anti-modernizing stance even in the atmosphere of
political repression, discrimination and police terror accompanying the royal dictatorship. Observers began to redefine Croatian
identity and compared it negatively with progressive Yugoslavism.
Ther suggests we should not ask how in mixed populations in the
eastern regions of the German Empire, for example, 'the Polish
national movement influenced the German one and vice versa' but,
rather, how they depended on each other and how their histories
were intertwined.[31] Similarly we should ask how the new Croatian
national stereotype related to its intertwining with the history of
twentieth-century Yugoslavia rather than trawl the past in search
of evidence proving an historic (or, as some were to put it, gen-
etic) Croatian predisposition towards ultranationalism. The resolution of the problems of national integration faced by the (ideal)
Yugoslav state depended on the identification, negative definition
and disappearance of its apparent rivals or enemies. Onlookers
observed internal grievances through the prism of the necessary
and preordained Yugoslav state and in the context of international
commitment to its permanence as a precondition for peace and stability. This background highlights the flaws in the approach that
starts from the position that the problem of perennial nationalist
obstructionism was the root of the state's troubles. It also alerts us
to the fact that transnational encounters were not necessarily progressive or cooperative[32] and that the state's governing elites made
Yugoslavia's malcontents.

The Sources

I draw on a range of writings that capture the essence of the discussions and debates taking place at various moments in Yugoslavia's
history. In particular I refer to the work of academics and other
prominent commentators on Yugoslav affairs who set the agenda
for discussion on key points and concepts such as the nature of
the Yugoslav 'race' and the geopolitical significance of the South
Slav state. I have gained insights from the vast magazine literature
as well as the memoirs and correspondence of commentators on

international affairs. I have used Yugoslav materials for background but I have not duplicated here what can be found elsewhere in the secondary literature by way of argument or evidence from Yugoslav sources, because the book has a different trajectory. All of the good general histories available in English draw on and synthesize Yugoslav sources and historiography but present few significant variations in argument or approach. Much of the material I use flowed from the pens of British observers, but French and American perspectives are also important at different points. Where there is an emphasis on the Anglophone viewpoint it is because of its breadth, importance, interest and representativeness.

The evidence available in the sources is so rich and voluminous that each of the book's chapters could have constituted a monograph. According to Jürgen Kocka, among the potential problems of transnational history are its range and span, which may make it seem 'merely speculative or feuilletonistic'.[33] However, Kocka also recognizes the real insights that can come from breadth and from asymmetrical comparisons. In a book like this, covering a period of over one hundred years and treating a range of themes rather than a series of events or political confrontations, it has been impossible to devote equal attention to everything important. I have been selective in the topics covered, the comparisons evoked and the sources used. I have sought novel perspectives on familiar and less familiar themes rather than attempted a comprehensive history. The sources allowed me to tell a story that complements and at times diverges from the more familiar tales of Balkan intrigue and disorder.

The Story Unfolds

There is a substantial literature on the evolution of the South Slav ideal and its early variants. While the emergence of native Yugoslavism is a fascinating story, for our purposes its complexities are largely secondary. What is important for us to recognize is that what came to pass in 1918, and then with the first constitution in 1921, could not have been predicted from the aspirations of the non-Serb proponents of Yugoslavism in the nineteenth century. In the 1830s Croatian writers, known as the Illyrians, projected the first Yugoslav ideal, which was a product of the period of romantic nationalism. Panslavism was another important variable, and these writers looked to their Slavonic brothers for inspiration. While the (largely Croatian) conception of an affinity between South Slavs attracted intellectuals and cultural figures, it did not engender a mass movement. It did not penetrate deep into local cultures or historical memory. Moreover, the first Croatian 'Yugoslavs' defined themselves in opposition to Austrian and Hungarian hegemony rather than in terms of a pre-existing and coherent South Slav 'race' or nationality. However, the South Slav ideal merged with the idea of the nation-state as the natural administrative, social and spiritual expression of a people's identity. Yugoslavism thus gained its national (or racial) pedigree and 'Yugoslavs' their rightful claim to statehood. Disaffection from the first Yugoslavia came quickly as the idea of Yugoslavia became indistinguishable from that of Great Serbia. How those first notions of the Yugoslav ideal, a loose federation of South Slavonic peoples, came to be disfigured in the course of the twentieth century to the point where Yugoslavia became a state purged or 'cleansed' of virtually all South Slavs and then vanished, is one of the themes of this book. I do not argue that there were three Yugoslavias, as does Sabrina Petra Ramet, but rather suggest that the idea of Yugoslavia had become so perverted by the 1990s that it did not seem odd to the likes of the Serb leader, Slobodan Milošević, or absurd to outsiders, to call the state of Serbs and Montenegrins 'Yugoslavia'.[34]

Chapter 1 establishes a number of the underlying premises of the book. I argue that we cannot understand developments in the Kingdom of Serbs, Croats and Slovenes without recognizing the long-term impact of the ideas about the Yugoslavs formalized in the nineteenth century and up to 1914. It is this emphasis on the early period which contributes to the debate concerning the inability of the first Yugoslav state to establish its legitimacy. What made the situation problematical was that the constructed Yugoslav 'race', as it was envisaged by outsiders, never fully embraced the existence of multiple South Slav histories. This accounts for the tone and dimension of wartime lobbying of outsiders in support of the successor state. It explains how outsiders came to believe that the establishment of a South Slav state would reunite a single race dispersed after a long separation, the product of foreign occupation and oppression, rather than bring together a group of distinct peoples in a single state for the first time. The nineteenth- and early twentieth-century context also explains the easy international acceptance of the notion of a Yugoslav national revolution in 1918. Chapter 1 provides evidence contradicting the view that Yugoslavia was hastily constructed,

while recognizing the contingent and negotiated nature of its formation over time. In Chapter 2 it becomes clear that the general reflections of our
nineteenth-century travellers and academics directly influenced
the promotion of a South Slav state during the First World War.
Without the gradual seeping of the earlier literature into common
currency there would not have been the receptivity to the intense
propaganda in its favour. At the same time the war threw up new
realities and what was once merely imagined became a 'necessary'
fixture on the map of Europe. Images of one's allies and enemies,
the destruction, tragedy and triumph, would mark indelibly the way
our outsiders thought about the war and the way in which countries interacted with each other in its aftermath. We will see that
in the state's foundational narrative the First World War figured
as the heroic event which spawned the Yugoslav state. The state's
creation was projected as the product both of the general will and
international recognition and acceptance of that will. The dismemberment of Austria-Hungary was not an aim of the war until late in
the piece but nor was there any desire among the Allies to retain
the Central European empire, let alone defend it. On the contrary,
its rapid disappearance suggests an indifference where there was
not outright hostility; it suggests too that the Yugoslav Kingdom was
far from rashly conceived. The pseudo-scientific talk of the dyna-
mism of the dominant races and Darwinian tropes about the inevitable triumph of the superior nations, grafted onto the post-war
landscape of loss, mourning and regret, made the prototype of the
Yugoslav state highly attractive. For the same reasons, that vision
was also difficult to sustain, and unsustainable over time. It was a
prototype built on falsehoods and upon which the great hopes for a
New Europe would founder.

Chapter 3 shows that many viewed the new South Slav state as a
mere extension of 'Gallant Serbia'. It was not that official rhetoric
denied the existence of the other nations; indeed the (cumbersome)
name of the state, the Kingdom of Serbs, Croats and Slovenes, highlighted that three 'tribes' were thought to form the Yugoslav race.
However, the racial discourse of the day held that all South Slavs
originated from Serbian stock, or had branched out from a single
and solid Serbian trunk. Thus the South Slavonic ideal, transformed
by the First World War, was superseded by another conception of
Yugoslavia which came to life as the highly centralized Kingdom.
Its constituent 'tribes' were submerged and dominated by the ruling

Serbian dynasty, the Karađorđevićs, as the Yugoslav state was now in search of its constituent race or nation. Now, too, there was a new set of variables to incorporate into the vision for a New Europe, not the least being the fact that a terrible war had been fought and won at great cost in order that 'enslaved' nations, including the so-called Yugoslav nation, might enjoy liberation. In the interwar years our outsiders were, at times, vexed by the fact that almost immediately it came into existence the new state's legitimacy was subject to interrogation, often by the very people who had preached the Yugoslav cause during the war. The possibility that they had miscalculated the extent of grass-roots attachment to the 'Yugoslav revolution' was incomprehensible and insupportable to men like Seton-Watson, even when they were critical of King Aleksandar's dictatorship.

In Chapter 4 we will see that the Yugoslavs' experience of war between 1941 and 1945 was brutal. We will also see that the only way to understand that experience is in the context of ideological confrontations in a total war of unprecedented dimensions, not within the framework of an exceptional Balkan bloodbath. Through a closer study of people's behaviour in the war we can continue to map the failings of the first Yugoslavia. It is true that Axis military successes and Allied strategic imperatives shaped the wartime situation; but Yugoslavs brought to the war experiences and memories that would inevitably have some bearing on their choices between 1941 and 1945. It is in the course of the Second World War that the Yugoslav voices begin to rise above those of their counterparts abroad. There are a number of reasons for this including, most importantly, the fact that during the war the Yugoslav ideal underwent another radical transformation: the federal version of Yugoslavism (preferred by the first generation of Croat Yugoslavists after 1918) started to edge out interwar understandings of the state as an extension of Serbia or as 'Serbia re-united'. This is one of the reasons why Tito, the Croat communist leader of the guerrilla resistance movement, the Partisans, won the support of the Allies. Like King Aleksandar, Tito was a hero and a loyal friend in a war that had to be fought and won whatever the cost. He would do as an almost-equal because he could be no worse than what had come before and because he had proven more effective in battle than his Serb counterparts, the Chetniks. The second Yugoslavia, like the first, was forged in war and this had a bearing on its capacity to fulfil its post-war promise.

No single communist leader outside the Soviet Union emerged from the war with the appeal and reputation of Tito. Stalin could not curb his ambition or intimidate him into submission. The new leadership's role in the war and the way the war was to be remembered and commemorated affected the standing of the Yugoslav state as had occurred after 1918. The communist ruling elite represented and monopolized the anti-fascist struggle and then defined itself in relation to a particular reading of wartime history. Chapter 5 argues that in this and other senses there was a strong strand of continuity between the two Yugoslavias. The international (generally long-distance) love affair with a version of the Yugoslav ideal continued and flourished. Tito eventually emerged as the favourite of the European Left. His split with Stalin, in 1948, triggering the Yugoslav's pledge to forge a new socialism, revealed to sympathetic outsiders that one could deviate from the Soviet path without betraying communist principles. Depending on their nation's wartime record, dissidents within Yugoslavia were perceived either as regrettable casualties in the pursuit of a modus vivendi in the new world order, or completely undeserving of attention. Another layer of memories of war settled upon those of the First World War. Commemorations of the anti-fascist struggle and the celebration of active resistance established the primary link between the new Yugoslavia and its international supporters. Because the state was in large part the product of the imperatives of war, the search for consensus was going to be as difficult as it had been in the Kingdom. Communist defectors themselves were to realize that once the partisan epic lost its allure, it was not possible to build a viable state purely on a socialist and materialist base or on filtered memories and the partial telling of the story of the struggle against a foreign enemy and local collaborators.

As the generation that was defined by a certain reading of anti-fascism was passing, the wartime memories and myths no longer sufficed to nourish the state. At first the conflation of the person of Tito, anti-fascism, dictatorship and Yugoslavism made the obligation to contain opposition that more urgent. We will note also important continuities between the Kingdom and communist Yugoslavia, both from the perspective of internal politics and outside perceptions. The difference after 1945 was that there was the experience of the old Yugoslavia, which was universally seen to have failed, to draw on. While the idea that Yugoslavs constituted an integrated race was no longer plausible, most people still thought of them as very closely related, indeed barely distinguishable, as the official use of the hybridized 'Serbo-Croat' language inside and out testifies. It became increasingly apparent that the triumph of Yugoslav communism was a triumph of hypocrisy and corruption. For all the talk of the special and more liberal Yugoslav socialist path, in essence the regime was just like any other communist regime. As always, the contrast between the rhetoric and the reality of life under the one party dictatorship was striking. After Tito's death in 1980, attempts at preserving the integrity of the state, and international yearnings for what some still imagined 'might have been', were futile in the face of mounting Serbian nationalism, and in the international context of Mikhail Gorbachev's policy of *glasnost* and *perestroika* (openness and restructuring). The explosion of politics accompanying the Polish Revolution and the fall of the Berlin Wall in 1989 was too much for the Yugoslav state to bear, but outsiders did not recognize this and through the first stages of the collapse continued, incredibly it seems now, their vigorous defence of the 'necessary' Yugoslav state. It was not until the world became aware of the tragic proportions of 'ethnic cleansing' and the genocide committed by Bosnian Serbs, most dramatically at Srebrenica in 1995, that the majority view of outsiders regarding the Yugoslav ideal changed definitively. Fewer and fewer people believed that Yugoslavia remained a necessity and thus fewer and fewer believed in its viability. There was less international tolerance for the abuse of human rights on the Continent and the beginning of the recognition that Yugoslavia never was and never could have been what others had imagined or wished it to be. Finally, when transnational forces no longer had the same interest in preserving the state and when it was plain that there was nothing holding the imagined South Slav family together, they abandoned it.

1 Imagining Savage Europe and Inventing Yugoslavia: 1850–1914

Work on the Construction Begins

The following quotation from *The Living Races of Mankind*, a lavishly produced and illustrated account of 'the customs, habits, pursuits, feasts and ceremonies of the races of mankind throughout the world', gives us a sense of the stereotypes about South Slavs that had entered the popular imagination through widely read ethnographic and travel literature by the early twentieth century.

> The Servians [*sic*] are a physical stalwart race. They are hospitable, energetic, and brave. Though proud, quick-tempered, and apt to fight on comparatively slight occasion, they are fond of social intercourse, and cling to old customs and old beliefs. ... The Servians are thoroughly democratic in their institutions; each family owns the ground it tills, so that in the country day-labourers are scarce. Few will consent to become household servants, and cooks and men-servants come mainly from Croatia or Hungary. ... The Servians are an eminently pious race. The fasts of the Church are rigidly observed, and the peasant never fails in the morning to invoke a blessing on the coming day.... The Croats are a branch of the Slav race and are closely akin to the Servians. They differ in being Roman Catholics and in using the Latin alphabet. ... [They] hav[e] for their physical characteristics black or very dark brown hair, and greyish or blue eyes, with a countenance suggestive of cruelty and suspicion. They are lazy and

intemperate, but good-humoured and hospitable. Their women, who do most of the work, are both ignorant and superstitious, and do not rank high in the scale of civilization.[1]

This is a fitting introduction to our discussion of perceptions of races and nations prior to the formation of the South Slav state. We will see that the construction of this state was possible because of the convergence of a particular understanding of the relationship between nations, states and races and the interests of Great Powers. This chapter traces the emergence and significance of racial stereotypes and of the attitude that the establishment of a South Slav state was as natural as it was necessary. We will observe the way in which a South Slav nation and race was imagined and described in the writings of (predominantly British) observers of the Balkans and the peoples of the Habsburg Empire, and note that these writings projected the contours of the future Yugoslavia earlier than is ordinarily thought to have been the case. Todorova, discussing the impact of the international situation on Balkan history, observes that 'the size, shape, stages of growth, even the very existence of the different Balkan states were almost exclusively regulated by great power considerations following the rules of the balance-of-power game', claims to historic state rights and calls for self-determination among various peoples notwithstanding.[2] It is not my intention to argue that the South Slavs were but pawns in the hands of the Great Powers that merely pursued their own interests. However, the ambitions of South Slavs themselves were neither coherent nor were they generally compatible. In the last decades of the nineteenth century through to the Second World War, outsiders exerted substantial influence in creating and maintaining the Yugoslav state and sought out the indigenous groups and individuals whose views chimed with their own. It is for this reason that the story of the construction of Yugoslavia begins first with the view from without and above.

Discussions about South Slav unity (as opposed to the independence of, for example, the Serbs or Montenegrins) were Croatian in origin. Ljudevit Gaj (1809–72), romantic poet, writer and publicist, was a leading proponent of the Illyrian movement. Initially its aspirations were to promote the Croatian literary language and reinforce Croatian cultural identity within the multinational Habsburg Empire. Illyrianism, influenced by Panslavism, also sought greater understanding between South Slavs on cultural and linguistic grounds. The Croatian liberal Bishop of Djakovo, Josip Juraj Strossmayer

(1815–1905), whose argument against Papal Infallibility at the First Vatican Council (1869–70) secured his international reputation, became one of the South Slav ideal's most illustrious advocates. He was known as a founding father of Yugoslavism and twentieth-century Yugoslavists often projected back onto Strossmayer their own views about the state. How the romantic ideas and aspirations of the nineteenth-century Croat Yugoslavists were to be acted upon was eventually determined by the place of the South Slav question within the constellation of the Great Powers' colonial interests and their geopolitical objectives and rivalries. This does not, as I have already intimated, deny the agency of South Slavs. Rather, it recognizes first, that the interests of the Great Powers and relations between them did not remain fixed, and second, that these interests influenced politics and state-building on the Continent.

The cultural, at times idiosyncratic or emotive, aspect of international politics and diplomacy remains under-explored and undervalued in so far as it affected policy. In the case of Yugoslavia we will see that it is an area full of interest and significance. Andrew Hammond, drawing on travel writing, and the 'representation and power' contained within it, suggests that Britain did not seek to dominate the Balkans by traditional methods, as it might seek to dominate a colonial possession or colonial interest outside Europe. However, the region's primary utility lay in its capacity to be manipulated to the end that the accepted order be maintained to Britain's advantage.[3] Todorova, while recognizing that 'there was always a plurality of British sympathies in the East', states that the 'correlation between the tone of the majority of British travelers' accounts and the main trends in foreign policy is clearly discernible'.[4] A number of my conclusions are consistent with these observations.

There is an argument that the majority of Entente politicians and activists deemed a South Slav state acceptable and desirable only when the outcome of the First World War was no longer in doubt, and only with a certain regret or resignation at the passing of the Dual Monarchy. The evidence at hand suggests a different interpretation. The image of the West as blissfully ignorant on matters relating to Central and Eastern Europe – in Britain's case said to be partly a product of isolationist foreign policy – is also misleading. There were many articulate commentators on the lands where 'East meets West' who wrote of the importance of these territories for the continued balance of power in Europe. Perhaps the British 'experts' on Southern Europe and the Balkans visiting the region in the course of their careers as academics, journalists and anthropologists were less numerous than the 'orientalists' or classicists. They were also less numerous than those who studied European countries closer to hand. There was, however, an important body of literature that influenced perceptions of the Habsburg and the Balkan South Slavs and which in turn laid the foundation for the formation of the Kingdom of Serbs, Croats and Slovenes.

The publications of travellers to the region reveal some of the formative processes in the development of perceptions of the Balkans. These works continued in the tradition of eighteenth-century travel writing with waverings between late Enlightenment and pre-Romantic views of primitivism, 'otherness' and noble savagery.[5] The writings to which I refer, however, deviated from earlier examples of the genre in that they more clearly situated their subjects in an international political context. Travellers to the Balkans in the late nineteenth century expanded on the notion of the Grand Tour and were, on the whole, more intrepid than those Victorians and Edwardians evoked in John Pemble's book, *The Mediterranean Passion*.[6] Our travellers were venturing into country, as they said, 'untouched by Macadam'.[7] Some of the routes they took were reasonably well traversed, for example the eastern shores of the Adriatic, which had also been a popular summer destination for Habsburg elites. The English architect and designer, Robert Adam (1728–92), found his way to the palace of the Emperor Diocletian in Split and, in a sumptuous book produced in 1764, skilfully depicted the way in which the very fabric of the lived city bore witness to its ancient past. Other routes, like those through Montenegro, Albania, Bosnia-Herzegovina, Serbia, Macedonia and Bulgaria were more exotic and revealed the blending of cultures in what was known as 'Turkey in Europe'. In many respects, these lands were considered semi-barbarous, not surprising given the classicists' traditional understanding of the less than civilized status of this region. It was, after all, the first stop in Harry de Windt's 1907 tour of 'Savage Europe', which extended into the heart of Russia.[8] On the eve of war, in 1913, the observation that the Near East began at Vienna was representative of the perspective of many western European, British and American travellers and indicative of a view elaborated over the preceding 60 years. It suggests that the Balkans comprised a potentially assimilable, but as yet 'unfinished', body of nations.[9]

Georgina Mary Muir Mackenzie (later Lady Sebright, 1833–74) and Adeline Paulina Irby (1831–1911) were among the women travellers who are as interesting for the lives they led as for the writings that are their legacy.[10] Mackenzie and Irby wrote articles and pamphlets as well as the substantial book, *The Turks, the Greeks and the Slavons. Travels in the Slavonic Provinces of Turkey-in-Europe*, parts of which appeared in different formats and under different titles between 1861 and 1877. Gladstone wrote the preface to the 1877 edition published after Mackenzie's death. The women said they were motivated to write the book to provide English readers with basic information, but most of all they sought to bring 'moral enlightenment' to the places they visited.[11] The subjects of the writings of these benevolent improvers are appreciated less for what they are than for what they might become. So, on the death of her collaborator, Irby, known as a 'Serbian patriot', continued their work promoting the Christian education of Bosnian Serb girls and then of refugees fleeing the disturbances against the Ottomans in 1876. Mackenzie and Irby's published works were expanded upon by others, most of whom tended to refer to their predecessors' writings as a matter of course.[12] There are overlaps in the cultural, social and historical themes within nineteenth-century narratives on the South Slavs, but one can trace a shift in perspective from about the 1850s and an intensification of focus on the promotion of independent Balkan states from the 1870s and 1880s. This is indicative of what we might call a process of *embourgeoisement*. There is a shift in the writings away from the formerly (aristocratic) preference for support for the Ottomans to the modernizers' and liberals' concern for national movements among Christian peoples and disdain for the perceived decadence, backwardness and corruption of Ottoman rule. As we will see, this change also coincided with the election of Gladstone as prime minister in 1880 and possibly reflected his interest in the Eastern Question as well as Home Rule.

We must recognize that not all Balkan peoples or South Slavs were treated as one and that there was a hierarchy among and between them. They compared themselves with each other, with western European countries and with the Ottomans. Todorova and Vesna Goldsworthy have stressed the extent of the penetration into popular and academic culture of the images and stereotypes abounding in writing in Britain and elsewhere about the obscure, often derisive, Balkan types, Goldsworthy's 'Ruritanians'.[13] These stereotypes varied, evoking the primitive, the heroic, the humorous and the disdainful. Goldsworthy's focus is English literature and especially popular literature, which was marked by a proliferation of Balkan or Central European characters and settings from the late 1800s to the mid-twentieth century. Todorova's work draws on a range of writings about different Balkan peoples, notably the Bulgars. She charts the processes whereby the shadowy and little known Balkans and the diverse peoples of the peninsula were first described and then 'classified'. They were classified according to seemingly objective standards of development or progress and according to degrees or levels of civilization and the cultural and racial hierarchies so popular in the late nineteenth century. As we have seen, Todorova argues that these hierarchies were not based on a universally applicable standard, but on the narrow experiences and prejudices of the 'classifiers' who had drawn their conclusions from an often partial literature. She writes about a shift in attitude in outsiders' works in the course of the nineteenth century from one of 'benign arrogance' to a fixation on the savage or barbarous Balkans, which was born out of racial and cultural stereotyping, among other factors.[14] The label 'savage', however, did not apply to everyone equally, and the zeal of the eventual British attachment to the cause of the Bulgars shows clearly that a number of variables affected the evolution of stereotypes, positive and negative.

The Last Hurrah of British Turcophilism

The policy of supporting the Ottomans against encroachments on their sphere of influence by other Great Powers, notably Austria and Russia, remained one of the cornerstones of British foreign policy and of the Eastern Question for a large part of the nineteenth century. The rationale for this position (the balance of power in Europe) did not change, but by the end of the century a reversal was evident, with Britain's virtual abandonment of the Ottomans and its rapprochement with France in 1904 and Russia in 1907. The goal was to block the aggrandizing aspirations of the Habsburgs and Germany, deemed the greatest threats to equilibrium on the Continent and beyond. Before that, it was Russia, with its seemingly constant attacks on the Ottomans since the eighteenth century, that caused concern in Britain. The Crimean War (1853–6) and the Russo-Turkish War of 1877–8 confirmed the seriousness of the intentions of Russian expansionists. At the same time, it was thought Russian Panslavism would inspire national and revolutionary movements across a large geographical area. The task of calculating the risk of Russia increasing its territory, westward or eastward or in both directions, engaged many outside observers of Balkan affairs and was a major preoccupation of British politicians and the Foreign Office. Eventually however, the administrative weaknesses of the Ottomans, and their failure to modernize and reform, resulted in their gradual retreat from Europe, necessitating a reconfiguration of the old alliances.

The Eastern Question, how it was perceived in all its stages, and the diplomatic problems it posed, shaped the literature about Balkan nationalities and South Slavs. This literature was read and discussed by politicians, academics, lobbyists and humanitarians. The relative strength of Austria-Hungary, the Ottomans, Russia, Germany and, inevitably, Britain, had a bearing on responses to the Eastern Question. Writings on the various South Slavs (whether they enjoyed independence or autonomy, as did the Serbs and Montenegrins, or whether they were inhabitants of the lands held by the Dual Monarchy or the Ottomans) broached economic, strategic and military concerns, the eventual rivalry between Russia and Austria in the Balkans being especially important. This rivalry, and Britain's underlying concern for its own commercial interests, notably its preoccupation with a clear passage through the Mediterranean and its reluctance to see Russia encroaching too closely on the region around Constantinople, had been at the root of continued British support for the Ottomans. Their social and political 'backwardness' was no more offensive to British Turcophiles than Russian autocracy. Regardless of the outcome of the Crimean War, many continued to fear that Russia still aspired to fill the void, should the Ottomans withdraw from the Balkans, and fuel Panslavism on the peninsula.[15] This fear was particularly prevalent in Britain, where economic progress depended on unimpeded access to India and other eastern trading partners. Access to India was a recurring and underlying theme in British appraisals of Great Power interests in the Balkans for many years after the Crimean War. Our travellers also took a certain comfort from the thought that the Ottoman presence served to block the aggrandizing tendencies of both Russia and Austria. However, in the last decades of the nineteenth century the idea of bolstering the Ottomans to Russia's, or even Austria's, disadvantage began to lose credibility.

A growing number of commentators, often moved by a sense of justice or liberal high-mindedness, or both, sympathized with the 'little nations' described as oppressed by 'the Turk'. These nations had 'pluck' and seemed to be reaching 'maturation', indicating they had the capacity for progress and reform. Championing the independence of these nations would become the British strategy for ensuring stability in an area of potential and actual rivalry among the Great Powers. The revolts and altercations involving the Montenegrin (1853), Bosnian and Herzegovinian (1875) and Bulgarian (1876) Christians and the Ottomans sharpened the focus of the debate about the latter's status. It was the Bulgarian Atrocities (March 1876), that is, the killing of some 12,000–15,000 Bulgars by the Turks (as punishment for their uprising), and official British indifference (in particular that of the Prime Minister, Disraeli) to the massacre, that truly mobilized a large number of British observers on the perceived plight of Christian Slavs under 'the yoke of Turkish rule'. This mobilization marked the first signs of the general collapse of Turcophilism in Britain. In some circles the once widely held view persisted that as the Ottoman presence had become a fact of life in Europe, the Turkish influence, culturally and administratively, was benign, even on occasion advantageous for those privileged indigenes who may have been selected for a life in the Empire's administrative structures. In one 1875 account, for example, we read that over time a significant number of Slavonic Muslim converts had risen to assume high positions in the Ottomans' administration, which was not centralized and which allowed for a relative degree of regional autonomy.[16] The Ottomans also exhibited a tolerance for Christian institutions. Their *millet* system (though in decline by this stage) had allowed for a measure of local self-government and independence along national (in effect, religious) lines, accepting as it was of the continued activity of the autocephalous Orthodox churches. The Serbian Church, for example, gained from this state of affairs and continued to exert influence in the region. However, the number of British observers subscribing to this interpretation of a benign Ottoman presence began to drop significantly in the 1870s.

Russia's rehabilitation, in the minds of British observers, resulted in part from the recognition that even if it had been instrumental in the Balkan Slavs' bid for independence, Russian influence did not persist once a degree of autonomy had been attained. Writers offered a number of explanations for Russia's 'arm's-length' attitude, including the nature of the Orthodox Churches, which were quasi-national institutions, and the robustness of the Balkan national movements themselves. In addition, it eventually became apparent that Panslavism was not a monolithic movement advocating Russian supremacy. Panslavism had a strong appeal and did inspire various forms of national activism, and Russia had used it in its bid to erode Austrian influence; but there were limits to its attraction. For the Poles it meant nothing short of Russification. Radical Russian proponents of Panslavism envisaged that all Slavs would adopt Russian culture and did not realize that, for example, the Czechs, among others, were not about to sacrifice what they had held on to for hundreds of years of foreign rule: their language and 'national individuality'. Nor did these Russians realize that Panslavism was embraced as a vehicle for national liberation, not for submission to another foreign power, no matter how sympathetic. This was evident in 1867 from the negative response of the various participants at the Moscow Slavonic Congress and visitors to the Ethnographical Exposition to the suggestion that they should all speak Russian.[17] In 1874 we read in the *Fortnightly Review* that 'the growth of Panslavism in Servia has reduced Russian influence with the South Slavonians to a minimum'.[18] Nor had the Russians themselves embraced Panslavism unambivalently. Russian diplomats working towards closer cooperation with Germany and Austria at the time of the Three Emperors' League in the early 1880s saw there was more to be gained from an alliance between powerful like-minded empires than from nurturing and protecting the national aspirations of various Slavonic peoples. Seeing its way to Constantinople 'through Vienna', Russia therefore did not go out of its way to support the Serbs in their confrontation with the Turks, for example.[19] Russia's attractiveness as an ally increased the more conciliatory it appeared.

In the late 1870s there were those who agreed that it was in Britain's interest to maintain its policy of 'neutrality', of keeping the peace by staying out of smaller disputes unless they impacted directly on the country's commercial concerns.[20] Henry Reeve (1813–95), foreign editor of *The Times* between 1840 and 1855 and editor of the *Edinburgh Review* for 40 years from 1855 until his death, wrote in 1876 that even if Serbia was 'the advanced guard of Russia', Britain ought to remain neutral until its interests were truly 'assailed'.[21] The ultimate goal of preserving British interests shaped the attitude of Disraeli and Salisbury, the Foreign Secretary between 1878 and 1880, at the time of the Congress of Berlin. The Congress, overturning as it did elements of the San Stefano Treaty signed after the Russo-Turkish War of 1877–8, left the Serbs and Bulgars, among others, dissatisfied. It was Gladstone's high-profile divergence from traditional British attitudes towards the Ottomans, evident in his emotive pleas from 1876 onwards on behalf of the Empire's Slavonic Christians, that set the tone for future discussions about independence movements and the union of the South Slavs. Gladstone was in opposition at the time and his sympathy for the persecuted Bulgars prompted him to write on the subject and to address parliament and public meetings. His pamphlet *Bulgarian Horrors and the Question of the East* (1876) calling for withdrawal – 'bag and baggage' – of 'the Turk' from the region stopped short of advocating the dissolution of the Ottoman Empire. It did, however, anticipate the view that the problems of the nationalities in the region were interlocking. He wrote that 'one of the latest artifices is to separate the question of Servia from the question of Herzegovina and Bosnia and of Bulgaria'.[22] At numerous speaking engagements Gladstone communicated his views vigorously and emotively to large audiences who were roused to act on behalf of the Orthodox insurrectionaries. Not all Liberal politicians shared his passion and some feared that Gladstone's effusive expressions of solidarity with the Bulgars would lead to a split in the party.

Gladstone's spirited action mobilized public opinion, stimulating the emergence of a number of (voluntary) aid agencies and an enormously successful fund-raising campaign.[23] Individuals who were often associated with each other personally and professionally produced a large body of writing on Slavonic Turkey and on the Habsburg Slavs. This was the case with Arthur Evans (1851–1941), the acclaimed archaeologist and discoverer of Knossos, who knew Irby, visited her school and promoted her work in his extensive writings about his travels through the region. Evans's father-in-law, E.A. Freeman (1823–92), was Regius Professor of Modern History at Oxford and another prolific commentator on the plight of Balkan Christians. Robert Seton-Watson and Henry Wickham Steed (1871–1956), European correspondent and then editor of *The Times*, would also be close to Evans and his circle and take up their cause. By the time Seton-Watson began writing his chapters for *The War and Democracy*, which appeared in 1914 and in which he expressed unambiguously his support for South Slav union, he had travelled widely, become a friend of the main promoters of the new hybrid Slavonic nationalisms, Yugoslav and Czechoslovak, and embarked on his own extensive researches that led to numerous articles, pamphlets and books.[24]

From the 1880s up to 1914 a steady flow of articles appeared on the Eastern Question, especially as it impacted on Europe. Many of these articles criticized Disraeli. With the return of Gladstone as prime minister the Eastern Question loomed larger in some quarters. Freeman admitted that while the issue did not galvanize all Gladstone's supporters, they nonetheless took up his 'righteous cause', that of the Bulgars: 'we follow [Gladstone] gladly'.[25] Freeman had been active in collecting money for the Herzegovinian rebels in 1876 and the backing for the cause had been bipartisan until Disraeli declared his support for Turkey. Freeman pondered Disraeli's decision and concluded that perhaps in addition to the fear of Russia, the prime minister's own 'Asiatic' (Jewish) background explained this preference. According to Freeman, the deaths of thousands of Christians obviously meant little to Disraeli.[26] Others did not go so far but argued simply that the 'disproportionate dread' of Russia had blinded Disraeli and Salisbury to potential threats from the Austro-German alliance as well as to the futility of any expectation of reform from within the Turkish provinces. Such reform would not be forthcoming without strong urgings from Britain and without the 'European concert', not a policy in itself but a valuable 'instrument' of policy. According to this argument it was to Gladstone's credit that he had gone beyond the narrow conservative view that maintaining Turkish influence in the region was the only way to advance British interests.[27]

Arthur Evans, as we have seen, was to become a friend and collaborator of Seton-Watson. Evans was a future associate of the Serbian Society of Great Britain and the Serbian (Jugoslav) National War Aims Committee. He also contributed to *The New Europe*, Seton-Watson's influential magazine drawing together advocates and publicists for the successor states. Evans wrote in 1880 that the Treaty of Berlin marked the beginning of a 'great Revolution'. He believed that the 'spell of Turkish dominion in Europe' was now 'broken forever': 'The policy of insurrection has been justified, and at the same time in these very lands the motives for it have been doubled.'[28] The underlying fear was, however, that Austria-Hungary would impede the revolution that had barely begun and prevent it from reaching its natural conclusion. Why it could be said to have barely begun was because the main centres of commerce, industry and learning remained outside the newly established countries, some 'rotting still in this Asiatic Slough of Despond', others in Austria's greedy possession. More bloodshed was to follow, Evans predicted, as the 'hurricane' had 'already drawn into its vortex the whole Slavonic world'. He wrote that the 'eruptive energy' in the Balkans was greater than ever.[29]

What made observers more likely to focus on that 'eruptive energy' was the emergence of Germany as a major force in Central Europe. Germany came to rival and threaten Britain's colonial and naval supremacy and after the turn of the century 'Berlin–Baghdad' signified much more than a rail route. Behind Austria, which had supported Britain's anti-Russian stance at the Congress of Berlin, stood Germany, and Austria's Slavonic territories were thus more closely scrutinized by critics of official policy. Critics also questioned the wisdom of Britain's decision to support the occupation by Austria of Bosnia-Herzegovina following the Congress in 1878. The occupation was a thorn in the side of Serb nationalists because, as a result of it, Serbia inevitably came more closely into Austria's orbit. Russia again played an important role in these calculations. Whereas rivalry with Russia had influenced the positive view of Austria as the buffer to the Panslavonic movement in Europe, eventually hostility towards Germany drew out the (latent) negativity of France and Britain towards Austria. Russia became a more appealing ally as Panslavism seemed less and less ominous. In 1880 Evans described Germany's attitude towards Austria in relation to its aggrandizing mission in the Lower Danube as a 'warming-pan', preparing the bed that Germany would not occupy until it had been made 'quite comfortable'.[30] Two years later Freeman wrote that the Austrian power was 'a singular curiosity, unlike anything else in the modern world', and behind Franz Joseph stood 'the mightier form of Bismarck'.[31] Thus the focus on the mounting Central European threat to traditional spheres of influence placed Russian advances in an altogether different and far more favourable light, leading in due course to Franco-Russian and Anglo-Russian rapprochement. At the same time there were fewer and fewer impediments to British acceptance of Balkan and Habsburg Slav national movements.

From Evans's impassioned pleas in the name of the nationalist forces of progress, we note that nothing was treated in isolation. The question of the 'little nations' was broached against an international backdrop. While Evans's treatment of the nationalities question was sweeping and triumphalist, others were more circumspect. For example, the view that multinational states were viable and even in some instances the norm occasionally softened mounting hostility towards Austria-Hungary. Indeed, the example of the British observers' own 'united kingdom' was tangible evidence of the potential success of such a state.[32] Thus, in some quarters, 'realism' in the form of a (sometimes) grudging acceptance of the territorial integrity and

Great Power status of both the Ottomans and the Dual Monarchy continued. Another 1880 article, entitled pointedly 'Home Rule in Several Countries', argued that decentralization was in general a good thing and that the Austrian system of 'Home Rule' which allowed provincial diets some local power was a preferable model to that of Hungary, which attempted to suppress local autonomy, notably that of the Croats. This author, in stark contrast to Evans, was among those, a minority it must be said, who assessed positively the Austrian (as opposed to the Italian) impact on the eastern Adriatic in Dalmatia.[33] The writer, however, had other motives, too, in speculating on Home Rule: Britain itself could take note and embark on a policy of devolving power to the provinces and consider in this light the position of Ireland, the 'only country in Europe in which peasant tenures have not been enfranchised'.[34] However, while the outsiders did not speak with one voice, and while there were different opinions about the appropriateness of the presence of the old empires across Central and South-eastern Europe, there was less caution about the process of national unification in 'Illyria'. In part this was because outsiders' projections depended upon the contingencies of the time.

Chief among these contingencies were the unification of Germany and of Italy. They were the background to the acceptance of a 'united Illyria', however defined, because they represented a process of necessary territorial rationalization to champions of the nation-state. The new 'Teutonic' nation, racially homogeneous and vigorously expansionist, would prove a challenge to British supremacy. British opinion was generally very favourably disposed towards Italian nationalists and their cause, especially in so far as it challenged Catholic authority. Giuseppe Garibaldi's visit to England in 1864, when 'his name was already a household word throughout the kingdom', attracted considerable attention. He was as much in demand among liberal elites as among workers' associations. Even though Garibaldi's visit was cut short due to the embarrassment it was causing the government, his celebrity status and cult-like following gives some indication of the capacity of the romantic nationalist quest to fire the British imagination.[35] In this context Austria and its ruling house were to become the chief object of disdain and no longer regarded as necessary to offset Russia's westward creep. Some did accept that Austria needed (and perhaps even justifiably sought) access to the sea. However, negative images of the Central European empire dominated the magazine literature and few commentators would concede it had any rights at all to seaports. Evans argued in 1880 that the inclination to prop up Austria (the 'residuary legatee') as Turkey retreated from Europe replaced the conservatives' 'unqualified Turcophily'.[36] Evans believed transferring one's allegiance to Austria-Hungary from Turkey was unwise because the former did not manage especially well the mix of nations under its mantle. A host of conflicting and contradictory positions, 'centralism, dualism, "trialism", federalism [and] disruption', all had their 'adherents', as indeed did the proponents of expansionism in the form of 'great Romania' and 'great Serbia'.[37] Freeman, echoing his son-in-law Evans, noted that in the event of radical territorial changes, the South Slavonic Latins (Catholics) were least likely to be heard outside the Dual Monarchy. Nevertheless, Austria had no right to the regions under its control along the Adriatic coast. While Austrian rule was not 'a rule of habitual gross outrage, like that of the Turk', it was 'dull, wearisome, ungenial, unnational, [and] utterly unscrupulous in case of opposition'.[38] Thus, continued Freeman, the 'good old prayer' of the English, 'From Pope and Turk defend us both', was also that of the 'ancient churches of the East since Pope and Turk first began to trouble them'.[39] Freeman was articulating what became the alternative position to that of balancing out the influence of the Great Powers in the region: strong new nation-states would negate the need for a stabilizing force and the need for either Austrian or Turkish overlords who were reactionary and out of step with the times.

Increasingly harsh anti-Habsburg sentiments informed (positive) attitudes towards the future of the Balkan nations. So, other than on the basis of their 'union of various races', there was, according to the *Times* correspondent in Rome, American-born W.J. Stillman (1828–1901), no point of comparison between Austria and England: Austria's government was 'reactionary and despotic by instinct and inclination, and progressive only by compulsion'.[40] The apparent loyalty extended towards the Dual Monarchy by its Slavonic subjects could not be genuine. In Evans's view, it was the loyalty of 'the ignorant and the frivolous ever oscillating between flunkeyism and superstition', a 'cheap commodity'.[41] It was also exploitative of those who had bravely fought off the Ottoman yoke. For example, a Russian woman, Olga Novikoff, writing in the *Contemporary Review*, noted in 1882 that the Serbs suffered at the hands of Austria-Hungary. The latter's control of Serbia's export trade and its commercial treaties meant that the Dual Monarchy made use of the principality 'for the benefit of her Jewish speculators, to almost any extent'. Novikoff's view was that the Serbian Orthodox Church, embroiled at that time in a dispute regarding taxation, had to maintain its independence in order to help present strong opposition to Teutonic expansionism.[42] Austria was at once illiberal and a haven for 'Jewish speculators': all potentially negative bases were being covered in a blanket condemnation.

Advocates of what, in effect, would amount to a radical reshaping of European borders and spheres of influence (especially as they pertained to Austria-Hungary and the Ottomans) generally agreed on two key points. First, that the national movements, in principle, had merit and as such ought to be promoted; and second, that the Great Powers (notably Britain) had a duty to present permanent solutions to the question of Slavonic nationalism in order to stabilize international relations and hasten the civilizing process. The extent to which the duty to civilize coincided with the safeguarding of Britain's interests and its premier trading and naval position is noteworthy. The collective voice of the Great Powers had promised peace and mutual respect so long as the cost of bestowing these gifts was contained. Some may have justified such diplomatic machinations by arguing that they would ensure an equitable distribution of economic and social progress. In fact they resulted in a precarious peace and unequal progress. Evans was representative of those who never viewed Austria's occupation of Bosnia, for example, as anything other than a violation of Slavonic independence and as Austria's 'excellent stepping-stone for the ultimate advance on Salonika', even though at the time many Englishmen had welcomed this buffer to Russian expansion.[43] In the 1880s, however, outside observers became less accommodating of Turkey's snail's pace of reform. Moreover, for them it appeared the Congress of Berlin presented merely short-term solutions to difficult problems of national demarcation and further exposed Britain's markets and possessions in the east.[44] The lack of sympathy for the Dual Monarchy was evident right through to the outbreak of war in 1914 and then intensified. Paradoxically, its 'unnational' nature provided the foundation for the popularity of loose interpretations of national and racial self-determination adhered to by the advocates of the multi-ethnic hybrids, like Czechoslovakia (an example, according to later cynics, of double-barrelled nationalism) and Yugoslavia. In the first instance, one of the chief principles of classification our outside observers applied in their assessments and definitions of the new or little nationalities was religion.

Religion and Nation

Religion was a recurring, indeed inescapable, theme in many writings about the South Slavs and had a role in shaping views about their relative merits. There were some who argued that religious dogma was an encumbrance to the modern state as it addressed its multiple functions, including foreign policy. According to this line of argument, the very idea of defending Christians against the 'Infidel' was a scandalous evocation of sectarianism of the worst kind: the days of the Crusades were (thankfully) long gone.[45] We will see that this seemingly rational approach to the subject in fact obscured a deep, collective disdain for 'Papists' and 'Mahometans'. The Catholicism of the Habsburgs, said to be under the spell of the Pope's widely detested 'army', the Jesuits, generated open hostility.[46] For its part, Muslim rule was socially backward and endemically corrupt: in a word, unreformable.

What troubled so many of our British observers, especially after the Crimean War when their government's policy firmly reinforced the Ottomans, was that the Slavonic Christians could not turn to them for assistance but seemingly had recourse only to the Russians. It was not so much a question of a strategic loss (though such a loss could not be ignored) but of Christian solidarity.[47] As noted above, at the time of the Slavonic Christians' clashes with the Ottomans in the 1870s a large battalion of British volunteers – including doctors and nurses – arrived to provide all manner of assistance to the casualties and refugees in this modern crusade. The Manchester Evangelisation Committee, one of many local organizations to do so, sent its own agent out to Serbia to help the wounded and manage relief work.[48] A devout member of the Netherlands Reformed Church, Jenny Merkus (1839–97), went so far as to join the Serbian army as a volunteer after having participated in the revolt in Bosnia-Herzegovina and purchasing Krupp cannons for the rebels. Wearing a Montenegrin cap and a man's cape, she was reported to have said that she did not wish to nurse wounded soldiers but 'to help liberate Christian people and all Christ's land from the sovereignty of the Turks'.[49] Irby also found herself deeply critical of her government's Turcophilism on religious grounds. This wave of volunteers laid the foundation for the collective humanitarian endeavour of the men and women who left for Serbia as volunteer relief workers in the First World War. For many of them religious and political conviction blended indistinguishably.

The British championed the Orthodox Churches as the true manifestation of South Slavonic religiosity and sympathized with them as victims of 'Mahometan' persecution. Overwhelmingly, British travellers felt a far greater affinity with Orthodox Slavs, Bulgars, Montenegrins and Serbs, than with Catholics. Anglicans strongly identified with Orthodox Christians because theirs were both Erastian national churches. The state has ascendancy over Erastian churches in ecclesiastical matters, in marked contrast to Rome's claims to universality, which were deplored at the time by most Anglicans. The late nineteenth century saw the eclipse of national Catholic Churches with the First Vatican Council condemning the Gallicans in the French Church and emphasizing the authority of the Holy See over all Catholics. The Orthodox Church was one of the pillars of modern state-building in Serbia and a defining characteristic of Serbdom. The heresy of phyletism, excessive nationalism, was first identified in the Bulgarian Church and condemned in Constantinople in 1872. According to Stevan Pavlowitch, the Serbian Church's marked tendency towards phyletism led to isolation and parochialism, allowing it to be manipulated by extreme nationalists.[50] By its nature the Catholic Church could not have the same role as Erastian churches in state-building; it was targeted by the secular state as anti-national and anti-modern, as evident in the virulent anticlerical campaigns in Germany and France in the late nineteenth and early twentieth centuries.

Catholic Habsburg Slavs were therefore unattractive for a number of reasons to our outsiders, including the belief that Vienna suffered political backwardness since having crushed its Protestant reformers. Wherever Protestantism flourished so, too, had reforms and local democratic institutions (or diets). Evans found schism in the Bosnian medieval Church, Bogomilism, and called its adherents, 'the first Protestants', rebels against the 'ferocious tyranny of Catholic kings, magnates, and monks'.[51] Elsewhere Evans had used the metaphor of an (ongoing) counter-revolution in an exposition of Austria-Hungary's desire to hold back progressive movements. In its treatment of Protestants, those influenced by the ideas central to the French Revolution and, in the 1880s, the proponents of the 'principle of Nationality' against 'the tyranny of alien statecraft', Austria exhibited its repressive tendencies. In Metternich, its Foreign Minister who had presided over the Congress of Vienna (1814–15), Evans identified 'the executioner of liberty', the personification of an Austrian reaction that persisted through the nineteenth century.[52]

The anti-Catholic strain is also evident in appraisals pitting the positive effects of Hungary's Protestantism against the failings of the 'bigotedly Catholic' Habsburgs.[53] (In the early twentieth century, however, Hungarian authoritarianism and Magyarization campaigns in Croatia would be roundly condemned.) Propaganda in favour of the Czechs and their nationalist aspirations during the First World War was to focus on the career of the Bohemian reformer, John Huss (c.1372–1415), who suffered excommunication and then imprisonment and death by burning and whose close identification with the English theologian and reformer, John Wycliffe (1330–84), made good copy.[54] Where they existed, Protestants were preferred. However, in the absence of strong pockets of Protestantism, there was unanimity in the outsiders' preference for Orthodox Christians. A predominantly Catholic France did not champion Catholic Austria or, after the First World War, Catholic Croats. In French governing circles an anticlerical impulse prevailed and the ties between former allies were more sacred and stronger than those of 'international Catholicism'.

Orthodoxy, far from alien or pejoratively 'Balkan', had an aesthetic and practical appeal for our travellers. Goldsworthy and Todorova, among others, have argued that the 'easternness' of Orthodoxy meant Catholic nations were regarded more favourably and as higher-order Europeans. Similarly, many supporters of Yugoslavia in the 1990s held that Catholic Slovenes and Croats eventually fared better than the Orthodox Serbs in the propaganda wars because of the West's greater affinity with Catholicism. The evidence for the nineteenth century (and the 1990s for that matter) does not support the view that Catholicism triumphed over Orthodoxy in the eyes of our commentators. On the contrary, what is noticeable in the late nineteenth century is not simply an aversion to Catholicism, but an overt preference for Orthodox nations. This had much to do with Erastianism, as we have seen, but there is also the fact that high-church men and women got their doses of art and ritual without contending directly with Popery. The more evangelically inclined, on the other hand, whether Anglican or non-Conformist, perhaps related better to a married clergy or the austerity of eastern monasticism, and thus avoided being tainted by Rome and its 'decadent' strain of Christianity. For most of our authors, however, its twinning with national liberation struggles set Orthodoxy apart from Catholicism.

In 1880 Stillman's was not a lone voice when he wrote that, by its very nature, Orthodoxy suited modern state-formation. Orthodoxy, federative in character, was preferable to Catholicism, which was highly centralized. With its autonomous bishoprics, Orthodoxy resembled closely the Anglican and Episcopalian churches. It became 'invariably the ally of every effort for independence'. By contrast, Stillman continued, Catholics in Bosnia were 'spiritless and denationalised', even more morally bankrupt than the 'Mussulman'; the priest in the service of Rome no longer called himself a Serb but a 'Latin'. (Here it seems for Stillman the Catholics were Serb 'converts'.) With no 'national aspirations, little love of independence and...no fight' the 'foreign' (Catholic) cleric compared poorly with the Orthodox priest who was 'a Serb before everything': 'the whole force of the Orthodox sentiment goes to rebuilding his nationality; that of the Roman Catholic, to obliterating it, and substituting for it a foreign dictation'.[55] If the Catholic priest was better educated, his Orthodox counterpart was a man of the people. Married, he avoided 'the scandals which now and then throw such a lurid light on the condition of the Catholic priesthood'. In times of trouble, the Orthodox priest was the 'first fighting man': 'As his church belongs to the nation, he belongs to his village, and often he pays the last debt of the patriot as well as the martyr, giving his life for his people.'[56] The comparison with Anglicanism imbued the Orthodox Church with the former's perceived positive attributes: naturally liberal inclinations and a national outlook. Orthodox churches were thus 'always...an aid to the state' and never sought to 'usurp civic powers'. The example of Bismarck's 'war of culture', his *Kulturkampf*, directed against Catholicism as an alternative sphere of (foreign) influence, would thus be unthinkable in an Orthodox state. Orthodoxy's peculiar combination of 'liberality' and 'intensity of attachment' accompanied by 'a higher tone of patriotism' (a perception of Serbian Orthodoxy that continued through to the 1990s), Stillman concluded, set it apart from the Catholicism of people of the 'same stock'.[57]

The Russian, Novikoff, mentioned above, wrote that in 'all Orthodox lands the State is much more the creation of the Church than the Church the instrument of the State'. Further, the relation between the Orthodox Church and State was like the 'relation between soul and body'. Conscious of the Great Power rivalry underlying English fears of Russian expansion into the Balkans, Novikoff indicated that while Serbia was indeed Russia's protégé, it was not Russia's tool. She expressed a commonly held view when she noted, in a fashion strangely prescient of the extreme religious rhetoric of the 1990s, that it was wrong to argue, as did some, that Serbia had prospered under the Turks (unlike the Catholic Poles who, Novikoff averred, had thrived under Russia's mantle). The Church which, during the 'dark centuries', had 'alone kept alive in the minds of the Serbians the consciousness of their nationality and their aspiration for independence', had to maintain its pre-eminent place in Serbian society. Otherwise, Serbia would simply become 'the avant-garde of the Hapsburg [*sic*] on the Balkan peninsula'. Novikoff's intention was that of writing as a Slav 'pleading the rights of the Slavs'. She was promoting the cause and 'legitimate aspirations' of the 16 million Slavs under Austrian rule.[58]

Rebel Orthodox Slavs, Montenegrins, Bulgars and Serbs, while not as free as Protestants were, nevertheless, seen to be aspiring to forge states that championed both liberty and Christianity. The Serbs, it was claimed, would thereby be able to bring liberty without revolution to their South Slav brothers. They would follow on from the Montenegrins, who had been responsible for 'saving Venice from the Ottomans'. As the Montenegrins repulsed the invaders, 'liberty and Christianity took refuge on the mountain-tops'.[59] The belief that Orthodoxy was predisposed towards and spawned liberation movements prevailed in British minds. Catholics, on the other hand, were seemingly incapable of forging that connection between the pursuit of liberty and religious practice. The vexed question of Home Rule in Ireland may well have had a bearing on this observation regarding the incapacity of Catholics to be responsible and accountable governors and citizens. As we have seen, articles on Austria and Central and Eastern Europe referred explicitly to the notion of 'home rule'. In 1862, 16 years before their occupation by Austria, Mackenzie wrote that Bosnia and 'the Herzegovine' (described as Slavonic and as belonging to the 'Eastern Church') had 'little disposition to place themselves under [the Austrian] government [which was] both Germanizing and Papistical'.[60] Further, South Slav nationalism did not find its natural expression in Agram (Zagreb) because that city was too narrowly linked to the Latin Church and its culture 'too local' for 'general interest'.[61] Evans noted 14 years later, in 1876, that the Catholic influence in Bosnia was a 'lever' in the hands of Austria. Catholic clergy in Bosnia-Herzegovina seemed, oddly to him, to prefer Austrian and even Turkish rule to any form of hegemony by the

Serb principality: they 'betrayed a lively repugnance to the Great Serbian idea'. That the Catholic priesthood 'shrinks from Serbia with more horror than from Stamboul' was deplorable to him.[62]

The negative treatment of Catholicism varied according to the broader subject under discussion. Some, like Mackenzie and Irby, believed the nationalist principle or 'national sympathy' between those who variously worshipped the 'Greek' and 'Roman' churches would not be held back by 'sectarian antipathy' and thus glossed over religious issues. The real division was between Christians and Muslims.[63] Others were not so convinced.[64] In their eyes, if 'sectarian antipathy' were to subside other factors had to come into play. There was, therefore, also talk of the eventual blending of peoples and the triumph of the 'rational' science of nations over the 'irrational' rule of religion. Edith Durham, on the other hand, argued in *Burden of the Balkans* (1905) that the struggles, as they were depicted between Christians and Muslims, constituted not a religious but a 'racial' or 'national' struggle.[65] By underemphasizing the national rivalries and reducing them to seemingly lesser 'religious' problems, there existed, she reasoned, presciently we see now, the potential for actual national, cultural (or, in the language of the time, 'racial') differences to be ignored, with significant repercussions in the long term. Hers was a strong expression of a position finally embraced by some commentators at the time of Yugoslavia's collapse almost a century later.

Evans highlighted the significance of religion but, unlike Durham, he did so in order to argue for the superiority of Orthodoxy over Catholicism. He noted that Serbian nationalism marshalled religion in the cause of national unity. While for the Serbs the national spirit was 'more than a political conviction' and resembled a religion, 'almost a fanaticism', religion itself had become the 'humble handmaid of nationality'. The Serbs' national propaganda was not to be found in 'Jesuit intrigues', but in 'a thousand heroic lays on the strings of the Serbian lyre'.[66] His father-in-law, Freeman, held similar views. As we will see, Freeman was to save some of his most immoderate language for his attacks on Islam. At the same time, there was no question in his mind that Austria posed the greatest threat in the region and its greed and intrigues had to be denounced: 'Every man there knows full well that the plots of Nihilists, Communists, Internationalists are weak and harmless compared with the plots of an Apostolic King.' Furthermore, the Dual Monarchy's rule was not systematic. On the contrary, it represented the whims of an individual who regarded the lands and nations under his control much as one might regard a family estate rather than a modern economic and national unit.[67]

Outsiders also generally reserved a deep disdain for the Muslims. There was no hint of romantic exoticism or liberal tolerance in appraisals of them and there were fewer echoes of official Turcophilism over time. In the isolated and barren wastes where Slavonic 'Mahometans' were forced to eke out a miserable existence, the British travellers regarded them as more backward and more fanatical than the Turkish Muslims living further east in the cosmopolitan cities, where they were exposed to 'civilising' influences. Mackenzie regarded the expulsion (or, euphemistically, 'exodus') of Muslims from the Serbian principality in the early 1860s in a positive light. Oriental decadence, which held back the Slavs, would now be a thing of the past. Admittedly, she continued, all Muslims were not equally corrupt but there were those, like the 'Turks of Sokol', the 'offspring of renegades', who stood out: 'Sprung of Serb stock, and speaking the Serb tongue, they are the enemies of their brethren, the scourge of their fatherland.'[68] When the 'incorruptible' Serbs united the entire region, they would ensure that Christian and Muslim Slavs would cooperate because, under Serbian leadership, the common Slav identity would triumph over religious difference.

We know Freeman was among those academics who protested vigorously at his government's support for the Ottomans and its seeming lack of concern for the Orthodox Christians after the Bulgarian massacres. 'Would you fight for the freedom of the Empire of Sodom?', he asked.[69] In 1877, he wrote:

> The Saracen was once an unnatural excrescence on the southwestern corner of Europe. The Ottoman still is an unnatural excrescence on the south-eastern corner of Europe. He cannot become a real pupil of Christian civilization; he cannot take real root on European soil; he can only remain for ever the alien and barbarian intruder which he was at his first coming.[70]

Descriptions of veiled women, proof absolute of backwardness, and the unsanitary squalor of Turkish quarters in towns and villages often accompanied anti-Muslim statements. In 1880 Freeman noted that 'the Turk cannot reform as long as he remains Mahometan' because 'the great principle of the Mahometan religion is that he shall not reform'.[71]

In the same vein, a June 1880 article in the *Nineteenth Century* was scathing of Turkish attempts at reform. As they retreated from Europe, the Turks left nothing. The Muslim had 'no desire for education, and has not the means of obtaining it if he had'. A 12-year-old English schoolboy could glance through a newspaper more capably than a Turkish scholar, whose greatest failing was his belief that he had no need for European culture. In addition, the Turkish system was incapable of reform without prompting from outside.[72] The election of Gladstone as prime minister in 1880, we read, brought panic to Turkey because it was obvious that he was serious about reform. Disraeli, on the other hand, oblivious of the national undercurrents, indulgent towards Turkey and through lack of vigilance, would have allowed Austria to expand through to Constantinople.[73] Another article in the same magazine two months previously had praised Gladstone's sensible approach to Russia. Instead of seeing it as a rival power, it was more profitable to consider 'despotic Russia' as ripe for enlightenment, which, the author suggested optimistically, would follow in the wake of free trade. Further, the Treaty of Berlin was a mere patch-up job on the part of Disraeli and his cohort and had left England 'mother of free nations', without 'moral influence' on the Balkan Peninsula and without influence over the Christian populations there. A sensible approach was necessary for the prosperity of all: 'Let us in concert with Europe make up our minds what settlement in the Eastern Peninsula is best for Europe in general and for the inhabitants of the Balkan Peninsula in particular: we may be perfectly certain that what is best for all will be best for us.'[74]

It was during the Balkan Wars (1912–13) that this lack of sympathy for Muslims, and in some cases deeply felt prejudice against them, became even more marked. Some were put out by this intolerance. The *Edinburgh Review* ran an article criticizing the lack of interest of the British public in general in the nature of the Balkan Wars and the course they were to take. It noted that the expulsions and massacres of Muslims from Macedonia (one of the contested regions) sparked no angry protest from the British. The once rebellious voice of a Freeman who championed only the oppressed he believed deserving was, 30 years later, the voice of British officialdom. The article further observed that it was the lack of debate that was most remarkable and, in comparison with earlier wars in the region, most uncharacteristic: 'It may be said without fear of contradiction that modern history furnishes no parallel to the atrocities inflicted by the allied invaders upon the helpless Moslem [*sic*] inhabitants of Macedonia.' Albanians had been 'slaughtered in wholesale fashion by the Servian troops, no mercy being given even to old men, women, or children'. The article added: 'A strange silence has been observed with regard to these happenings by the English Press.'[75] However, this was a minority view.

The extent of British identification of Bosnia-Herzegovina religiously with Orthodoxy, Catholicism or Islam and 'racially' with Serbs or Croats is important for an understanding of the evolution of the South Slav 'nation' in the minds of outsiders. Bosnia-Herzegovina came to be regarded as predominantly Orthodox and therefore, by nature, a Serb possession, which, once won over and occupied by the Turks, had been destined to remain backward. Inhabitants of Bosnia-Herzegovina who were not Orthodox were in some sense 'foreign'. They might be descendants of weaker Serbs who had converted or of proselytizing Catholics, emissaries of Rome and the tools of reaction. The Serbs' future depended on their possession of Bosnia-Herzegovina, which was to provide access to the Adriatic coast through its 'natural' connection with Dalmatia. Some questioned the premise that the Muslims of Bosnia were originally Serbs because it was unthinkable that Serbs would have converted en masse, Orthodoxy being inseparable from nation in Serbia.[76] However, the consensus emerging from the 1860s was that Bosnia-Herzegovina, the potential lifeline of Serbia, was itself Serbian; and Serbia's passage to the sea would be secured via the (re)acquisition of another of its 'rightful possessions', Dalmatia.[77] A similar logic was at work in appraisals of 'Serbian' Macedonia. As we will see, however, in the First World War the Serbs were not willing to look westwards for the 'reunification' of Illyria if it meant sacrificing what they held to be (sacred) Serb lands further south and east.

In the placement and classification of South Slavs by outsiders, religion was an important criterion. In our context Orthodoxy was neither 'oriental' nor (pejoratively) 'Balkan'. Rather, it was the source of, or at least a main contributor to, national identity. Unlike its 'supranational' rivals in the region, Catholicism and Islam, Orthodoxy could be relied upon to provide continuity and cohesion, and thus stability, in a time of change. Further, its identification with national liberation struggles afforded it a progressive identity irrespective of the nature of the practice of the faith itself and the political outcomes of those liberation struggles. Orthodoxy would provide one of the pillars of identity in the construction of the

Yugoslav race and nation in the writings of our travellers, a topic to which we now turn.

Race and Nation

Cultural factors affected the evolution of a Yugoslav race in the imaginings of our outsiders. Religious history, the story of embattled Christianity in its Orthodox guise, retrospectively provided authenticity and a long national pedigree allowing for the easy acceptance of the view that Catholicism and Islam were 'foreign' and a-national or anti-national, and therefore out of step with the times. Science also had an important role to play in the construction of the Yugoslav race. We know theories about racial hierarchies informed by social Darwinism gained particular currency in the late nineteenth century. Accordingly, ethnographers and anthropologists presented their findings about the South Slavs in pseudo-racial terms which came to underpin political arguments in favour of establishing a South Slav state. In an article by Edward Willoughby appearing in *Fraser's Magazine* in 1877, we can read that while Slavs stood 'at the head' of the races of Europe 'numerically', they lagged behind 'socially and intellectually'. Yet it was also true that races and their civilizations rose and fell. Thus, the article continued, 'it would be rash to deny that the Slavonians may have a future'. Indeed, great changes seemed imminent. Willoughby concluded that 'the Southern Slavs will not long remain in subjection to Mussulman rule'.[78] Permutations or inversions of the classification system as described by Todorova and as evident here from the particular example of the establishment of Yugoslavia were not necessarily based on fixed views about what constituted higher cultural or 'racial' planes. In the first instance, peoples might move between and within planes for reasons that related to factors beyond their control, international patterns of trade or the territorial aspirations of one of the Great Powers, for example. However, as early favourites among nations lost their mobilizing potential, it became obvious who (alone) would be capable of leading the Ottoman and Habsburg South Slavs to freedom.

At first the Montenegrins, much admired as the small nation of mountain warriors who had heroically struck out at their Turkish oppressors, were the chosen people. Montenegro (Crna Gora or Black Mountain) assumed near legendary and romantic status as a principality whose superior fighting force of warrior-princes saved it from the infidel's yoke.[79] In 1862 Mackenzie argued that Britain should support Montenegrin independence. Such support would counteract Russian influence there and at the same time prove advantageous to Britain. The principality, as it sought to develop commercially, must look to Britain, not Russia, for help, she argued. Like the 'vine-dresser', Britain must plan for the future by planting young shoots prior to cutting back the old stock:

> Now, a sprout of the right sort is Montenegro. A vigorous, healthy, Christian nationality, let Britain take her by the hand. Let Britain's vote accord to her that place among European States for which she has so long, so nobly struggled; let British influence be extended to obtain for her such a territory as shall enable her worthily to maintain her new position throughout her future history as a free government and a commercial power.[80]

Montenegro's most important leader of the modern period was Petar II (Petrović Njegoš, 1813–51), Orthodox Prince Bishop between 1830 and 1851. A poet, he drew on folk motifs and oral traditions of storytelling and his best known work is the epic, *The Mountain Wreath*. Published in 1847, it concerns the fate of those among them who had converted to Islam, thereby weakening the resistance to the foreign invader. The epic centuries-long struggle of the people of the Black Mountain had an impact on the (romantic) Western imagination, which is today largely forgotten. It is important for our story because of the eventual merging of these tales into an invented South Slav literary canon. Selective references to the poem figured in propaganda promoting the idea of a long history of South Slav unity through to Tito's Yugoslavia.[81] Tennyson's poem 'Montenegro', written and published in the first half of 1877, gives us a sense of the Black Mountain's capacity to conjure heroic images of another era and to layer those images onto a modern quest for nationhood:

> They rose to where their sovran eagle sails,
> They kept their faith, their freedom, on the height,
> Chaste, frugal, savage, arm'd by day and night
> Against the Turk; whose inroad nowhere scales
> Their headlong passes, but his footstep fails,
> And red with blood the Crescent reels from fight
> Before their dauntless hundreds, in prone flight

By thousands down the crags and thro' the vales.
O smallest among peoples! rough rock-throne
Of Freedom! warriors beating back the swarm
Of Turkish Islam for five hundred years,
Great Tsernogora! never since thine own
Black ridges drew the cloud and brake the storm
Has breathed a race of mightier mountaineers.[82]

In the same issue of the magazine Gladstone wrote a review article on a number of books about Montenegro. He referred to his 'friend' Tennyson's poem and praised him for at last finding a way to communicate Montenegro's history more broadly.[83]

Gladstone referred to the Montenegrins' role in protecting Europe from the Ottomans and fighting 'with a valour that rivalled, if it did not surpass, that of Thermopylae and Marathon': in 1835 ten Montenegrins had held an historic castle against 3000 Turks for four days.[84] Gladstone also spoke of this 'bishop-led community, which held fast its oasis of Christianity and freedom amidst the dry and boundless desert of Ottoman domination' and had 'done a work for freedom, as well as for religion, never surpassed in any country of the globe'.[85] Referring to the Spencerian concept of survival of the strong in harsh conditions, Gladstone also speculated on the racial strength and superiority of the Montenegrins. Unlike weaker peoples destined for extinction, he noted, they were 'men of exceptional power and stature'.[86] Two potential drawbacks were the Montenegrins' treatment of women and their propensity to commit atrocities in war. A mark of civilization in any society was the status of women, wrote Gladstone, and he noted that Montenegrin women were without power and completely subjected. However, as they were also highly respected and never 'violated', there was a state of almost happy equilibrium which, he rationalized, seemed to suit the women themselves. Gladstone was also able to gloss over, if not justify, the problem of the culture of cruelty in war and especially in the treatment of prisoners. Turks, he wrote, committed equally cruel, perhaps crueller, acts. It was possible that the atrocities were not actually committed by the Montenegrins but by their allies. One had to bear in mind, however, that theirs was a harsher culture, one in which agricultural work was women's work, where death in battle was valued and where it was better to cut off the head of one's fellow-soldier than allow him to be taken by the enemy.[87] Gladstone's words are important for us because they contained all the themes, social, scientific, religious and political, that ran through the works of so many of our authors and that had a formative role in establishing the racial identikit of the South Slav. Gladstone wrote that 'the indifference, or even contempt' with which his countrymen regarded 'this field of history, ought to be displaced by a more rational, as well as more honourable, sentiment of gratitude'.[88] As it turned out, the Montenegrins did not have the overall strength in numbers and therefore lacked the military capacity to lead their South Slav brothers. Plans for Montenegro's expansion and potential leadership in the region would eventually be subsumed by the hopes invested in Serbia. It was not long before the Serbs came to be regarded as the dominant power among the South Slavs in a process that involved the Montenegrins and Croats, among others, being defined racially as one with the Serbs. Before the Serbs' ascendancy was complete, however, Bulgars were also championed by many British voices.

Humphry Sandwith (1822–81), veteran traveller, former correspondent for *The Times* and army surgeon, had assisted the wounded in Belgrade during the Serbo-Turkish war and joined the great influx of the first wave of British 'Balkan volunteers'. He then collected a total of £7000 in England for the Serbian refugees in 1877.[89] In 1865, when he wrote the preface to Mackenzie and Irby's *Notes on the South Slavonic Countries in Austria and Turkey in Europe*, Sandwith compared the Bulgars with the Serbs, revealing his slight preference for the former partly because they were 'less warlike' (though he admitted this might change under different circumstances).[90] In early projections of a South Slav state, Bulgars were seen either as potential leaders or as equal partners with the Serbs. The 1876 Ottoman massacres of Bulgars, as we have observed, first evoked widespread indignation and disillusionment with the notion of British neutrality or 'peace with honour', so dear to Disraeli and his supporters, and then popular sympathy for the Orthodox Christian Slavs. This sympathy made the Eastern Question a European question. There was thus a bridging of the gap between Britain and South-eastern Europe accompanied by a more cynical approach towards Turkish rule there. The Bulgarian victims were worthy of compassion, and once deemed so, their champions argued that there was also a moral obligation to attend to their legitimate claims to freedom and autonomy. Yet, over a decade previously, Mackenzie and Irby had written of Belgrade, not Sofia, as the natural capital of a South Slav state. Some suggested that the Serbs could combine forces with the Bulgars, thus forming a large state or Balkan

Slavonic confederation. Eventually such a conglomerate would seem too unwieldy and unrealistic to those advocating the establishment of a South Slav state. In addition, the inclusion of Bulgaria in such a state or federation would make that entity far too strong from the point of view of the Great Powers. The Serb-Bulgar war of 1885 put an end to these speculations as it became evident that there were territorial disputes between these 'tribes' that had yet to be resolved.[91] Bulgaria remained an unpredictable force in the region, as its cooperation with the Central Powers in the First World War was to show.

As I have already intimated, distinctions between the South Slavs were often (and confusingly) blurred, but were then rapidly clarified once the preferred racial identikit emerged. In the proliferation of charts, tables and maps showing the 'national' and 'racial' character-istics of geographical regions, if they figured at all, Croats became one with the Serbs or were identified as 'Serbo-Croats'. Examples of this tendency are more pronounced from the late 1870s. Croatian cities became Serbian cities and all manner of inaccuracies and baseless assertions were transmitted in articles whose authors, para-doxically, so often prided themselves on their mission 'to inform'. That Croatian papers edited and printed in Zagreb were not written in the Cyrillic script seemed to puzzle the relatively seasoned trav-eller Andrew Archibald Paton (1811–74) in 1862.[92] Observers might, on occasion and briefly, prove favourably disposed towards Croats: Hungary oppressed them and the independence of their diet (*Sabor*) in Zagreb was stunted by Magyarization.[93] Overall, however, it would be true to say that Croats as Catholics were far from favourable, even unloved, and certainly no one's pet nation. 'The Croats themselves belong to the Serb branch of Slavs', wrote Evans, but they were vastly inferior, even, at first sight, 'repellent'.[94]

A series of articles on the Slavs appearing between 1878 and 1882 in the *Journal of the Anthropological Institute* illustrates well the rela-tionship between the process of ethnic stereotyping and the estab-lishment of racial hierarchies. The articles by Sir Henry Hoyle Howarth (1842–1923), barrister, public figure in Lancashire polit-ics and author of over one hundred scientific papers covering geol-ogy, ethnology, history and archaeology,[95] argued that Croats and Serbs were originally 'one race, speaking one language, and hav-ing one history'. Croats had 'retained their practical independence, although subject to the Hungarian Crown', but people should 'never forget that in origin and in race [Croats] belong to the great Servian stock'.[96] Freeman wrote in 1877 that, among the 'Southern Slaves [sic]', the Croats are 'the branch which makes the smallest figure in general history'. Like other weak 'tribes' they would fade from view, either blending imperceptibly with their stronger neighbours or pruned from the great Serbian trunk. The Croats' moment, fleeting as it was, had passed and now 'the Servian race, in all its forms and all the shiftings of its territory, has a higher interest'.[97]

These speculations were possible because of the currency of Spencerian (and later, social Darwinian) metaphors relating to strong and weak races and because our travellers were convinced of the seemingly uncontestable fact that the Serbs were the 'hope and pride' of the surrounding populations. From the 1860s it was already stated that with their naturally occurring, almost instinctive, egalitarian and democratic principles of communal organization (the zadrugas), and in the absence of a 'mob', there was much to recommend Serbian leadership of the region. It was in 1867 that Mackenzie and Irby described 'the story of Serbia' as consisting 'of four parts – growth, glory, fall, and rising again'.[98] The view of the South Slavs as a homogeneous 'race' yearning for a state of their own grew out of this view of Serbian history and national renewal. In this scenario the region as a whole was 'salvageable'. Mackenzie and Irby wrote that it was acceptable, indeed laudable, that the Serbs should be seen to avenge the 1389 'victory of the Muslim at Kossovo [which] plunged the wide lands between the Black Sea and the Adriatic into the darkness of Turkish barbarism, and opened to the janissary the road to the Danube, Buda, and Vienna'.[99] In 1874, while the 'dissolution of Turkey' was still the central point of the Eastern Question, 'the key of that question' was in Belgrade rather than Constantinople. Belgrade 'did not possess many imperial attributes' and was not yet ready to assume leadership of a South Slavonic empire or federation, as Serbia was not of the same standing as Prussia. However, its time would come.[100] In 1880, Stillman wrote: 'The Serb is at least the equal of the Magyar in all the virtues and capacities of civilisation; and the tenacity and vitality he has shown in his struggle of four centuries augurs well for the future of the empire in which he must play so important a part.'[101] The fact that 'every Serb is a gentleman' was also a point in Serbia's favour.[102] Sweeping geographic and racial generalizations were the essential components of a policy which had to be simultaneously rationally (or historically) and scientifically (or racially) justifiable as well as politically and economically viable. Nation-formation thus constituted a natural, evolutionary process enhanced by timely human intervention. It was true that a cloud hung over the Serbs from the perspective of their 'breeding'. For example, de Windt, our chronicler of 'Savage Europe', was to remark that in Serbia there was no aristocracy to speak of 'in the English sense of the word': 'How should there be when less than a century ago the ruler of the country was a pig-drover who could not sign his own name?' There were, nonetheless, agreeable types in Belgrade who had 'intermarried with the best families of Austria', the result being 'a so-called "society" which ... is to an outsider rather novel and attractive'.[103]

A country comprising South Slavs (and excluding Bulgars) was taking shape in the minds of people living far from the territories South Slavs inhabited. The Montenegrins and Bulgars had lost their primary position in the hierarchy of Balkan favourites well before the end of the century. The principality of Serbia (which became a kingdom in 1882) gained greater prestige at their expense. Alternative options put forward by various writers for the future of the Habsburg and Ottoman Slavs were discarded one by one. The appeal of the idea of Bulgaria joining with its South Slav neighbours had been short-lived, even though Bulgaria had its advocates in the Anglophone world through to the First World War (and beyond) who understood its dilemma (stemming from its unfair treatment after the Second Balkan War) when it took up with the Central Powers. To begin, people inside and outside the region writing about a South Slav state often meant quite different things. Some had envisaged the transformation of Austria-Hungary into a 'monarchical and Slavonic Switzerland'.[104] The so-called trialist solution to the problem of the unfulfilled national aspirations of the subject nationalities posited that Austria and Hungary accept a third and equal governing partner in the Habsburg South Slavs. Trialism remained popular among some groups of Slovenes and Croats through to 1918. However, our observers were to discard it as an unrealistic option: given the autocratic tendencies of Austria and the national chauvinism of the Hungarians, it was thought trialism would be a sham and no better than dualism.[105] By the 1900s, and especially after the Balkan Wars, outsiders understood the concept of Yugoslavism as Serbia enlarged, an entity that would 'reunite' peoples derived from the same racial stock taking different 'tribal' names. Other South Slav groups were not to feature particularly in this discussion. Slovenes, for example, were mentioned even less often than Croats. There was no question, however, that the Slovenes' national yearnings would be fulfilled in a state run from Belgrade rather than Vienna.

Nurturing Nature: The Foundations of a New Nation-State

Anthropologists and ethnographers had identified a hierarchy among South Slavs that, coincidentally, dovetailed with the prevailing geopolitical objectives of Britain at a time of increasing rivalry between the Great Powers and when 'the Turk' was 'retreating' from Europe. What was 'natural' was also, serendipitously, strategically advantageous. However, nature needed some nurturing, as attested in Mackenzie's image of Britain cultivating the national 'vines' of Europe, carefully pruning the young shoots in the interests of greater productivity and order. The happy outcome of 'nurturing nature', the marriage of science and politics, was that developments would seem to be both inevitable and the result of the general will. Put bluntly, strategic and economic concerns shaped Great Power attitudes to the Eastern Question while, increasingly, the language of national liberation and a reforming liberal high-mindedness, characteristic of the times, also left its stamp on foreign policy. The 'Nationality Principle', so firmly established in theory, was never rock solid in practice. This was in part because of the difficulty of allocating distinct geographical areas to a single national group. It was also in part because only stable and viable economic units (that is, units of a particular size) with which one might conduct trade and which would maintain stability and the balance of power in the region could be promoted. (One result of such calculations was the creation of national hybrids, the 'Czecho-slovaks' and 'Yugo-slavs'.) There were a number of ways of establishing who was worthy and who was not, which nation was the 'natural' leader and which was not. The comparison with Britain, which successfully brought together different people under a single government, was applied to the Serbs but not to the Austrians, for example. This was because, to outsiders, certain national groups were either dispensable or blendable or both. An 1898 article with the telling title 'A Dissolving Empire' looked to the future with apprehension. It observed, somewhat fatalistically, that the 'ramshackle and antiquated tenements of the House of Austria' were held together simply by the German language. The smaller nationalities, 'whose grievances are real, but whose expectations are far greater than is the capacity to realize them', were 'strong enough to endanger the Empire but not strong enough to protect themselves when they have shattered the present structure'.[106] In this context we can see that it was not surprising that the ideal of self-determination could only be applied unevenly after the First World War. Czechoslovakia emerged with a disproportionately high percentage of the former Empire's industrial capacity and with one-quarter of its population German-speaking. Yugoslavia (but not Austria) had a plenitude of seaports in response to the obsession of promoters of the Serbian cause up to 1914 (and beyond) that Belgrade be accorded its 'rightful' access to the Adriatic.[107]

Pragmatism modified the tone of those who championed the nationalist aspirations of the subject nationalities, as did the view that Austria-Hungary itself was no longer viable. Arguments for a new suite of independent European and Balkan states became compelling well before the Balkan Wars. The various Slavonic nationalisms, described as popular protest movements rising in opposition to the hegemony of Austria-Hungary, captured the imagination of outsiders even when those movements had failed to mobilize cultural and social elites within, let alone support at grass-roots level. Willoughby's 1877 article in *Fraser's Magazine* on the 'Slavonian races', mentioned above, suggested that 'great changes are imminent' and that the South Slavs were ready to overthrow 'Mussulman rule'. It also implied that they would 'revive the memories' of Serbian preeminence under the medieval leader, 'Stephan Dushan...in once more asserting the ascendancy of the Cross over the Crescent, and erecting a Christian state or federation of states from the Adriatic to the Black Sea'. Willoughby was in no doubt that the Serbs would do this, 'though how soon we may be unable to say'. At the same time, he recognized that Austria would continue to work towards realizing its goal of a true *Österreich* because Panslavonic aspirations were on the ascendant.[108]

If the nationality principle might be negotiable in the sense that the definition of a nation or nationality could vary according to prevailing interests (Bulgaria, as we have seen, fell outside the South Slav family in due course for that reason), the idea that the Dual Monarchy was no longer viable because it was not nationally-derived became an obsession. One commentator wrote in 1885 that Austria was 'not an independent and homogeneous State such, for example, as France or Italy, or indeed even second-class states of strong and compact nationality', but a 'political combination tolerated by the rest of Europe for the sake of preserving the balance of power'.[109] As such, it could not last. Evans argued (in 1880) that 'real parliamentary liberty is an impossibility in a state so fundamentally artificial' as Austria-Hungary whose 'monarchy cannot even call itself by a single name'.[110] He wrote freely and enthusiastically of 'great Serbian' aspirations as legitimate and dynamic. The Serbs were noted for their 'national instinct of self-preservation'. Their 'abhorrence of Austrian rule and absolute distrust of Hapsburg [sic] promises' had been maintained over centuries. The Serbs would not succumb to the repressive policies of Austria-Hungary, which did not constitute a real state because it was not 'backed by an united people'.[111] On the other hand, Evans attacked the scheme of 'Great Croatia' with its 'Latinising innovations' and its bigoted Catholic priesthood in Bosnia for whom the Cyrillic characters of the alphabet were 'an invention of the devil'.[112] The 'artificial' state of the Habsburgs could not hope to offer a solution to the Eastern Question. Indeed its presence on the Balkan peninsula in the modern age could only be temporary or transitional. In effect, Habsburg rule merely united all those it oppressed, 'Mahometan, Serb, and Latin, in common antagonism to herself'. In contrast, Britain was in a position to settle the Eastern Question in a 'triumphant and lasting manner' because it had at its disposal a 'mighty engine', the 'principle of Nationality, as the true basis of reorganisation'. Evans saw two possibilities for the Balkan Peninsula, Russian incorporation or national union, and concluded: 'our Government may take its choice'.[113]

The speeches and writings of Gladstone had marked a symbolic turning point in attitudes towards the region from the late 1870s. The relentlessly optimistic tone of the rhetoric in favour of applying the nationality principle to the South Slavs could not negate completely the view expressed in 1899, that it was to Austria at least (if not Hungary) that the Slavonic nations owed 'the preservation of their distinct nationality and language' and, by implication, their national awakening. Thus, while there was room for parliamentary reform in the Dual Monarchy, for a small number of our outsiders the sprawling geographic and national mosaic nevertheless had a role to play in the new century.[114] Just a few years later, however, this was the (extreme) minority view, not that of mainstream liberals or of popular opinion. The Monarchy's lack of a homogeneous core, the fact that it was 'a fortuitous concourse of racial atoms', stood against it, especially in anti-Austrian propaganda during the First World War.[115]

Serbia, however, had yet to obtain all the necessary requirements for successful leadership. Notably it lacked the potential for economic expansion. Thus, in all discussions about the emerging South Slav state, the question of a Serbian outlet to the sea dominated from at least the 1860s through to 1918. We know that as early as 1865,

Mackenzie and Irby wrote that Belgrade, 'situated at the junction of two large rivers, and forming the natural terminus of railroads uniting four seas... is evidently declared by nature, if not, as has been said, the capital of a south eastern empire, at least the capital of the South Slavonic lands'. Belgrade's position marked it as 'the port of regions far wider than the Principality of Serbia'. At the time this assessment grew out of an anti-Austrian sentiment as well as the view that support for a strong South Slav state would extend British influence in the region while keeping Russia in check.[116] But without access to the sea, the capital would be stunted. It became necessary to speak of 'restoring' to Serbia what it was imagined it had once possessed. As academics denied or negated the ethnic integrity of other South Slav nations, the extent of Serbia's 'former possessions' grew proportionately. Already the 'Latin' presence in Bosnia-Herzegovina was repudiated. The blending of all South Slavs into the Serbian nation meant it was much easier to speak of a 're-union' of all the lands in the region, including eventually and inevitably the valuable coastline, under its ('rightful' and 'restored') Serbian leadership. In 1873 Sandwith wrote of the 'appearance of Bosnia, Herzegovina and Montenegro on the map' as 'strangely incomplete without a seaboard'. That Dalmatia (which, he wrote, was 'naturally and essentially a part of Bosnia') was in the hands of Austrians left the fine inland provinces 'isolated, cut off,... poor and barbarous'. He continued: 'Probably Bosnia will be incorporated with Servia, and then a great and rich province will refuse any longer to be strangled by the hand of Austria.'[117] Evans, writing later but still in the 1870s, consolidated these thoughts with his ruminations on the relationship between Bosnia-Herzegovina (hence, by default, Serbia) and Dubrovnik. Their futures were bound together: 'The plodding genius of the Serbs needs to be fanned into energy by these fresh sea breezes – their imagination languishes for want of this southern sunshine!'[118] Montenegro similarly, argued Freeman in 1880, needed more land and greater access to the sea.[119] There was a strong sense that provinces, kingdoms and regions might feasibly be connected (or 'reconnected') to form a workable nation-state. The Eastern Question, wrote Freeman in 1882, could never be 'closed' until all South-eastern Europe was free. This necessitated the departure of Austria and Turkey: negative responses to Austria's occupation of Bosnia-Herzegovina showed that national movements there and in Dalmatia could not be 'put down'.[120]

For Freeman all of the national groups belonged to a single race. It was the same for most Yugoslav lobbyists through to 1918 and, for a significant proportion of them, well beyond that. In the early 1880s Freeman wrote of the 'fragments of nations unnaturally parted from their brethren' by the imperial powers and of fragments that 'yearn to be joined to their natural countrymen and their natural princes'. (In much the same way, 30 years later, Seton-Watson was to argue for the 'reunion' of the three South Slav sisters, Serbs, Croats and Slovenes.) Continuing in this vein and extending the truncated body metaphor, Freeman wrote in 1892 that the South Slavs had been cut off from each other by non-Slavs. Though the occupation of Bosnia-Herzegovina by Austria was not to everyone's liking, Freeman noted that it was natural that the 'body and mouth' (Bosnia-Herzegovina and Dalmatia) that were 'parted asunder' and 'unnaturally kept asunder' in an 'extreme case of unnatural disunion' were now connected. Like his predecessors (Mackenzie and Irby, for example), he promoted the cause of a mythical past with his evocation of the 'great continuous Slavonic mass': when Illyria (whose boundaries are not delimited) was 'united', it had 'flourished'.[121] Ideas advanced about South Slav unity by Croats in the Illyrian movement were thus to be described as the first step not in the union, but in the reunion of South Slav Siamese twins (then triplets) separated, it seems, by some violent primitive surgery performed in stages first by the Ottoman and then the Austrian imperialists. Indeed, one writer in 1913 discussed the Serbian people's 'long cherished ambitions' and belief that they were the 'inheritors of the territories of the old Illyrian Empire which extended from the Adriatic to the Aegean, and from the mountains of Thessaly to far beyond the Save [River]'. He then referred to the proposed Serb state as 'united Illyria'. It was the 'manifest destiny of the Serb race to be united in one community', in 'one great homogeneous state'.[122] This idea of the Serbs' 'manifest destiny' fitted well with the heroic evocation of Serbs reclaiming the hallowed ground of Kosovo and Macedonia and assuming their 'natural' claim to a seaboard with the acquisition of the Dalmatian coast. In all the apparently reconstituted nations that emerged, or were to emerge after 1918, there were large minorities inhabiting contested lands. Generally, the closer a state was to being established, the greater the ease with which those contested lands, and the contradictions or omissions in the historically justified claims and master narratives of the dominant 'races', were overlooked or ignored. Ultimately there was no room for historical variants in the Yugoslav nation-building narrative.

Realpolitik, merging with idealism and liberal supremacist views on religion, race and nation, led ineluctably to the imagining of a country which met the requirements of outsiders' perceptions of what the region needed and what constituted a functional modern state. These imaginings were justified by the scientifically observed information, the 'facts', uncovered by racial theorists and anthropologists, as well as the selective and often self-serving reading of history. If there was any doubt as to the unity of the newly defined race then, again, the example of the United Kingdom was testament to what could be achieved by a multinational state and to its possibilities over time. What was natural then, coincidentally, would also be economically viable, and thus stable. Some commentators were more cautious and warned that the dissolution of the Turkish Empire did not necessarily present a solution to the Eastern Question. For example, Reeve had written in 1876 that the story of allegiances was not as simple as some observers liked to think, in particular on the question of Bosnia, whose fate in a Serb-dominated state he predicted would be in question. What, he asked, would be the prospect for half a million 'Sclavonian' Muslims if they were incorporated into Serbia which had already 'expelled every Mussulman from her own territory'? On the other hand, he wondered whether that would be as bad as the prospect of half a dozen or more new states springing up. These small states would embroil all of Europe in their disputes. More than anything, he wrote, Europe desired peace. As 'the whole of Turkey-in-Europe' was 'charged with combustible materials', it was the duty of 'every sound English politician and every rational man, not to seek to fan this flame, but if possible to extinguish it' and work towards restoring peace.[123] So the new entity (or entities) had not only to be viable, but also had to put an end to seemingly unrealistic quests by small nations for autonomy, while preserving stability.

Some of the critics of those whose imaginations had been fired by 'the cry of the oppressed nationalities' were alarmed by the potential havoc that would result from the 'absolute application' of the national principle they advocated. Thus on the question of the future of Albania, we read in an October 1881 article in the *Edinburgh Review* that '"Autonomy" is a benefit conditional on the character of the organisation which it serves to shelter and develop. Independence becomes an evil, and ceases to be a right, when destructive anarchy, not peaceful progress, is fostered by its sway.'[124] Albania was among those nations that had 'none of the qualities requisite to form a united nation', and only became someone's 'pet' or favourite 'little nationality' when Durham made her trips to the Balkans about twenty years later. For the vast majority of our outsiders Albania had no naturally ordained or historically derived coherence, geographical, political, social or religious. The waves of conversions to Islam there (resulting from a general preference for 'apostasy to persecution') set a 'general conformity ... to Mahometanism' against the 'savage independence' of the Catholic faith, in contrast to the laudable independence of the Orthodox faith elsewhere. There were critics of the idea that a 'community of descent alone' (the integrated race or nation) constituted reason enough to support a movement for independence: both 'unity of history and nobility of institutions' were the fundamental requirements for a successful transition toward independence.[125] Interestingly, then, the constructed 'unity' of an ancient, monolithic South Slav history and its cultural monuments was (and would remain) an underlying theme in the propaganda of Yugoslav activists of the region as well as their outside supporters. Furthermore, the criteria for the conditional support of national liberation movements outlined, as we have seen, so unselfconsciously by Reeve, influenced perceptions of Yugoslavia and its 'national question' throughout the country's history.

The Legacy of the Balkan Wars

By the time of the Balkan Wars, much of the polemical writing on the racial and historical unity of the South Slav nation had achieved in its readers' minds the status of fact. The Balkan Wars were important in further promoting the view that there was a need for a firm position on the future of Habsburg and non-Habsburg South Slavs. These wars established Serbia's prestige as the superior force; its standing soared and its suitability as the future leader of its South Slav brothers was definitively established by virtue of its military prowess. Moreover, the Serbs had become the best known and reputedly most deserving of the South Slav nationalities. Through a series of rebellions, they had won their autonomy as well as acclaim as a heroic nation of independent warriors. The story of their journey from Ottoman vassal to Kingdom came to rival and then eclipse Montenegro's tale of audacity against overwhelming odds in its quest for independence. Inevitably, it seems, outsiders superimposed a social and democratic struggle onto the Serbian (and Montenegrin) national struggle against, and triumph over, foreign oppression. Having endured a kind of cultural and national hibernation after the 1389 defeat on the Kosovo plain at the hands of the Turks, the Serbs were now assuming their rightful place as leaders of the South Slavs. Serbian liberation from Ottoman rule came to be seen as a revival of the fortunes of the distant past. The theme of national resurgence after a long night of foreign control and cultural slumber dominated Serbian political and national rhetoric throughout the period under review in this book. It struck a chord with our Yugoslav sympathizers decades before the First World War. Aspects of the liberation struggle, including the bloody rivalries between the Obrenović and Karađorđević (Black George) dynasties, were unpalatable to outsiders. The 1903 regicide by Serb officers of the Austrophile Obrenović king, Aleksandar, and his queen, Draga, led to the reinstatement of the Karađorđevićs and did not reflect well on the Serbian state. It alienated the ruling houses of Europe and led Britain temporarily to cut off diplomatic relations with Serbia. The damage to Serbia's reputation was short-lived, however. The new king, Petar I, had a glowing reputation as a man with a thoroughly modern outlook, having lived most of his adult life under the civilizing influence of Western Europeans. Having translated Mill's *On Liberty* into Serbian, he was expected to usher in a 'Periclean era' of democratic and cultural progress.

The First Balkan War (October 1912–May 1913) led to the final expulsion of the Ottomans from Europe by a coalition of Balkan states, Serbia, Montenegro, Bulgaria and Greece. Serbia had doubled its territory and Greece won much of Macedonia. The Second Balkan War (June–August 1913) broke out when Bulgaria attacked Serbia because it was unhappy with the territorial readjustments after the First Balkan War. The Serbs, supported by the Greeks, Romanians and Montenegrins, trounced the Bulgars. Serbia was triumphant again and, while it had not gained access to the Mediterranean, it secured a pre-eminent negotiating position in the region. Its international stature was at its height. It was during the Balkan Wars that Durham became disillusioned with the Serbs because of their treatment of the Albanians and the atrocities committed against them. Albania had become an independent state after the First Balkan War but there were substantial Albanian minorities outside its borders and under Serbian jurisdiction. As we will see, Durham's efforts to

bring this potential problem to the attention of other more powerful commentators came to nothing. Her impotence on this topic
was a product both of the fact that she was pleading the cause of a
group that elicited little sympathy and attracted few devotees, and
of the fact that its claims went against those of the dominant voices
within and without the region. Similarly, the Balkan Wars brought
into sharp relief the problematic question of Macedonian identity.
The issue of the place of Macedonians (or 'South Serbs' as they were
known in Serbia) in the new South Slav nuclear family would surface
again in due course.[126] But the moment of triumph in 1913 was not
an opportune time to consider in any detail such anomalies. Soon
another war, one of international proportions, would lead outsiders
to dismiss these concerns as trivial in the grand scheme of things as
they nurtured the 'natural' leaders of the region.

The 'outgoing Turk' may not have been demonized equally by
all our observers, but the fear of the vacuum left by his departure
had brought to the fore the rivalry towards Russia (on the part
of Austria-Hungary) and Germany (on the part of Britain). Great
Power consensus did not survive this shift in allegiances. Inevitably
some solutions to the problems such a vacuum might precipitate
were deemed more attractive (or more historically justifiable) than
others. Most importantly for us, it was in 1913 that the South Slav
'nation' seemed poised for 'reunification' after decades of preparation. While the Balkan Wars had led to its rapid expansion, Serbia
still required its 'natural' outlet to the sea, and so any future attempts
at 'European Reconstruction' and the establishment of the borders
of 'United Illyria' would have to take full account of Serbia's most
pressing economic need.[127] Discussion in the magazine literature
spanning many years affirmed that it was just and fitting to ratify
Serbia's territorial aspirations in 1913 because they represented the
aspirations of a nation, fully formed yet frustrated by its fragmentation. After the assassination of the Archduke and his wife in Sarajevo,
Francis Gribble (1862–1946), an Oxford graduate and prolific writer
of books on court and cultural life in Europe, who described his rec-
reation as 'continental travel',[128] contemplated the prospect of the
establishment of a new state, 'United Servia'. He drew on the examples of Italy and Germany, noting that 'racial problems' and 'the
emergence of new nationalities based upon racial self-consciousness'
had been a dominant fact in European development over the previous 50 years.[129] In this article, aptly titled 'Servia Irredenta', Gribble
held that the overwhelming majority of South Slavs were Serbs who

shared the same goal. While he thought the potential existed for some difference of opinion within the Catholic (that is, Croat) 'branch' of the race – called by some the 'Croato-Serbs'[130] – Gribble concluded that 'the tendency of the times, throughout the world, certainly is for racial self-consciousness [nationalism] to increase, and for dogmatic fanaticism [religion] to diminish in intensity'.[131] It is easy for us now to understand how effortlessly notions of Serbia, United Serbia, Great(er) Serbia and Yugoslavia would come to be intermingled in the minds and writings of our outside observers of South Slav affairs. It was not an intermingling entirely based on ignorance or selective blindness. We know that by the end of the century those who made it their business to write about the Balkans did so with confidence and on the basis of their own travels and researches or those of others, often their like-minded friends and colleagues. Perhaps their spellings were inconsistent but Montenegrins, Macedonians, Croats, Serbs and Slovenes were all familiar to them. The racial intermingling was the outcome of a process of rationalization whereby a state whose establishment was geopolitically desirable had to be seen to be emerging from a pre-existing nation.

There had always been a balancing act between idealism and realism in the possible solutions to the Habsburg nationalities question. Realism born of self-interest or ideological predisposition brought together individuals who might have nothing in common otherwise, as would be the case in the First World War. If the view that the Dual Monarchy had to be expunged from the map of Europe was not based on reasoned argument but on prejudice, it did not matter because the goal of 'freeing' peoples, of providing them with the opportunity to 'reclaim' the vast territory and independence they allegedly had once had and of forming nation-states, was so laudable. This goal, in keeping with the spirit of the times as well as geopolitical priorities, overrode or obscured any negative motives. Great effort was expended establishing that the dominant view was popularly acclaimed and was as historically justifiable as it was inevitable. A distant past spoke to the present and the future as Illyria was to be reunited.

2 The Expansion of Gallant Serbia into Yugoslavia: 1914–1920

Robert Seton-Watson made the following pronouncement in the book, *The War and Democracy*, he co-wrote in 1914 after the war had begun:

> We are witnessing the birth-throes of a new nation, the rise of a new national consciousness, the triumph of the idea of National Unity among three Southern Slav sisters – the Croats, Serbs, and Slovenes. Fate has assigned to Britain and to France an important share in the solution of the problem, and it is our duty to insist that this solution shall be radical and permanent, based upon the principle of Nationality and the wishes of the Southern Slav race. Only by treating the problem as an organic whole, by avoiding patchwork remedies and by building for a distant future, can we hope to remove one of the chief danger-centres in Europe.[1]

For Seton-Watson it was 'inconceivable' that South Slav union should be held back: 'So far … as the Southern Slavs are concerned, the triumph of the Allies ought to mean the creation of a new State on the Eastern Adriatic, the expansion of gallant Serbia into Jugoslavia … and the achievement of Unity by three kindred races, Serbs, Croats, and Slovenes.'[2] This view, shared by many others, prevailed well before the end of the First World War. The idea that the allies should apply the 'principle of Nationality' in a 'radical and permanent' solution to the challenges facing what had become known as the South Slav race was well established, but war made it a possibility. It was an idea that was decades in the making and falsely imbued with an even longer historical and cultural pedigree in order to justify the creation of a Yugoslav state.

The collapse of empires in 1918 necessitated the reorganization of former Habsburg lands, and the experience of war affected the shape the successor states would take. Seton-Watson and his circle were deeply involved in mapping the New Europe. They were as interested in the emergence of Czechoslovakia and an enlarged Romania as they were in Serbia's expansion and the union of the Yugoslavs. Tomàš Masaryk (1850–1937), 'father' of Czechoslovakia and close confidant of Seton-Watson, took up a lectureship at the newly established School of Slavonic Studies at the University of London in 1915. He may not have attracted the same adoring attention as Garibaldi had when promoting the Italian nationalist cause in England in 1864, but he was certainly politically active and his presence was celebrated; the prime minister himself congratulated King's College on Masaryk's appointment, which Seton-Watson had arranged.[3] Individual 'Yugoslavs' did not enjoy such a high profile, but a wide public embraced their cause with gusto, as indeed did Masaryk, who had been a strong influence on South Slav activists for many years. The Kingdom of Serbs, Croats and Slovenes was not a makeshift creation of the war but part of the vision for a New Europe. The international situation between 1914 and 1918, the nature of the war and the relationships forged in the war, confirmed to outsiders what many of them had come to accept in the decades prior to the assassinations in Sarajevo: that a state comprising South Slavs was as necessary as it was historically justifiable. Historians are often accused of placing too much importance on the acts of significant men and ignoring the wider social or cultural forces at work at 'turning points' in history. I argue that in the case of the promotion and establishment of the Kingdom of Serbs, Croats and Slovenes, the importance of such men and the transnational forces they represented has been undervalued. The literature on the emergence of the new 'nation-states' after 1918 focuses more on the (apparently) popular base of Yugoslav nationalism than on the careers and influence of individuals. The relationship between outsiders and the creation of the successor states is important and should be written back into the story of the New Europe. As important and almost completely ignored is the link between twentieth-century champions of Yugoslavism, like Seton-Watson, and the ideas of the earlier generation of propagandists encountered in Chapter 1. Even if we ignore the long view and point only to the rapid disintegration of the Yugoslav ideal in the 1920s and 1930s within the Kingdom itself, it would seem reasonable to ask what it was that led a man of Seton-Watson's learning and standing in the international academic and diplomatic community to argue so vigorously and passionately the case for the expansion of 'Gallant Serbia into Jugoslavia', one of the cornerstones of the peace-making at war's end.

The war years were decisive in the shaping of Yugoslavism; but receptivity to the view that the dismemberment of the Dual Monarchy and the establishment of the successor states were vital for European stability was so great that the seeds had to have been sown well before the war and to have fallen on particularly fertile ground. The new nationalism's momentum, such as it was, was manipulated from above and also from without. In our case it was imagined and announced and then given a name: Yugoslavism. During the war, champions of the new state argued that they were articulating the will of a broad cross-section of people and that a national revolution, the product of a mass-based popular movement, was afoot. Yet Yugoslavism had not penetrated deeply into the local national cultures, and the quest for unification remained an ideal shared by a politically and culturally disparate elite. Where they did exist, the groups of individuals from different nationalities who shared the vision of a South Slav state often had little in common politically or culturally. The Yugoslav Committee was led by a group of Croats close to Seton-Watson. These men had diverse political experiences and beliefs but shared Seton-Watson's anti-Habsburg views as well as his ideas about self-determination. The Yugoslav Committee lobbied for the unification of South Slavs as equals, in some cases as an undifferentiated whole, and rejected the idea of Yugoslavia as Serbia expanded but, overall, had little impact on the Entente powers or on the ruling Serbs. It was predictable that the monolithic view from without about the new race and nation would subsume contrasting (internal) visions of the Yugoslav ideal, which were too divergent to provide solid underpinning for the new state.

The Kingdom rose from the ashes of the war and on the foundation of the enormously successful lobbying and fund raising on behalf of Serbs by the Allies. While there were some among the Allies who made a distinction between Serbs and 'Yugoslavs', most did not, and used the terms almost interchangeably. The image of the South Slavs in the First World War was that of Serbia, triumphant, embattled, martyred and triumphant again. Serbia's entire history was condensed and superimposed onto the future Kingdom. Hence the new Yugoslav state would be the culmination of a 500-year cycle of Serbian glory, defeat at the hands of the Ottomans, decline and gradual resurgence. At the same time, the role of Europe's protectors and saviours, the 'guardians at the gate' who held back the infidel, divided the parties. Prior to unification Serbs, Croats, Slovenes and Montenegrins all claimed they had saved Europe. After 1918, however, this would no longer be possible, and whoever won the title of the protector of peace and civilization in Europe would garner favours that lasted at least until the outbreak of a second world war.

The Archduke's Visit to Sarajevo: 'An Act of Provocation'

The assassination of the Archduke Franz Ferdinand in Sarajevo on 28 June 1914 was universally deplored. While recognizing that the conspirators had had dealings with elements in the Serbian military and intelligence, our onlookers' near unanimous response was that the Serbian government was not responsible in any way for the actions of the young assassin, a Bosnian Serb, Gavrilo Princip, and his accomplices in what has broadly come to be known as the *Mlada Bosna* (Young Bosnia) movement.[4] Belgrade Serbs sympathetic to *Mlada Bosna* included military officers who were members of the Black Hand. This group, also known as 'Unification or Death', which aptly described their commitment to the goal of bringing all Serbs together into one considerably enlarged state, had facilitated the traffic of arms to Bosnia to the would-be assassins among others. Aware of the general mood of the young radicals across the border, sympathizers from Serbia proper pulled back from the planned assassination but only when it was too late to make a difference. Leading members of the Black Hand had been involved in the assassination of the last ruling Obrenović in Belgrade in 1903 and were themselves eventually shot for treason after the Salonika trials of 1917.[5] The fact that Franz Ferdinand was known to support some kind of federal solution to the South Slav nationality problem was proposed as a reason for Serbia's apparent tolerance (or perhaps its fomenting) of anti-Habsburg plotting within and in close proximity to its borders: a federalist solution would thwart Serbia's territorial aspirations. According to this reasoning, Serbia's Prime Minister Nikola Pašić (1845–1926) and his ruling Radical Party had no reason to inhibit the activities of anti-Austrian elements in Bosnia. However, the Serbian government's behaviour after the assassination was seen to be exemplary, especially as it was held that it had previously warned Vienna of the danger of such a visit by the Archduke.

By contrast, Austria's reaction to the crime, its insistence on participating in the Serbian government's inquiry, gained the Dual Monarchy nothing by way of sympathy from outside observers. It caused even those who may have raised some questions regarding Serbia's possible negligence to turn against Austria-Hungary and take up the cause of the Serbs. A general theme to emerge was that the visit of Franz Ferdinand, so 'inconsiderately' planned to coincide with the anniversary of the defeat at the Battle of Kosovo, could have been interpreted by Serbs as an act of provocation on the part of Austria.[6] After all, asked Sir Valentine Chirol, the author of a 1914 Oxford Pamphlet entitled *Serbia and the Serbs*, why would the Serbian government be implicated in a plot that did not serve South Slav interests? He continued, noting there were 'many mysterious features about [the] tragedy', that not enough precautions had been taken and that the demands of Austria were 'outrageous'.[7] Wartime propaganda regularly restated this position. In a 1916 article the Swiss-based publication, *La Serbie*, explained why the assassination was 'to be expected' in Sarajevo at that time and concluded there was 'nothing extraordinary' about a crime committed in 'such circumstances'.[8] Princip was much like the Austrian socialist, Friedrich Adler, who assassinated the Prime Minister, Count Stürgkh, in October 1916. There had been no conspiracy in either case, argued *La Serbie*, and both men were individuals killing individuals in order to 'kill the system'.[9] The paper claimed the Austrians would stop at nothing to silence opposition and so, when in the war they began to commit atrocities against the Serbs, they were avenging an 'imaginary crime'.[10] It was common to accuse the Austrians of failing to take the necessary precautionary measures and failing to provide adequate protection for the Archduke and his wife. It was clear to the Dual Monarchy's enemies and critics that the Austrian governor in Sarajevo, General (later Field Marshal) Oskar Potiorek was the guilty party, not Pašić.[11]

The Austrian 'act of provocation' was much more than an imprudent visit by the Habsburg heir and his wife to a city allegedly smouldering with 'national revolutionaries'; more broadly it comprised the Empire's plan for aggrandisement in the region. It was a direct challenge to Serbia's allies, notably Russia, because they would not tolerate the violation of Serbian sovereignty or German and Austrian dominance in the Balkans. The first and possibly most long-lived truism about the war was that the assassination of the Archduke in

Sarajevo was not the cause of war, but provided Austria with the pretext it needed to issue its ultimatum to Serbia in July 1914 in a bid to retain its control in the region.[12] Germany, having promised to come to Austria's aid in such an event, had the opportunity it finally needed to activate its plans for launching a European (if not a world) war. According to this almost universally accepted argument, Serbia was thwarting Germany's and the Dual Monarchy's drive eastwards and had to be put in its place. So another of the earliest potent and enduring truths of the war – the innocence of Serbia – became one of the essential tenets of Western historiography of the outbreak of the war and the foundational tenet of the new South Slav state.

The opening quotation from Seton-Watson's *War and Democracy* indicates clearly the path he was to take on the nationalities question from the outset. This is further confirmed by a letter he wrote to his wife on 6 August 1914:

> From now onwards the Great Serbian State is inevitable; and *we* must create it. I find Steed and Strachey are absolutely at one with me in this. You must not say much of what I write to you, but this much is clear. Dalmatia, Bosnia, Croatia, Istria must be united to Serbia: at the final settlement we must save the Diet of Agram [Zagreb]. Romania must have all her kinsmen.

Seton-Watson's sons, Hugh and Christopher, note his was a program 'of the amputation of the monarchy', not its destruction.[13] The Monarchy's chance of surviving such an amputation would depend on a number of variables, among which was the changing status of other nationalities including the Germans, Magyars, Czechs and Slovaks. As Seton-Watson would also be advocating further 'amputations' that amounted to a radical restructuring of Europe in accordance with the 'nationality principle', the Dual Monarchy's prospects for emerging intact after the war were not promising.

It was common for wartime propagandists to address the strain of violence in Serbia's political history in order to highlight that it was a thing of the past. In his 1914 pamphlet, referred to above, Chirol wrote that in some circles, if Serbia was known at all it was only for the 'revolting brutality' of the act that sent 'a thrill of horror throughout Europe' in 1903. But Serbia's 'splendid gallantry' in the field in the Balkan Wars meant that it was a fighting power 'of no mean value'.[14] This was a typical observation. Another 1914 publication noted that if the Serbs had once exhibited 'an unhappy

fondness for assassination and intrigue', the result of the machinations of powerful cliques, or the *čaršija*, those days were long gone.
The Second Balkan War may well have shown 'that these passionate little peoples could attack one another more fiercely than they
had fought their old Moslem masters' but, also, that the Serbs were
'born fighters' and made 'excellent soldiers'.[15] While the report on
atrocities committed in the Balkan Wars produced by the Carnegie
Endowment for International Peace in 1914 reflected badly on all
parties involved, many noted that for the Serbs there were extenu-
ating circumstances.[16] They had been freeing themselves from
'Turkish tyranny'. It was also plain that the Serbs were both 'a more
heroic and a more kindly people than their enemies, the Germans
of Austria and the Magyars of Hungary'.[17] These were constant
themes in Allied propaganda for the duration of the war and, we
will see, in the commemorative practices recalling wartime comradeship in the interwar years. The combination of military prowess
and their loyalty endeared the Serbs to their allies. Seton-Watson, in
his characteristically persuasive style, claimed that the events of 1912
and 1913 and 'all of the past fifteen months have forever exploded
the false and superficial estimation of Serbia with which the news
service of Vienna and Budapest had so skillfully inoculated our
press'.[18] Serbia's innocence was never in question and never would
be in the eyes of the majority of our international observers. At the
same time, historians have argued that the role of Austria has been
diminished in much that has been written on Germany's guilt for
the outbreak of the war. Samuel Williamson, for example, believes
that in the effort to establish Germany's blame, Austria's culpability
and its long-term aims vis-à-vis the proposed subjugation of Serbia
are glossed over. He is an advocate for more focus on the culpability
of the aggressors, not less.[19]

Deploring the assassination of the Archduke was not incompatible with a position that was firmly anti-Austrian. This was because
Austria's reaction was still more deplorable and its demands seen
to be completely unreasonable and out of step with the times. Post-
1945 communist historiography all but romanticized the activities
of the *Mlada Bosna* movement and then gave it a popular, or at least
a cross-class and cross-national, profile. This historiography also
celebrated the South Slav revolutionary inclination and underplayed
the bearing of outside forces on the establishment of Yugoslavia.[20]
Youthful assassins, one step beyond boyish pranksters, it would
seem, provided the 'warlike party in Vienna' with 'an unexpected

gift from the God Mars'; this was the pretext it needed finally to take action against the Serbs.[21] Princip's act was made to speak for all Serbs, Muslims and Croats in the province and beyond. According to Seton-Watson, nationality among the Slavs was like an 'inrolling tide': 'If their emancipation is one of the results of this gigantic clash of arms, the misery and suffering of Europe will at least have a compensation.'[22] This was a local issue with global repercussions if left unresolved. Intellectuals, peasants and merchants alike, the argument went, were increasingly wedded to the idea of a South Slav struggle for 'national liberation', creating the atmosphere in which Princip felt free, indeed justified, to act as he did. This atmosphere made it possible for Princip and his accomplices to think of assassination not as a last resort but as the first step, an appropriate method of bringing to the world's attention their aspirations. Nobel Prize-winning novelist Ivo Andrić (1892–1975) retrospectively idealized what he perceived to be an inherently revolutionary Yugoslav impulse in his acclaimed novel *The Bridge over the River Drina* which, interestingly, he wrote during the Second World War and which was first published in 1945.[23]

In 1927, Hamilton Fish Armstrong (1893–1973), the editor of the influential American journal *Foreign Affairs*, posed the question, 'Who was Gavrilo Princip?' His answer was, 'A mere cog in the ponderous machinery propelling Europe toward the catastrophe of the World War.'[24] The greater the complexity of the discussion of the causes of the war, the more distant, mysterious and irrelevant the assassins became. They could be cast as sympathetic figures because they had attached themselves so passionately to 'progressive' ideas of freedom and national independence in the smoky cafés of Sarajevo. Theirs was the voice and collective conscience of a (non-existent) 'nation' in a just campaign in opposition to its multinational oppressors and their endless acts of provocation. The 'revolutionary' aspirations of the new nationalists were fundamental to the establishment of Yugoslav legitimacy internationally and were celebrated in the work of interwar and post-1945 historians and publicists as well as writers like Andrić.

The War in the Balkans

Austria-Hungary declared war on Serbia on 28 July 1914, four weeks after the assassinations in Sarajevo and five days after sending the ultimatum. The early months of the war saw Austria embarrassed by three Serbian victories in August, September and November 1914. The Dual Monarchy had underestimated the difficulty of the terrain and the resolve of the enemy. Austria's military capacity, both in terms of manpower and *matériel*, was weaker than that of the other empires, including Russia. The Austrians were poorly equipped and poorly staffed and it soon became clear that the Empire had not maintained its military capacity. In fact, it had spent much less per capita on the military than the other Great Powers.[25]

Initially it was the Belgian martyrs, closer to home, who were to take centre stage in the Allies' propaganda campaigns. Similarly, from the perspective of Germany, action against the Serbs in the Balkans was only occasionally considered of principal importance, with more resources directed towards the war against the Russians. Austria realized it was a poor second to Germany, both in leadership and initiative, as the war turned against the Central Powers. The propaganda on Serbia's behalf, discussed above, reveals that if there had been any doubt as to the moral worthiness of Serbia as an ally, its exemplary heroism in these first months of the war reassured the sceptics. At the time Serbia's perceived political culture, notably its seeming propensity for political assassinations and regicide, meant, for some, that its recent history was not 'unblotted'. But, as Chirol noted in 1914, its victories against the 'Austrian Goliath', whom it had 'smitten ... hip and thigh', showed Serbia had 'the splendid pluck' to wipe out 'even worse blots'.[26] The outpouring of sympathy for the Serbs recognized them as fearless and loyal allies as the following 1915 excerpt from the *Contemporary Review* attests: 'This, indeed, is a war of defence of small nationalities, and so far as courage, combined with able generalship is concerned, Serbia can take her stand by the side of Belgium, and claim that she has shown herself worthy of the blood England and France have shed on her behalf.'[27] Just like the Belgians, the Serbs were subjected to atrocities. The Austrians were accused of 'waging a war of extermination' in what was for them 'a punitive expedition'.[28]

The Serbs, whose army included veterans of the Balkan Wars, held back the Austrians after their advance in September 1914. The Austrians, under Commander Potiorek, launched their second attack on 8 September, came to a standstill and then attacked again on 8 November. The Serbs, commanded by their much admired military leader Radomir Putnik, evacuated Belgrade and after a brief respite triumphed in December. Italy's entry into the war on the side of the Entente, the April 1915 debacle at Gallipoli (which thwarted plans to knock Turkey out of the war to support Russia and to win over the Balkans) and Austria's preoccupation with the war in the east, notably the advances of the Russians in Galicia, all had a bearing on the Central Powers' performance on the Balkan front. Reflecting on these events after the war in 1921 Gordon Gordon-Smith, a Captain of the Royal Serbian Army,[29] wrote that the Germans had underestimated Serbian military strength and that Serbia's efforts were of great importance. Indeed the title of this article was 'The War Won on the Eastern Front'. Gordon-Smith wrote: 'There is not the slightest doubt that Serbia, by her gallant resistance, saved Europe. If she had given way in the first four weeks of the war Europe would have been doomed.' Moreover, the failure to come to Serbia's aid between July and September 1915 was the 'most shameful page for the Allies in the whole history of the war'.[30] This was the prevailing view of Serbia's contribution to the war effort.

After the flurry of activity in late 1914 a stalemate ensued. The Austrians did not have the resources to mount a counter-attack and the Serbs, in the absence of vital supplies from their allies, could not wage a continuous offensive. In 1915 operations on the Balkan front proved disastrous for the Entente. It was the German Chief of Staff Erich von Falkenhayn's goal to open up the line to Turkey by ousting Serbia, and the entry of Bulgaria into the war on the side of the Central Powers was to help achieve this. The French presence in Salonika under the command of General Maurice Sarrail was ineffectual in the face of the combined forces of the Germans, Austrians and Bulgars. Serbia, like most other countries, was not prepared for a long war. The lack of ammunition, uniforms and supplies took its toll. The Serbs' energies were spent and after the loss of Belgrade (8 October 1915) they embarked on their long retreat, thus saving what remained of their army from the Austro-German forces led by General (later Field Marshal) August von Mackensen. The Serbian 'exodus' proved a national disaster, and the Balkan impasse was a setback for the Entente powers. As they withdrew the Serbs passed through the wintry desolation of Kosovo and Albania. Iconic images of this exodus, including the ageing Soldier-King, Petar I, slumped on a litter pulled by oxen, accompanied by a number of historic national relics and thousands of his subjects, touched all who read about it.

While casualties in the field were high, more lives were actually lost through disease than on the battlefield in the Balkans and Mediterranean.[31] The Italians, who were suspicious of Serbia's war

aims, refused to come to its army's assistance. It was the view of some
that Serbia's territorial ambitions clashed with Italy's own irredentist
claims to large areas of Croatian- and Slovenian-populated lands.[32]
The 'secret' 1915 Treaty of London, by which the Allies had drawn
Italy into the war against the Central Powers with the promise of territory on the eastern shores of the Adriatic, put Yugoslavs, especially
the Slovenes and Croats, on guard. Seton-Watson was very critical of
the Treaty and its implications for the South Slav project and urged
concerted action on the part of the Yugoslav Committee when he
became aware of its terms. Indeed, he drafted a memorandum on the
subject which was to be signed and circulated widely by Committee
members.[33] The dominant Serbian perception of the Italians was
also that they were intransigent, and had imperialistic designs on
'South Slav' lands on the eastern coast of the Adriatic which they
themselves coveted and which had been described as 'historically'
Serbian by our nineteenth-century travellers. This did not change,
and the call for the 'reunification' of Serbia with 'its coastline' filtered
though much Entente propaganda.[34] The claims of the Serbs and
the Yugoslav lobbyists became more urgent, while the deteriorating
situation on the Balkan front made some of them more amenable
to compromise. Frano Supilo (1870–1917) would eventually leave
the Committee feeling the Croats were being forced to give up too
much in the negotiations. The retreating Serbs, who had reached
the Adriatic coast, were transported to Corfu by British, French and
Italian ships in early 1916 to recover and reconsider their position.
French troops under Sarrail were fortifying Salonika in the first
half of the year in preparation for the re-taking of Serbia. Serbian
survivors and new recruits arrived in May to support the action,
having been 'clothed and equipped by France'.[35] While there was
some support from the Italians and Russians, from this point France
and Serbia provided the main thrust of the campaign. This period
of the war laid the strong foundation of the bond between France
and Serbia which lasted through to the interwar years. French children prayed for their Serbian counterparts and *La Serbie* celebrated
France as the torchbearer of human rights and freedom.[36] There
was a melancholy note in the observation by Emily Simmonds, an
American nurse writing under the pen name 'Americano', that some
of the Serbs she encountered were dressed in the 'faded horizon-
blue uniform' of the French *poilu*.[37]

The political divisions in Vienna which had led to the neglect of
military budgets before the war also resulted in poor generalship.

Interestingly, the charge that the multi-ethnic composition of the army was a disadvantage is countered by the argument that this was not evidently the case until late in the war and that there was a high degree of loyalty towards the Monarchy among Habsburg Slavs, including Serbs. Desertions, first of Czechs and Serbs and then of Croats and Slovenes, ultimately did create difficulties for Austria. Rudolf Jerabek argues that unrest precipitated by desertions and the return of prisoners of war after Russia's withdrawal posed problems that were more socially and politically revolutionary in nature than national.[38] The Allied Armies of the Orient were not well supplied, either. The Bulgars held firm and the offensive in May 1917 under Sarrail 'fizzled', according to Keith Robbins. The final offensive in September 1918 under Franchet d'Esperey (Commander in Chief of the Allied Forces in Greece) and launched from Salonika saw the Bulgars retreat, a rapid advance of Serbs reclaiming their own territory and the French pressing forward through Bulgaria to Romania. Robbins writes that this was 'a modest achievement for an army of 350,000 men whose presence had not disturbed the supply line between Germany and Turkey for the duration of the war'.[39] In spite of this assessment, the determining factor regarding Serbia's standing in postwar negotiations was the decisive and victorious assault in the last months of the war. This advance against the Central Powers was one of the war's turning points and, because of its impact, at war's end Serbia enjoyed a negotiating position of military strength, honour and moral superiority.

The Politics of International Aid

In order to appreciate fully the place of Serbia in the international imagination at this time it is helpful to turn to the work of volunteers who took up its cause. The Balkan front did not attract the same attention internationally as the battles on the Western and Eastern fronts, either at the time or in the war's aftermath. This is unsurprising given the perspective of most historians that developments on the Western front determined the direction of the war in the Balkans, and by association, the eventual deliberations regarding the break-up of the Dual Monarchy. Nonetheless, descriptions of certain aspects of the Allies' war in the Balkans, chiefly surrounding the loss of life suffered by Serbia both in the field and as a result of deprivation and disease (the typhus epidemic, typhoid, tuberculosis, diphtheria, malaria, smallpox and so forth) were shocking and evinced a humanitarian response on a truly international scale. It was reminiscent of the activities of the volunteers of the 1870s, though it extended over a longer period and engaged many more people. Aid workers responded to 'a profound medical as opposed to military emergency'.[40] The retreat to the Adriatic which had led to the evacuation of the Serbs to Corfu communicated movingly in words and images the sufferings of Serbs on a global scale. The Karađorđevićs were seen to be exemplary in their leadership and heroism. They were not distant rulers but directly involved in the battles; anachronistic, perhaps, on their horses and in their rough carts, but all the more sympathetic for being so. Aleksandar, named regent in June 1914, was the warrior-prince, his father the ailing hero-king. King Petar and his son, in retreat from a marauding enemy, became heroic figures of another era, more than worthy of the respect of their allies, whom they had supported in the difficult early stages of the war with a touching constancy.

Serbia's greatest advocates included the remarkable entourage of women who embarked on the work of providing medical aid. Mabel Anne St Clair Stobart (1862–1954) had led the 'first-ever all-women medical unit' in Bulgaria during the First Balkan War and travelled to the front in 1915 with her husband and the second Serbian Relief Fund unit.[41] Her unit comprised 75 people, including 15 doctors. Only four of the team were men and they were orderlies. On arrival the unit immediately set to work helping to keep in check the typhus epidemic.[42] As the military situation deteriorated they were forced to withdraw. Mrs Stobart, given the temporary commission of Major in the Serbian army, ended up leading a column of refugees, including an entire Serbian medical corps, in the retreat. She had witnessed 'the tragedy of a nation wrenched by the roots from nationhood', and though this tragedy was 'not describable in a magazine article', she wrote of her experiences nonetheless. She hoped simply to give 'a few personal reflections' and 'glimpses of the misery diabolical endured by the Serbian people'.[43] As they passed through evacuated towns and villages the houses were deserted and 'shops shuttered': 'all eyes, as it were, closed that they should not see the scenes of sorrow as the fugitives fled in silence through their streets; that they should not witness the galling spectacle of the triumphant entry of the enemy'.[44] From her position as leader of the column, Mrs Stobart observed: 'Truly remarkable was the dignity and orderliness with which, from start to finish, the retreat of the Serbian Army was conducted. And the silence!.... No laughter, no singing, no talking. The silence of a funeral procession, as indeed it was.' And when 'all hope of help from the Allies had vanished... the intensity of the tragedy for the Serbian nation was revealed'. Food became harder to find and they passed corpses on the roadside, 'their eyes staring at the irresponsive sky'. The refugees finally reached Shkodra (Scutari) on 20 December (1915), eleven weeks after leaving Kragujevac.[45] Mrs Stobart's group had covered 800 miles and she did not have to report any deaths or desertions. Hers was an extraordinary feat.

Thus it was that volunteers, doctors, nurses and other relief workers, displaying remarkable courage, dedication and tenacity in deplorable conditions, responded to the needs of the Serbs. Closely documenting and publicizing Serbian distress, they communicated their experiences in a deeply personal fashion. As a result, Serbia's 'martyrdom' led to multiple expressions of sympathy, and multiple acts of salutary generosity. Many other women, from the farthest corners of the British Empire (including high-profile individuals such as the Australian writer, Miles Franklin), were prompted to join the medical units in Serbia and Macedonia or create their own. The story of these women is a tale of self-abnegation and heartfelt loyalty towards the Serbs. The foreigners struck extremely close ties with local populations and lobbied hard, along with their contacts at home, to provide assistance to the Serbs. This was the popular face of Allied diplomacy in the Balkans and it was not uncommon for volunteers to suggest that their assistance was all the more necessary, given that military aid had not been forthcoming when it was needed most. Foreign Secretary Sir Edward Grey intimated that the women doctors and nurses constituted the informal or 'political' rather than military arm of British influence in the region. He had at one point promised British military aid to Serbia, but when the policy changed he supported and praised the work of the volunteers, saying their (highly visible) efforts were 'of inestimable benefit to the common cause'.[46] Flora Sandes (1876–1956) was one of the English women who went to the front to assist as a nurse with the Serbian Red Cross and worked with Emily Simmonds. Just as 40 years previously Jenny Merkus had fought dressed as a man so, too, Sandes ended up donning the Serbian army uniform and fighting alongside men as the 'Serbian Joan of Arc reincarnate', and said of her efforts: 'I represented England.'[47] Sandes was the only woman to be accepted into a Serbian regiment and she was decorated by the Serbs for her bravery. During the war she regularly

returned to England to raise funds and was 'phenomenally successful' in publicizing the Serbs' cause. Surviving the war she attained
something akin to a legendary status. Sandes married and settled
in Belgrade, dedicating the rest of her (public) life to collecting
money for Serbs devastated by the war. She went on international
lecture tours and kept in touch with members of her old regiment
who somehow never grew accustomed to seeing her in a dress.[48]
When in 1927 she published her autobiography, the *Times Literary
Supplement* described it as an important work for 'students of Balkan
affairs' and diplomats whose job it was to 'preserve the peace' in the
region. It is evident that Sandes successfully combined the 'dual political function as combatant and diplomat'.[49]

Sir Thomas Lipton, the tea-merchant, was also moved to help the
Serbs. He sailed his yacht, the *Erin*, which was full of much-needed
hospital stores, to Salonika. Lipton spent three weeks among the
Serbs and the volunteers and, according to his biographer, 'these
travels were, of course, attended with all the limelight, if not the
comfort to which he was accustomed': 'It was not only that the *Erin*
conveyed a Red Cross unit and large quantities of medical equip-
ment, but that [Lipton's] presence publicised Serbia's problems in
England and America in a way that no ministerial oratory could
have done.' Lipton subsequently wrote a public letter about Serbia's
plight which was printed in 'practically every newspaper'. He continued raising funds and later returned to Serbia on the *Erin* with
more supplies. In their gratitude, the Serbs decorated Lipton, who
became a Grand Commander of the Order of St Sava.[50] He was
just one of many British, Dominion and United States citizens decorated by the Serbian government for their wartime contributions to
Serbia's cause.

Various organizations funded and coordinated relief work in
Serbia during the war. These included the Serbian Relief Fund mentioned above, the Scottish Women's Hospitals and the Red Cross;
other groups such as the Miners' Union also gave assistance to the
Serbs. As we have seen from the example of Lipton, individuals
initiated their own projects and went to Serbia independently of the
existing structures administering aid to the Serbs. The involvement
of women in this activity was extraordinary and cannot be overesti-
mated. The war office did not encourage women doctors to serve –
indeed, early on many volunteering for medical service were turned
away – but they were welcomed by France, Belgium and Serbia. They
managed and maintained all aspects of medical care on the front

line and behind it in Serbia and Macedonia.[51] Members of these all-women units drove ambulances, performed operations, trained locals to do basic tasks and set up dispensaries that could be moved easily and quickly. They saved thousands of lives. Mrs Stobart noted that, as many of the Serbian doctors had died in the almost continuous warfare Serbia had waged since 1912, and as the local population had little knowledge on minimizing the effects of the typhus epidemic, her roadside dispensaries were particularly valuable for intensive bursts of activity across a large area.[52] Dame (Louise Margaret) Leila Wemyss Paget (1881–1958) was another tireless relief worker and a founding member of the Serbian Relief Fund. She was married to the diplomat Ralph Spencer Paget (1864–1940), who had been posted to Belgrade in 1910. He became assistant under-secretary for foreign affairs in August 1913. Lady Paget was an energetic and effective volunteer who had the experience of having administered aid during the Balkan Wars. She wrote in a 1915 report:

> For the Serbians, so suffering and so courageous, I feel that nothing one can do is too much, and the trust and the gratitude they give back is one of the most touching and beautiful things I have ever known, not too dearly purchased by any sacrifice. That this feeling is shared by my staff is fully shown by the wonderful efficiency and devotedness of their work.[53]

The local populations paid tribute to the British women in particular. For their part, the French assisted with the evacuation of refugees. Some ended up on Corsica with a group of British nurses attached to the Serbian Relief Fund and Scottish Women's Hospitals. Having arrived after the retreat, these women had not been able to enter the enemy-occupied territories. (Some of the units had remained in place as the Central Powers advanced, while others were evacuated and then resumed functioning as soon as the British medical personnel were given leave to return to their posts.) On Corsica there was a great effort at rehabilitation of the weak and wounded. Kathleen Royds, who had hoped to participate in the immense humanitarian enterprise and did not get beyond Salonika, ended up accompanying the refugees to the French island and wrote: 'One is in a perpetual state of wonder that people can lose so much and recover so rapidly.'[54]

Memorial plaques, fountains and gardens commemorate the British women's wartime work in Serbia. Dr Elsie Inglis (1864–1917), for example, after having been informed that the War Office had no need of her medical expertise, contacted Seton-Watson for advice as to the best way to help. He urged her to begin work with her Scottish Women's Hospitals in Serbia as soon as was practicable. She had hoped to be able to fund one unit but had so many contributions that she was able to dispatch several. Inglis was responsible for a number of innovations in health care at the front and behind the lines. She died in 1917 after also having served on the Eastern front. A fountain was built in her honour and that of the volunteers with the Scottish Women's Hospital in Mladenovac (south of the capital) in 1915, and in 1919 the Belgrade hospital was named after her. Among other visible and ongoing manifestations of the bond between the allies were the memorial tablets and streets named after British volunteers (for example Lady Paget Street in Belgrade).[55] In March 1917 another dedicated volunteer, Mrs Harley, died after a bombardment in Bitola (Monastir). Here a principal road was named after her and in July (1917) 'the Serbs had a beautiful ceremony at which they unveiled a memorial which they had built on her grave'. The religious ceremony, with 'many Serbian priests in their flowing, brilliant vestments, their curious tremulous voices making one feel melancholy in spite of oneself', was one of the indications that this was 'entirely a Serbian affair':

> one felt that they wanted to keep it quite to themselves and to show that, although she was a daughter of England, she belonged entirely to Serbia, as she died helping them. It was for them, therefore, to honour her thus and not for her countrymen. The inscription on her monument reads: 'On your tomb instead of flowers/ The gratitude of the Serbs shall blossom./ For your wonderful acts your name shall/ Be known from generation to generation.'[56]

This voluntary work is crucial to our story of the evolution of the Yugoslav ideal. It provides evidence of the continuity of the commitment by a vocal international community to certain groups of people in the region and a pressing desire to identify with them and publicize their cause. It shows how the Serbian cause continued to pique the interest and imagination of our outsiders and that even if there was not continuous action on their part on behalf of the Serbs, the new generation built on the experience and legacy of the old. One Scottish woman, who gave cooking classes in a girls' school and volunteered with the Red Cross in her spare time, was so moved when she heard Dr Inglis give a single lecture on the great need for help that she immediately came forward to offer her services, and shortly afterwards (July 1916) left to work as a cook in one of the field hospitals in Serbia.[57] The work our new wave of 'travellers' undertook would be of great import for a long period (and for the duration of Yugoslavia's existence), given the personal commitment and ties forged with allies in the field, the extensiveness of their actions, the magnitude of the war itself and the impact of the memory of war on politics and international affairs after 1918. Many of these women, like Sandes, retained an interest in the fortunes of the Serbs and their new state through to the Second World War. (Interestingly, as we will see, a number of the women were commemorated anew in the Serbian national revival of the 1980s.) The work of the volunteers indicated an ongoing commitment to the resolution of what were by now deemed 'longstanding' national problems of the 'race' of South Slavs as represented by the Serbian struggle. There was no intermingling of peoples in these first-hand accounts of life on the front: Serbs fought for Serbian land and Serbian interests, which were one and the same as their allies' interests.

Rarely do historians make a connection between these vital transmission belts of influence and South Slav policy formation. This oversight may be attributed to a number of factors, including the gendered understanding of the impact of the different wartime fronts, even in cases when our female volunteers were in the firing line. For example, while historians are very familiar with the story of women as doctors and nurses on the Balkan front, seldom is the connection made with a broader civic contribution or participation in the British war effort and the extension of British interests in the region or of the region's interests in Britain. Sandes herself insisted that she acted both as an Englishwoman and a Serbian soldier. She 'valued her Englishness as a moral virtue and in particular extended this morality to England's obligation to support the Serbs'.[58] At the same time, the British authorities valued Sandes's public position because it was a 'visible sign of support' for the Serbs when relief and supplies were not forthcoming. Further, the Serbs valued and respected Sandes because of her nationality and her class or standing as 'a lady', proof absolute that their cause was morally justifiable. The formerly near obsessive focus of historians on the narrow question of the extent to which the war was an emancipatory experience for women (that is, on the outcome of wartime experiences) led to a neglect of the range and depth of their contribution in all manner of action (notably voluntarism) during the war itself. While few Western women assumed the authority and respect of Sandes as soldiers, many hundreds of thousands more engaged in activities which clearly had a bearing on the war and clearly had an impact on public life and opinion beyond the confines of the home.[59] Another impediment to our capacity to integrate these tales into a coherent history of the impact of the war on the place of Yugoslavia in the public imagination has been the narrow approach to diplomatic history. The activity carried out on the Serbs' behalf in Britain reveals another side to the role of the 'informal diplomatists' in the war as well as the popularity of Serbia's cause and the effectiveness of its outside advocates.

When the committee outlining 'Serbian (Jugoslav) National War Aims' met in 1918 at Mansion House, London, the first five rows of the auditorium were reserved for representatives of 'societies, working for or in connection with' Serbs and Yugoslavs in Great Britain. These included the Serbian Relief Fund, the Serbian Red Cross, the Scottish Women's Hospitals, the British Red Cross, the War Refugees Committee, the Dr E. Inglis Memorial Fund, the Royal Agricultural Fund for Allies, the YMCA and the Serbian Church Fund.[60] Vicars hosted teas in aid of the Serbian Relief Fund in parish halls and medical units were kitted out and received ongoing funding through the dedication of legions of volunteers. The political implications of this activity were not lost on the devoted South Slav propagandists. The Serbian Relief Fund enjoyed some of its greatest successes when its functions coincided with the anniversary of the defeat at Kosovo. Seton-Watson, a founder and an executive member of the Serbian Relief Fund, was also involved with the Kossovo [sic] Day Committee and the Serbian Society. He often lectured on the plight of the Serbs, including at the public school, Sherborne, where he presented a version of his 'school address' in 1916 on the occasion of the anniversary of the Battle of Kosovo. Seton-Watson became one of the most influential British voices in favour of the dismemberment of the Central European empire and the establishment of the successor states, of Yugoslavia in particular. Writing to a fellow lobbyist in July 1916, he described why the committee postponed a public meeting to agitate on the Serbs' behalf:

The real reason for our decision was a very satisfactory one. The Kosovo Day agitation was so extraordinarily satisfactory that only the very big kind of meeting with a large group of the most prominent speakers, would have seemed anything but a 'come down'. ... Meanwhile we have had a large number of very successful minor meetings all over the country – some of them, like Oxford and Birmingham, Lincoln, York etc, crowded to the door and with all the local bigwigs taking an active part. We circularized over 23,000 clergy and a great many responded. ... Over 12,000 schools in England alone read the school address on Serbia on the day. Many schools hoisted the Serbian flag. Over 30,000 copies of the Serbian anthem were sold. Over 1,000 cinemas produced Serbian films, and there was a special lecture for a week on Serbia at the Scala. A number of the theatres played the Serbian anthem that evening and included slips of explanation in their programmes. ... Above all we distributed an enormous amount of literature and sold a very great deal more. That the response to our propaganda would be splendid, we were absolutely certain from the first; but it is no exaggeration to say that it far exceeded our expectations. The press propaganda was also very successful – special articles and notices in practically every London and provincial daily, and in most of the weeklies and monthlies as well. I wish you could have seen the St Paul's celebration, which was really most impressive and at which the Archbishop preached a real Yugoslav sermon. Everyone was much impressed by the singing of the Serb boys afterwards – certainly the first time Serb has ever been sung in an English church.[61]

The Lord Mayor then invited 300 Serb boys to Mansion House for a reception. The Australian Prime Minister, William Hughes, after having given a fine address on the subject in Oxford, was present. Such propaganda, which was wide-ranging and, by all accounts, more effective than its promoters could ever have hoped, had an impact on subsequent understandings of and international receptivity to the Yugoslav ideal.[62]

A Revolutionary Synthesis?

The unification of the South Slavs was justified by commentators at the time and historians subsequently on the grounds that it represented the aims of a popular and revolutionary national movement. This was one of the founding tenets of the Yugoslav state. In the last years of the war, during the interwar years and in post-1945 (communist and non-communist) historiography the majority of our commentators emphasized the importance of the indigenous revolution and de-emphasized the impact of external forces, especially in cases where their careers or research interests were closely tied to the fortunes of the Yugoslav state. This did not preclude them from also recognizing that the war was a necessary precondition for the Yugoslav revolution. Few now argue that such a revolution took place in 1918 but it is important for us to understand what led many to maintain that it had and why it was so vital to earlier generations of historians' understanding of Yugoslavia.

The chief British and French activists on behalf of the Serbs (and by extension the 'Yugoslavs') were closely connected to the Croatian-led Yugoslav Committee and Serb politicians. Members of the Yugoslav Committee were an internationally focused elite group of men. Some were motivated by a specific experience of national life under the Habsburgs. For example, the Croats from Dalmatia might be Yugoslav in orientation as a defensive measure against Italian claims to Croatian lands. Similarly, Slovenes were conscious of the greater capacity for resisting a new wave of Germanizing and Italianizing influences within a South Slav state. Supilo was among those Croat members of the Yugoslav Committee expressing concern that Serbia might negotiate its own separate peace and thereby leave the Croats and Slovenes vulnerable to further Italian encroachments. So, along with his colleagues, he courted Serbian support. As he came to realize that the goal of a federal South Slav state was slipping from collective view, however, Supilo became disillusioned and abandoned the whole enterprise. (He died before the end of the war.) The Yugoslav Committee (unlike the Czech and Polish National Committees) had no official status and in the absence of international recognition and legitimacy it deferred to Serbia's greater diplomatic and military weight and standing.[63] Compromise and negotiation on the run were the order of the day.

The Yugoslav Committee alone could not have precipitated or even anticipated the popular reception its cause eventually won abroad. It is the merging of Serbian and 'Yugoslav' war aims that explains the enthusiasm with which outsiders embraced the Yugoslav ideal. Few distinguished between the aims of the Yugoslav Committee and the Serbian government, and the rhetoric of both groups did nothing to change that. Always the emphasis in the propaganda was on what brought them together, not their potential differences or those of the populations they purportedly represented. When our British publicists detected a lack of flexibility on the part of the Serbs, in particular the Prime Minister and Great Serbia advocate, Pašić, who shunned the idea of a federal state, the Serbs were quick to respond by rejecting the criticism. This had been the case in 1916 when Seton-Watson's journal, *The New Europe*, ran articles condemning the intransigence of certain Serbs on the question of a truly Yugoslav union based on equality and liberal ideals. A response to this criticism, published in *La Serbie*, for example, was emphatically 'Yugoslav' in orientation.[64]

Representatives of the exiled Serbian government conducted talks with the Yugoslav Committee on the island of Corfu. The negotiated goals of the Yugoslav Committee and the Serbian government were formally articulated in the Corfu Declaration in July 1917 when the end of the war still seemed some way off. Overriding the Serbs' December 1914 Niš Declaration,[65] the Corfu Declaration 'called for ... a democratic, constitutional Kingdom of Serbs, Croats and Slovenes under the Karađorđević dynasty in which cultural and religious rights of all three would be preserved'.[66] (The constitution would be decided upon after the Kingdom was established.) Writing in the American magazine *Current History* in 1922, Gordon-Smith described the Corfu Declaration as 'the Magna Carta of the Yugoslav race'. It had been freely signed; adhesion was 'purely voluntary'. He wrote that subsequently all had unanimously and 'solemnly' confirmed the declaration in Belgrade: 'This act was only natural. Serbia had been the rock in the tempest; she had behind her a century of freedom and independence, she possessed a king, a Parliament, an army and a Government and was, therefore, the natural rallying point around which the new kingdom of 14,000,000 souls would be grouped.'[67] In truth the Serbian government had been ambivalent on a number of matters broached in the Corfu Declaration, including the state's borders and the form it would take. In its attempt to realise its wartime goals, Serbia looked for support east and west, respectively, depending on its perception of the war's progress and its relationship with the Allies. However, the Russian Revolution was a terrible blow to the Serbs who felt they had lost their Great Power sponsor when Russia withdrew from the war. It was, of course, through its alliance with Russia that Serbia's cause became that of France and Britain in 1914 and that Serbia was to become a part of the 'victorious coalition'. Further, the Serbian royal family lost a close spiritual ally and counsellor when the Tsar

was deposed. (The prince regent had received some of his education in Russia and was Tsar Alexander III's godson.) Above all else,
Serbia wanted to bring all Serbs under one government by whatever
means and acquire a seaboard, not just a port or two. The changing
circumstances forced Serbia to focus on the west in search for more
powerful friends and propelled it towards a 'Yugoslav' worldview
when it was pragmatic and necessary to do so.

For its part, the Yugoslav Committee emphasised its affinity
with the Serbs. Hinko Hinkovitch, for example, in his pamphlet
entitled *Les Croates sous le Joug Magyar* (1915), wrote that the union
of 'the race' would herald 'the resurrection' of a larger, free and
independent 'Napoleonic Illyria' and 'the triumph of civilization
over *Kultur*'. The Serbs, whose heroism had earned them 'the admiration of the whole world', would lead the charge: 'we other Yugoslavs
who are not yet free, await with trembling impatience the liberating
armies of our brothers'.[68] The second pamphlet in the Southern Slav
Library (published in 1916 on behalf of the Yugoslav Committee in
London), *The Southern Slavs: Land and People*, states that 'the Serbs,
Croats, and Slovenes are one single nation known by three different names', that 'the Jugoslavs are a homogeneous nation, both as
regards their language and their ethnographical characteristics',
and that 'the Serbs and Croats form an absolute linguistic unit.
Their literary language is identical; their spoken language varies
locally according to the dialect'. Further, South Slavs 'gravitated
towards' Serbia, 'the centre of attraction for all our provinces... the
state which is destined to realize our national unity, and to gather
the different units of our people about herself, just as a crystal
plunged into a saturated solution attracts all particles of the same
nature contained in that solution and groups them about itself'.[69]
(Imagery of this kind was not novel and predated the war by at least
three decades.) Nevill Forbes, reader in Russian at the University of
Oxford, wrote in 1914 that 'nobody knows that the Montenegrins
are Serbs'. Forbes admitted that the Yugoslav cause was not entirely
straightforward but that this was because of religious and political,
rather than 'racial', differences. He mentioned the 'Serbo-Croatian
race', noting that Serbs and Croats were 'identical in kind but different in name' and 'two halves' of one nationality. Croats might insist
they were different and 'maintain their individuality with the utmost
desperation' and even if they were misguided, it was still an underlying concern.[70] This position, evident in descriptions of Croats in
the pre-war period, was less prevalent during the war because of the

need to treat them as one with the other South Slavs in propaganda for union, but surfaced again in the interwar years. The November 1918 report in *La Serbie* – that most Croats placed the 'idea of integral union above regional particularism' and rejected the 'caricature of Great Croatia'[71] – was a sign of the way in which words like 'particularism' (and then 'separatism') would be used henceforth. In the 1920s and 1930s, for example, those who did not accept the notion of a centralized Kingdom administered from Belgrade were routinely labelled particularists. For the most part, however, Croats were seen to be in agreement with their South Slav brothers and striving, as Hinkovitch wrote, to free themselves from the 'yoke' of Hungary's repressive rule.[72] *La Serbie* presented the Croats as having accepted the moral leadership of the Serbs, self-proclaimed liberators 'fighting to death' for the freedom of all Yugoslavs and the 'integral and total emancipation' of their 'nation' in a war that was forced upon them.[73] Ivo Banac has shown definitively how far these simplistic characterizations misrepresented the views of people from all the national groups and from different parties, even those advocating the establishment of a Yugoslav state.[74]

Depending on one's outlook and status, one might describe the union of South Slavs as a federation of nations in an independent country, a unit of equal worth to that of Austria and Hungary within the Empire (trialism), or a unitary state governed by the Karađorđević dynasty from Belgrade. It was the South Slavs remaining in Habsburg lands and participating in the political life of the Empire during the war, namely certain groups of Croats and Slovenes, who clung to the trialist solution for the longest. The idea of a revolutionary synthesis implies that what had started out as the quixotic gesture of a small group of individuals without mandate on the part of the Yugoslav Committee, and a series of compromises by the Serbian government often arrived at by default and against its leaders' political inclination, transformed itself into a popular social and democratic national movement. But there is no evidence to suggest that Serbian lobbying for the new state was founded on a highly evolved set of ideas based on the notion of a distinct and integrated Yugoslav identity. The lack of consensus regarding the nature of the future state among the people who would live in it attests to that. The contradictory aims of the Yugoslav propagandists and the fact that war did not provide an atmosphere conducive to establishing a new 'nation-state' worked against consensus. Rather, the atmosphere of war and international crisis falsely invested each stage in the move towards union with a disproportionate historical and political significance.

War thus shaped the way in which native Yugoslavism evolved among the Allies, notably the Serbs, and among the Habsburg South Slavs. At the same time the war also affected attitudes towards Austria-Hungary as its fortunes changed and precipitated what Janko Pleterski calls the 'radicalization' of the demands of the Habsburg South Slavs. For example, those Dalmatian Croats and Slovenes who were active in the Viennese *Reichsrat* began to take a more vigorous role in shaping their 'Yugoslav' future in the last year of the war as they abandoned hope in a trialist solution to the nationalities question. The Slovene-Croatian parliamentary club of deputies in Vienna metamorphosed into the Yugoslav Club in early 1917. A declaration followed in May 1917 in which they demanded a democratic, independent territorial entity and called for peace, self-determination and an end to the 'German War'. This process of radicalization, Pleterski argues, occurred independently of developments on Corfu. He notes the support of most groups, including the charismatic Stjepan Radić's (1871–1928) influential Croat People's Peasant Party, and activism at the grass-roots level in Slovenia and Bosnia-Herzegovina. (Many of the Croats would live to regret bitterly their adhesion to the Yugoslav movement.) The relative inaction on the part of the Croato-Serb Coalition, the strongest voice for collaborative action in the pre-war period, had seemingly emboldened others, principally Slovene clericalists and Croats from Dalmatia and Istria.[75] The Frankists, followers of Josip Frank (1844–1911), who had broken from Ante Starčević's Croat Party of Right in 1895, seemingly alone however, continued to consider Croatia's future in terms of its independence from other South Slavs and retained their loyal regard for the Habsburgs through to the end of the war.

The significance of the agitation of self-proclaimed 'Yugoslavs' from within the Empire is that it provided the Yugoslav movement, which had gained an extraordinary momentum from without, with greater legitimacy, and the Serbs with greater authority as they participated in the Salonika offensive with the French and retook their lands. Serbia's position regarding 'Yugoslavia' continued to be determined by the changing circumstances of the war. The Niš Declaration and the Corfu Declaration which superseded it were products of a defensive state of mind. Self-preservation was paramount for the Serbs but any evocation of a Yugoslav state was predicated upon the understanding that it would fulfil Serbia's goals of the union of all Serbs both within and outside its borders, and the territorial expansion that would entail.[76] During the Balkan Wars Serbia had increased in size more than twofold, from 39,000 to 87,000 square kilometres.[77] However, it did not gain an outlet to the sea and lost its ethnic homogeneity, two factors which made a 'Yugoslav' solution to their problems all the more acceptable. The acquisition of Bosnia-Herzegovina, at the very least, was critical for the realization of the burning aspiration for ports on the Adriatic because, as we have seen, the province was described as the 'natural hinterland' of Dalmatia.

In 1918 there was a convergence among chief Yugoslav strategists internally and externally. At the same time the trend, begun in the nineteenth century, of describing all 'South Slav lands' as Serbian continued apace. Forbes's 1915 pamphlet referred to above, for example, explained that Dalmatia was 'purely Serb' but not widely recognized as such because it came under Austrian rule. According to Forbes, the Serbs had 'never been able to put to any practical use the coast which by rights is theirs'.[78] There are countless other examples of this kind of reasoning, concluding that Serbia had lost the opportunity to be drawn closer to Western Europe and Britain because of its enforced isolation. Historian G.M. Trevelyan, who had written extensively on the unification of Italy and travelled among the Serbs with Seton-Watson, wrote that 'Serbia was cut off from England, because it was cut off from the sea by geography – not natural or racial geography, but the artificial geography of the map of Eastern Europe, as drawn by Austria-Hungary for her own ends'.[79] As Wickham Steed averred:

> a *restored* Serbia, even enlarged with an outlet to the sea, would ... be a strong guardian of the gates of the East and at the same time the guardian of peace in the Balkans – the best friend of her neighbours and of her friends today, a home of freedom, justice and individual rights and an upholder of the principles which are at stake in this war.[80]

This was a commonly held position. The Cambridge don R.G.D. Laffan's well known 1918 book pleading the cause of Serbia as leader of the Yugoslavs, bore the title *The Guardians of the Gate*.[81] When, in 1918, Serbia was advancing triumphantly with the French under Commander Franchet d'Esperey and pushing back the Bulgars, its sense of its future in the Balkans was much more ambitious than it had been just over eighteen months previously on the island of Corfu. Serbia's victory underpinned the new South Slav state and determined the form it would take. It thus transpired that although it was a small group of Croats who had been the architects of the South Slav ideal in the nineteenth century, Serbia became the unchallenged 'Piedmont of the Yugoslavs'. To the very end, comparisons were made with the Piedmontese who, under Cavour, had agitated successfully for the unification of Italy. In the light of postwar political developments, some commentators in the 1920s and 1930s would observe, wryly or mournfully, depending on their disposition, that it was possibly more appropriate to refer to Serbia as the Prussia of the Yugoslavs rather than their Piedmont.

The period at war's end, when the National Councils of Zagreb and Ljubljana assumed control and direction of affairs, was considered one of the high points of the so-called Yugoslav revolution. We should exercise considerable caution when evoking this image of a 'nation' in revolt. It is true that social, civil and military disobedience, including desertions and the formation of the 'Green Army' fomenting agrarian disturbances, were reported among the Habsburg Slavs in 1918. This disorder was in keeping with experiences elsewhere (notably France, for example) in 1917, a most difficult year of the war, and in the aftermath of Bolshevik-inspired unrest and Revolution. The extent of the impact of the Russian Revolution is difficult to determine exactly, but we know that there were South Slav prisoners of war (the future Croat communist agitator, Josip Broz, later known as Tito (1892–1980) among them) who were, if not directly radicalized by it, at least struck by the language of rights and freedom associated with the Bolshevik seizure of power. However, the absence of a 'social platform' among Yugoslav propagandists distanced them from strands of progressive thought gaining momentum across Europe and among groups of South Slavs themselves.[82] The 1918 mutinies in Boka Kotorska and in Slovenia, the rebelliousness in Bosnia-Herzegovina and the disturbances in the Croatian countryside in fact often led to greater conservatism among decision-makers. Politics, here as everywhere, was more polarized in the wake of the Russian Revolution: some Yugoslav activists became more radical, others more conservative. But it would be wrong to impose a revolutionary – social or national – impulse on all unrest as we know that much of it stemmed from wartime conditions and war-weariness at home and on the front. The successful Serbian assault and the expansion of its army late in the war, the lobbying of exiles and emigrants especially in Britain and the United States, and the Croatian and Slovenian National Committee's declaration in May 1917 converged with outside aspirations for a South Slav state. At the crucial moment, in December 1918, the National Committee rallied to the Yugoslav Committee and the Serbian government in Belgrade, bringing to a close the first phase of the 'revolution'. From here there was no turning back.

Yet the merging of idealism and realism led to inconsistencies in the appraisal of the Yugoslav revolutionary synthesis. As the architects of the New Europe would claim to hold the moral high ground, discordant voices were easily ignored and subsequently would not be tolerated. Gordon-Smith, writing after the war in response to criticism of Serbian domination in the Kingdom (made more visible by the fact that the Serbian Army, as opposed to the multi-ethnic Adriatic Legion, had become the state's military force), stated that a description of the Serbian Army as 'an army of occupation' was outrageous. Anyone who had ever had any knowledge of that army, 'the freest and most democratic in Europe today', he added, 'knows that it could never be made use of as an instrument of oppression'.[83] This and statements like it that appeared in an abundance of publications reveal that the ground for European restructuring was generally well prepared. More specifically, international acceptance of a certain kind of South Slav state existed long before the last stages of the war. For that state to have been truly viable in 1918, however, the 'national revolution' would have had to have been informed by a rich, cross-national associational life based on the ideals of South Slav unity. And for such a state to have been seen as the product of a revolution from within, rather than one that was coordinated and propped up from without, there would have had to have been a clearer sense of purpose and a stronger (communal and home-grown) sense of its future on the part of the leaders of the Yugoslav cause. None of these factors was evident in 1918.

The New Europe

The Kingdom did not emerge as a result of a coherent dialogue between the interested parties or as a result of the weaving together of the strands of a nascent or synthetic Yugoslav culture or a shared Yugoslav identity. The situation had changed for internal negotiators in the course of the war. Their motives and aims in 1918 were often quite different from their motives and aims in 1914, and yet there is a tendency to invest the Yugoslav movement from within with a greater prescience and authority than it had because of the radically changed circumstances in 1918.

It was the imaginings and musings of the outsiders over several decades, combined with the experience of war, that determined the plans for a Yugoslav state and that invested what internal agitation there was with a significance and authority it could not have had of its own accord. A fundamental and legitimating premise of the newly-formed Kingdom would be that it had support from across all the South Slav nationalities or 'tribes' and from within a range of social groups. Some historians therefore vehemently insisted that social unrest channelled into the 'revolutionary synthesis' pre-cipitated the move towards the establishment of a South Slav state. Anti-Yugoslav discourse before the country's demise in 1941 and then again in the early 1990s, on the other hand, argued that the Yugoslav ideal in 1918 was without broad social and national sup-port. At the time of its establishment, however, the Kingdom's uni-fication of the three tribes of a single race into one state had to be seen to be the climax of years (in some cases, centuries) of sacrifice and yearning and the result of a national revolution. That is, it had to be the very opposite of an 'artificial' creation and the furthest thing imaginable from a product of the machinations of intellec-tuals and diplomatists out of touch with the feelings of the popula-tion at large, let alone an elite group of outsiders who would never live or work there. As we saw in Chapter 1, the Yugoslav ideal was not born of the war or at the eleventh hour when Austria-Hungary was 'dissolving'. It was well established (but ill-defined) long before there was talk of a national revolution from within. The old arguments for the territorial reorganization of the area developed by outsiders governed wartime discussions on the successor states and deliber-ations at the Peace Conference in Paris. The problem was that the layering of outside expectations onto internal agitation was not an organic process and a new 'race' or 'nation' could not be constructed in such a manner, regardless of the great efforts to invest it with pol-itical and historical legitimacy.

The Yugoslav ideal triumphed in 1918 because the international community came to accept the establishment of several successor states as a necessary precondition for peace, future stability in the region and the balance of power in Europe. Czechoslovakia was invested with a similar historical legitimacy and, as we have seen,

Masaryk, a friend and collaborator of Seton-Watson, widely regarded as one of the great minds of the New Europe, was respected internationally. Historians often observe that the 'insiders' lobbying for a Yugoslav state did not find an especially receptive audience among diplomatic leaders until the war was almost over. The disestablishment of the Dual Monarchy, the argument goes, did not become a war aim until 1918 and so policy makers were not amenable to solutions to the 'nationalities problem' predicated upon its dissolution until they had eliminated all other alternatives. (This theory of ill-thought-out deliberations at war's end and the 'unforeseen' and 'unplanned' dismemberment of Austria-Hungary is especially important when evaluating the arguments of historians wishing to emphasize that the Yugoslav revolution was indigenous, long in the making and propelled by the general will.[84]) Yet at the crucial moment 'alternatives' were abandoned with ease and with relatively little regret, suggesting their viability, and the commitment of the international community to them, were in question long before. The changing fortunes of the Serbs and their allies on the Balkan front; the apparent collapse of civil and military authority in the Dual Monarchy; the Bolshevik Revolution in Russia; the increasingly vocal national independence movements; the broadening of the international support base of those movements; and the influence of Wilsonian rhetoric about self-determination: all these factors led many to what then seemed the inevitable conclusion, that there was no choice but to establish a series of states in order to negate German influence on the Continent and serve as a buffer against the spread of communism.

It is true that for some the resolution of the nationalities question had not always presupposed the demise of the Dual Monarchy, but merely an 'amputation' or two. However, we must also recognize that the absence of a war aim expressly stipulating the dismemberment of Austria-Hungary did not of necessity (if at all) translate into support for the Empire or lack of support for the policy of establishing the successor states. Austria-Hungary had few defenders in 1918. As the Habsburgs' centuries-long rule over Central Europe ended quite unceremoniously with the stroke of a pen on 11 November 1918 at Schönbrunn, their summer palace just outside Vienna, our observers' centre of focus was elsewhere. Few outsiders regretted the passing of Habsburg rule and none considered doing anything to prevent it. Most compelling of all was the fact that the Yugoslav question was 'a European question' and it was a 'European necessity' that it be resolved 'in its fullness': 'only a complete solution can assure the results for which the Triple Entente has gone to war'.[85] What that meant in 1918 was that Yugoslavism was projected on both sides of the channel as a movement that was 'as intense and as profound [as] and even more generalized' than the Risorgimento. 'One voice' across all the South Slav lands favoured Yugoslav union: 'If one does not hear it ... one is blocking one's ears.'[86] The European context was always at the forefront. Seton-Watson had noted in early 1918 that Austria-Hungary presented a problem because it was not 'an island in the Pacific' but an 'essential part of the machinery upon which the life of the European community depends'. (Interestingly, 42 years previously almost exactly the same reasoning was a factor in assessing Britain's position regarding the Ottoman presence in Europe: 'Now, if the Turkish Empire stood isolated from Europe altogether, an island in the Atlantic, it might, perhaps, be left to work out its own destiny.'[87]) Seton-Watson, we know, had become fixated on the consequences of the malfunctioning of the Central European empire: the fact that 'it is clogged and out of gear, gravely affects the efficiency of the whole machine and the general interest demands its reparation or remodelling'. As a 'relic of the middle ages' the Dual Monarchy was 'abnormal' because within it state and nation did not 'coincide'. Even an 'Austrian nation' did not exist except in the 'imaginations of a few thousand a-national bureaucrats', whereas state and nation were made to appear as if they did coincide in the proposed new countries.[88] By the time of the Balkan Wars, perhaps in part because of them, men like Seton-Watson held that there was no option but that gallant Serbia should be expanded into 'Jugoslavia'. An ever-growing number of people agreed with this position, regardless of the fact that the exact dimensions of this imagined Yugoslav state had still to be determined. Seton-Watson was also representative in that while he may not have spoken overtly of the destruction of the Dual Monarchy, all his actions and statements from the commencement of the war, consciously or unconsciously, were predicated on the imminent fall of the Habsburgs and the disestablishment of their Empire and make no sense otherwise.

The Kingdom of Serbs, Croats and Slovenes was accepted as a *fait accompli* at the Peace Conference in Paris. There were differences of opinion among the diplomats and politicians there. Some were more concerned to establish nationally coherent successor states, others with economic viability. Seton-Watson, commenting in 1921 on Czechoslovakia's new borders, for example, perfectly summarized the pragmatic approach that underpinned his 'ideal-ism' when he stated that the 'Czecho-Slovaks' had acquired 'the frontiers of history supplemented by the additions demanded by the necessities of economic life'.[89] At the Conference the views of men like Clemenceau dominated. They wanted to punish Germany for its aggression and Russia for its 'treachery', isolating the socialist contagion.[90] Most of the discussion surrounding the new South Slav state concerned not its legitimacy or its nature but its borders, an issue which remained vexed throughout Yugoslavia's history. The relative facility with which the state was seen to be acceptable and viable by peacemakers may be seen as the result both of the experi-ence of the war itself and of longstanding views of the inappropri-ateness of 'Teutonic' hegemony in the region. This convergence also coincided with the high point of thinking about the nation-state as the ideal unit to secure international peace and 'racial' harmony.

Harold Nicolson (1886–1968), diplomatist, politician and pro-lific author, known for his critical appraisal of the peacemaking negotiations in which he played an important role as a member of the British delegation, was sceptical of Wilsonian principles of self-determination. He believed, among other things, that these princi-ples were applied cynically and suspected that 'America was asking Europe to make sacrifices to righteousness which America would never make, and had never made'. He noted this expectation led to 'a mood of diffidence, uncertainty, and increasing despair'. In 1919 he wrote that the 'Fourteen Points were hailed as an admirable method of extracting motes from the eyes of others'. But, he asked,

> would any great and victorious power apply them for the pur-poses of extracting beams from their own body politic? The most ardent British advocate of the principle of self-determination found himself sooner or later, in a false position. However fervid might be our indignation regarding Italian claims to Dalmatia and the Dodecanese it could be cooled by a reference, not to Cyprus only but to Ireland, Egypt, and India. We had accepted a system for others which, when it came to practice, we should ref-use to apply to ourselves.[91]

Nicolson, taking the long view, was among the first to recognize the potential negative consequences of the uneven application of the principles of self-determination. Others had no doubts about the pro-ceedings in Paris and celebrated the birth of the new nations.

Todorova identifies the paradox that the use of the term Balkanization dates from a period when the only newly established Balkan states actually reversed the process of what we understand by that word. Yugoslavia, like Czechoslovakia, did not contribute to parcellization but constituted a 'synthesis', a hybrid perhaps, while the other Balkan states had been discernible entities for almost a century.[92] This striking image of inversion and the fluidity of the nationality principle serves us well in attempting to understand the energy (or lack of it) expended on thinking through alternatives to the rule of the Habsburgs and Ottomans in the region. In fact alternatives were unthinkable because 'history' and the irrepressible force of the popular will demanded but one outcome. There were difficulties of national definition or 'classification' that writers did not overlook but addressed superficially in their desire to treat the issues 'comprehensively', as Seton-Watson had put it in 1914. One of the keys, then, was the understanding of Yugoslavia as a country comprising not all South Slavs but a selection of the most fraternally disposed subgroups, or 'tribes', with a few unnamed offshoots from the main trunk and unrelated minorities thrown in for good measure. The First World War was the occasion of Serbia's sacrifice and the Kingdom of Serbs, Croats and Slovenes its just reward. But 'Plucky' or 'Gallant' Serbia had been firing the imagination of British observers for decades. Serbs had taken over from the Bulgars as the most fashionable 'pet' nationality in the region. Its remarkable feats of expansion over the nineteenth century, culminating in its victories in the Balkan Wars, confirmed that Serbia was the force to be reckoned with. The First World War then sealed the fate of the South Slavs for the next 70 years.

3 A State in Search of a Nation: the Kingdom, 1920–1940

The impact of the First World War is the single greatest factor to take into account in a transnational history of the Kingdom of Serbs, Croats and Slovenes (renamed the Kingdom of Yugoslavia in 1929). The outcome of the war determined who had power and who did not and therefore which conception of Yugoslavism would prevail. Further, the devastating loss of a generation of young men in 'the war for democracy' and the search for stability and a new balance of power in Europe led to the investment of a great deal of hope in the successor states. The unshakeable view that peace had to be maintained above all else, and that it depended on the presence of a strong South Slav state, permeated the way outsiders framed their discussions about the Kingdom's progress and determined its place in international affairs.

I do not contend that the state was doomed from the start but that the impact of war on its foundational myths impeded the Kingdom's ruling elites from aspiring towards establishing legitimacy. The failure to do so was their undoing. The authority conferred by the actions of the proponents of the 'Yugoslav revolution' in 1918 was not grounded in a shared Yugoslav identity. Their inability to recognize the significance of this was the first mistake of the new Kingdom's leaders and of their international supporters. Collectively, they promoted a mythopoeia inappropriate for a modern and complex democratic state. Most importantly, the mythology related only to the numerically strongest national group, the Serbs, and enshrined partial truths as well as falsehoods about the

'Yugoslav' past. These partial truths rested on a series of assumptions: that everyone wanted the state, that everyone needed it, that it fulfilled the historical destiny of the South Slavs as an integrated race, that it was justly conceived and that there existed no other options for South Slavs. Above all of these assumptions was the most important foundational tenet of all: that the war was fought and torrents of blood spilt by the leading (Serb) nation to create this state. These ideas became popular currency locally and internationally and they were bound to gratify those to whom they appealed and applied, and marginalize those to whom they did not. As 'South Serbs', Macedonians were often written out of the First World War epic, for example. This was despite the fact, as we will see, that many of the important battlefields and sites of commemoration visited by French veterans on their pilgrimages to the Kingdom after the war were Macedonian.

The symbolic domination of the Serbs in this mythopoeia was matched by their actual domination in the Kingdom. The passing of the controversial centralist constitution in 1921 effectively ensured the primacy of Serbs and Serbian institutions in the new state. To many outsiders this did not seem problematic at the time. They argued that the vigorous constitutional debate touched only a few recalcitrant politicians and would prove inconsequential because in due course the shared sense of (underlying) racial unity or nationhood would transcend it. However, the constitution represented a betrayal for many Yugoslavs. The notion of Yugoslavism as the expression of unity in diversity in the form of a loosely federated amalgam, as propounded by certain Croat groups, for example, could not coexist with the view of the state as the natural end point of a progressive Serbian revolution or as Serbia's reward for its sacrifice in war. The immediate effect of the passing of the constitution was that it created political and national dissatisfaction and disaffection from the governing process. Much of this was confusing and alienating to our outsiders because it seemed to undermine their great work and went against the 'historical forces' which they believed had led to the establishment of the state. Thus the view of the Kingdom as actually or potentially racially homogeneous remained popular among a large group of influential outsiders for the entire interwar period, and seemed to have wider appeal in some circles the greater the crisis the state was facing. When they observed progressive systemic malfunction, they often reasoned that where racial coalescence was not already evident, it was both desirable and attainable. This inflexibility on a key point had the effect of limiting the possibility of compromise because it cast any alternative perspectives in a completely negative light and failed to allow for workable modifications to the system to emerge. In this atmosphere Yugoslav politicians aspiring towards general reform by advocating federalism over centralism for example, had little hope of effecting any change and could only be seen to be 'obstructionist' when confronted by a wall of indifference at best and hostility at worst. As we will see, the fate of the leader of the Croat Peasant Party illustrates this well.

There were 'Yugosceptics' from the outset within and without. They had virtually no impact, in spite of the fact that there was little evidence of an emerging Yugoslav synthesis either in the 1920s or the 1930s, and much evidence suggesting that integral Yugoslavism had not been a widespread force prior to 1918 and could not capture the imagination of enough Yugoslavs to give it vitality and momentum in the new state. Forging a Yugoslav identity from above, as King Aleksandar attempted to do by means of his dictatorship from 1929, proved impossible.[1] However the royal dictatorship would be justified on the grounds that it safeguarded the integrity of the state. Unsurprisingly, the loudest voices in support of the Kingdom continued to be the architects of the New Europe, the outsiders who sought peace above all else and who would selectively sacrifice the democratic ideal, for which they claimed they had fought and won the war, in the hope of securing it for the future. Thus those who spoke for the disaffected in the Kingdom, including the victims of the police state, were overshadowed by men like Seton-Watson. While even he found it increasingly difficult to reconcile the idea of the Yugoslav national revolution with the political realities he observed in the Kingdom, Seton-Watson kept trying to do so. There were a number of reasons for this, not the least being that he felt it was the duty of men like himself to make a contribution to political life; he wrote and lectured on the public role of modern historians in shaping the world they inhabit.[2]

Thus in the name of peace, reason, progress and, it would seem, self-respect, Seton-Watson identified and sought to address the pre-existing or 'historical' problems which thwarted Yugoslav progress. Notably, he identified an historic Croatian propensity for being against the ruling power, whatever its character. He thought one had to take Yugoslav opposition voices with more than a pinch of salt because they were anachronistic and did not respond to the political realities of the time. It was only after it became evident that the ruling Serbian elites were abusing their power and had no intention of reinstating democratic processes that Seton-Watson considered the way forward lay with greater regional autonomy. The British Ambassador to Belgrade, Sir Nevile Henderson (1882–1942), on the other hand, articulated the pragmatic approach which dominated all other conceptions of Yugoslavism. Henderson unequivocally championed Serbian centralism and the king to whom he was personally drawn. Above all else he sought stability in the region and the extension of British interests there. The tension between the positions taken up by our outsiders reflected tensions within the Kingdom and how and why views about the state evolved or remained fixed over time.

This chapter has as its focus evocations of the memory of war and international responses to two spectacular acts of political violence, the murder of Croat Peasant Party politicians in the Belgrade parliament in 1928 and the assassination of King Aleksandar in Marseilles in 1934. While few histories fail to mention these events, I believe that they are emblematic and shed light on the problems within Europe as they were played out in the Kingdom. They also amplify our understanding of the reasons for the collapse of the first Yugoslavia. These incidents were not aberrations in the history of an otherwise peaceful and progressive regime, but are linked to each other and to the way political life developed in the Kingdom. A study of international reactions to them reveals why Yugoslav ideas continued to elicit sympathy throughout the interwar years and why this was often misplaced.

The Memory of War

A vast historiography surrounds the subject of the memory of war and twentieth-century history.[3] We know from the example of France that if the First World War was not a totally transforming experience, socially, culturally or politically, it was nonetheless a cataclysmic event in the life of the nation. Different French men and women remembered the war in different ways. A socialist municipality may have commemorated its lost sons with a poignant evocation in stone of the humble *poilu*, while a Catholic municipality may have sought comfort in raising a version of the Pietà, evoking the universal character of maternal mourning. The overwhelming sense of a nation united in bereavement was not compromised by this plurality of memories. It was not diminished but strengthened in a process whereby the local, regional and national or collective rituals of commemoration accommodated the individual, or personal and familial sense of loss. What has been described as the 'exuberance of civil society' provided for the needs of the state and its diverse citizens at a time of national mourning.[4] There had been a potentially destabilizing period of social, economic, political and military unrest in France in 1917. In spite of this, the final victory and the collective bereavement assumed a dimension that was as 'national' (if not triumphalist) and as inclusive as possible, given the range of opinions accommodated in the French Republic.

In contrast to France, evocations of the First World War were to complicate and perhaps even thwart the project of state-building in the Kingdom of Serbs, Croats and Slovenes. The First World War helped forge Yugoslavia, as it had the other national hybrids among the successor states. However, the experiences of Yugoslavs during the war and their subsequent memory of those experiences were not integrative forces in the new state. For a start, Yugoslavs had fought on both sides. For the most part, it was the Serbs who fought alongside the victors. In the emergent narrative of Yugoslavia's making, it was, in effect, one people, the Serbs, loyal allies of the Entente powers who had begun the battle valiantly, suffered terrible defeats as well as the pain of evacuation, then rose triumphant to liberate and 'reunite' their South Slav brothers. This became the Yugoslav story of the war, but it could not be applied to the population as a whole. Nor did the Serbs transmogrify into 'Yugoslavs' at war's end. However much one might have chosen to argue that the establishment of Yugoslavia was a reflection of the general will (or the product of a 'Yugoslav revolution'), the war experience and the memory of it could never be a unifying thread in the new state, as even the briefest overview of the Kingdom in the interwar period demonstrates.

To many outsiders the words Serbia and Yugoslavia continued to be interchangeable. French and British diplomatic correspondence from Belgrade in the 1920s routinely referred simply to Serbia, rather than the Kingdom of Serbs, Croats and Slovenes.[5] This was understandable. The Allies fought on the Balkan front not with 'Yugoslavs', but with Serbs. Moreover, wartime propaganda overwhelmingly projected Yugoslavia as the Serbs' reward for their unique suffering. It was common to speak of the 'expansion of gallant Serbia into Jugoslavia', or of the Serbs' final triumph in 1918 as a progression 'from Serbia to Jugoslavia'. This language did not sit well with the idea of the national revolution.[6] That the other nationalities, the Croats in particular, might take umbrage at being treated as the 'spoils of war' rather than equal partners in a contractual relationship hardly occasioned any comment.[7] If the Yugoslav state did attract criticism on that score, the vigorous retort was that as Serbia was the first of the South Slav nations to have won its freedom, it was therefore, as Gordon-Smith declared in 1922, the 'standard-bearer of the other Serbo-Croats' national aspirations', their 'champion'. Due to its sacrifices in the war, Serbia 'nobly justified the trust placed in her'.[8] What made state-building problematic was the fact that other symbols, which could not be universalized in the forging of a Yugoslav identity, were superimposed onto the Serbian victory of 1918. An unfinished monument in a Belgrade park to Serbia's triumphs in the Balkan Wars, for example, was recycled in 1919 as the First World War victory monument.[9] A pragmatic move, perhaps, but not an especially diplomatic one given that a large percentage of the 'Yugoslavs' were not involved in the Balkan Wars. Moreover, the nations embroiled in the second of those wars were attempting to negate the identity of another group of 'South Slavs', the Macedonians, whom the Greeks, Serbs and Bulgarians fought not to liberate but to colonize and assimilate. The Macedonian experience of the First World War was either conflated with that of the Serbs or buried and forgotten. This illustrates the complexity of evocations of the South Slavs' war. There were similar problems in Czechoslovakia, where Sudeten Germans, for example, remembered the war differently from the Czechs.[10]

The memory of war had an impact on attitudes towards the Kingdom's place in Europe. Studies of the memory of the First World War, while rich and varied, have focused more on cultural memory, including remembrance practices, literature, art and education, than on political relations and power.[11] Traditionally, historians have been less attuned to the multiple ways in which memories of the war fashioned the history of Central and Eastern Europe and the Balkans in the 1920s and 1930s.[12] Diplomatic histories of the new alliances, the Little Entente and the Balkan Pact, for example, abound; but the wider impact of the relationship between memory and the political perceptions governing the new alliances is also instructive. While few fail to note that the Kingdom was born of the war, there is virtually no attention accorded to the way in which memories of wartime alliances, variously expressed, affected the nature of the new state or to the way those memories affected the international standing of the Kingdom.[13] The war experience bound people who influenced policy inside and outside the Kingdom to particular positions regarding its evolution and its future. These positions, potentially fluid to begin with, became fixed. According to Jan-Werner Müller, for 'realist' historians, the connection between memory and politics, or memory and foreign policy, is tenuous. Posing the question 'money or memory?', they argue that memory is but 'window dressing' for hard, material interests, or 'money'. An ampler view, Müller argues, is that memory and material interests 'become interdependent' and that memory can define and shape interests, perhaps unconsciously and in ways that are difficult to quantify. I believe Müller's approach, which he largely applies to post-1945 Europe, provides a useful framework of investigation for the interwar years.[14]

The territorial integrity of the Yugoslav state came to be seen as an essential cornerstone of peace in Europe. At the same time, however, it was more than just one new country among others. For example, the special attachment between France and its wartime ally, Serbia, was evident in different ways. It affected perceptions of the Kingdom's ruling elites and the status of those South Slavs excluded from, or subsumed by, its foundation myths.[15] The large-format fortnightly magazine, *L'Illustration*, covered many stories relating to the First World War: the process of rebuilding and repair, physical and psychological, the commemoration of the war dead and the recollections of prominent wartime civil and military leaders, as well as the new artistic and political movements, including Italy's fascism. The magazine also manifested a particular attachment to France's wartime allies and Europe's newly fêted royal families, including the Karađorđevićs. *L'Illustration* recycled all the accepted truths about the New Europe. It promoted the proclamation of the Kingdom of Serbs, Croats and Slovenes as the culmination of centuries of longing on the part of the South Slav 'race' for liberation from their oppressors but, in fact, Serb and Yugoslav became synonyms. Articles in *L'Illustration* on the Kingdom might appear under headings such as 'En Serbie', 'Une fête française à Belgrade', 'L'Amitié franco-serbe', and so forth.

L'Illustration's articles on King Petar's funeral in 1921 were replete with references to the First World War, linking the outcome – the new state – with Serbia's long and tortured path towards independence. Indeed the whole event was, in the eyes of *L'Illustration*'s correspondents, like a 'living tableau of the great pageant of Serbia's history'.[16] On his death the magazine reproduced a full-page portrait of Petar from *L'Illustration*'s archive. It was not a formal 'official' photograph but one from 1917 when the 'joy of victory' was still over a year away. The ageing king, in uniform, short and unimposing and supported by his cane, had a longish beard, the caption noting that it was a Serbian tradition that men in mourning let their beards grow. Petar had done this when his wife died and in the dark days of 1915 to mark the suffering of his army and his people in retreat.[17] After the funeral service in Belgrade, the king's body was transported by train to the Karađorđević family mausoleum in Oplenac, near Topola, south of the capital. Here 'Petar the Great, the Liberator' (*Oslobodilac*) would join his humble 'friends' who had suffered with him in the war and whom he had known intimately. Having witnessed first-hand their bravery and shared their sorrows, he sought their eternal companionship in death. The usual conflation of Serbian and 'Yugoslav' symbols marked this story as it would many others: the Serbian flag draping the coffin representing the 'national colours', the mute crowd recognizing in the king the man who had brought the Serbian victory over 'the Austrian armies'.[18] In another article about the funeral we read that the distinctive cross and sword on top of his temporary sepulchre represented the faith and courage of the glorious king whom 'Great Serbia' venerated as its liberator.[19]

Recollecting Petar's life, *L'Illustration*'s correspondent evoked the war, its painful memories still vivid, and looked towards a future full of hope. The *comitadjis*, the irregulars, who had had been important in the 'great Serbian battles', earned a special mention and would remain in the popular imagination through to the Second World War and the celebration of their 'heirs', the Chetniks, as the true resisters in Yugoslavia.[20] The French correspondent had travelled to Belgrade, the 'capital of Great Serbia', on the Simplon Express, which he thought of now as the 'train of the Entente', linking more closely nations whose destinies were intertwined as a result of the war.[21] At the same time attention was drawn to the king's strong ties with France: his military training at St Cyr, his enthusiastic participation with his French friends as 'Lieutenant Kara' in the Franco-Prussian War and then his loyalty in the First World War. He had the demeanour, mentality and spirit of a French officer. Further, his 'French intellectual formation' gave him the capacity to take his place as king after the 'Byzantine tragedy', regicide, ended the Obrenović's rule.[22] Petar Karađorđević's long association with the civilizing influences of Europe, far from his Balkan home, reflected well on him, especially as he had actively chosen exile among democratic peoples while his rivals were in power. In countless books and articles published in his lifetime and after his death his translation of Mill (mentioned above) remained his great claim to fame, showing that he had the highest regard for progressive political thought.

L'Illustration also covered the 1923 Bastille Day ceremony in Belgrade marking the regrouping of the graves of the French war dead. There was present a crowd of over 3000 people, including members of the clergy, various patriotic societies, 'young nationalists', veterans and the war wounded. Wreaths laid at the French graves attested to the recognition of the French sacrifice, all the more gratefully received on France's national holiday. In his response to the various speeches, the French envoy spoke of the brotherhood of arms and linked the 'attachment to the cult of our dead' to the loyalty towards 'alliances'.[23] This was just one of many commemorative events taking place during the interwar period and marking the strong affinity between the Serbs and the French at the local level. The relationship between the impact of the memory of war on the prestige of Yugoslavia and on the international reputation of its constituent nationalities is significant across Yugoslavia's entire history. It is well known that the polemical manipulation of the memory of the Second World War was a formative influence on Serbian nationalist literature of the 1980s. However, people's receptivity to that revisionist propaganda can only be understood in the light of the impact of the memory of war on nation-building in the 1920s and 1930s.

Yugoslavism as Centralism

In the aftermath of the First World War, Yugoslavs, like other peoples coming to terms with a set of newly realigned borders, experienced difficulties ranging from threats to their territorial integrity to agreeing on a new constitution. In addition, within the Kingdom members of different social, political and national groups were expecting to find their place in the new governing system. The establishment of the Kingdom was not associated with large-scale celebrations or a particularly joyful atmosphere. There was a demonstration in Zagreb on 5 December 1918 involving people who were against the union or the way it came about or both. Many were calling for a republic as they made their way to the main square. The forces of the National Council of Serbs, Croats and Slovenes shot and killed 15 of the demonstrators and wounded a further 20.[24] The fundamental political problem from the Kingdom's first hour to its last was that the ruling parties lacked legitimacy and popular cross-national support. We may attribute the successive governments' lack of moral authority and the rapid disaffection from the state of former promoters and supporters of the Yugoslav ideal, particularly its Croat exponents, to a number of things. In the first instance, it was the form the state would take.

The political storm surrounding the passing of the new constitution in 1921 was bitterly divisive. Retrospectively, polarization around this issue seems natural given that those involved came from different political cultures, that the national groups had different expectations of South Slav unity and that within national groups themselves there was diversity, with opinions changing with the changing circumstances. Possibly, then, the tribes had been too long apart for the 'reunion' to be harmonious. The constitution which, according to Banac, 'sanctioned the untenable centralist solution of Yugoslavia's national question', remained controversial and never enjoyed general acceptance. Indeed many Croats, for example, thought it illegal because it was passed not by the two-thirds majority 'proposed by some autonomists and enshrined in several pre-unification documents', but by a narrow simple majority. A large number of politicians (161 out of 419), rejecting the very basis of the constitution, boycotted the procedure. The final vote was 223 members for the constitution, and 35 against. There would have been 196 against had those who abstained voted to reject it. The constitution, passed by a mere 13 votes, was modelled on the 1903 Serbian constitution. It became known, most inappropriately, as the Vidovdan constitution because it came into force on 28 June, St Vitus's Day and the anniversary of the Battle of Kosovo, a date which figured significantly in the Serbian national calendar.[25] It was also the anniversary of the assassination of Franz Ferdinand. Few of our outsiders foresaw any problem with the identification of the new constitution with a Serbian day of commemoration. During the First World War the anniversary of the Battle of Kosovo was, as we have seen, the occasion of enormously successful fundraising in Britain and the occasion of rallying to the Serbs' cause in France on the *Journées serbes*, falling on or near 28 June. International opinion held that Franz Ferdinand's visit to Sarajevo on 28 June 1914 constituted an act of 'provocation', but the passing of a contentious constitution in Belgrade on such an anniversary apparently did not.

Discussions in the magazine literature on the constitutional question touched on all the problems successive interwar governments faced. Differences of opinion revealed in *Current History*, for example, show that some believed the constitutional debate was not especially serious but a rarefied discussion of little or no significance to the common people that would fail to attract much interest in the long run. The government, 'progressive and far-sighted', was more than capable of dealing with any underlying problems.[26] On the other hand there were those who saw the constitution as 'an extension of the old instrument to cover new territory, rather than a totally new instrument for the administration of Government'.[27] Another 1922 article in *Current History* was entitled interestingly but misleadingly 'Drifting towards a Jugoslav Federation'. It noted that the constitution highlighted that '"Jugoslavia or Greater Serbia" [was] the "to be or not to be" dilemma facing the Kingdom',[28] a dilemma that it avoided confronting.

In November 1922, just months after the passing of the constitution, *Current History*'s Ludwell Denny wrote that the 'Croatian protest was so general that it was subdued only by what was virtually martial law'. It was evident that 'Belgrade did not keep the faith' on the question of 'provincial equality'. What were the pacifists' weapons if not 'non-co-operation and civil disobedience', Denny went on to ask.[29] Elsewhere the problem was put slightly differently: debates about centralism and federalism drew attention to a nationalist discourse (unity versus autonomy) whereas in fact they masked the true division which was between those advocating 'semi-autocratic rule' on the one hand, and the 'new popular forces which are clamouring throughout south-eastern Europe for a true parliamentary government' on the other. Romanian-born political scientist David Mitrany (1888–1975), who was committed to the formation of effective peace organizations, implied that a reasonable objection regarding a political question was transformed into an unreasonable nationalist dispute. This left those who opposed the constitutional developments with no recourse for action and without a sympathetic hearing.[30] On the other hand, Gordon-Smith, whom we have encountered above as the self-proclaimed champion of Great Serbia, denied even the existence of a constitutional problem. While these responses typify the disparity in outside reports on the challenges to Serbian dominance in governing structures in the interwar period, they also underscore the pervasiveness of the paradigm which pitted 'Yugoslavs' against 'autonomists', 'federalists' and 'anti-Yugoslav' nationalists.

Historians are careful to point out that it is too simplistic to attribute all the Kingdom's troubles to the national question or to the struggle between Serbs and Croats. For example, all centralists were not necessarily unitarists, that is, not all centralists accepted the notion of an integrated Yugoslav race. Some centralists believed ethnically distinct Yugoslavs might still develop under the mantle of protection afforded by Serbian leadership in Belgrade.[31] How that position might have been perceived from the periphery varied. As we will see, on the whole it was quite acceptable to Slovenes. It is also important for us to recognize that oppositionists generally advocated the reform of the state, not amputation or separation. Further, Yugoslavs cooperated with each other across ethnic lines on various occasions. The Serbs did not speak as one, nor did the Croats. However, the question of national and minority rights was not resolved satisfactorily and there was discrimination along national and ethnic lines. The three 'tribes' were recognized as constituent peoples in the new state but the minorities, including Albanians, Macedonians, Germans and Hungarians, were not. Minorities had citizenship rights but Serbs treated Macedonians and Albanians as Serbs. Leslie Benson notes that it was never resolved whether the Yugoslavs were one people or three. Serbs, Croats and Slovenes approached this question differently, and herein lay the fundamental contradiction of the new state.[32] Whether Yugoslavs constituted one nation or three was largely overlooked – even an irrelevance for some of our outsiders – in the interwar period. In practice, Yugoslavism meant rule by Serbs and domination by Serbian cultural and political institutions. At the time of the dictatorship, when Aleksandar claimed to be forging an integrated Yugoslav nation by extinguishing old national particularisms, it was still the case that state institutions were dominated by Serbs. The project for a Concordat resulted in a political storm in 1937, with the Serbian Church excommunicating ministers and deputies who voted in favour of it. Administrative boundaries did not correlate with peoples and their historic territories until the eleventh-hour agreement between Serbs and Croats in 1939.

One of the unforeseen problems with the adoption of the centralist constitution was that it made Serbs appear to be ersatz Yugoslavs from the outset. Many of those who approved the constitution may well have been Great Serbs or Pan-Serbs in camouflage, but it would not have been their intention to appear so. An early discussion on the impact of the differences between centralists and federalists by Franjo Šuklje, which appeared in the *Slavonic Review*, argued this point, noting that centralism was a disastrous policy. Whether or not Serbs were truly working towards a Great Serbia was almost irrelevant, because 'it is so widely believed they are'.[33] Others spoke of the unfortunate identification of the new state with Serbian 'village pump centralism'.[34] At the same time St Vitus's Day had become a national holiday honouring the war dead, the Serbian martyrs and heroes. Melissa Bokovoy tells us that about two hundred war memorials and monuments were constructed in the interwar period and that tens of thousands of Vidovdan services commemorated and honoured a distinctly Serbian past and a Serbian experience and recollection of the war. This process also drew almost exclusively on memories of Ottoman oppression while virtually erasing the South Slavs' Habsburg past.[35]

As the dictatorship was not formally established until 1929, abuses in the system in the years before tend to be glossed over, especially in histories emphasizing division along ethnic lines. There were some outsiders, a minority, who argued that active discrimination against non-Serbs in political, military, professional, administrative, diplomatic and financial life and the overt nepotism and corruption in Belgrade were more corrosive than the national question per se.[36] Interwar Yugoslavia was a highly centralized state, a 'quasi-French' system divided (monstrously, according to critics at the time[37]) into 33 administrative units or districts on the model of French departments. Each of the districts had prefects appointed by the king. Benson writes that with the exception of Slovenia, the king appointed overwhelmingly Serb officials to the prefectures and that electoral lines were drawn 'to create Serb majorities or failing that to prevent any other nationality from becoming one'.[38] All men over 21 had the vote and theoretically one candidate was elected for every 3000 inhabitants. However, the electoral system failed to take into account demographic changes (especially Serbia's population losses) resulting from the war and was therefore weighted in favour of Serbian districts. The constituencies created by the Electoral Law of 1922 were based on pre-war census data and 'the effect was to enfranchize the Serbian war dead at the expense of the other nationalities'.[39] Mitrany's 1925 article in *The New Republic*, mentioned above, commented disparagingly on the electoral system and its malapportionments, noting that Croat parties won a seat for every 6600 votes cast whereas Pašić's

Radicals won a seat for every 4944 cast, giving the latter 107 seats instead of 82.[40] Seats in the unicameral legislature remaining empty after the final count (that is, where none of the parties attained the minimum number of votes required to win the seat) were distributed among those parties with sufficient votes overall; this added to the inconsistencies and exacerbated the problem of gerrymandering. The king appointed ministers and could veto legislation. Wayne Vucinich, among others, showed that interwar Yugoslavia was dominated by and favoured Serbs. In the period 1918–41, only one non-Serb, the Slovene cleric, Anton Korošec, was appointed prime minister, and that was for just six months, between July 1928 and January 1929, after the shootings in the Belgrade parliament. He also briefly served as Interior Minister. Prior to the establishment of the dictatorship, that is, between December 1918 and January 1929, every minister in each of the 24 cabinets was a Serb.[41]

Significantly, this feature of Yugoslav political life did not unduly concern the Slovenes. As we have seen, most of their districts comprised Slovenian majorities. For them Serbian domination was but a temporary irritation in a situation that was, on the whole, a considerable improvement on their previous fragmentation, notwithstanding the Italianization of Croats and Slovenes inhabiting the contested areas living in what was known as the Julian March, after the Julian Alps. For the Croat Peasant Party, on the other hand, surrendering all power to Belgrade had been unacceptable and its response was to abstain from the political process in protest until 1925. In 1924, at a time when its leader, Radić, was reconsidering this strategy, Korošec wrote that he appreciated and respected the Croats, whose territories in some measure the Austro-Hungarian monarchy had recognized and who had thus succeeded in preserving their 'autonomy to a considerable extent'. He continued: 'the Croats therefore have lost so much to the new state that their unyielding opposition to it is most understandable'. But the Croats had to understand the Slovenes' position too, he argued, for they had achieved 'noteworthy gains'. So long as Slovenes were represented in the government and had the power to administer Slovenian territory as they wished, they were satisfied: 'Although I realise that this centralising system cannot maintain itself very long, I consider it wise to profit from the circumstances as they exist and to obtain a few favours in the bargain.'[42] For others, like some Macedonians and Croats, Serbian hegemony was more and more unacceptable because they came to believe it threatened their very existence as distinctive peoples.

In some quarters outside Yugoslavia there was a general perception that the political leadership of the ruling Serbian parties was in an advanced state of ossification. In the early period the Serbian Radical and Democratic parties dominated. They had their roots in pre-war Serbian political culture which, many argued, was a shortcoming. Two political forces with great mobilizing potential immediately after the war were the Croat People's Peasant Party and the Communist Party of Yugoslavia. The Communist Party, banned in 1921, could not fulfil its early postwar electoral promise. Anticommunism was one of the features of politics in Belgrade and this policy was driven by Aleksandar for whom, we recall, the Russian Revolution was devastating. Radić found himself under constant surveillance and periodically under house arrest. He was gaoled without trial in 1919 and 1923. As a consequence, the Peasant Party never exerted an influence proportional to its electoral support, even on the occasions when its leaders abandoned their abstentionist tactics and agreed to participate in the governing process in the mid-1920s. The Peasant Party had a different political outlook from that of the two main Serb parties, though its critics also attributed its perceived failings to its development prior to the establishment of the Kingdom. Unlike them, it was formally republican.[43] It was also socially progressive and had strong local support networks. Winning 50 seats in the first elections after the war in 1920 and 70 seats in 1923, it had a wide popular base. The party had a broad social vision and its education programme aimed to raise literacy levels in rural Croatia. The Peasant Party's appeal was not limited to the agrarian vote, as its electoral success testifies.[44]

Much outside commentary on Yugoslav political life centred on key personalities. Prime Minister Pašić, for example, may have seemed like 'an ornamental figure with a venerable beard', but to the initiated, wrote one observer in 1922, 'he stands for all those practices of devious intrigue, evasion and prevarication which have given the word "Balkan" in its political sense so unpleasant a sound'.[45] A photograph of Pašić which appeared in 1927 in *Current History*, after his death, evoked politics from another era: with his long, bushy white beard, Pašić stood for an outdated political (and conspiratorial) state of mind which characterized the Yugoslav ruling elite.[46] Overwhelmingly, however, Pašić was regarded as the great uncle of Serbian political life, protector of Serbian interests, and as a relic of Radical Party politics which had reached its high point between 1903 and 1914. After the war, the Radical Party, like its French counterpart, became the party of vested interests and represented Serbian hegemony in the Kingdom. It was Pašić's political manoeuvring that led to the passing of the Vidovdan Constitution, because he had negotiated successfully with the Muslims of Bosnia and the Sandžak (an area in western Serbia with a Muslim majority) to vote in favour, giving him the small majority he needed. On his death in December 1926, tributes to Pašić from all over the world praised his intuitiveness and flexibility. A man who allegedly did not condone violence himself, Pašić nonetheless saw the opportunity that the assassination of the Obrenovićs in 1903 afforded to pursue his nationalist agenda in Serbia. With the return of the Karađorđevićs, in the person of King Petar, Pašić set himself the task of undoing the damage to Serbian interests wrought by the Austrophile Obrenović dynasty. He was, paradoxically, hailed as the creator of modern Yugoslavia and the Serbian equivalent of Washington or Lincoln by his supporters. As he turned 80 *Current History* praised Pašić: a devoted, tireless reformer, he had been in and out of favour but always remained true to his beloved nation. Pašić was thought not to have conspired with the 1903 assassins but recognized their actions were 'for the good of the Serbian people' and he was committed to reviving 'Yugoslav civilisation' which had flourished before the fall of the Serbian Empire in the battle of Kosovo in 1389.[47] He was not implicated in the Sarajevo plot in 1914, we read in the same journal one year later, but it was true that he was more interested in 'Greater Serbia' than many Croats and Slovenes would have wished. On Pašić's death Serbian students in mourning made an offering of a crown of thorns, 'symbolising the suffering of the wars through which [he] had led the Serbian people'. At the same time he was described as having been instrumental in achieving the unity of the new state, which would not have been possible with 'solder less tough than his inflexible determination'.[48]

The Croatian politician attracting the most (and largely negative) attention was Radić. He was seen to be the greatest impediment to the successful transition to a smooth-functioning Yugoslav state. Radić's petition to the Peace Conference, containing over 115,000 signatures and requesting international support for the Croats' right to self-determination, indicates the extent of early disaffection and division over the nature of the new state. Radić, in gaol at the time, articulated the 'Croatian position', which, as we have seen, was republican and federalist in the first instance, though he later reconciled himself to working with the monarchy. In May 1921 *Current*

History noted that Radić accepted Yugoslavia but not subjugation by the Serbs. Radić also appealed to the Genoa Conference (April 1922) and to the League of Nations in August of the same year. His Memorandum, which he was not permitted to present to the League in person, stated that the Croat people had not approved the South Slav union and asked that the League recognize their 'political and national individuality', to the end that the Serbs might also be persuaded to do so. Radić wrote of the impossibility of harmony in a state where the Croats would always be outvoted in Belgrade and where there was not fair and equal political representation. The abuses to which Radić drew attention included the reintroduction of corporal punishment for men and women which had been banned in Croatia-Slavonia in 1870.[49] The 1922 article, 'Drifting towards a Jugoslav Federation', and mentioned above, described Radić as a 'great patriot, fearless [and] self-confident': 'We did not destroy Austria in order to have Budapest in Zagreb, Belgrade or Sarajevo', he had said in his defence when tried by the regime for high treason or 'crimes against the fatherland'.[50] Further, he argued that 'the principle of self-determination is not concerned only with territorial boundaries but also with the right of establishing a form of government such as the people desire'.[51] As the 'intrepid apostle of Jugoslav federation' and the 'idol of all oppressed Jugoslavs', Radić had a strong following among Croats.[52]

We have much evidence of international disapproval for Radić and indifference to the source of his criticisms of the new state. The foundational work of the Croats in the Yugoslav Committee and the support among Croat intellectuals for union, combined with Serbia's position of strength at the end of the war, meant that the nonconformists, no matter how widespread their electoral appeal, were ignored or silenced. Overall, there was little receptivity to Radić's plea for self-determination, which was deemed unrealistic. Furthermore, he was simply not liked. For example Denny, in *Current History*, recognized Radić's patriotism and adherence to federalist principles but also expressed distaste for Radić himself, and his attitude was representative. Denny described Radić's non-participation after the passing of the constitution as Croatia's 'pacifist revolution' but took a swipe at him, noting that the strength of the 'autonomy movement' was borne out by the fact that it could 'survive such heroic but absurd leadership'. The fact of the matter was that Radić's 'paper republic' was 'naïve' and unworkable and the continuing dissension, together with new repressive laws, made it possible for the Serbs to continue to mistreat the Croats and 'terrorise [them] in a manner comparable to the worst deeds of Magyar misrule'.[53] Prime Minister Pašić's 'two weapons to use against the Croatian movement were suppression and denial', but they were not 'sufficient' and the optimistic conclusion was that, as there were forces for good on each side, Yugoslavia could be made 'a homogeneous economic and racial unit'.[54] There was still hope for synthesis under the banner of centralism if the Croats would sensibly cooperate.

The uncompromisingly democratic Radić's image among his critics was that of a disruptive rural populist. Radić raised the ire of the intensely anti-communist Belgrade politicians by travelling to Moscow in 1924 at the invitation of the Praesidium of the Peasant International and the Soviet Commissar for Foreign Affairs. The Croat leader had no sympathy with Bolshevism but admired the Soviets' promise of self-determination.[55] Radić was not succumbing to the Bolshevik temptation as his critics claimed, but nor was his party to become the rural voice of the new (or old) Right. Unlike the agrarian parties in Weimar Germany, which were won over by the Nazis in the late 1920s, for example, the Peasant Party did not act as a lever in the hands of the radical Right, some defections by its members to the Ustaše notwithstanding. It was common for outsiders and insiders to remark that Radić was one of the greatest impediments to Yugoslav unity. Writing in the early 1920s about the 'open ferment' in Croatia, Šuklje argued that the ferment was 'increased by the rodomontades of the peasant leader, and by the psychology of a people which has never learnt moderation in the school of political freedom and self-government'.[56] In contrast to the Slovenes, who seemed more cool-headed, the Croats were too impatient and utopian, and not mindful enough of the fact that they were playing into the hands of 'hostile neighbours': Italian and Hungarian revisionists, given half the chance, would divide them up and separate them from their 'Serbian brethren'.[57] The 'demagogue' Radić thus 'manufactured' grievances among Croats. This was the position of Yugoslav propagandists and most outsiders prior to Radić's death in 1928.

Another Act of Provocation

On 20 June 1928, Puniša Račić, a Montenegrin Serb deputy and member of the Serbian Radical Party, shot five Croatian politicians, including the leaders of the Croat Peasant Party, in the Belgrade parliament (*Skupština*). The shootings were the culmination of a difficult period in parliament in the first half of 1928 over a series of measures including the so-called Nettuno Conventions, which gave special privileges to Italians who owned property in Croatian and Slovenian territory. The Croatian deputies had strong views opposing these agreements with Italy. On the day of the attack, discussion was spirited. Račić produced a revolver and started firing. Of the five Croatian deputies he shot, Stjepan Radić's nephew, Pavle, and Ðuro Basariček died immediately. Stjepan Radić died two months later, in August, of complications from his wounds. The attack and Radić's passing led to demonstrations violently put down by the police, resulting in a number of deaths, resignations from parliament, and renewed calls for federalization.[58] The assassination was a shocking event, unprecedented in Croatian politics. The impact reverberated wherever Croats lived, including the United States.

Described as having a 'magnetic hold over the masses', Radić was not tolerated as a man of Pašić's ilk had been. Men like Seton-Watson may well have regretted the shooting and feared repercussions for the stability of the country, but the event did not evince collective international outrage or disquiet. Even his potential supporters criticized Radić. In his 1929 article in the journal of the Royal Institute of International Affairs, C. Douglas Booth wrote of the plight of Croats in the new state, noting that the 'outstanding feature' in Yugosavia's short history was that it had managed 'to retain even the appearance of national unity'. He also remarked, in a tone guaranteed to irk the likes of a Seton-Watson, that the plight of Radić showed the 'folly of allowing a backward race to govern a more civilized people'. However, even though Booth described Radić as 'brilliant' he was also 'erratic' and 'incorrigible', vilifying opponents in 'an unjustifiable way' with 'all the gifts and disabilities of a demagogue'. Booth's Balkanist framework of interpretation argued that historical factors produced differences in political culture and that, while Croatian opposition historically expressed itself in parliamentary disputes, Serbs resorted to political violence. Thus Booth accounted for the 1928 assassinations by saying that they were not the result of 'a single spontaneous act' but made possible by an atmosphere and feeling generated openly in Belgrade and by its press. Serb deputies and organs of the ruling Radical elite had called for the death of Radić and then celebrated his passing as the victory of the state against one of its enemies. That Serbs were known to be baptizing their sons 'Punisha Ratchitch' threw 'light on

Serbian psychology'. In 'more chauvinistic Serbian circles' he had become 'almost as much a hero as Gavrilo Princip'. In fact Booth's view was not the norm but, like others, he spoke of Radić 'exasperating his assassin', which chimed with the dominant perception of the Croat politician.[59]

It was very common for outsiders at the time to suggest that Radić provoked Račić. Seton-Watson wrote that the death of Radić highlighted the Croats' 'purely oppositional outlook upon life' and the Peasant Party's leaders' weaknesses. They were doctrinaire, changeable and, though well read, their knowledge was 'ill-digested'. Serbs, on the contrary, were naturally democratic and defended social stability. The opposition in parliament 'was provocative in the extreme' and Radić, with his 'wild language' and 'rash inroads', was the main culprit. His killer expressed, albeit in an 'extreme and criminal form', the exasperation and frustration others were feeling.[60] Radić was therefore 'virtually assassinated' for his 'unbending resistance to Italian dominance in Yugoslavia' and his nature *tout court*. This neatly sums up the way many felt as well as the way in which a general problem, cultural and political domination from Belgrade, was reduced to a dispute about policy.[61] As an indefatigable advocate for Croatian rights, Radić aggravated his political enemies with his vacillations between abstentionism on the one hand and involvement in the governing process on the other. What made his stand confusing was his commitment to working for greater Croatian autonomy within the Yugoslav state. This view of Radić acting in a provocative manner and precipitating his own demise persisted into the 1990s, especially in studies lamenting the fall of Yugoslavia and interpreting its collapse as the result of the continuation of the Croat nationalists' anti-Yugoslav 'pathology'.[62] A 2005 textbook on European history reiterates those interwar prejudices, calling Radić 'a rabble-rousing demagogue who wanted an independent Croatia' and whose party 'emerged as the most troublesome parliamentary faction in Belgrade'. Radić was '[a] loose cannon careening between boycotts of parliamentary proceedings, a spewing of verbal abuse on party rivals, and seemingly disingenuous offers of cooperation that invariably ended in a return to obstructionism' and, predictably, he 'damaged Yugoslavian democracy'.[63] At the time and in subsequent accounts many also argued that Račić's act, though regrettable, was personal rather than political. In this context the political consequences, or antecedents, for that matter, of his act were of little import. The Slovenian politician, Korošec, who had explained the Slovenes' attitude towards Yugoslavia as one of pragmatic self-interest, was reported to have said that the *Skupština* shootings constituted an 'isolated and personal act of a single misguided' man.[64] The Yugoslav National Assembly, wrote Frederic Ogg, an historian at the University of Wisconsin and regular contributor to *Current History*, 'is not noted for its orderliness'. But, he added, while 'violence both of language and of action marks almost every session. ... fortunately such things as happened during the sitting of June 20 do not often befall'. Further, Račić declared he was 'moved to his desperate act by considerations of self-defense' and the source of his behaviour was the 'perennial hostility between the Serbs and Croats'.[65]

According to an anonymous 'Croat view', published in the *Slavonic Review* after Radić's death, the tendency of outside observers to gloss over the crime was short-sighted. Many 'Pan-Serbs' treated it 'as merely "a regrettable event due to personal issues"'.[66] This author described the Kingdom as 'a rather sudden experiment in blending two elements which in their nature showed but little powers of cohesion', and concluded: 'Indeed there has been all too little sign of racial symbiosis.'[67] The search for that 'symbiosis' continued, and those who denied its existence were often also seen to be preventing it from eventuating. The assassinations aroused distress and anger among Croats across the political spectrum and when, a year later (June 1929), news came of Račić's comparatively lenient sentence of 20 years' imprisonment, and that the charge was murder and attempted murder without premeditation, it sparked further outrage.[68] After all, what had Račić actually planned to do with his revolver that day in the *Skupština*, if not shoot people? The responses to Radić's death abroad revealed how little interest there was internationally in whether or not the Kingdom remained (or indeed ever was) true to the democratic project of the First World War. The shooting of their deputies in the Belgrade parliament alerted Croats to the precariousness of their political standing in the Kingdom while the excuses made for the Serb nationalists who had buoyed Račić seemed curiously reminiscent of those made for the circle around the assassins of the Archduke.

The obstinate Croats, as we read in *L'Illustration*, had proven 'a headache for the king'. Their non-cooperation had frustrated their opponents and their assassin, but nothing could mar the October celebrations marking the tenth anniversary of the 1918 victories. Even in such an atmosphere, or perhaps because of it, five months after the assassinations the king was determined to commemorate the anniversary with pride and pomp. Envoys from Romania, Greece, Italy, the United States, Czechoslovakia and the United Kingdom were present. Marshal Franchet d'Esperey represented France. It was a stunning affair, as much a display of military might and Serbian 'renewal' as an indication of the king's power and charisma. No one, *L'Illustration* reported, seriously entertained the idea of a 'bicephalous Kingdom' with capitals in Zagreb and Belgrade, as the local and international support for the military display demonstrated.[69] The unity forged in war was safe and when, three months later, the king declared his dictatorship, he did so in the belief that as long as he promised to preserve that unity, the international community would not seriously question his leadership, let alone undermine it.

Dictatorship Tolerated and Defended

The response of the king to the death of politicians who argued for equality of peoples and for their democratic and social rights was to rescind ethnic and political rights, allegedly in order to protect them. Aleksandar proclaimed a dictatorship in January 1929, after which he embarked on a concerted programme of national homogenization. He dismantled all religiously and nationally based associations. The administrative restructuring of the country into nine *Banovine* was also designed to undermine further pre-existing national affiliations. This first attempt to instil a sense of a common Yugoslav identity from above was backed by force. The formal renaming of the state as the Kingdom of Yugoslavia in October coincided with an intensive and relentless campaign of 'denationalization', notably among Croats. This was evident in the very foundation of the *Banovine*, which, apart from the (Slovenian) Dravska *Banovina*, eschewed national and historic borders in an attempt to stimulate wider identification with Yugoslavism and to re-establish tighter controls from the centre. Linking Yugoslavism with dictatorship and state terrorism just ten years after the Kingdom's formation would have serious consequences, including the departure to Italy in early 1929 of a group of Croat oppositionists under the leadership of Dr Ante Pavelić (1889–1959), who formed the Ustaša (Insurgent) movement. Theirs was to be a separatist solution to the 'Croat question'.

International reactions to the dictatorship varied. Some commentators were immediately critical. Others chose to reserve judgement until the nature of the regime could no longer be ignored. Others yet again were defensive and sympathetic. Whatever one's position, it was difficult to overlook the basic facts: that there was strict censorship and the regime's opponents, real and imagined, could be arbitrarily arrested and gaoled without trial. Political prisoners who had been psychologically brutalized and tortured were often either killed in custody or committed suicide. Croats, predictably, made comparisons between the execution of young Croat nationalists merely suspected of anti-state activities and Račić's seemingly mild sentence. National and international figures like the acclaimed Croat academic, Milan Šufflay, were among the regime's victims. Šufflay's murder in 1931, committed when his police guard mysteriously abandoned their post, led to an outcry against the terroristic methods of the regime from notables including Albert Einstein.[70] The revisionist *Danubian Review* deplored the travails of Croats – killings, torture and all the indiscriminate methods used to subdue them – alongside those of the sizeable Hungarian minority in the Kingdom who were without municipal representation. The 'fiction of "National Unity" concealed Serb hegemony' and exploitation and the paper went on to suggest 'dictatorship has generally one more companion besides despotism, namely corruption'.[71] The more common viewpoint was expressed in the *Revue de Paris*: the king had no choice other than his recourse to a dictatorship in order to overcome the 'heightened state of excitation' and the impasse created by the Croats. Radić was not the victim but the cause of instability and had brought his death upon himself. The author restated the dominant position, drawing on the foundational tenet of racial homogeneity, that all Yugoslavs branched out from 'the Serbian trunk', in the face of more and more evidence suggesting the contrary.[72] The 2005 European history textbook referred to above again provides a contemporary version of this shallow interpretation and demonstrates the longevity of its appeal: 'Weary of the chaos, King Alexsandar established a personal dictatorship.'[73] The king seemed to have considerable confidence in his ability to withstand potential and actual criticism of his dictatorship. In part, at least, this confidence may have derived from the rhetoric surrounding the establishment of the state and the attachment of outsiders to its foundational myths, rooted as they were in the memory of war.

The theme of international tolerance for the transgressions of a wartime ally recurs in Yugoslav history. In the first year of the dictatorship the *poilus* of the French Orient Army made a pilgrimage to the graves of the French war dead on the Balkan front. This pilgrimage was the occasion of much reflection on the ties of friendship and mutual respect that bound the French to the Kingdom. The splendid *monuments aux morts* in Bitola (Monastir), Skopje and Belgrade were the sites of civic and military services, occasions on which the local population greeted the *poilus* with enthusiasm. How moving it was for the 'pilgrims' to see that the French war graves, though maintained with subsidies from the French government, were the focus of the tender attentions of those living nearby. Handmade candles rather than mass-produced ones flickered on these graves on the appropriate feast days and days of commemoration. Serb mothers watched over the dead sons of French mothers, and this sight reassured the pilgrims that their comrades could rest in peace here.[74]

L'Illustration covered the 15-day visit of over two hundred French veterans in three articles in October and November 1929.[75] The group left from Marseilles on 23 August and nothing could have prepared the French for the reception they received on their arrival. The invitation had been 'warm': 'Come! We are waiting for you.... We have to show our gratitude, to show you that we have forgotten nothing, to spread out before you...to whom we owe our life, more than our life, the honour of being your brothers...the harvest from the seed you have sown.'[76] The French veterans were overcome by emotion during the pilgrimage. The whole country, *'toute la Yougoslavie'*, was involved in preparing, greeting and thanking. The event unfolded like a 'beautiful fable'. Everywhere crowds came out to greet them. The outcome was an even closer friendship than was evident in 1921 at the time of King Petar's funeral, an indestructible alliance between men after the 'bloodiest of wars' and in the midst of a 'most precarious peace'. Eleven years on the gratitude towards the French had not abated, but was greater than ever: 'This people knows what their liberty cost them and what ours has cost us.'[77] The Yugoslavs had 'forgotten nothing'. What did they want from the French now? Only 'fraternal love and advice' and 'our approbation and criticism', when it is called for. Moreover, the Yugoslavs were a worthy ally, having helped win the war and then honouring the collective sacrifice with their efforts at moral and physical reconstruction. Never had they lost sight of their ultimate goal, their liberty, not even in the darkest moments of the war. Nonetheless, like the French, they had taken from the war an understanding of its horrors and the desire to preserve the peace. 'You saved us' was the Serbs' constant refrain, reassuring in an age when nations thought 'only of themselves' and their own achievements.[78]

The pilgrims made their way to Bitola, the resting place of some 6000 soldiers of the French Orient Army, where a choir sang *The Marseillaise* in four parts. The crowd of close to 10,000 people included 'loyal *mahométans*', who deserved now to be called 'Yugoslavs'.[79] From Bitola the pilgrims and their hosts travelled in a convoy of 68 cars to the next way station. The landscape was familiar and, apart from the French graves, there were other reminders of the sites of battles, including the then prince regent's headquarters, the castle where Aleksandar stayed after re-taking Bitola. This Macedonian stronghold became the 'first capital of a reconquered Serbia'. It was also nearby that Aleksandar had given the cross he wore around his neck to a dying French airman. In response to the Frenchman's cry of thanks the prince regent had said: 'My friend, my brother, you thank me when I give so little to you who have given us everything.'[80] How could one describe this man who was now the king? He was of the military, to be sure, but also 'tender, sensitive, ... [one] who knows how to command and does not blush at showing his soft heart, riches for a man'.[81] There was not even passing reference to the dictatorship or Yugoslavia's political instability.

At another of the Macedonian way stations, a bishop who had been a volunteer in three wars spoke, moving those present to tears. Planes dropped flowers which the mountain breezes scattered across the countryside. The Frenchmen were decorated with the 'Serbian *Croix de Guerre*' by order of the king. Small cemeteries dotted on the side of the hill among the pines made of the entire mountain 'an immense, splendid and terrifying ossuary'.[82] It would remain a monument to the success of the Serbs, the 'most eloquent symbol of the nation': the 'small and courageous Serbia' of yesterday had become the 'great Yugoslavia' of today.[83] From Skopje, cars drove the pilgrims to the nearby French cemetery. The spot had marked a dramatic moment in the war, with 100,000 Bulgars of the Eleventh Army forced to capitulate in open country.[84] The *poilus* drew on memory and imagination and saw not the new buildings of Skopje, but the old town of white minarets and rounded roof tiles. Here, again, the township was decked out to impress and a panoply of civic dignitaries, veterans, soldiers, members of various voluntary associations and local peasants welcomed the French.

The 1929 pilgrimage shows how the Serbian war experience was transposed onto all Yugoslavs, including the Macedonians. Those who were not members of the international family of victorious veterans at least knew how to express gratitude and paid tribute to the

French accordingly. In the case of the Slovenes, who had few opportunities to participate in this process of memorialization, there were
other vehicles for the expression of solidarity with France. One comprised a curious twist on the cult of the Unknown Soldier, the unveil-
ing of the monument to an unknown soldier of the Grande Armée,
the army of Napoleon's Empire, in Ljubljana in October 1929. In
an issue of L'Illustration that appeared between the first and second
reports on the pilgrimage was a three-page account of the ceremony
in which the Slovenes paid tribute to the civilizing mission of the
French in the Illyrian provinces in the early nineteenth century. A
Slovene poet's tribute, an Ode to Napoleon, was read and the obelisk
bore the following inscription: 'Under this stone we have placed your
ashes, unknown solder of the army of Napoleon, that you might rest
among us, you who in going to battle for the glory of your Emperor
fell for our freedom.' The centenary of the French decrees relating to the Illyrian provinces could not be celebrated in 1909 under
the Habsburgs but now, in 1929, the Slovenes were free to contemplate the visionary stance of Napoleon who had, for all intents and
purposes, founded the first Yugoslavia.[85] The fact that the highly
centralized Kingdom borrowed much from the French model of government and administration seemed simply to confirm that view of
ongoing and constructive French influence in the region.

High-ranking British officials and public figures shared the show
of support for the king by the French veterans, although some British
observers were more sceptical. Three individuals in particular, the
British Ambassador, Henderson, Seton-Watson and Durham serve
as our focus to illustrate the subtle, and sometimes not so subtle,
differences in approach to the Yugoslav question. Each reflects an
external perspective on internal developments. Assessing the relative impact of the ideas of these individuals enables us to get a sense
of the main points of contention on the Yugoslav question while
avoiding the (often predictable and at times flawed) generalizations
arising from an exclusive focus on high politics within the Kingdom.
Henderson, best known as British Ambassador to Berlin from 1937
until the outbreak of war in 1939, was posted to Belgrade in the
crucial years between 1929 and 1935. He was the kind of man who,
in early 1914, thought nothing of helping to smuggle 200 revolvers
and 2000 rounds of ammunition into Donegal for his Protestant
brother-in-law, whom Henderson himself described as 'one of the
most fanatical of Ulstermen and one of the most energetic of its
gun runners'.[86] When he first heard of his posting in Belgrade

Henderson was in Paris and, he later wrote, the news 'shocked and horrified' him because he believed he would be travelling to a backwater. His six years in Belgrade proved to be the happiest and most interesting years of his life. Henderson 'had no preconceived dislike of authoritarian government as such'.[87] In Berlin he would become the voice of appeasement and his critics held he went further than merely upholding his government's policy. Lord Cadogan, head of the Foreign Office, wrote at the time that Henderson was 'completely bewitched by his German friends', as evidenced by his reports on the Nuremberg rally he attended in September 1937. The rally sent Henderson into a veritable ecstasy. The effect of the lighting, Henderson wrote, was 'both solemn and beautiful ... something like being inside a cathedral of ice'.[88] In his final report to the Foreign Secretary after the outbreak of war Henderson wrote:

> It would be idle to deny the great achievements of the man who restored to the German nation its self respect and its disciplined orderliness. The tyrannical methods which were employed in Germany itself to obtain this result were detestable, but were Germany's own concern. Many of Herr Hitler's social reforms, in spite of their complete disregard of personal liberty of thought, word or deed, were on highly advanced democratic lines ... typical examples of a benevolent dictatorship.[89]

Such admiration for Hitler's 'benevolent dictatorship' may in some part be attributed to the fact that Henderson had cut his teeth on the dictatorship of King Aleksandar prior to his Berlin posting. Peter Neville argues that Henderson has become the scapegoat for critics of the policy of appeasement. He adds that Henderson simply followed instructions by adopting a more 'sympathetic, emollient line' towards the Nazis and that while he was sympathetic to Germany, he was not pro-Nazi. However, at the same time Henderson was known for his hero-worship of the king, which he later transferred to Göring. He was also notoriously partial and widely known to be promoting Aleksandar's dictatorship. Neville suggests that Henderson was sent to Berlin because he had proven he could 'get on with dictators'.[90] Significantly, Henderson had served in the diplomatic mission in Serbia (in Niš) in 1915 and his memoirs, correspondence and reports from Belgrade to the Foreign Secretary reveal the extent to which he had imbibed the views about the South Slavs that triumphed in 1918. Serbs and Montenegrins had taken the key role

in fighting for South Slav freedom and unity and so, 'not unnaturally', he wrote, 'the Serbs at Belgrade ... played the predominant part
in the new union'.[91]

Henderson justified and defended the dictatorship, ostensibly for
the higher purpose of protecting British interests and maintaining stability in the region. He wrote that according to Aleksandar,
'the question of a federation of Yugoslav States or of a centralized
Government at Belgrade was one which time alone could solve and,
rightly or wrongly [the king] believed that until the Yugoslav principle was more firmly established and generally understood, the
course most likely to promote union rather than tend to disunion,
was centralization'.[92] Henderson held that the king had no relish
for the dictatorial powers which he had been 'forced' to assume and
which he felt were in the best interests of his country. The dictatorship, according to Henderson, allowed the king to concentrate on
the pressing question of foreign policy, including reaching a *modus
vivendi* with Italy regarding its claims to a large part of the Adriatic
coastline. Taking the union of Scotland and England as his model
for successful 'unions' elsewhere, Henderson wrote in a volume of
his memoirs published posthumously in 1945 that time would heal
all wounds and solve all problems in due course.[93]

Henderson's was the official voice of British policy towards the
Kingdom and his goal was to silence critics of Yugoslavia. The British
press and the Labour Party were among his targets. Exceedingly
irritated by those in Britain who were critical of Yugoslavia's dictatorship, he wrote: 'all dictators [are] in principle anathema to
good democrats, quite oblivious of the special circumstances which
may have created a dictator in "less happier lands" than ours'.[94]
Henderson asked that Seton-Watson refrain from publishing articles damaging to the dictatorship. Seton-Watson was responsive
to Henderson's pleas for 'silence' but did not commit himself to
remaining aloof from the situation indefinitely. Prior to agreeing
to Henderson's request, Seton-Watson had begun to feel a certain
impatience with the king of whom he, too, was very fond. Like
Henderson, he believed in Aleksandar's good faith. Initially Seton-
Watson had blamed the deterioration of political life in Yugoslavia
on the negative influence of three men, Pašić, Pribičević and Radić.[95]
He said this after Radić and Pašić were dead and after the dictatorship was established. Seton-Watson's perspective generally was that
of a man entirely committed to the Yugoslav principle. Convinced
of its rationality and necessity, he could identify precise internal

reasons to explain the Kingdom's failure to live up to expectations. Unsurprisingly then, at first Seton-Watson needed no prompting from Henderson to hold back from judging Aleksandar's dictatorship. In January 1929 he delivered a lecture at the Royal (formerly British) Institute of International Affairs just after the dictatorship was proclaimed. Like Henderson, he noted that the king was not the kind of man who liked being a dictator, or the kind of man who would 'impose his will by violent means': Aleksandar was in a 'cruel dilemma' and, before proclaiming the dictatorship, exhibited 'great reluctance, patience and restraint'. He had governed with 'moderation under long years of provocation'.[96]

In his lecture Seton-Watson mentioned the 'party chaos' – the corruption and intrigues determining party leadership – and the social chaos resulting from the activities of war profiteers and the 'jobbery' and 'nepotism' that came with 'exaggerated centralisation of all administrative, judicial and economic functions'. He expressed his 'intense dislike for dictatorships' but 'common fairness' compelled him 'to point out that the Jugoslav dictatorship belongs to a special category of its own'.[97] Moreover the king and his ministers had made 'absolutely explicit statements that their action is not either Fascism or a Dictatorship, but that as soon as they have done the work which they regard as necessary, a new and more workable constitution and a new Parliament will take the place of the old'. Seton-Watson could say this knowing that the king's guiding principle was 'one state, one nation, one king'. He drew on the founding myths (to the formation and diffusion of which he had devoted so much of his energy) and stated categorically that the union of South Slavs was not artificial but, like that of Italy and Germany, 'spontaneous' and 'inevitable'. Yugoslavia came into existence through the 'efforts and will of the Jugoslavs themselves', even when the Entente powers opposed them. To support this claim he reasoned backwards by remarking on the 'impossibility of dividing' those who had not in fact previously been united (and whom he had done a great deal). He said that to 're-unite' 'no human ingenuity could draw a dividing line between Serb and Croat'. Differences between them were not racial, linguistic or religious but 'psychological', and arguments focusing on the supposed distinctions occasioned by the historical East–West divide were a 'preposterous exaggeration'. He exhibited little sympathy for the victims of the killings in the parliament the previous year, drawing attention to their irascible nature. Croats had the 'habit of constitutional thinking' from their association with Hungary and, with their inherently negative attitude, were always 'agin the government', whatever its complexion.[98] He rationalized that the Croats would therefore be happy with the abandonment of a constitution they had never embraced.

Serbia's nature, according to Seton-Watson, was 'absolutely and fundamentally democratic', if primitively so. Serbs killed for democracy while Croats, as it would be argued with particular vigour after 1934, did so for their own base and unreasonable (or 'extreme') nationalist ends. Essentially Seton-Watson's lecture was a justification of the state itself, irrespective of its leaders' abuses of their power. His position was even more intransigent than that of others who were equally Yugoslav in orientation and inclination, as the comments after his lecture reveal. Carlisle Aymer Macartney (1895–1978), an historian of Central Europe who was also an adviser to the League of Nations, was present. He commented that it was 'very disquieting' that at this difficult moment the king 'should have chosen to rest his power' on the army which was 'not a Jugoslav force but...a Serbian force'. Arthur Evans, Seton-Watson's longstanding collaborator and contributor to *The New Europe*, whose writings on the subject began with his travels in the 1870s, was also there. He said, surprisingly, given his proven and well-known commitment to the Yugoslav ideal, that 'centralisation at Belgrade must cease'. Ignoring Seton-Watson's dismissive comments on the 'exaggerated' emphasis on cultural and religious divisions and donning his archaeologist's hat, Evans called for 'some kind of Home Rule' for the Croats because the divergence between East and West dated back to Diocletian's Rome.[99] Sir Edward Boyle, formerly Honorary Treasurer of the Serbian Relief Fund, Acting British Commissioner for Serbia, Member of the Serbian Red Cross and decorated by Serbia with the title Grand Officer of the Order of St Sava, made the classic slip by referring simply to 'Serbia' when he wondered aloud what would bring peace to 'the Serbian State'. His answer was 'compromise': the Serbs should get less and the Croats more. He said that everyone present wanted the best 'for Serbia'; they wanted the approval of loans 'to Serbia' but acknowledged these should not be forthcoming in the absence of confidence, and stability bred confidence. Apparently unmoved by any of the discussion following his address, Seton-Watson concluded by saying the dissolution of the old parties was a good thing, as political life could start afresh. Neither 'dualism' nor parcellization along national lines was an option because Croats and Serbs alone did not inhabit the country and because 'Serb and Croat [were not] coterminous with Serbia and Croatia'.[100] In due course events would force him to modify his hard line against ethnically and historically-derived administrative units, though most of his other views on Yugoslavia remained remarkably uncompromising.

By the end of 1929 Seton-Watson began to distance himself from the king. Henderson, not wanting negative publicity about Aleksandar, wrote to Seton-Watson in June 1930 assuring him that there were hopeful signs in Belgrade. Henderson brought up the comparison of which he was so fond, the union of Scotland and England, and pleaded with Seton-Watson to keep the long-term perspective before him: 'in some ways this people is not much more civilised than we were a few hundred years ago'. In addition, Henderson noted, the country had to be made as amenable as possible to British influence and interests, and communism was a menace in the Balkans. France's relentless overtures towards the countries of the Little Entente were a direct threat to British interests. For these and other reasons he believed it was imperative not to 'indispose the British public' against Yugoslavia.[101]

Henderson's recurring lament was France's privileged status in Belgrade. Visits to the country by the former Commander in Chief of the Allied Armies of the Orient, Franchet d'Esperey, for official functions commemorating the wartime alliance and paying tribute to the war dead (as observed in our discussion of the 1929 pilgrimage of the French *poilus*), took place with great fanfare. The International Federation of Veterans also held their tenth annual general meeting in Belgrade in the first year of the dictatorship. It was a source of constant irritation to the British in Belgrade that the French held this special place, given that they believed France had no real concern for the well-being of the Yugoslavs and cared only for the preferential trade agreements that allowed for the easy export of French goods. In short, France was capitalizing on the wartime comradeship and seemed to want to monopolize this relationship by acting as if the 'French alone' had liberated the country with the Serbs. Yugoslavia's real friends and supporters were the British as their investments and loans now attested. However, instead of taking the upper hand, they allowed the French to dominate in Belgrade. What made the job of the embassy staff still more difficult was negative commentary in the British press on political life in Yugoslavia.[102] Henderson succeeded in convincing Seton-Watson to withdraw, temporarily at least, from the fray. It was imperative, Henderson argued, that at this delicate time a man of

Seton-Watson's influence should not compromise British interests. In February and March 1931 Seton-Watson wrote to Milan Ćurčin, a Serb colleague who had edited the Zagreb-based *Nova Evropa* and was by then living in France, saying he would 'remain quite inactive' on this question: 'Out of deference to Henderson's wishes... I have refrained from writing anything on this side of the channel for the last six months: but as Pharaoh has so obviously hardened his heart, this attitude on my part cannot last indefinitely. But meanwhile it is useless for anyone to ask me to do anything for Yugoslavia.'[103] When he did break his silence, Seton-Watson was critical of the dictatorship, but there was a limit to his capacity to question his own deeply felt premises about the state.

In three articles he published between December 1931 and January 1932 Seton-Watson's views become clear.[104] He no longer believed that the dictatorship was benevolent or transitional. He was less indulgent towards the king, whom he accused of being responsible for the abuses of the regime, and he was more circumspect about the appropriateness of the lenient treatment of Radić's killer. Significantly, Seton-Watson remained fixed on two key points and these reflect not just his personal views but also the trend of the times. There was no doubt in his mind first, that the Croats remained the principal cause of disruption, and second, that the Yugoslav state was popularly acclaimed, well conceived and one of the crowning achievements of the First World War – in short, a 'necessity'.

At his December 1931 talk at Chatham House (published in January 1932) Seton-Watson spoke of a 'political terrorism and repression' worse than that of Austria-Hungary towards Croatia and Southern Slavs.[105] He spoke, too, of the torture of Croats, 'mysterious deaths in prison' and Šufflay's murder as the result of police collusion.[106] In the third article on this subject, also published in January 1932, Seton-Watson added more detail on the forms of torture, including the caning of the victims' feet, the beatings suffered by political prisoners, the mental anguish suffered by victims of the police state and murders covered up as suicides. He also cited actual cases of suicides of internees, mistreated to the point of having 'lost their reason'.[107] Further abuses came with the 'complete muzzling of the press' and the opposition and with public ballots. (Troops and the gendarmerie intimidated peasants, whom they drove to the polling stations, into voting for government candidates.)[108] Possibly the greatest dismay for Seton-Watson was the realization that the king, of 'purely democratic pedigree' and of the 'purest Serbian blood', had betrayed this fine tradition. Dictatorship was not a last resort but Aleksandar's first choice in dealing with the problems he faced. Europe suffered 'different types of nightmare, varying from the super Tsarism of Lenin and Stalin to the tyranny of Mussolini'. However, there was 'no instance of a King who has with his own hands destroyed a constitution which he helped to create and to which he had taken an oath only a few short years before'.[109] There were different contributing factors to his lapse, including the influence of autocratic Russia, where he had spent his boyhood, his extended military service[110] and the 'autocratic leanings' of his mother's Montenegrin family.[111] The return to constitutional government in September 1931 had proven a sham, which was even more difficult to accept from a man 'whose fine war record is well known and who possesses many of the qualities which go to the making of a great King'.[112]

If Seton-Watson had not defended Radić's attacker he had been generous in his interpretation of the violent act, in his view a spontaneous outburst by an individual acting independently. He did reconsider this position when he wrote that the consequence of the tolerant attitude towards earlier abuses of power and lapses in judgement by the Kingdom's ruling elite was more, not less, injustice. The glaring contrast between the treatment of Vladko Maček (1879–1964), Radić's successor as leader of the Peasant Party, arrested and gaoled without trial on suspicion of treason, and Račić, was a case in point.[113] Seton-Watson then went further, acknowledging the danger of justifying, and in some cases glorifying, Radić's murderer. Our expert was therefore capable of reassessing some views but not others. He did not deviate from the position that Radić had argued for a programme, the 'Croat humanitarian republic', which was 'quite unsuited to the realist world in which he lived and was simply incomprehensible to the more mundane Serbs'. The Croats made the system unworkable because their 'tactics towards Belgrade' were 'false and irritating'. They took 'their own superior culture for granted, using the glib catchwords of "Byzantinism" and forgetting the heroic role of the Serbian army and the sacrifices of the entire Serbian population in the cause of unity'. Their 'carping and negative attitude' was bound to draw some reaction against the Croats: 'the Serbs would not have been human' if they did not resent it.[114] The Croats had by definition to be 'unreasonable' because history and Austria-Hungary made them that way and because they were now incapable of distinguishing between a state that was good for them and a state that was not.[115]

After all this, and after his indictment of the 'Police State, which governs by the suppression of all opinion and the intimidation of its opponents',[116] Seton-Watson could still write that Yugoslav unity, 'rest[ing] upon solid foundations', was a 'European necessity' and would more than likely emerge from the 'present crisis stronger than ever'.[117] This confirmed his rededication to the South Slav ideal and the principles of 1918 the previous month: 'I have no fear for the unity of the Yugoslav state. I believe as firmly as ever that Yugoslavia has come to stay, and that this is desirable, both for the peace of Europe and for the progress of South-Eastern Europe in particular.' He admitted the Yugoslav 'salad' had been difficult to mix but it was clear 'it can never be unmixed again'. Still recovering from the wars and upheavals of 1912–19 the Yugoslavs, he wrote, 'virile and highly intelligent' people that they were, would eventually recognise cooperation was in their best interests. Such blurring of the lines between Serbian and 'Yugoslav' experiences of war was, as we have seen, the norm.[118] Moreover, Seton-Watson was privy to the extent of the manoeuvrings prior to the formation of the state, and he was not about to entertain the idea of exerting anything near that effort on 'unmixing' the salad he himself had spent enormous energy tossing.

Henderson wrote to Seton-Watson in an attempt to silence him again, insisting that the state had to be strengthened and that under the circumstances dictatorship was the path to this end. Among Seton-Watson's Serb correspondents were men critical of Henderson, including Ilija Jukić and Pribičević, who was living in exile in Paris at this time. For example in 1933 Jukić described Henderson as 'inclined to fashist [sic] conceptions', while Pribičević called him an ordinary bureaucrat who, relishing the atmosphere of the palace and the company of the king, sent back to the foreign office only the most favourable reports. It was hard enough battling the dictatorship, Pribičević wrote, without having also to battle against those foreign governments who supported it.[119] It was not surprising that Henderson should have provoked such a reaction. His personal devotion to Aleksandar knew no bounds. Henderson's loyalty persisted through the worst of the Belgrade terror. In April 1934 he wrote to Seton-Watson that criticism of the dictatorship would only encourage the 'disruptive efforts' of 'separationists' living in exile.[120]

While Seton-Watson tolerated Henderson's views and respected his wishes up to a point, he had no patience with Durham. The differences of opinion between the three reflect differences of opinion between Yugoslavs and it is for this reason the interactions are important. Seton-Watson remained a leading authority on Yugoslavia until his death in 1951. He focused his tireless activism and research on the situation in Central and South-eastern Europe and corresponded with key figures in political and cultural life across the whole region. Durham participated in debates on Balkan issues but with considerably less impact than Seton-Watson and his circle, in part at least because the latter effectively marginalized her. Durham is a significant character in our story precisely for the reason that her impact was limited. Her fortunes show why some transnational forces prevailed over others and why some internal protagonists were more successful than others in marshalling the support of powerful outsiders.

Durham was a recognizable 'type' by the interwar years. We have seen that an extensive secondary literature documents the great adventures and writings of women like her who, for a range of reasons, ventured beyond the Mediterranean in their travels and left their mark on the places they visited in different ways.[121] Rebecca West referred specifically and disparagingly to Durham in her classic work, *Black Lamb and Grey Falcon*. West implied that Durham was gullible and that she was 'the sort of person devoted to good works and austerities, who is traditionally supposed to keep a cat and a parrot'. Durham's lawyers held up the publication of West's book and had Durham's name removed from one of the offensive passages.[122] However, the attack, coming so late in Durham's life, could not add too much to the harm that had already been done to her credibility in those circles in which it mattered what one thought and wrote about the Balkans. West was building on a pattern of Durham-bashing firmly established by Seton-Watson and others in academia, politics and journalism. During the war Evans had written to Seton-Watson about Durham's 'meddling'. In 1916 she was commenting unfavourably on the projected South Slav union. Evans hoped that Seton-Watson would ensure timely ripostes from right-thinking colleagues would belittle her views.[123] The 'Durham problem' for these men was at least twofold: she did not fit their academic (or quasi-academic) mould and she did not share their views. Durham had undergone a transformation of sorts as a result of what she had witnessed in the Balkan Wars. Her first love had been for Serbian culture and traditions, which she described in her early writings.[124] When she went to work with Albanian border villagers she witnessed their suffering at the hands of Serbs and Montenegrins. According to West, Durham's work was flawed because of her very nature and because she favoured the Albanians. On the other hand, Seton-Watson, though strongly (and acceptably) 'anti-Austrian', was level-headed because he 'had no favourite among the Balkan peoples'.[125]

Evidently the concern with Durham was not so much what she said, but the people about whom she said it. For there was nothing particularly unusual about British writers speaking intemperately or in a prejudicial (even bigoted) way about Balkan or Yugoslav peoples. The problem was that Durham decried the Serbs. She had become, according to Seton-Watson, a Serbophobe. Worse still, because in many people's minds Serbia and Yugoslavia were interchangeable, hers was an attack not just on Serbs, but on the legitimacy of the international deliberations after the First World War. Durham's perception of events warrants attention because it gives us a unique insight into a view that was scorned and the reasons for that.

Seton-Watson and Durham publicly differed on a number of issues. In every sense Durham was the underdog in what became for Seton-Watson an uneven battle of wills. Durham was persistent and thought that their shared interests would eventually provide enough common ground for discussions and future collaborations, but she became as irrelevant as those whom she championed. She and her loyal group of friends in Britain and Europe resigned themselves to their marginalization, but never gave in. They kept their spirits up through voluminous correspondence in which they criticized and mocked many of the views expressed in *The New Europe*. They took some satisfaction from the fact that much of what its editorial committee and contributors predicted concerning the future Yugoslavia proved wrong so quickly. Durham and her friends were, indeed, put out by the fact that they had difficulty getting their letters published in *The Times*, whose editor in the immediate postwar years, Wickham Steed, was among Seton-Watson's confidants. For his part, Seton-Watson ridiculed Durham's work, refusing an invitation from as eminent a colleague as Arnold Toynbee (1889–1975) to work with her on editions of documents outlining the causes of the war. Finally, he sought to isolate her, often by following her, or having others follow her, to speaking engagements and attacking the views she expressed. When Durham was to give a talk in December 1924 on 'Serbian Responsibility for the War' at the Institute of International Affairs, Seton-Watson wrote that even though it was not a 'public occasion', there were 'likely to be some serious people present' and he intended to go 'to make the sparks fly'. He hoped Steed would also attend.[126] These men openly rebuked Durham while privately

deriding her as 'waving a tomahawk' and one of Serbia's 'raving
enemies',[127] 'a rabid and disgusting Serbophobe'.[128] Seton-Watson
wrote a witheringly dismissive review of Durham's book implicat-
ing the Serbian government in Franz Ferdinand's assassination, *The
Serajevo [sic] Crime* (1925). According to him, Durham used all manner of unverified and unverifiable sources uncritically, had 'no ink-
ling of what is meant by historical evidence' and accepted 'as gospel
the merest pothouse gossip or braggadocio'.[129] The following year
(1926) Seton-Watson published his own book on the assassination
arguing that Berlin and Vienna were responsible for the outbreak
of the war.[130] The vehemence of his attack on Durham suggests this
was not merely an academic quarrel based on her perceived lack of
judgement and uncritical use of primary sources. It seems reasonable to conclude that Seton-Watson took her stance to be an attack
on Yugoslavia's legitimacy and that he could not allow such an attack
to pass unchallenged.

Seton-Watson's response was rooted in his and most external
observers' unswerving attachment to Yugoslavia's creation narrative.
While he was critical of Aleksandar's dictatorship and the police
state, he never stopped believing that Yugoslavia, one of the crowning achievements of the war, was viable, historically justifiable and
necessary. Durham, who was present at Seton-Watson's lecture in
early January 1929 discussed above, recognized this unyielding
attachment and drew attention to it. Her comments at the time
included a critique of the accepted view of the South Slav revolution: the Kingdom was not the happy outcome of a movement for
unification but 'formed by violence' before the people were 'ripe
for union'. She also referred to the 1903 regicide, saying the ruling Karađorđević dynasty 'was floated to the throne on a wave of
blood after one of the most ghastly murders that had ever been
committed, and the murder gang had never ceased to influence
the policy of the country'.[131] That Durham's comments fell on deaf
ears is confirmed by the general discussion following Seton-Watson's
December 1931 talk at Chatham House. There, Durham, provocative as always, asked how it was that Britain did not break off relations with a country 'governed by a murderer', the prime minister,
General Živoković, whom she described as one of the chief plotters of the 1903 regicide. Yugoslavia was 'founded on a crime', the
Sarajevo crime, and was led by 'the Belgrade party' which never
took the Corfu Declaration seriously. Why did Seton-Watson blame
the king's Montenegrin heritage for his transgressions when it was

clear the Karađorđevićs were self-serving and profited from murder and intrigue to rule Serbia and then Yugoslavia? The fate of
Radić epitomized the regime's failure to 'Serbize' the Croats and
the need therefore to murder their leaders. Seton-Watson declined,
as he put it, 'to embark on a controversy with Miss Durham'. There
was no proof the Serbian government was involved in the Sarajevo
plot, the prime minister was but 'the least important' of the 1903
conspirators and one of the worst of the *agents provocateurs* was, predictably, a Croat, the Zagreb police chief. In short, Durham's claims
were 'fantastic' and the king was a good man who had made some
bad political choices.[132]

In fact it was Durham who asked the most pertinent question of all:
'What use was a Constitution which could not punish Raditch's murderer?' She added: 'If the Croats could not rely upon justice there
was no hope.'[133] Like others she also referred to the Macedonians,
whose very existence the Serbs denied and whose problems outsiders either ignored or belittled. Durham took much more to heart
the death of Radić than many others and did not blame the victims
for the shootings. Indeed she referred privately and in her notes to
'poor Stefan [*sic*] Radić', whom she had met when he was in London
in 1923 for a period of several months studying and lecturing and of
whom she was fond. It was 'poor Radić' who had discussed with her
the injustices perpetrated in the new state and he who alerted her to
the plight of the Macedonians, saying: 'Under the Turk Macedonia
was a cupful of blood. Today it is an ocean of blood.'[134] In retrospect,
it is clear that Durham was more attuned to the possible long-term
consequences of events within Yugoslavia than were other commentators. But for those who had chosen the path of least resistance
and supported the new ruling elite with a constancy that was inex-
haustible, Durham was exasperating. In the grand scheme of things
Radić and, by association, his constituency, were casualties of little
consequence for them, but Durham insisted the short-sightedness of
this attitude would have repercussions long into the future.

Durham had written to Seton-Watson after the January 1929 lecture and mentioned the possibility of their discussing some of the
issues he had raised. On 12 February 1929 he replied curtly:

> We seem to differ fundamentally on almost every fact connected
> with the whole Jugoslav question, and certainly on what is or is
> not, evidence: and I do not therefore see what possible good it
> can do to discuss these matters on the same platform. I refrained

from answering you at the Institute, not because I had nothing to
say, but because I resent most intensely your whole treatment and
interpretation of the question and did not wish to be led into too
sharp a retort.[135]

For her part, Durham was conciliatory and guilelessly keen for further contact. She wrote that she was 'surprised and grieved' by his
letter. The idea that he should 'resent' her interpretation of 'these
very serious questions' was 'inexplicable' to her:

> Surely we are all free to draw our own conclusions from the facts
> we have lived through. For many years I was in such close contact
> with the South Slav question. In fact I believe I began to work for
> S. Slav rights before you did. I have never opposed the extension
> of Serb rule over what I had found to be places mainly inhabited
> by them.

Hers was a long letter, going over ground that could not conceivably
have made Seton-Watson want to discuss the issues with her, publicly
or privately. She returned to the topic of political murder and conspiracy among the Serbian military and ruling circles, the injustices
faced by 'annexed peoples', the inability of the Belgrade government to provide stability, and British complicity in the perpetuation
of injustice: 'As I said the other night, the fault is not so much that
Jugoslavia has been created but that it has been artificially and pre-
maturely formed.' Durham also made it clear that she was well aware
of Seton-Watson's attitude towards her:

> I have never resented criticisms you have made about me. You
> said nasty things about me in Belgrad [sic] papers I am told. ... I
> do not understand why you are not willing to meet and talk things
> over – in private if you prefer it. To me this is all history – a thing
> outside myself – and all personal feelings are quite passed out.
> If you will tell me what, if any particular things I have said, have
> offended you we might be able to make peace. Personally I con-
> sider all squabbling is silly ... life is too short for it.[136]

Unsurprisingly, perhaps, she did not succeed in establishing cordial
relations with Seton-Watson.

There were inconsistencies in Durham's arguments about politics in the Balkans. She was not an academic or a diplomat and did

not speak or write like either. However, Durham had done what most of her male counterparts never contemplated doing: muck in and talk plainly about the people she had studied at very close quarters and assisted with her humanitarian work. As far back as February 1920 Durham had written to Seton-Watson in her capacity as Honorary Secretary of the Anglo-Albanian Society about the plight of Albanians who found themselves within Yugoslavia's borders. There was a lot of fuss about the injustice of Jugoslavs being Italianized, but 'what of the Albanians being Slavized?', she asked.[137] Durham was not a visionary but her opinions were based on personal observation and experience in the field, not on self-interest, British interests, diplomatic expediency, or indeed on the perception of herself as a primary actor in world affairs. She had no academic empire to protect or expand. Her principled belief was that an injustice inflicted on the weak and the voiceless would have far-reaching consequences. Durham's threshold for violence and injustice was low, whereas Henderson's was high. Seton-Watson did not care for it personally, but made certain calculations which took into account Britain's interests and those of Europe as he perceived them. He did not like to go against Henderson's wishes and did not do so until he could no longer be silent and retain his credibility. Even then, Seton-Watson's criticism did not extend to questioning what he saw as the fundamental nature and necessity of the state of Yugoslavia itself. He could not undermine the entity in whose existence he had invested so much of himself and which was the product of the First World War. On that question he would not abide any difference of opinion and felt no compunction in using any means at his disposal to belittle even the most insignificant opponent. In many respects history proved the instinctive Durham correct, or at least more prescient, on several of the points on which she and Seton-Watson differed: the formation of Yugoslavia, the impact of its history and 'pre-history' on its future and the consequence of the injustices suffered by non-Serbs, as responses to the assassination of Aleksandar in Marseilles attest.

The King is Dead! Long Live Yugoslavia!

We have already noted the significance of the memory of war on early developments in the Kingdom. The memory of war also blurred the focus around the more reprehensible aspects of the dictatorship.

Men like Henderson sought not simply to overlook the fact of the dictatorship but to defend it. However, the death and 'martyrdom' of Aleksandar, the Hero-King, did more to confirm people's belief that the difficult South Slavs actually needed the firm hand of a dictator than was ever possible in his lifetime. The king was assassinated along with the French Foreign Minister, Louis Barthou, in Marseilles on 9 October 1934 at the beginning of a state visit to France. Emigré Croatian and Macedonian separatist groups – the Ustaše and the Internal Macedonian Revolutionary Organisation (IMRO) – planned and carried out the killing. The king's trip came after Barthou's very positive reception in the Belgrade parliament four months previously. While in Yugoslavia, Barthou had sought to restore Yugoslav confidence in the Franco-Yugoslav alliance, which had suffered in the wake of French diplomatic overtures to the Soviet Union, including French support for admission of the Soviet Union into the League of Nations. Barthou wanted to show that in spite of some French criticism of the royal dictatorship France recognized the legitimacy of Aleksandar's regime. Most importantly, Barthou's presence in Belgrade served to confirm France's anti-revisionist position vis-à-vis the successor states and allay any Yugoslav apprehensions regarding Franco-Italian cooperation, which seemed all the more pressing in the wake of the Nazi seizure of power.[138] Aleksandar's reciprocal visit was intended to restore confidence in an alliance, shaped by war, but now under some pressure given the competing interests of Germany and Italy, and the former's threat to France's increasingly fragile sense of security. Thus, the unstated reason for the king's visit was to help open the way for the consolidation of the Franco-Italian rapprochement, which was difficult to achieve without Yugoslav cooperation. France also hoped to offer Yugoslavia diplomatic alternatives at a time when Nazi Germany was on the ascendant and the virulently anti-communist king was establishing closer ties between the two countries.

On the eve of his arrival in Marseilles, the king was the subject of much press coverage in France. Descriptions of Aleksandar focused on his qualities as a military leader in the first instance. In those 'sombre' days of 1915, recalled the correspondent of *Le Temps*, it was the then Prince Regent Aleksandar, Commander in Chief of the Serbian forces, who had been 'everywhere', had shared in 'the privations of the most humble of soldiers, given the example of endurance, and of sang-froid, rekindled courage [and] galvanised people's spirits'. Thus, Aleksandar became the 'hero-king'. But he was also the 'unifying king' (*Ujedinitelj*): a military man as well as a man of state who, according to the writer in *Le Temps*, had undertaken the difficult task of 'forging a homogeneous nation out of elements united by race and language, but separated by recent history'.[139] The meaning of the word 'recent' here was relative because, as we have already seen, for many Serbs and others, the time between 1389 and 1919 seemed to have been especially 'condensed'.[140] We should also note here the ready evocation of the long-awaited reunification, rather than unification, of South Slavs.

Once in Marseilles, before doing anything else, the king was to have laid a wreath at the *monument aux morts* of the French Orient Army. Within minutes of setting foot on French soil, both he and Barthou were shot. Sadness mixed with horror was the immediate response conveyed in *Le Temps*' coverage of the assassination. The idea that foreigners had so cruelly abused France's generous hospitality and its long, chivalrous tradition of providing asylum intensified the humiliation of the terrible crime having been committed there.[141] Aleksandar had survived attempts on his life in the Kingdom and travelled to all sorts of insalubrious destinations, reported the fascist paper, *Je suis partout*. For example, police protected the king admirably during his recent visit to the capital of his country's former foe, Bulgaria, which was teeming with Macedonian plotters. Nor were there any incidents in Istanbul or Athens. However, the report went on, Aleksandar 'had not been able to spend one hour on the soil of friend and ally, France'.[142]

In the first weeks after the murders the emphasis, for the most part, was not on placing blame but on reaffirming the solidity of the friendship between France and Yugoslavia. Marshal Franchet d'Esperey, recalling Aleksandar as his 'companion in arms' in a 30-page address delivered in Paris on 3 November, said that 'A pact of friendship links the people [of France and Yugoslavia], both committed to maintaining peace by respecting treaties, both conscious of their strength, and each assured of the support of the other in the defence of its just cause.' However, there was also a bond of 'mutual affection' between them. King Petar had fought for France in 1870 and in his son the French had observed the 'most sublime example of a knight and leader'. The Marshal concluded that 'Such profound and heartfelt sentiments are indestructible; the alliance between France and Yugoslavia will endure as long as the two peoples themselves [endure] – and we know them to be immortal.'[143] There was an emphasis in France on the commonality between the two nations,

as evidenced in their shared wartime experiences. *L'Illustration* presented its readers with images from many stages in the king's life,
the underlying theme being that companions in battle would remain
friends in perpetuity.[144] At the same time there was a feeling in
France (and Britain) that excessive zeal directed against the countries outwardly seen to be responsible for harbouring the terrorists (revisionist Hungary and Fascist Italy) ought to be avoided in
the interest of maintaining peaceful relations between all parties.
King Aleksandar's work on the international front (with the Little
Entente and the Balkan Pact) was to be maintained above all else,
given his role of peacemaker. Thus the hero-king, decorated by the
French government for his role in the First World War was, in addition to being a military giant, both *l'unificateur* and *le pacificateur*.[145]
Fundamental to this fulsome praise was the premise of the durabil-
ity of the bond between France and Yugoslavia.

The soldiers of the French Orient Army led other *anciens combattants* in the memorial services and rituals in various cities after
Aleksandar's death. The fact that 11 November was so close stamped
the tone of the reporting of these events with a special quality. Moreover, the death of France's wartime president, Raymond
Poincaré, not a week after the assassinations, symbolized the passing
of the generation that had led France through the ordeal, and made
the process of commemoration in the context of the First World War
more affecting. Three new medals, struck and released simultaneously, bore the profiles of Poincaré, Barthou and Aleksandar.[146] The
service at the Arc de Triomphe on Armistice Day itself was to focus
on honouring the dead king. On the preceding day, 10 November,
his death mask and a huge standard bearing his coat of arms provided the centrepiece behind an altar for the all-night vigil at the
Arc de Triomphe prior to the Armistice Day solemnities. Cardinal
Verdier, representatives of Orthodox Churches in Paris and other
dignitaries and politicians including the President, Albert Lebrun,
made their way to pay tribute, while through the night a constant
stream of *anciens combattants* ensured there was not a moment when
there was not someone silently keeping watch.[147] Yugoslav papers
noted all of this, in particular the services organized by veterans,
and the fact that French war widows sent condolences to the queen
in an act of sympathy and solidarity.[148] *L'Illustration,* early in the
New Year, also covered the pilgrimage of the veterans of the French
Orient Army to Aleksandar's tomb in the Karađorđević mausoleum in Oplenac. The 250 'pilgrims' who participated were met by

enthusiastic throngs of people on all the platforms of all the stations through which they passed on their way to Belgrade. How reassuring it all was in the wake of the tragedy the previous October. Now, more than ever, the memory of their wartime comradeship had to be maintained.[149]

The common experience of war and suffering provided the framework in which mainstream French opinion largely justified and supported the Yugoslav state and the royal dictatorship. Not surprisingly, many sought comfort and guidance in Aleksandar's alleged last words, 'Conservez ma Yougoslavie!', which were widely reported. After his death many commentators depicted his regime in a favourable light. It has been suggested that prior to Aleksandar's death France did not hold Yugoslavia in such high regard because of the abuses of the dictatorship. François Grumel-Jaquignon, in his detailed 1999 study of Franco-Yugoslav relations between 1918 and 1935, argues that well before the assassination France enjoyed less prestige in Yugoslavia than it had done in the wake of the war and that the Kingdom's cultural, economic and military policies reflected this.[150] (Barthou's visit to Belgrade, as we have seen, was designed to bolster relations between the countries.) Yugoslavia's perceived disenchantment with its French ally was also, in part, a product of France's obsessive search for security through alliances, its 'pactomania', as evidenced by its desire for closer ties with Italy (seemingly) to Yugoslavia's detriment. Early French enthusiasm for the Kingdom gently subsided in some quarters as it became clear that Aleksandar's methods for dealing with political and national problems were authoritarian and, on occasion, inflammatory. Following the 1928 assassinations in the Belgrade parliament and Radić's death two months later, French diplomats had expressed their most serious reservations about the Yugoslav government. French critics of the regime, both liberal and Left, were unimpressed with the extent of political violence tolerated in the Kingdom, the Serbian ruling elite's disregard for the rights of the other nationalities, its abandonment of democratic rule, and its receptivity to German trade and investment with the coming to power of the Nazis. The Yugoslav dictatorship was a point of negative focus in the French socialist and communist press as well as in some diplomatic circles.[151] Léon Blum, leader of the Socialists and future prime minister, said his party had always been critical of the 'fascist dictatorship' but rejected the methods adopted by its opponents. In January 1934, when there was talk of the royal visit to France, the Communists arranged a demonstration in Paris against it and against the Yugoslavs' 'fascist dictatorship', which was celebrating its fifth anniversary. According to the communist paper, *L'Humanité*, 'democratic France's ally' oppressed minorities and workers and was responsible for 'unspeakable crimes'. Communists subsequently greeted the king in Marseilles in October by singing *The International*.[152] After the assassinations, *L'Humanité* expressed concerns about the way in which the government might deal with other foreigners, workers in particular, who had sought asylum and a better life in France.[153]

Grumel-Jaquignon describes the process of the gradual collapse of 'the Serbian myth' – the positive image of the supremacy of Serbia in the region – within some French circles. However, he also shows that there was an overwhelming and persistent French attachment to that myth.[154] The king's death did much to restore it and led to a renewed commitment to the state. Mainstream opinion and opinion on the Right blithely praised the dictatorship for its 'moderation'. British diplomatic reports continued to bemoan the fact that France remained Britain's greatest rival in the region. Radical, republican and anti-clerical France came out in full force, it appeared, in defence of a royal dictatorship. Moreover, it seemed to matter little at the time that during the First World War much French and British propaganda about the Dual Monarchy focused on its autocratic powers and the intertwining of self-determination and democracy in the Allies' goal to establish the successor states, Yugoslavia especially. French opinion had long demonized the Austro-Hungarian Empire and sought its dismemberment on the grounds that it would be replaced by a more fitting 'suite' of states. Now the crusade for democracy had lost its urgency and relevance.

Reports on Aleksandar's funeral emphasized the universality of the suffering and the way in which it brought together all classes and peoples in Yugoslavia. According to *L'Illustration*'s correspondent, the fact that Yugoslavia was a new country made the event more important than the funeral of an English monarch, for example. Forces working against stability and harmony had to be shown to be representing only the smallest minority. Thousands of people declared themselves ready to avenge the death of the king and to show their sympathy for the young heir, the future Petar II (1923–70). The large numbers of people who had gathered in Belgrade for the funeral, the colourful peasants in national costume, the youth from the state-sponsored Sokols, ordinary men and women, white-collar workers and politicians, all reportedly came together to mourn as one and defend 'the work accomplished between 1914–1918'.[155] According to *Le Temps*, this display of solidarity also showed that Aleksandar had been building the edifice of his state on an indestructible foundation no senseless act of terror could undo.[156]

International opinion thus took comfort from the observation that all parties in Yugoslavia paid tribute to the dynasty in mourning and mistakenly concluded that they also sought its preservation. This attitude was reinforced by a miscalculation on the part of both the French and the British that the near universal abhorrence in Yugoslavia for the crime, and the compassion for Aleksandar's widow and the boy-king, were the same as support for the system Aleksandar had instituted. The French analysed Yugoslav opposition within this context, interpreting the obviously sympathetic response as widespread grass-roots endorsement of the dynasty per se, not just in its bereavement. Thus, French writers could argue, a great deal of fuss about the dictatorship came not from legitimate opposition, but from the permanently recalcitrant whose criticism 'poisoned' the last years of Aleksandar's reign.[157] Plainly, according to elements in the French press, this negative criticism by Yugoslav oppositionists was unreasonable. Noted, with a complete absence of irony, was the fact that even Maček, the leader of the Croat Peasant Party, who at the time of the 1934 assassination was in gaol on political charges after his show trial, had sent condolences from his prison cell to the Yugoslav Queen.[158] This was presented as evidence of the unanimity of support for and affiliation with the state, revealing once again the remarkable capacity for self-deception among outsiders.

In some ways such rationalisations were reminiscent of the imbalances in descriptions of the gun-wielding deputy entering the Belgrade parliament in 1928 and shooting 'spontaneously' after having been provoked. But what was different in 1934 was that commentators concentrated on the circumstances of the Marseilles killings almost to the complete exclusion of an analysis of the possible reasons for the assassins' recourse to regicide. Perhaps the focus on the event rather than its causes was predictable, given the assassination of Austria's chancellor, Engelbert Dollfuss, by Austrian Nazis in July 1934. Equally important were the riots in the wake of the Stavisky financial scandal in February 1934 (involving French politicians and the police), and the wave of anti-fascism that ensued. The focus on the alleged fascism of the groups responsible for the king's death, which were themselves harboured, in exile, by fascist states or revisionist states deemed all but fascist, deflected attention

from the nature of the royal dictatorship. A pamphlet which ful-
minated against the Macedonian separatists and their role in the
assassination quoted from pacifist Henri Barbusse's vigorous 1928
denunciation of IMRO. Barbusse, like others after him, noted the
'absolutely indisputable' fact of 'the collusion of autonomists with
fascism', but wrote nothing of the discriminatory treatment of
Macedonians prior to the war and in the successor state.[159]

In many regards Aleksandar's dictatorship itself was arguably
more coherently fascist than its Yugoslav critics in both its rhetoric
and its methods. Defending one's support for such a regime on the
basis of an anti-fascist stance was at best tenuous. This changed, up
to a point, when the popular frontism of communists everywhere led
to a different view of the successor states and an end to Moscow's
policy that separatism in the Kingdom was to be supported for its
national revolutionary potential. 'Versailles Yugoslavia' had once
been viewed by the Comintern as the quintessential product of
the imperialist war, the 'prison house of nations'. It became more
acceptable on the understanding that it could be reformed along
more equitable lines because this would hasten social change and
precipitate the second (social) revolutionary wave. As we have seen,
some Left and liberal commentators in France, as elsewhere, linked
the troubles in Yugoslavia to its repressive centralism, to the Serbian
king's hegemonic and homogenizing policies on the question of the
'founder-peoples', and to the ruthlessness of the police state that had
itself set the precedent of political assassinations and terror. But this
was not widely accepted. On the contrary, the lesson of Marseilles
was not that dictatorship and the rescinding of rights were inappropriate strategies for solving the problems Yugoslavia faced, but that
these were necessary and acceptable. The dictatorship was therefore
a 'pre-emptive strike', necessary because of the nature of the unruly
opposition a 'weary' King Aleksandar had to wipe out. Thus, it was
argued, the crime 'beyond expiation' committed in France in 1934
was of such an order that European civilization risked being plunged
back into 'the darkest centuries of its history'. There had to be a
united front of civilized nations against terrorists. Words like 'shocking', 'vile' and 'barbarous' were common in reports on the assassination. It was an act, according to Le Temps, that indicated that the
'instincts of primitive beasts' were being unleashed in the heart of
Europe.[160] Presumably political assassinations in the parliament of
Belgrade were less threatening to European civilization. The widely
accepted stereotypes of Balkan political culture combined with a

reliance, almost at any cost, on a system of pacts and alliances in the hope that another war would be averted, shaped international attitudes towards Yugoslavia. Self-interest thus merged with an idealism borne of war and suffering, producing a mindset which was almost impossible to dislodge.

Like others, Seton-Watson categorized the Marseilles crime as one outside the normal and acceptable bounds of political discourse, and did not consider that it was in itself indicative of a deeper systemic malaise.[161] By 1934 Seton-Watson had certainly lost all patience with Aleksandar's promises of reform. Describing the problem as a crisis of state and conceding the open 'glorification' in Serbian circles of Franz Ferdinand's assassin, Princip, had sanctioned an atmosphere which implicitly legitimated assassination as a political strategy,[162] he nevertheless maintained an unshakeable attachment to the Yugoslav ideal. Democracy was expendable in the overwhelming imperative to preserve the peace. In any case, democracy was seen as an unrealistic goal for the partially civilized Yugoslav peoples. The example of Henderson illustrates this position particularly well. On Aleksandar's death, the Foreign Secretary, Sir John Simon, wrote: 'A strong, contented and united Yugoslavia is a vital European necessity.' These much-quoted words, described as a fitting epitaph to the late king, are further evidence of the predominance of the mentality I have described.[163] Durham, on the other hand, could only consider the killings in Marseilles in the context of the killings in the Belgrade parliament in 1928, in Sarajevo in 1914 and in the palace in Belgrade in 1903. For her these assassinations were linked. For others there were only endless rationalisations and recourse to the double standard. Radić was but a rowdy populist, a peasant leading peasants, while Aleksandar was the wartime hero turned head of state. For Durham, who knew Radić and liked him, his death was a tragic event, one that grieved her and one that she predicted would have grave repercussions. Our more academic and detached observers denied a connection between these events because it would undermine one of their fundamental premises about the New Europe.

The Kingdom's legitimacy was in question almost immediately it came into existence, but Western democracies did not have the will or the capacity to respond to this problem at any stage of the country's history. Constant references to the First World War and its associated camaraderie were a critical element of the Franco-Yugoslav relationship and to the international standing of Yugoslavia more generally. This was evident at the time of crisis in 1928 and again in 1934. The historiography of the memory of war provides an explanation for the persistence of 'the Serbian myth' internationally. It also allows us to place the history of the Kingdom through to its collapse in 1941 in a wider context. The foundational tenets of Yugoslavia became more important, more inflated, more inflexible and more exclusive the more unstable the country became.

'The Croats have continued restless'

There was a direct relationship between the abandonment of parliamentary democracy, the attempt to forge an integrated Yugoslav identity from above, the institution of the despotic police state, and wide-scale political repression on the one side, and the radicalization of Croatian politics on the other. The initial shock of the assassination in 1934 led to the promise of reform, but in fact there followed the progressive Rightward push of politics in Belgrade. International tolerance for and justification of injustice made this possible and, to a degree, inevitable. Further miscalculations unavoidably followed the seemingly wilful determination to describe the state's problems in narrowly ethnic or national terms. In September 1935, as some of the rigours of the dictatorship were being relaxed following Aleksandar's death, one could read in *Current History* that, 'without any promise of autonomy from government sources, the Croats have continued restless'.[164] Herein was encapsulated the way in which discussion about the Yugoslav nationality question would be framed for at least another fifty years. It related both to a specific context and a broader discourse. The Croatian response to the social and political question, inequality, the lack of representation, the rescinding of rights and repression, was interpreted as a threat to the integrity of the Yugoslav state and counteracted by an extreme anti-Croat retort.

The charge that political life in interwar Yugoslavia was hampered by 'troublesome' Croatian nationalists is partly true. However, the roots of the 'restlessness' were not to be found deep in the Croatian past or in a selective and teleological reading of nineteenth-century Croatian nationalist polemics, but in the nature of the Kingdom itself. People's lived experience, rather than a 'natural' predisposition, determined the degree of 'restlessness' they felt. It could also be suggested that the issue at stake was political and civic. It did indeed seem as if Europe was turning its back on democracy in the interwar years, but people were not consciously fleeing into the arms of dictators. Ruthless men imposed dictatorship from above, generally with the complicity of conservative or military elites. With the tacit and open support of democratic countries willing to sacrifice anyone's rights in the interest of preserving the peace, as we saw with France and Britain's reaction to the assassination of Aleksandar, autocrats and dictators impeded the spread of democratic principles and practices and openly marginalized or 'neutralized' their opponents. 'Contented people', Durham argued in 1934, 'did not plot across the border', while 'people who found peaceful means useless in the end resorted to violence'. This was a reference to the fact that the Macedonians' deputations to the League of Nations in Geneva regarding the 'cruel persecutions' they endured went unheeded and resulted in continued suffering and then direct action on their part.[165] There were those who drew attention to the causes of Yugoslavia's problems and to the fact that if these causes went unchecked then the king's death would have no repercussions other than further abuses and instability in the region. The way forward, according to Sir Edward Boyle, was 'not militarism but democracy, not force but justice, not autocracy but freedom'.[166] While deploring the brutality of the dictatorship, Seton-Watson was compelled to assert that Croats and Slovenes had 'rushed into the union' and that the former, regardless of the persecutions they suffered now, were to blame for the early successes of the Serb centralists because of their abstentionism in the 1920s. They had brought their travails on themselves, as epitomized by the fate of Radić.[167] This was and remains the most common way of explaining the Kingdom's failure. If it was not flawed from the start, one of its constituent 'tribes' was.

The trivialization of the crimes of the royal dictatorship and of the Croats' experience in interwar Yugoslavia, in particular attempts at submerging their distinctive identity and denying their political rights, led directly to the radicalization of one strand of Croatian nationalist politics. The constitution, Belgrade's recourse to nepotism, corruption and repression and then the dictatorship shaped the opposition. Yet even when these factors were not ignored our observers sought a deeper reason for the failure of the state and they found it in the Croats' 'difficult' nature. Thus commentators resorted to a number of platitudes. Some said the Croats did not like the rough and tumble of politics, whereas the Serbs did. Others insisted that the story of Serbian hegemony was inflated and a convenient excuse for the non-participation of Croats in political life. Croats were uncooperative and, as Seton-Watson had declared, perpetually obstructionist and 'agin the government' because they were historically predisposed to behave in such a fashion. As this was their permanent state of mind and not a reasoned or even justifiable reaction to what outsiders regarded as passing inequalities, it was not necessary to reproach the regime under which they expressed this obstructionism because it would have been the same under any government. As this chapter has shown, such explanations were inadequate at the time and remain so.

Croats and Macedonians were also routinely described as extremists. After the banning of the Communist Party in Yugoslavia, the government only had to contend overtly with one kind of extremism, national extremism. This was measured by an individual's or a group's attitude towards the control of government, the bureaucracy, the policing agencies and the military, by Belgrade. The Yugoslavism adopted by the state in 1921, allowing as it did for Serbian domination, meant that by definition only non-Serbs could fall into the category of national extremists. In the interwar years the aspirations of Serb nationalists had begun to be met within the Kingdom, which brought together all Serbs into one state. In this context, Aleksandar's intensive campaign to create a Yugoslav nation after 1929 could not be an expression of extremism, national or political, even if it precipitated greater Serbian domination under a fascist-leaning dictatorship. Serb democrats who suffered under the dictatorship and who agitated for a return to democratic processes generally projected their opposition within the acceptable framework of the unitary or centralist Yugoslav state and, by default, could not be extreme. On the other hand, Radić, the democrat and pacifist, could only be seen to be extreme because he questioned the nature of the state itself. It was from this environment that the Macedonians and Croats responsible for Aleksandar's assassination emerged.

One of the consequences of the Marseilles killings was the further radicalization of Yugoslav politics, with the formation of a government with greater fascistic mobilizing aspirations under the auspices of the Yugoslav Radical Union. The new ruling elite was equally (though less ostentatiously) committed to Aleksandar's organizing principle, 'one state, one nation, one king'.[168] Aleksandar's cousin, Prince Paul, was one of three regents appointed after the king's death. Regent Paul had no military experience, was a political novice and interested in culture and travel. Educated at Oxford, Paul retained close ties with his English friends, including Member of Parliament and socialite Sir Henry (Chips) Channon, who visited him on a number of occasions in Belgrade.[169] Under Prime Minister Milan Stojadinović the country became more dependent on trade with Nazi Germany. The voices of 'reason' accepted Yugoslavia's cooperation with the Third Reich: the new nation had to make its way and establish economic independence. However, these rationalizations could not hide the fact that whereas in 1929 Yugoslavia's imports from Germany constituted 16 per cent of the total and its exports to Germany 9 per cent of the total, by 1939 the figures had risen to 39 per cent and 42 per cent, respectively.[170] Yugoslavia was thus emerging as a 'client state' of Germany. Stojadinović proclaimed himself the leader or *Vođa*, introduced a fascist-style salute and established a mass youth movement, members of which wore green shirts.[171] R.J. Crampton, quoting Seton-Watson, has called the regency between 1934 and 1941 'a dictatorship without a dictator'.[172] The amnesty granted to a number of political detainees in 1935 could not hide the fact that strict controls were still in place.

Seton-Watson eventually came to the conclusion that the realization of the Yugoslav ideal was not possible without some administrative reform. In 1937 he was arguing that Yugoslavia had a 'Croat problem' and had to address it. The crucial point of a settlement, he argued in a memorandum and an article entitled, predictably enough, 'Jugoslavia and the Croat Problem', was 'the acceptance of the Federal principle'. He went on to outline what ought to be under central control and what ought to be under local jurisdiction, delimiting what were essentially to be the post-1945 republican and autonomous units of government. Certain technical matters had still to be considered but, according to Seton-Watson, there were plenty of skilled people to work their way through those outstanding issues. With mutual goodwill they could draft a new constitution based on greater equality and local autonomy.[173] It seemed there could be some 'unmixing' of the salad after all.

The fate of Czechoslovakia and the prospect of another war led to a more conciliatory mentality in Yugoslavia. The August 1939 *Sporazum*, or agreement, between the more moderate Serb prime minister, Dragiša Cvetković, who had replaced Stojadinović, and the Croat, Maček, on the restructuring of the administrative boundaries along more ethnically and historically coherent lines, was an attempt at addressing the problem of the alienation of the Croats.

The *Banovina* of Croatia now comprised about 30 per cent of the country. It had its own representative or *Ban* and its *Sabor* resumed functioning. Similar plans were afoot for the Slovenes and Serbs. However, coming just months before the outbreak of the Second World War, the *Sporazum* could not save the state. Moreover, the agreement itself was divisive. There were Croats who supported this change and who felt a workable system could still be achieved within the state of Yugoslavia; others rejected outright the state's authority, legitimacy and viability. Further, the *Sporazum* earned the Croats who had negotiated the agreement the ire of both Serb nationalists and Serb oppositionists. The former resented Croatian 'expansionism'. The latter believed Croats had caved in to the ruling clique and sacrificed higher principles, including democratization, to further their narrow nationalist aspirations. Thus one of the dominant lines of interpretation became that Croats, caring less for democracy than independence, had compromised the process of reform for their own 'particularist' interests. This reasoning seemed logical because it built on two decades of a discourse which identified and privileged what was seen as a naturally occurring Serbian 'democratic impulse' over a Croatian 'nationalist obsession'.

The historiography of the memory of war amplifies our understanding of interwar Yugoslavia and the reasons for its collapse in 1941. The experience of war advanced a particular and partial reading of the South Slavs' past, enshrining myths of origin that facilitated Serbian domination in the Kingdom. The belief that national homogenization was not just possible but desirable, and then necessary, made the situation worse and led to the underestimation of the long-term impact of the political abuses of the centralist and dictatorial regime. The assassination of Aleksandar in Marseilles brought to the attention of the world many of these issues. However, those outside observers whose views were informed by an idealism born of war and a pragmatism demanded of them by 'realism' in the sphere of politics and international relations were immovable on the question of Yugoslavia. The old diplomacy had not been buried with the countless war dead, as was promised in 1918, but thrived in the New Europe. In the case of the Kingdom, this had the effect of exacerbating a situation that was not, primarily, of the Yugoslavs' making and that prepared the ground for the next wave of destruction in Europe. The Second World War was to give rise to another set of conflicting memories of war, the reconciling of which, as it turned out, would not be possible so long as Yugoslavia existed.

4 'The future lies with the federative idea': War and Dissolution, 1941–1945

Communist Yugoslavia was a product of the Second World War. The Yugoslavs' experience of that war and the way it was interpreted by outsiders and historians shaped the nature of the new state and how it was perceived through to Tito's death. The memory of war was a crucial factor in the resurgent Serb nationalism of the 1980s prior to the final collapse of the country, and it is commonly held that revisionist interpretations of the Second World War fed into that nationalist rhetoric. Commentators drew on the received understanding of the war in their explanations of events in the 1990s. Often the Wars of Yugoslav Succession were depicted as a re-enactment of aspects of the 1941–5 conflict. Clearly, the war invites serious reflection from historians, and there are a number of valuable books on the subject. Yet nowhere is the general poverty of Yugoslav historiography more obvious than in works relating to the period 1941–5. A partial explanation for this may be found in the decisive shift in international thinking about what constituted Yugoslavism that took place in these years and the impact of this shift on the Yugoslav state in the postwar world.

Among our outsiders there was a core group for whom Yugoslavia would always remain Serbia's (deserved) reward for its sacrifice in war, but in the late 1930s others, like Seton-Watson, came to the conclusion that Belgrade had to make concessions and allow for a degree of regional autonomy for the state to fulfil its early promise.

Seton-Watson came to argue this less from a sense of the inherent injustice of the system than from the belief that the abuse of power from the centre engendered instability. After the invasion by Germany in 1941 outsiders considered the impact of Yugoslavia's interwar history on its capacity to withstand the enemy and its dependability as an ally. The desire to defeat Germany at any cost governed Western European attitudes towards the Yugoslavs for the duration of the war. Eventually, concerns about the need for a new balance of power in a Soviet-dominated Europe also came into play. In short, perceptions of Yugoslavia's past, present and future position on the Continent influenced the reconfiguration of the Yugoslav ideal during the war. At the same time, insiders were rebelling against the old regime and, as it was in the interwar years, the people whose views chimed with those of the men shaping the Allies' strategic objectives gained the upper hand. In saying this I do not deny the agency of Yugoslavs; on the contrary, as the example of Tito testifies, at no other time up to this point had they had more impact on their destiny. Tito was ideologically and personally tied to the Soviet Union, which relayed information on the success of Partisan resistance to its Western allies, but in due course he also had the nearest thing to a direct line of communication to Churchill through British personnel stationed in the Balkan theatre of war, and benefited from this connection. However dependent Tito was on outside aid, moral and material, he was not subservient to its source whether it came from the West or the East. The Tehran Conference at the end of 1943 revealed that the Big Three were sympathetic to his demands for aid and recognized his authority. Tito went on to become the leader of possibly the most celebrated resistance movement in Europe.

As we locate Yugoslavia's war in the general European context, we will see that the Yugoslav government-in-exile in London lost its credibility relatively soon. When the Allies made decisions about how best to assist Yugoslavia, they considered the objective of winning the war as well as the competency of the London Yugoslavs. By adopting the traditional framework of treating collaboration and resistance as polar opposites we will come to see the war the way outsiders saw it. Two case studies focusing on the Catholic Church and women in the resistance will highlight the deficiencies in the crudely dichotomous approach to collaboration and resistance that prevailed during the war and in postwar historiography. It will also become clear that the Allies viewed various groups within Yugoslavia from the perspective of their capacity to strengthen the Yugoslav state until the crisis subsided. The communist partisans under Tito were eventually preferable to Serb resister-turned-collaborator Draža Mihailović (1893–1946) and the Chetniks he led. Tito's was a more effective force against the Axis powers because his support was cross-national. He could garner this support because he fought collaboration and occupation relentlessly and because the vision he projected for postwar Yugoslavia was more nationally equitable. Further, he roundly denounced interwar Serbian hegemonism.[1] The layering of the memories of both world wars made state-building as complex in 1945 as it had been after 1918, only this time there was no pretence that the war had been fought for democracy

Europeanizing Yugoslav Historiography of the War

One of the goals of this book is to 'Europeanize' Yugoslav history and historiography, from which much is to be gained in respect of the period 1941–5. Ute Frevert refers to the restoration of the Europeanizing process in Germany as well as the Europeanizing of German historiography after 1945, the former more attractive when Germany was shattered for a second time in less than thirty years and then divided, and after a war in which it had tried to Germanize Europe. Europeanizing German historiography eventually came to be seen as more historically illuminating than the exceptionalist approach to German history and more politically acceptable further afield when the country was weak and broken up.[2] Europeanizing Yugoslav historiography is more straightforward now that the country no longer exists. Historians cannot become enmeshed in an ongoing Yugoslav state-building project: apart from focus, there is nothing to be gained or lost politically by the (purely academic) enterprise of Europeanizing Yugoslav historiography.

The Yugoslav story of the war is suffused with tales of the confrontations between resistance and collaboration, with particular focus on the national question, the armed struggle, high politics and the bureaucratic and administrative aspects of the wartime regimes. That story reflects the most pressing concerns of outsiders both during and after the war. It also emphasizes excess, with some stating that this theatre of war bore witness to an endemic and unparalleled genocidal impulse.[3] The preoccupation of interwar observers with the 'extreme' nationalism of the Croats and their troublesome political nature provided the foundation for this obsession with

Yugoslavia's 'unique' war. By contrast, Western European works dealing with the National Socialist revolution, total war and the Holocaust, for example, have explored different themes including the impact of the relationship between ideology and the social history of the period by focusing on the lives of ordinary people or on cultural institutions. Historians have also sought to understand more fully what it meant to resist the Nazi occupation and local collaborators by looking beyond male-dominated resistance narrowly defined in military terms, and incorporating detailed observations of the behaviour of women and young people, for example, into a more comprehensive picture of nonconformism and dissent in daily life. Yugoslav historiography of the war remained out of step with these developments and the result was that the Yugoslavs' war, studied in isolation, became an 'exceptional' war. It was exceptionally brutal and racist. It was exceptionally complex and tragic. This is an outdated understanding of the war in Yugoslavia.

One of the reasons for the persistence of the exceptionalist approach to the war in Yugoslavia is that the new state was founded on a fixed understanding of a blanket term, the anti-fascist struggle, the nature of which could never be truly open to interpretation under a one-party communist dictatorship. Anti-fascism in a general sense brought together politically disparate allies in a temporary coalition that, Davies argues, would be recalled in a nostalgic and ahistorical fashion as the 'defining event in the triumph of Good over Evil'.[4] Certain topics were either under-researched or not addressed at all. Even points of fact posed problems if they called into question the 'Allied Scheme of History'. Davies uses the example of the refusal of the Soviets to accept responsibility for the Katyn massacres to illustrate this point.[5] In Yugoslavia, questioning the official numbers of victims of the war from all causes was unacceptable. The figures for the numbers of Serbian war dead, for example, though widely recognized within Yugoslavia to be inflated by several hundreds of thousands, in extreme cases by one million, were not officially modified until the 1980s.[6] The politicization of Yugoslav historiography of the war resulted in generalizations and accusations on the one hand and defensiveness on the other. The so-called 'Ustaša complex' among Croat historians and politicians, for example, led to a kind of immobilism, an inability to move beyond the black and white portrayal of these years and beyond the position that anyone who was not obviously against the Ustaše must have been for them. Nowhere was this more symbolically apparent than in the 'parallel lives' of two Croats,

Pavelić, the arch-collaborator, and Tito, the hero of the resistance. The Serbs' experience was projected differently and this meant that in the long term there were not going to be serious obstacles to the rehabilitation of Mihailović, who emerged in revisionist histories as a martyr of non-communist resistance to the Nazis.

In addition to the communists' official line of interpretation there was the generalized difficulty, shared by all Europeans, of dealing with the immediate and traumatic past. The historiography of Fascist Italy and Nazi Germany evolved as a series of debates and controversies that led historians to question established views. For example, some had feared that studies of daily life and the social history of the Third Reich would lead to the historicization of the regime, which in this case meant anxiety that a new generation of researchers might contextualize and make understandable the Nazi past to the point where it could seem to have been somehow 'normal', if not acceptable. In France there was a similar process of historiographical evolution. As historians attempted to integrate different aspects of the country's wartime history, especially the Vichy government's collaboration and its anti-Semitism, into a coherent narrative of France at war, the phenomenon of resistance came under closer scrutiny. It became evident that Vichy's relationship with the German occupiers had been underplayed in studies of the 'dark years' and the demythologization of resistance proceeded apace in the wake of the generational revolt of the late 1960s. An inversion then took place as the nation of resisters became the nation of collaborators and it was subsequently almost impossible to speak of the French resistance without referring to it as a myth. New elastic and inclusive definitions of complicity facilitated this process and rendered the term collaboration almost meaningless in a number of contexts.

When social historians of the Third Reich began to explore aspects of life under Nazism that eschewed the narrowly political and military it was remarked that these researchers had, at last, 'discovered the German people'.[7] Historians of the war in Yugoslavia have yet to make a comparable discovery. The deconstruction of resistance after Tito's death was problematic and premature. It did not emerge from a deep understanding of the social history of the war or from a nuanced understanding of complicity and dissent. The place of ideology in daily life and the multiple (ethical) ways in which people in wartime Yugoslavia might have expressed their views and beliefs have scarcely been touched upon. We have little precise information about the levels of penetration of racist ideology, public opinion in the war, the role of cultural institutions, the impact of intellectuals and writers and the impact of total war on daily life. Obviously it is beyond the scope of the book to redress the imbalances that have been the hallmarks of Yugoslav historiography of the war for over 60 years. Rather, I will touch on some of the key themes related to the status and perception of Yugoslavia and Yugoslavs at this time of international crisis, paying particular attention to the impact of interpretations of collaboration and resistance, at the time and subsequently, on the national question. More Yugoslavs will become more visible in the course of this chapter. Our outsiders remain important, however, both because they provide us with a strand of continuity and because so much depended on the Allies' understanding of events in Yugoslavia before and after its fall in 1941. The debates about collaboration and resistance make no sense unless we accept that they have been filtered through the prism of Yugoslavia's place in the strategic priorities of the Allies. Nor do they make much sense when treated in isolation. All Europeans confronted similar problems, including the radicalization of politics of the Left and Right at this time of crisis. While local and national factors affected people's capacity to withstand the most destructive impulses of that radicalization, there were common features to the wartime experience. An integrated approach allows us to begin to piece together the somewhat fragmented history of Europe in the Second World War and to understand better the war in Yugoslavia.

War Comes to Yugoslavia

After a period of close affiliation, economic and political, with Nazi Germany from the mid- to late 1930s, Yugoslavia proclaimed it would remain neutral in the event of war. Then, on 25 March 1941, it signed the Tripartite Pact with Germany and Italy. Many Yugoslavs found the Pact unacceptable. A day later a coup, planned and executed by officers of the Yugoslav army with assistance from British intelligence ousted the signatories to the Pact including the regent, Prince Paul. Churchill declared, melodramatically, that the Yugoslavs had found their soul. Prince Petar was declared of age (six months short of his eighteenth birthday) and installed as King Petar II with General Simović, leader of the coup, at the head of the new government and Maček as its short-lived prime minister. This precipitated the German invasion on 6 April.

When the Germans invaded and overran the Kingdom in April 1941 the Yugoslavs' plight evinced sympathy from many quarters. Roosevelt wrote to King Petar noting that the American people were 'profoundly shocked' by the 'unprovoked ruthless aggression'. However, they were 'witnessing with admiration the courageous self-defence' of the Yugoslav people which constituted 'one more shining example of their traditional bravery'.[8] The British government expressed similar sentiments, noting that the 'savage outrage committed by Germany without the slightest provocation' had met with 'valiant resistance' by the Serbs, Croats and Slovenes: 'We renew the comradeship which in the Great War carried us through tribulations to victory. We will conduct the war in common and make peace only when right has been vindicated and law and justice are again enthroned.'[9] According to the *Contemporary Review*, early Greek and Yugoslav resistance to the Germans presented onlookers with the 'magnificent spectacle of two small nations fearlessly accepting the towering odds against them rather than bow[ing] the knee in shameful surrender'. Theirs was the act of 'gallant resistance…of the weak against brutal aggression on the part of the strong'. If the war had taught them anything, it was that 'those who do not oppose the aggressor are helping the aggressor'.[10] It was this basic calculation that guided Allied policy on Yugoslavia through to the defeat of Germany.

Surrendering to the Germans just 12 days after the invasion, members of the government fled and a Yugoslav government-in-exile was established in London. On 10 April Slavko Kvaternik, a founding member of the Ustaša, had proclaimed the Independent State of Croatia (*Nezavisna Država Hrvatska*, the considerably expanded *Banovina*, henceforth NDH) and Dr Ante Pavelić was declared *Poglavnik* (Leader) in absentia. Pavelić arrived in Zagreb a few days later. A German military government was established in Belgrade with the collaboration of General Milan Nedić and other Serb fascists and fellow-travellers. Germany partitioned and annexed a large part of Slovenia while Italy took possession of most of the Croatian coast, Montenegro and Kosovo (joining it to Albania). All of Yugoslavia's neighbours who had in some sense regretted and wished to revise the borders of 1918 got a slice of the Yugoslav pie as Bulgaria 'retook' parts of Macedonia and Hungary extended its border southwards. Croat nationalists in the interwar period tended towards republicanism and so the proclamation of the Italian Duke of Spoleto (Split) as King of Croatia was more than a

little absurd. (He never visited his 'Kingdom' and at the time outsiders commonly held that he was far from popular among Croats,
who 'utterly repudiate[d] the Kingdom' by a 'vast majority'.[11]) The
Italians and Germans had zones of influence in Croatia. One of the
consequences of the Balkan campaign extending to Greece was that
it retarded the invasion of the Soviet Union.

The Yugoslav government-in-exile comprised members of the
Serb ruling elite, the military and a representative of the Croat
Peasant Party. The young King Petar was not especially charismatic and was thought to be under the thumb of his advisers.[12] The
London-based Yugoslavs progressively alienated all but their most
loyal and assiduously anti-communist friends because of their bick-
ering, corruption and incompetence, because of their barely concealed attachment to Serb hegemony in Yugoslavia and because they
were dominated by Mihailović. An American intelligence report for
the Office of Strategic Services (OSS) from November 1943 noted
the government-in-exile was perceived to be run by 'traitors and
deserters'.[13] Over time the British were less inclined to consult with
the London-based Yugoslavs than to inform them of the preferred
Allied policies, especially as they had their own operatives in the
field (first with Mihailović, then with both Mihailović and Tito and
finally only with Tito). The British began to take the government
slightly more seriously again once the Yugoslavs moved from London
to Cairo in 1943 and once some of its members agreed to negotiate
with Tito. The pressure to move to Cairo had come from the British,
a move American intelligence reports applauded, adding that the
British should place still more pressure on the Yugoslavs because
'unless there is outside interference there will be another Pan-Serb
cabinet'.[14] It was clear that the principal Yugoslavs in London and
Washington were men of the old order who had neither the capacity nor inclination to provide adequate leadership for all national
groups, constituent peoples or minorities, in Yugoslavia.

Observers often suggested that Yugoslavia's rapid military collapse in 1941 resulted from the state's lack of legitimacy, which
rendered it weak and indefensible. This assessment figured significantly in the writings of Yugoslavists in the war. The Croat Bogdan
Radica (1904–93) was a publicist attached to the Yugoslav Embassy
in Washington and, along with the Slovenian emigrant and popular author Louis Adamic (1899–1951), among others, he lobbied in
support of Tito's Partisans. Radica described the *Sporazum* (agreement) leading to the establishment of the Croatian *Banovina* in
1939 not as a move towards true reconciliation but as eleventh-hour

cooperation.[15] American OSS reports noted periodically that the interwar regime had left much to be desired, as the dictatorship persisted with the promise of the 1931 constitution left unfulfilled. Background reports referred to the inequities in the electoral system, recalling that more than anything the elections of 1935 had shown the flagrant disregard for due process, with the Serb Bogoljub Jevtić gaining 82 per cent of seats with 60.6 per cent of the vote while the Croat Maček gained 18 per cent of the seats with 37.4 per cent of the vote.[16] In an article in *The Nation* from March 1941 we read that 'rarely was a state in a more helpless position' than Yugoslavia.[17] Reverting to the argument resting on the Balkanist paradigm, the article also noted that the state had found it difficult to function after the 'reunification' of peoples who had been separated for so many centuries. The ferocious struggles between 'Cross and Crescent, between the Habsburgs and the Sultans', had left 'flaming fires of enmity in South Slav hearts'. The (re)united peoples found it hard 'to quench very persistent hatreds' and thus in the interwar years Yugoslavs 'passionately killed each other'. At the same time outsiders believed Yugoslavia fell in 1941 because it had its own Nazis who were as 'fanatically authoritarian as German stormtroopers'. Referring to the Ustaše, *The Nation* reported that the Yugoslav Nazis would 'join the devil if thereby they could take vengeance on the Serbs'.[18] Moreover, Pavelić, infamous since the Marseilles assassinations, had been plotting abroad for ten years 'against the Jugoslav state'.[19] This general assessment of the South Slavs as driven by pre-existing hatreds and extreme nationalism and therefore in need of a firm hand, had emerged during the period of Aleksandar's dictatorship and in the wake of his assassination. It had become one of the key variables in ruminations on Yugoslavia's future. Others put forward less emotive explanations for the debacle in 1941, for example that the state was militarily ill-prepared for the German invasion and, in spite of the provocative nature of the coup in Belgrade, that the country had not fully mobilized for the near-certain invasion. It was therefore a military defeat by a superior enemy that had made short work of the Battle of France the previous May and June and whose allies could barely conceal their desire to cut Yugoslavia up into pieces.[20] Proponents of this argument noted that Yugoslavia had had its difficult moments politically in the 1920s and 1930s, but that there was no feeling that the state was about to collapse before 1941.[21]

One of the red herrings in the debate about Yugoslavia's collapse was the question of alleged Croatian fifth columnists. Did they make

Germany's task easier? Both the Ustaše and the Serbs claimed this to be the case for altogether different reasons: the Ustaše, to aggrandize themselves, the Serbs to convince outsiders of their own commitment to the Yugoslav state. There is no evidence to support the theory of Croatian fifth columnists wreaking havoc at the crucial moment. The Ustaše were a minor group, without extensive party structures and no mass mobilizing potential on the eve of war. For his part, Maček, and the popular Croat Peasant Party which he led, refused the German offer to take on any formal governmental or administrative role. After the establishment of the NDH the Ustaše placed Maček under house arrest for the duration of the war. The fifth columnists debate had its parallels elsewhere and, combined with the talk of political ineptitude and infighting leading to moral defeat or collapse, resembles the old argument that France's fall in 1940 was not military, but primarily moral.

Even though Tito and Mihailović met to discuss concerted action against the enemy, it became clear in the course of 1941 that their goals and motives were too different. Mihailović, as War Minister, was acclaimed as the European resister of the first hour. He was purportedly the leader of a Yugoslav Home Army but in reality his was a Serbian movement. Tito would outdo his rival and win support internationally because he was single-minded in his desire to overcome the enemy and local collaborators and because his appeal was cross-national. Out of his Partisan resistance movement Tito established the People's Liberation Army and the Anti-fascist Council for the People's Liberation of Yugoslavia. The Council met for the first time in 1942. A year later it reconvened to declare itself the government of Yugoslavia, rejecting the old order and its representatives. Historical accounts that are hostile towards Tito tend to emphasize his dependence on Soviet aid. In truth, there was very little material assistance from Stalin until late in the war. Radio Free Yugoslavia transmitted broadcasts celebrating the work of the Partisans from Soviet-controlled territory, but Stalin was wary of Tito's obvious determination and his personal appeal. The first material assistance of real significance came from the Americans after the fall of Mussolini and Italy's surrender in 1943. The Soviets did not want to alienate their Western allies by appearing to foment revolution across Europe and were so concerned to establish their good faith on this question that they disbanded the Comintern in 1943. Stalin constantly advised Tito to submerge his revolutionary intention and to concentrate on military priorities. Tito did not comply.

In the course of 1942 the British began to question the reliability of the Chetniks and to doubt the loyalty of Mihailović but maintained some ties with him for a year after that. Eventually Mihailović lost his position in the government and King Petar called on all Yugoslavs to rally to Tito. A number of German offensives against Tito's forces had failed to knock them out of the war and the People's Liberation Army became an all-Yugoslav fighting force that won the confidence of Churchill. The British prime minister met Tito in Italy in September 1944, reassuring him of his commitment to the Partisans' cause. The following month Tito, determined not to appear dependent on the West, flew to Moscow where he met Stalin for the first time. They reportedly discussed the plans for the final assault on Belgrade in October. Just as the Soviets had not wanted to alienate the British and the Americans, so the latter had wanted to prove to the Soviets that they were not averse to supporting another communist leader. This atmosphere worked to Tito's advantage and marked the beginning of his skilful balancing of the influences from the East and the West. The Soviets came to the Partisans' assistance at the time of the liberation of Belgrade in October 1944, but were out of the country by the following month, leaving Tito to oversee the final victory in May 1945.

Interpreting Collaboration

The communists might have regarded all collaboration, Croatian, Slovenian and Serbian, as equally deplorable during the war. But internationally the Ustaše attracted the greatest share of negative focus, in large part because of the atrocities they committed, but also because of the ambiguities in the Chetniks' role in the war and the dominant perceptions of Croatian nationalism. The division of the country after 1941 exacerbated this problem of perception, allowing for dichotomous, essentialist (national) interpretations of collaboration as allegedly deriving from certain ethnic proclivities and political predispositions that predated the war, rather than the circumstances of the war, for example. Thus it was that many observers noted that the Serbs (as Yugoslavs) were the first to resist and the Croats (as anti-Yugoslavs) the first to collaborate.

Historians are often concerned to establish the extent to which fascist or collaborationist regimes represented continuities in their respective national histories. These questions are relevant here. For example, whereas Vichy France resulted from the government's departure from Paris and the defeat and armistice signed by the new Head of State, the 'Saviour of Verdun', Marshal Pétain, in 1940, it is evident also that the nature of state collaboration and Vichy's promise of a National Revolution derived from strands of conservative and fascist thought predating the war years. Vichy replaced the revolutionary slogan, 'Liberty, Equality, Fraternity', with 'Work, Family, Homeland', and promised to rededicate France to its 'eternal' rural and spiritual values. At the same time the French ultra-collaborationists had nothing but disdain for the National Revolution, believing it meek and nostalgic, and placed their hopes in the National Socialist project and Hitler's New European Order. Similarly, the once fashionable view of the Italian fascist regime as no more than a parenthesis in the otherwise 'normal' history of the modernizing Italian state also led to a vigorous debate. That there existed a relationship between interwar social and political fragmentation and wartime collaboration is largely uncontested, though this assumption does not take adequate note of the impact of unforeseen circumstances and responses to the changes wrought by war. The question of continuities and the ideological coherence of the NDH is not straightforward, as perceptions of the Ustaše attest.

There was a degree of incomprehension at the developments in the NDH. Even the most damning articles and reports of the time often carried riders stating that Croats in general were alienated by the regime. Significantly, these riders were largely absent from postwar histories. After 1945 historians evoked a Croatian *Sonderweg*, a special path of right-wing nationalist politics proceeding in a straight line from the late nineteenth century and culminating in the wartime career of Pavelić. While it is productive to trace the roots of ultranationalist thinking, this approach fails to take full account of the fact that the regime was the product of foreign intervention, not a national or fascist revolution. Indeed, several variables generally thought to constitute the 'fascist minimum' were absent from Croatian politics in the interwar years, and the only self-proclaimed fascist parties in the Kingdom were in fact Serbian.[22] Further, in spite of the international outrage engendered by the Marseilles assassinations, there was a general perception of Croats as incapable of effecting their own liberation, their 'restlessness' notwithstanding. This view was based on their history, on comparisons between Croats and the far more militarily and politically successful Serbs and on their (inferior) political leaders.

Moreover, while the Ustaše were clearly and uncompromisingly anti-Yugoslav, other Croats were not.

Mussolini had no illusions about the revolutionary mobilizing potential of the Croats even at the height of Italian support for Pavelić (that is, before 1934).[23] The Ustaše in Italy did not hold a place of privilege as members of an elite 'fascist brotherhood'. Mussolini was distant, and after their implication in the Marseilles assassinations Croat émigrés were a liability and thus closely monitored. By the end of 1935 the Ustaše in Italy were interned, either on the island of Lipari with Italian criminals and anti-fascists or in Turin. Most remained under surveillance up to the invasion of Yugoslavia in 1941. Italian reports on Yugoslav separatist activity described Croats as 'quiescent' and lacking a 'superior man' who could impose himself on 'the masses'. Pavelić was not that superior man, in the Italians' view. He had limited experience and no well thought-out programme. Croats were not 'true Slavs' but 'docile as the lambs on the earth and the tuna in the sea'. The Serbs, on the other hand, were a superior race who had proven their worth on the battlefield, which was more than the Croats were even willing to attempt. A 'Croat revolution' was out of the question, the report continued, but should the Croats be foolhardy enough to attempt one, the superior Serbs would crush them. As Pavelić had no elaborate theoretical justification for his stance he had not known 'how to orient the movement correctly'.[24] Nor did he have the capacity to unite all Croats behind his movement. Pavelić did not seek greater autonomy for Croats within Yugoslavia but an independent Croatian state. He believed that Croatia could not survive within Yugoslavia: by its very existence, Yugoslavia was extinguishing Croatian identity. As the Yugoslav state was run and dominated by Serbs, and as there were no identifiable 'Yugoslavs' (other than Serbs) who were the oppressors, the enemy was Serbia. Herein lay the root of the corrosive hatred of the Ustaše for the Serbs and the violence and atrocities perpetrated against them during the war.

If the Partisans did not distinguish between different manifestations of collaboration, up to about the end of 1943 the Allies did. The British supported Mihailović and tolerated his deepening relations first with the collaborationist administration in Belgrade, then with the Axis powers, until they could no longer ignore his betrayal. This, in part, explains the predominance in Yugoslav historiography of studies of Croatian collaboration as a generalized phenomenon and of Serbian collaboration as representing the acts of a small group of traitors or individuals. Stanley Payne states outright that there is no comparison to be made between the acts of the collaborators in Belgrade and those of the NDH because the latter had more autonomy and the former were under closer German control.[25] The greater emphasis on Croatian collaboration can also be attributed to the nature of the NDH and the suffering of its national and racial victims.

There were structural as well as ideological reasons that approximately 80 per cent of the Jews, refugees and Yugoslav-born, living in Yugoslav territories perished in the Holocaust. This is practically the reverse of the figures for France. Twenty-five per cent of the total population of Jews residing in France did not survive the war. Of the 80,000 Jews living in Yugoslavia approximately 57,000 were killed. Approximately 28,000 of the 36,000 Jews who fell under the control of the NDH perished either as victims of the Ustaše or after having been deported to German camps. The Germans worked closely with Serb anti-Semites and the local collaborationist administration to isolate and 'remove' all the Jews residing in Serbia, known as the 'Serbian residual state', with a view to making it 'free of Jews', or *Judenfrei*. There were international reports of Jews and Roma being rounded up and shot in Belgrade's main square.[26] The fact of the German presence in Serbia has led historians to underemphasize religious and secular anti-Semitism and local responsibility for the Holocaust there, and to focus rather on the fate of the Jews in NDH territories. (This was as true of commentary during the war as it was after 1945, with the Serb collaborator Nedić often depicted in generally sympathetic terms by outsiders.) In the NDH there were different factors facilitating the Final Solution. Among the most significant of these were the establishment of concentration camps (notably the Jasenovac group of camps) and a collaborationist regime whose main target was Serbs, but which was also a willing partner in the racialist project of the Third Reich to which it was beholden.[27] Why precisely this was the case is difficult to establish from existing studies. Recent work attempting to identify the ideological roots of Ustaša-initiated racial policies suggests we should look to writings from the interwar period for the answer to this question. However, there must also be some attempt at establishing a connection between such polemical literature, its reception and the perpetrators of the crimes of the NDH for this line of argument to be convincing. While there is no question of the consequences of the NDH's racial policies, there is less agreement on their origins.[28]

Apart from being responsible for the death or expulsion of Serbs, the NDH was complicit in the genocide of Jews. Survivors' accounts and the testimony of witnesses tell the story of suffering and cruelty in the concentration camps of the NDH. Cultural, religious and political anti-Semitism, of necessity, had to have a role in the persecutions and killing, though there is less consensus among historians on the degree of the impact of pre-existing anti-Semitism on the Final Solution than one might expect. Evidently the circumstances of the war made genocide possible. It is also evident that local populations had to be complicit wherever Jews were interned and wherever they were killed.

Historians have offered a range of explanations for the differences in the levels of responsibility of different agencies and institutions in occupied countries for the fate of their Jewish populations. Some have said the relatively high proportion of Jewish survivors in France relates to the fact that French soil was liberated relatively early (from the summer of 1944), that there remained no opportunities for Vichy officials to act on their anti-Semitic impulse, that the government protected Jews who were French citizens (the majority) by deporting Jewish refugees first, and that there were resistance groups dedicated to rescuing Jews. Indeed, many French resisters recalled that it was the plight of the Jews that first prompted them to make a stand against occupation and against the German occupiers. Foreign Jews resident in France were most at risk, both because they were targeted for deportation and because they were more vulnerable, given that they had no established support networks. The infamous round-up of Jews in the Paris velodrome in the summer of 1942 led to the arrest of almost 13,000 men, women and children. The goal for that operation had been the arrest of 28,000 Jews, but tip-offs from the French police and assistance from Parisians, Jews and non-Jews, led to the remaining 15,000 escaping or being rescued on that particular occasion.[29] We know that approximately 48,000 Jewish children under the age of 15 escaped death as they were moved across the country to safety by resistance networks whose main goal was rescuing Jews. This involved the cooperation of people from all over France and from various walks of life.[30]

Pre-war fragmentation had an impact on behaviour in wartime Yugoslavia, as did the fact that the population was ethnically diverse. Fleetingly, links were established within Yugoslavia and they allowed for a certain set of actions on the part of those drawn into resistance structures whose success in a number of activities and in guerrilla warfare became legendary. But how far was Yugoslav resistance, successful as it was, limited both by the priorities of the leadership and the options available to those not drawn to the Partisans' essentially political cause? As we think about this question we must also bear in mind that most of the excesses of the NDH took place early, that the excesses led directly to disillusionment and resistance (as was the case in other countries) and that there were fewer victims as the war progressed. For example, Payne has noted that the regime became 'less lethal with the passage of time ... as contrasted with the genocide in the latter phases of the German regime'. He adds that had the NDH been 'a geographically and militarily isolated entity', that is, had it not been maintained by outside support, the resistance would 'soon have grown strong enough to have overthrown it directly'.[31] It makes more sense to connect these observations and to place them in the context of events in Europe as a whole than to treat them in isolation.

Pavelić enjoyed support when he was installed as *Poglavnik* in 1941. What that support signified in political terms is less clear. When charting the life of the NDH and its crimes we must take seriously the chronology of disaffection. Generalizations about Ustaša support have not to date provided the kind of nuanced profiles we have for collaborators elsewhere. Nor do we have studies that relate the ideological lineage of the NDH and the reception of propaganda and policies to the way in which the regime developed and then imploded. Analyses of French opinion during the war, for example, have resulted in a clear chronology of disaffection. The '40 million Pétainists' of June 1940 were soon on guard against collaboration, and whether or not they were resisters did not change the fact that there was near universal hope for an Allied victory. We know disaffection from the NDH came early, often within weeks. The Peasant Party, the preferred party of the overwhelming majority of Croats, had distanced itself from agrarian fascism in the interwar years and then from the NDH.[32] It became apparent that the NDH exercised little autonomy in most areas and none in those of real importance to Germany, including the requisitioning of labour and resources. The NDH, although priding itself on its nationalist vision, could not even organize to have brought to fruition the project of erecting a statue of the first Croat king, Tomislav, who reigned between 910 and 928, in a prominent position opposite the main railway station in Zagreb. Originally proposed in 1924 and subsequently blocked by internal squabbling and Belgrade, the statue was finally completed and raised in 1947 under the watchful eye of the new communist rulers.[33] The NDH's cultural project has yet to be explored fully but even its pet schemes, such as its language policy based on the desire to promote 'pure Croatian', met with a degree of ambivalence.[34] One might also ask how successful fascistization would follow from teaching materials such as the songbook prepared for primary school teachers in 1942 and approved by the Ministry for Education. It contained 153 songs, the overwhelming majority predating the regime by decades. There is one song that mentions the Ustaše specifically, and it is the Ustaša anthem. There are 24 so-called 'patriotic' songs, many with lyrics from the works of writers of the nineteenth-century Illyrian movement. One of the songs became communist Yugoslavia's anthem, with the word 'Croats' replaced by 'Slavs'.[35] In a similar vein, a high-quality publication celebrating (mostly modern) Croatian art contains 216 images of sculptures and paintings covering different genres. It would be a challenge to ascribe a 'fascist aesthetic' to works in this eclectic collection, including those of the great Croat and avowedly 'Yugoslav' sculptor, Ivan Meštrović.[36] Many would also question the legitimacy of an ultranationalist regime that was prepared to sacrifice to the Italians much of the Croatian coast in order to gain Bosnia-Herzegovina. Indeed this 'compromise' generated dissent immediately. It was not long before the Partisans began to register large numbers of recruits from among those who were disillusioned and turning away from the NDH and those who had never been won over to its politics.

Perceptions of the way the war was fought by Yugoslavs are important, as these had a significant impact on the historiography of the period as well as on the place that Yugoslavia came to assume in the international community. The Balkanist paradigm persisted and the Partisans would perpetuate it, drawing on it at appropriate moments. They knew that their internal struggle against 'backwardness' would be sympathetically received in the West and they constantly referred to the need for the Yugoslavs to shake off the burden of their 'pre-modern' social and economic relations. The Balkan and East European 'Quislingovitches', therefore, were always worse, more distasteful and altogether more extreme imitations of their German masters in part because of their retarded development.[37] It has become a truism that in the Balkans, but most notably in the NDH, were to be witnessed the worst horrors of the Second World War. Here 'barbaric', 'bestial' and 'notorious' people 'butchered' and 'slaughtered' their victims. The *Wehrmacht* officers used words like these freely in reports from Yugoslav territories.[38] Today it is unusual for a work on the war in Yugoslavia not to use such language.[39] Normally analyses of European collaboration discuss motivation and intention when assessing people's behaviour. Opportunity, geographical location, careerism, self-interest, disillusionment, racially-derived ideological commitment, the process of 'barbarization' resulting from total war and people's simple strategies for survival from day to day led to different kinds of behaviour and had different consequences. All of these distinctions are important in studies of degrees of complicity and culpability elsewhere and have only recently begun to be applied to Central and Eastern Europe.[40]

Croats were often described as fanatical terrorists, whether they were supporting the Ustaše or the Partisans, whereas the (Serb) Chetnik guerrilla fighters were not. The Chetniks may have been brutal in their reprisals but that was because of the brutality of the Serbs' communist foes whose goal was 'to establish a Communist tyranny'.[41] To make matters worse, the Serbs 'gave Croats their state' and the Croats repaid them by 'avenging' what amounted to 'merely political grievances in a sea of Serbian blood'. In this scenario interwar Yugoslav history had no bearing on the wartime situation. It was rationalized that the Chetniks, by definition, could not be collaborators in the same sense as the Ustaše because Mihailović would not have the support of the people if he were cooperating with the enemy. Mihailović 'almost defie[d] analysis by a Western mind'. He was 'unpredictable', 'quixotic' and worked within the framework of 'limited and outworn ideas of pan-Serbism'.[42] Nonetheless, it was claimed that he aimed to protect Serbs from further bloodshed for the greater good of Yugoslavia.[43] Croats as Croats (as opposed to Croats as Yugoslavs) continued to be described as unreasonable in their political expectations; irrational (at best) and bestial (at worst) in their political choices. The racially loaded generalizations about predispositions to violence and national character affected subsequent historical debates. Recently, there has been slightly less emphasis on the apparently atavistic nature of violence in the NDH and more emphasis on its inability to broaden its support base. Payne has argued that the problem with categorizing Croatian fascism and comparing it with other fascisms lies in the absence of at least one essential 'fascist minimum', mass mobilization. Yet he has also written that the NDH is comparable not to any European collaborationism but, rather, to the regime of the Khmer Rouge.[44] One of the reasons for this inability to integrate Yugoslav wartime history into the general historiography of the Second World War is the fact that collaboration and resistance have not been integrated into a coherent story of Yugoslavia at war and remain self-contained topics of research. The treatment of the Church in the war illustrates this well.

Religion in the War: A Case Study of Extreme Exceptionalism

The killing, forced conversion and expulsion of Orthodox Serbs residing in the NDH by the Ustaše implicated the Catholic Church in the crimes of the regime and led to the false depiction of the war and Ustaša policy as religiously inspired. The general historiography of religion at this time is controversial, often bordering on the polemical, and may be regarded as 'the Balkans' of the historiography of the war. The vast literature on religion in the war is also accompanied by a popular debate which, in turn, has had a significant impact on academic debates. Strident and highly contentious works often stirred more intensive academic research on the Church in the war. If appraisals of the NDH can be emotive and sweeping, appraisals of the Croatian Catholic Church are doubly so. According to John Pollard, the incessant focus on Pius XII has not advanced our understanding of the Church at this time, and he urges us to look more closely at Slovakia and Croatia, the latter in particular, where 'the general passivity' of priests and bishops and the involvement of Franciscans in concentration camps 'stands as one of the most shameful episodes in the history of Christianity'.[45]

In the religious historiography of the war there is a great chasm between top-down studies, focusing most obviously on the Pope and then members of the hierarchy, and those studies which aim to reconstruct the daily life of worship and worshippers. This has led to contradictory assessments of Catholic behaviour. For example, if they resisted, Catholics are said to have done so 'as individuals' separate from the institution of the Church. If they did not resist in the traditional sense, they were 'mainstream', or in France, the 'pious parishioners' of Marshal Pétain, reflecting the passivity of their accommodating bishops. Elsewhere I have discussed the deficiencies of this methodological approach to the study of religion in the war from the example of French Catholics. The social history of religious life 'from the bottom up' exposes a double standard in most studies of the Church in the war. Individual action is dissociated from Catholic institutional presence as well as from interwar Catholic history, and the local is disassociated from the broader ideological framework of religious belief and practice. An ideological war (as it was perceived by the Church) had to be fought on many equally important fronts. That was why keeping Catholic structures, including the scout movement and other works devoted to young people, independent of state incursions was one of the keys to winning the ideological war.[46] Historians have begun to disentangle the reality from the rhetoric about Church complicity in the crimes of the NDH by reassessing the career of prelates like the Archbishop of Zagreb, Alojzije Stepinac (1898–1960). It has been a protracted process, with one prominent historian of the Church and the Holocaust, for example, moving from condemning Stepinac in 2000 as one of the weakest prelates in wartime Europe, to describing him in 2008 as possibly the strongest Church critic of racial persecution.[47] Historians have found that Stepinac's enthusiasm for the NDH quickly subsided and that by the end of 1941 he expressed serious reservations, followed by protests and a rejection of the regime's racial policies. Pavelić complained bitterly about Stepinac and tried to have him removed. There were plots on the Archbishop's life and there emerged what can only be described as open hostility between him and the Ustaša leadership.[48]

Taking the single topic of forced conversions of Serbs in the NDH, Mark Biondich has shown that the policy was not centrally directed, that there were considerable variations in the manner in which it was adopted across regions, and most significantly, that it was not religiously inspired or justified in religious terms but a bureaucratic process. Biondich has not argued a revisionist line in defence of the Church, but clarified the real distance between the Church and the NDH on a crucial question. On the strength of this evidence he notes that Ustaša rhetoric on religion could not mask the fact that the aims of the leadership were far from Christian and their recourse to Christian symbolism instrumental. Biondich also sheds light on the haphazard nature of NDH racial policy, the waverings between exclusion, assimilation, expulsion and extermination. His approach teaches us as much about Croatian fascism as the Catholic Church's response to this policy and others. Biondich goes so far as to introduce, if a little hesitantly, the famous distinction between intentionalist and structuralist (or functionalist) interpretations of the study of policy formation and implementation in the NDH. He does so by looking closely at chronology and line of command.[49] At the time the French Consul in Zagreb commented on Stepinac's stance on the regime's racial and religious policies, which had won him no friends in the NDH's administration.[50] Interestingly, the French Catholic underground press also referred to Stepinac's protests against the regime's racial policies, and indicated that Croats were turning towards the Partisans because of the persecutions.[51] It was almost impossible for ordinary Catholics in Europe to retain links with each other during the war. It is therefore significant that wherever and whenever possible, Catholic resisters sought to explain their stance with reference to the example of the universality and coherence of the religious response to suffering set by the quintessentially transnational institution of the Church.

The place of religion in the interwar years is also an important consideration in this discussion. It provides us with a connection to our nineteenth-century observers and their critique of Habsburg Catholicism and to the interwar debates about the problems of the Kingdom stemming from the intertwining of religion and national identity rather than politics. It is true that Catholics had reason to feel like outsiders in the Kingdom. The interwar period was one of expansion for the Serbian Orthodox Church. It embarked on a building programme outside areas of strong Orthodox identity, ostensibly to cater for Serbs who had previously found themselves religiously isolated especially in predominantly Catholic regions. No comparable Catholic building programme existed either where Catholic population density was high or elsewhere, for example in regions which had experienced Catholic emigration, or in parts of Yugoslavia where Catholics were in the minority. Catholic conversions to Orthodoxy in the Kingdom were commonplace as a means of advancing one's career.[52] However, the 'Yugoslav nation', when it was conceived as broadly South Slav, provided ample room for Croatian Catholic identification with the state, or at least limited reasons for anti-state agitation. By contrast, Yugoslavia as a highly centralized unitarist state, dominated by a Serbian dynasty and Orthodoxy, was bound to elicit at least some (purely) Catholic reaction against Yugoslavism. At the same time, there was nothing in the behaviour of Catholics and Church leadership to suggest that they would condone and facilitate an orgy of violence when the Kingdom collapsed in 1941. There had been a strong pro-Yugoslav element in the Church at the time of unification and there was no Church-initiated anti-state agitation in the interwar years. The idea that the NDH represented the realization of the aspirations of 'Catholic Croatia' (even if such a coherent identity had existed) was a product of the 'primitive' phase of fascist historiography that has stuck.

The associational life of the laity in Yugoslavia did not translate into a straightforward political position on the part of Catholics and never could, because for them the relationship between active citizenship and politics was not that easy to define and because the Church discouraged direct political involvement. This was in contrast to the Orthodox Church, whose clergy stood for and won seats in elections. Croats, for the most part, did not seek to articulate religious concerns through political activism or political concerns through religious activism. They did not regard Catholicism as a defining characteristic of Croatian identity. Croats might embrace any religion or none at all. Nationalists focused on state and historical rights rather than religion. For example, their centuries-old continuously functioning assembly, *Sabor*, suspended at the stroke of a pen in 1918, had been central to their claim to statehood. The view that Croatdom drew on multiple sources made it possible for some (including many Ustaše) to classify Bosnian Muslims as the 'purest' Croats. The example of Radić is also instructive. For him religion had to be private; it did not belong to the world of politics. Radić, influenced deeply by the writings of Masaryk, who was well known for his view of Catholicism as backward and Protestantism as progressive, expressed an idea of citizenship that was not determined by ethnicity or religion.[53] Though firmly anticlerical, Radić was a great admirer of the Orthodox Churches, which, like our travellers, he believed were robustly independent and democratic. Radić took his degree in Paris in 1899, and would have been aware of the divisions in the Church, and French society as a whole, occasioned by the Dreyfus Affair and of the tensions leading to the separation of Church and State (1905). For his part, Stepinac was at the forefront of the drive for religious renewal in the secular world, the hallmark of interwar Catholic Action.[54] He followed the lead of Pius XI, with his condemnation in 1937 of National Socialism and Communism in two encyclicals. The Pope was especially critical of the extreme statism and materialism of both, the racialism of the former and the theory of class warfare of the latter.[55] The lay Catholic activism of Catholic Action at this time had to be above politics, or above the conflict between divergent parties.[56] Yugoslav Catholics as individuals (and like Catholics elsewhere) were dispersed across the political spectrum, embracing politics of the Left and Right. The tone of

Church deliberations at this time was low-key and Catholic leadership did not propel the nationalist or separatist movements in the Kingdom in the interwar years. This is the experience Catholic Croats carried through to the collapse and invasion of the country in 1941.

The indestructible link between Serbian identity and the Serbian Orthodox Church meant that the suffering of the two in the war would be indistinguishable. The Serbian Church endured significant losses (the 'Serbian Golgotha'), with large numbers of priests being killed and the destruction of Church property. It was the formative experience Serbs carried into the new Yugoslavia. The memory of the war made normalization of relations between Serbs and Croats difficult after 1945. Even if historians accepted uncritically the official interpretation of Catholic support for the Ustaše in the war, one might have expected some scepticism simply on the basis of the interwar history of relations between the Churches. After Tito's death and at the time of the collapse of Yugoslavia in the 1990s there were renewed attacks on Stepinac and the Church's alleged collaboration between 1941 and 1945. This propaganda was destructive and possible only because of the deficiencies in the historiography of religion in the war, notably from the perspective of social history. Church histories reverted to old clichés about faith and nation that bore no resemblance to the lived experience of worshippers but that had serious consequences in the Wars of Yugoslav Succession in which religion was harnessed to the Serbian nationalist cause.

Taken out of the context of the worldwide conflict the events in Yugoslavia, notably Croatian collaboration, have been described in an emotive language and made to stand apart. However, placed within the context of a war in which entire cities were razed to the ground, unprecedented numbers of civilians were displaced or killed indiscriminately and in which racial, political and territorial objectives merged in the genocide of Europe's Jews, then these events are far from exceptional. While it may have been a source of consolation for *Wehrmacht* officers to distance themselves from the Slavonic 'barbarians' over whom they exercised considerable influence and control, for us to reduce the struggles in Yugoslavia to the level of the irrational and, therefore, politically and historically inexplicable is at the very least, hypocritical. There is no danger of historicizing the crimes perpetrated by Pavelić and the Ustaše now. In the past this was only possible because the stranglehold on the telling of the story of the war in Yugoslavia elicited a reaction which was not tempered or regulated by open academic debate. There have been important advances in research on the period, although there is still much ground to be covered. This is borne out by the fact that as war broke out in the 1990s on this famous 'fault line of history' some commentators were moved to remark that such was the bloody and tribal nature of the political culture of these lands that it could be argued that here was the birthplace of fascism itself.[57] When we have stopped trying to relativize the crimes committed during the war, those committed by the Chetniks and other Serb collaborators as well as the Partisans, we will come closer to the truth of the story of the war in Yugoslavia and Europe. We can see how the paradigm described by Davies as the 'Allied Scheme of History' has underpinned the relativist approach to crimes committed by all combatants generally (and to those committed by collaborators in Yugoslavia in particular) and militated against an integrated analysis. For now we need only to recognize that when outsiders contemplated Yugoslavia's role in the war they eventually concluded that that the only tolerable option for action was to reject all collaboration, to reject the old ruling elites and to remake the state.

Integrating Yugoslav Resistance into the History of Hitler's Europe

Our understanding of European resistance was first shaped by historians who had lived through the war and then by those who grew up in the shadow of the war. This was as much the case for Yugoslavia as any other country. Among Yugoslavia's prominent Anglophone publicist-historians were F.W.D. (Bill) Deakin (1913–2005), Brigadier Sir Fitzroy Maclean (1911–96) and Stephen Clissold (1918–82),[58] all of whom served in Yugoslavia during the war and had very public careers after 1945. Maclean and Tito were especially close, Maclean having been sent to Yugoslavia as Churchill's special envoy. Perhaps the generational factor in the historiography of resistance was even more important in places like Yugoslavia and the German Democratic Republic, for example, given the communist parties' hegemony there and the pressing need to establish the new states on the strength of the memory of anti-fascism. As these two communist states were founded upon the success of the anti-fascist struggle, it was defined in clear-cut military terms. That image could not be sustained indefinitely. In its very promotion it became unsustainable because resistance meant so much more than the armed struggle.

One of the fears of historians of resistance has always been that we will end up with such an elastic, or diluted, definition of resistance that it will not take into account the heroism of the individuals who risked (and often lost) their lives. But, as I have argued, what we have ended up with instead is an elastic definition of collaboration. There is still a strong attachment to Robert Paxton's idea of 'functional collaboration' which describes the behaviour of most people other than active resisters.[59] The problem with the 'life went on' (or 'consensus') school of historians is that its adherents either tend to generalize from the aberrant or do not make clear the connections between accommodations and negotiations people made daily to survive on the one hand, and the success of fascist or collaborationist regimes on the other. We must also consider more seriously the fact that many people would have made the decision not to resist as guerrilla fighters. This did not necessarily mean they were collaborators, or 'bystanders', or unpatriotic. Perhaps they could not choose this form of resistance because some of its work was morally repugnant to them. However, they may well have made other (ethical) choices that also had a bearing on the success of resistance and the ultimate liberation of their soil.[60] In spite of the various ways in which historians define it, resistance generally involves certain objectives. Historians subscribing to a narrow view of resistance agree that these objectives must be political and explicitly so, with the removal of the offending or occupying regime as the ultimate aim of all acts of resistance. However, the extent to which that option was available, tactically preferable or morally acceptable differed according to circumstances. Furthermore, there was the consideration of the appropriateness of certain kinds of resistance in certain circumstances. German reprisals could be so extreme that the value of the resistance act might easily be negated. The German reaction to the death of Reinhard Heydrich, Deputy Reich Protector of Bohemia and Moravia (from wounds sustained in a spectacular attack by London-trained Czech resisters in the middle of Prague in 1942), is a case in point. The massacre by the Germans of the male inhabitants of the village of Lidice, which was then completely destroyed, and the eventual decimation of the internal Czech resistance horrified the Allies. An article on Mihailović appearing in the *Nineteenth Century and After* in August 1943 mentioned the story of Lidice and suggested that the situation in Yugoslavia was much worse.[61] It would be reasonable to suggest that the stories of German reprisals filtering out of Central Europe made Mihailović's policy not to embark on futile sorties acceptable to the Allies for much longer than it would have been elsewhere.

The broader social aspects of dissent in daily life have been neglected in studies of Yugoslav resistance because the national question and narrowly public, that is military and political, interpretations of resistance govern our perceptions of Yugoslav history generally and resistance history specifically. As I have pointed out, the simplistic dichotomy pitting resistance against collaboration has also tended to dominate Yugoslav resistance studies. Thus a lot of our conclusions about the nature of Yugoslav resistance and, by default, collaboration, still rest on assumptions about its potential or actual military success and failure, which is possibly one of the least interesting things about resistance activity in Hitler's Europe from the point of view of a people's history of the war. In France, the presence of Vichy and the ultra-collaborationists in Paris notwithstanding, there was a greater sense of security from the point of view of national integrity and social and physical cohesion (as well as the proximity of de Gaulle in London), leading to a plurality of ethical responses to occupation. In Poland the situation was different again. Recently an historian called for the reappraisal of the 'myth' of the Poles' near universal refusal to collaborate in the light of evidence of instances of cooperation with the Germans. An alternative position rejects this view as well as the claim that the Germans would not accept partnership with the 'inferior Slavs' and shows that, on the contrary, the Germans actively sought more Polish accomplices for a range of actions and that they were constantly thwarted and frustrated by the unresponsiveness of Polish people to German overtures.[62] We see here that the evidence of large-scale Polish resistance across many different kinds of activities, cultural, social and educational, informs the story of cooperation and complicity and should prevent us from generalizing blithely about the responsibility of so-called bystanders, another term, like collaboration, often very loosely and inappropriately applied. These examples alert us also to the logical fallacy in the argument that suggests the 'demythologization' of resistance, however defined, will of necessity reveal greater degrees of collaboration. Clearly there is still much historians can contribute to the definitional debate about the nature of resistance generally and resistance in Yugoslavia in particular.

In the case of Yugoslavia these general problems regarding our interpretation of resistance do need to be considered alongside the national question, but also alongside perceptions of the pre-war regime. It was not enough to be against the enemy, or even to be an anti-fascist. A positive vision, of the past or the future or both, had also to propel resistance. Whereas for many in France resistance might become a struggle for reasserting national integrity and political continuity by restoring the republic, the situation was different in Yugoslavia. It was, for all intents and purposes, a country that no longer existed, where there was no shared sense of continuity or shared history; what actually constituted national integrity had become difficult, if not impossible, to establish. Here the tolerable options for action in wartime were therefore even less clear-cut.[63] Yugoslav resistance, from the perspective of interwar history, ought to have been weak, divided along national and political lines and ineffectual. In fact it was the opposite, and only by treating collaboration and resistance in a coherent narrative can one begin to explain that seeming anomaly. The cross-national appeal of Yugoslav resistance related both to a generalized anti-fascist struggle and to local or regional factors, including the actions of the collaborators against which people reacted from an early stage.

In places like France the elevation of an unsustainable individualized heroic resistance ideal was one of the factors that precipitated the end of the resistance myth. The multifaceted history of dissent in everyday life did not dislodge the stereotype of the armed resistance struggle. In Yugoslavia and other communist countries a frozen image of the armed anti-fascist struggle was politicized and also led to glib and shallow stereotypes. The participation of women in this resistance occasioned little reflection after 1945 other than on the question of whether it led to full equality in the postwar period, which of course it did not, providing another example where the emphasis on outcomes over process obscured the complexities of the wartime experience. It was difficult for outsiders to avoid describing events in Yugoslavia without resorting to flat images of Balkan brothers and sisters fighting to the death against undifferentiated fascists in the name of a new national revolution. The great patriotic war and the anti-fascist struggle would have a similar resonance in all communist countries after 1945, with the heroic Soviet Union emerging as the state primarily responsible for the destruction of the fascist contagion on the Continent. In Yugoslavia, as elsewhere, one-dimensional histories of resistance failed to identify the multiple

ways in which people expressed their anti-collaborationist views
and how this contributed to the success of the resistance movement
as a whole. Henceforth the emphasis on collaboration remained
important, especially at key moments in Yugoslavia's history. For
example, insiders and outsiders drew on the memory of collaboration in isolation at the time of the postwar purges, in the protest
movement known as the Croatian Spring in 1970–1, on Tito's death
in 1980 and as Yugoslavia collapsed in the 1990s. The struggle for
the appropriation of the Partisan epic was also one of the features
of these politicized 'reminiscences'.

The First Wave of International Tito Acclamation

Outsiders celebrated Yugoslav resisters of the first hour. Almost
immediately there were two groups, the Chetniks and the Partisans,
engaged in active resistance against the Germans and their indigenous supporters. Attempts to bring these two groups together
failed and they remained at odds with each other for the duration
of the war. There was no Yugoslav equivalent of Jean Moulin, de
Gaulle's envoy who brought all the internal resistance in France
under the umbrella of the *Mouvements unis de la Résistance* and the
Conseil national de la Résistance before being betrayed, tortured and
killed at the hands of the 'Butcher of Lyons', Klaus Barbie. Romantic
evocations of the Chetniks under Mihailović drew on tales about a
centuries-old tradition of resistance and guerrilla warfare by a people who inhabited a mountainous terrain that schooled them well
for war. Mihailović was 'the eternal Serb rebel',[64] and the 'thousands
of soldiers operating as guerrillas in the mountains' were proof of
the fact that 'Jugoslavia', the 'first of the conquered countries of
Europe where armed revolts have been successfully organised against
the oppressor on an important scale', was 'beaten but not broken'.[65]
We can identify the reversions to Balkan stereotypes (in this case
positive) based on the region's imagined past, its bandits and its heroes, who had fought endless battles to shake off the foreign yoke of
the infidel. Chetnik resistance tales spoke of a warrior tradition that
had served 'the nation' well in the past. Repeatedly, writers commented on the contrast, territorially and politically, between Serbia
at the beginning of the nineteenth century and Serbia after the
First World War. Serbia had proven itself on the battlefields. It had
repelled the 'Ottoman dragon' to the point that at the time of the

Balkan Wars, the country stood unchallenged. Yugoslavia's foundation story remained firmly intact. In 1942 Lewis Namier, reviewing Rebecca West's acclaimed *Black Lamb and Grey Falcon*, recalled her reflection on the Kosovo defeat thus: 'A single battle sealed for five centuries the fate of the nation, condemning it to an existence which was "not life but sheer nonsense", to "a night of evil" during which the pain of Kossovo [*sic*] was "newly born, in acuteness for each generation".'[66] There is much that could be said about the persistent tendency to justify territorial expansion in terms of a battle fought over five centuries previously in another, very different, kind of war. It is sufficient simply to recall here the depth of the penetration of this legend outside Yugoslavia and its evocative power in a time of crisis. None of the other Yugoslavs could draw on such boilerplate rhetoric to their political advantage but, as had occurred during the First World War, it could envelop all of them indiscriminately, making it possible for the Kosovo lament to be absorbed by the Partisan struggle at the opportune moment, much to the eventual chagrin, and then resentment, of the Serbs.

According to Mihailović's champions, and there were many, disintegration under German rule would have advanced 'even further' had it not been for 'the indomitable spirit of a nation and of the man who has emerged as the leader of that nation ... a hero-patriot, and one of the greatest figures of the Second World War'.[67] In another positive account a year later, in 1944, when evidence of his collaboration was circulating widely, Mihailović was still a 'brave man of undeniable military capacity and possessing the mysterious power of appearing simultaneously in different places'.[68] Right to the very end his supporters ignored the fact that Mihailović was closer to Axis forces, and on occasion the Ustaše, than the Partisans. Magazines like the *Nineteenth Century and After* ran articles defending Mihailović over several months. Mihailović was described as a friend of the English who repaid his loyalty by denying him sufficient arms. Tito was a communist fighting for a communist 'socio-political revolution' that 'grafts itself onto the national revolution', whereas Mihailović was fighting for the king and democracy.[69] It was for this reason that many continued to advocate that the English back the Chetniks, not the Partisans, as Tito's goal was to 'consolidate and extend this "totalitarian" despotism' by destroying 'every genuinely popular movement in Yugoslavia'.[70]

Outsiders eventually understood that Mihailović was not aspiring to be a 'national liberator' and that his was the voice of Serbian interests. According to an OSS report, his 'wait and see' policy was as much about preserving Serbian lives as 'consolidat[ing] control in Serbia' which he would 'hand back to his Great Serb superiors' when they returned from exile.[71] This tactic hindered the Chetniks' mobilizing potential. In fact Mihailović's policy not only led to what the Allies saw as inertia, the population's 'complete passive attitude toward the whole situation', but also to collaboration with Nedić, the Germans and Italians. The Yugoslavs in London promised that the Chetniks would give 'the greatest possible assistance' at the time of the (anticipated) Allied invasion but in the interim were content with 'casual sabotage and destruction' with the 'least possible sacrifice in blood'.[72] From Tito's reported standpoint, Mihailović embodied 'the last remnant of armed power of the old, rotten, bourgeois order, [which] in no case wanted to struggle against the occupiers but, at all costs, wanted to safeguard the old bourgeois social order under the occupation'.[73] Supporters of the Partisans in the United States like Radica, for example, argued in 1943 that Mihailović might well have started out as a trailblazer but he had ended up as the 'servant of a clique', fighting battles of another era unrelated to the aspirations of most Yugoslavs. He represented the 'Serbian conception of a centralised state' and rule by Belgrade's corrupt political circle or *čaršija*, the blight of the first Yugoslavia.[74] The People's Liberation Movement in Yugoslavia, we learn from another October 1943 article by Radica, 'is trying to build a new Yugoslavia and a new Balkan order based on a commonwealth of free and equal nations'.[75] Henceforth true anti-fascists would have but one path to active resistance. Seton-Watson, who remained a dedicated promoter of the Yugoslav ideal, endorsed the decision to arm Tito and the Partisans when it emerged that the Chetniks were collaborating and that their tactics were shaped as much by their intention to re-create their Great Serbian vision of the (failed) state as their desire to save manpower until such time as the Allies would turn their attention to a Balkan offensive.[76] By then Seton-Watson had come to share some of the views of Durham who, months before her death in 1944, was still writing about the need for greater equality among the South Slavs.

The men determining Allied policy in Yugoslavia were eventually guided by the belief that Yugoslavia had to be remade, as one British magazine put it so aptly in January 1942, on the premise that 'the future lies with the federative idea'.[77] They were not simply looking for an excuse to justify abandoning their one-time favourite, the

Serb nationalist and royalist, Mihailović, for the Croat communist, Tito. Rather, they were turning their backs on the established
understanding of Yugoslavia, a unitary, centralized state dominated
by the Serbs, and advocating another which seemed fairer and more
workable for the times. We know that this was not a novel concept
and key Yugoslavists had argued for over twenty years for federalist structures, but it was more attractive to our outsiders in wartime in large part because it seemed that such a state would prove
a more effective ally. It was therefore not enough merely to defeat
and expel enemy occupiers from Yugoslav territories as it was obvious that in 1941, in the moment of crisis, the country had been of
no use to the international forces for good, the anti-fascist forces. It
had proven almost impossible to exploit fully the Kingdom's moral
and material resources against the Germans and their local followers until some alternative model of the nation with broad-based
cross-national support provided a positive (if chimerical) vision for
the future. Churchill famously claimed that politics had no bearing
on his choice to support Tito as he was only interested in assisting
the group killing the most number of Germans. When the Allies
decided to arm Tito's Partisans over Mihailović's Chetniks, they
therefore took several factors into account but Churchill's dictum
was never far from view. This was because it was equally apparent
that the most number of Germans would be killed not simply by
the best-armed resisters, but by those resisters able to cast their net
wide across all national and social groups and carry the greatest
number of people along with them, if only for the duration of the
struggle. As it was established in the course of 1942 and as has been
shown repeatedly in the works of prominent historians in the field,
the Chetniks were incapable of realizing this inclusive goal because
they did not share it.[78]

The change in Allied policy led to bitter attacks on the Partisans
by the Great Serb faction outside the country. In January 1944,
for one writer, Tito was still 'a non-entity', a Croat 'Apparatchik'
with no 'outstanding qualities'. Some of the British and American
magazine literature thus continued to deplore 'marauding', 'ter-
rorizing' Partisans who expropriated the holdings of 'relatively
well-to-do' farmers.[79] The American, Ruth Mitchell, who was living
in Yugoslavia at the time of the German invasion and who briefly
joined the Chetniks, was fulsome in her praise of Mihailović, whom
she described as a 'heroic, incorruptible Serb patriot and quite
possibly the most brilliant soldier this war has thus far produced'.

According to Mitchell, the 'so-called Partisans hardly exist today, and...they never did exist as an effective fighting force against the Axis except in the imagination of communist and Croat propagandists'. She also wrote that 'Croat officers' of the Yugoslav Army went over to the Axis 'by pre-arranged plan' whereas the Germans proclaimed Mihailović 'Public Enemy Number One'.[80] The *American Mercury*, running a pro-Mihailović line, repeatedly accused the Partisans of slandering Mihailović and lying about their successes. Among the Yugoslav voices joining Mihailović's detractors were expatriate Croats and Slovenes, like Radica and Adamic. Adamic, a successful writer, referred to pejoratively by his critics as the 'professional foreigner', a 'violently pro-Croat Slovene' and a paid agent of Stalin, was doing a thriving trade after having been taken up as a favourite by Eleanor Roosevelt.[81] Reviled by the Yugoslav ambassador in Washington, the royalist Serb Constantin Fotich, Adamic was undeterred, writing that Mihailović was 'working with the Axis' as the 'patriot-blunderer and blind agent of amoral interests which have been at large in the Balkans for a thousand years'.[82] Serbs and Chetnik sympathizers continued to attack Tito supporters as 'Serb-haters' (in the same way that Durham had been attacked in the interwar years), and as communists whose views were evident in papers such as the *Daily Worker* and *New Masses*.[83] Nonetheless there was a shift in the balance, so that just as Rebecca West had accused others of inherent bias in their descriptions of various South Slavs, now others pointed to the inherent prejudices in the work of West herself.[84]

Americans expressed concern that the London Yugoslavs, representing the 'old Serb anti-Croat clique', were embarking on an 'extended anti-Croat propaganda campaign'. The 'ardent Great Serb' Fotich was also conducting such a campaign in the United States.[85] The Yugoslavs in London were thought to be making anti-Croat mileage out of the massacres of Serbs 'committed by a small extremist group of Croats' and 'missed no chance to denounce the Croats, in the hope that they may get support for their plan to return to power as rulers of a Greater Serbia'. The real problem, however, was that the London Yugoslavs had failed to unite 'anti-Axis elements' at home and had no hope of doing so given that they were never representative of the popular will and, having fled the country, had lost 'what little claim to office they ever had'. The cabinet, full of the 'worst autocrats' of the old regime including 'the former head of the most notorious political prison in Belgrade', did not inspire confidence.[86] There was a definitive shift in perceptions in the course of 1943 so that by November of that year, for example, the Partisans were thought to be attracting all ex-Pavelić supporters as well as ex-Chetniks, 'displeased with [Mihailović's] policy of inaction' and who wanted to be on an 'active front'.[87] Intelligence gleaned from Ultra intercepts and Soviet dispatches as well as evidence from operatives in the field convinced Churchill that there was no other option but to pledge support to the Partisans. Maclean personally carried a letter to Tito from Churchill in August 1943 and when he later recalled that Tito stood 'head and shoulders above his fellows', he spoke for his generation.[88] An OSS report providing some biographical background on key personnel in the Partisan movement gives us a sense of the way in which the resisters could be glamorized and romanticized. Croat poets and artists were in the vanguard, including the sculptor Antun Augustinčić (1900–79), for whom both Pavelić and Tito posed. Other high-profile scientists and academics (including the winner of a Rockefeller Fellowship who had studied in London) and veterans of the International Brigade joined the Partisans. (Of the 66 Partisan generals at least 15 were veterans of the Spanish Civil War.[89]) Philosophers, intellectuals, 'wits' and lawyers all graced the rank and file of the Partisan movement. When the Yugoslav government moved to Cairo and was forced to negotiate with the Partisans, the guerrilla fighters turned up as heroes. They wore their improvised uniforms, comprising anything from bits and pieces of old Yugoslav army uniforms to shirts made from Allied parachutes, to great effect.[90]

The idealized projection of the Partisan movement was part of its appeal, as was the deliberate and pragmatic decision to underplay the ideological motivation of Tito and his forces. Many Partisan sympathizers and supporters, indeed many resisters themselves, were not adherents of the Communist Party nor ever would be. An OSS report on the Partisans from November 1943 (referred to above) suggested the Partisan resisters and fellow-travellers might include anyone from a 'clerical' to an 'agrarian democrat' and continued: 'there can only be an infinitesimal proportion of Marxist doctrinaire communists in the Partisan ranks, simply because the breed has never existed in Yugoslavia'.[91] Observers played down both the radical nature of Partisan ideology and the fears of some that the democratic posturing of the Partisans was 'a front' behind which 'someone is preparing a Revolution on the Russian model': 'there is nobody to revolt against and nobody to revolt'. The country

thus retained the capacity for an easy transition to peaceful democratic institutions once the Germans had been defeated.[92] It was
also held that the Partisans were especially careful not to make the
same mistakes as the Bolsheviks regarding religion. They approved
army chaplains and apparently had no religious 'bias'. Nor did they
engage in 'class warfare'.[93] When the NDH's nature became apparent there were also fewer impediments for the Partisans in Croatia
than in Serbia, where the Chetniks dominated. For example, a leading Croat Partisan, Andrija Hebrang, was charismatic and attracted
Serbs and Croats living in the NDH to Croatian Partisan units.
Hebrang was eventually removed and recalled to Belgrade ostensibly because he exhibited Croatian nationalist particularism but,
in fact, according to Banac, because his real failing was his pluralism.[94] Whatever the reason, the image of the restless and inward-
looking Croat nationalist was never far from the surface, regardless
of Hebrang's impeccable Partisan credentials.

If some outsiders were pragmatic, others embraced the Partisan
resistance movement simply because it had wider appeal than all
the other alternatives. In Australia, Croat immigrants raised funds
for the Partisans and lobbied hard against the Yugoslav Consuls
in Sydney and Perth who supported the government-in-exile and
the Chetniks.[95] There were similar gestures among the Croatian
émigré groups in America.[96] In spite of the persistent patronage of
the Chetniks in some British and American quarters, Tito became
the undisputed hero of the Yugoslav resistance and his victory in
propagandistic terms was spectacular. The Chetniks' stated tactic of preserving personnel by holding back and thus preventing
excessive reprisals from the Germans was morally and strategically
defensible only as long as the Serbs did not fight other resisters and
friends of the Allies and waste valuable matériel in the process. As
was noted in 1942 in *The Nation*, 'an inactive front is a decomposing
front'.[97] Others would reiterate this fundamental point at the time
of Mihailović's capture and trial in Belgrade in 1946. Some were to
realize retrospectively how lacking in foresight was the policy in support of the Chetniks, 'a guerrilla army which had not fighting but
waiting as its purpose'. The truth of the matter was that if one wanted
to fight the Germans, one joined the Partisans, as Tito was always
'active' and 'the theory of inactivity' led only to 'collaboration and
ruin'.[98] Tito's was the 'all people's war', with no holds barred regardless of the consequences. This may well have been ethically intolerable to many, but as long as the Partisans were active the front did

not 'decompose', and for outsiders this was the determining factor in decisions regarding whom to support. It was certainly not the case, as one English magazine reported in the autumn of 1944, almost a year before war's end, that everyone in Yugoslavia was relieved when they saw the Chetniks, those 'bearded, picturesque-looking men carrying super-modern arms including automatic pistols'.[99] Mihailović's failure was generalized across many Serbian interest groups and they would never recover from the shock of losing their position as the first among the 'equal nations' of Yugoslavia. The experience of women in the resistance illustrates well this unpredictable elevation of non-Serbs to a higher status from the outsiders' perspective at this time.

The Fighting Women of Yugoslavia

One of the singular features of Partisan resistance in Yugoslavia was the presence of women in all aspects of the activism, including in armed units. Accounts of the fighting women of Yugoslavia filtered out of the country and in reports where the lines between Chetniks and Partisans were blurred, it might seem as if women were fighting with the former. This was rarely the case. A March 1943 article in the British magazine *Nineteenth Century and After* argued that it was the 'fighting women of Yugoslavia' who made resistance on the Balkan front possible. It was through their 'devotion and assistance' that these women sustained resistance, 'vowing to fight to their last drop of blood' to save children and other victims of the 'Croatian quisling' Pavelić.[100] It became clear that the women resisters capturing the imagination of our outsiders were behind Tito's forces, not the Chetniks. Early in 1944 the *Times* correspondent in Alexandria reported on the 'Women Fighters of Yugoslavia' and focused on 'a fresh-faced girl named Anka Barich' who was in 'the camp of the Yugoslav partisans, mainly women, children and a few men incapacitated by wounds'. Barich, 'known to have been responsible for the killing of about 150 of the enemy', had been forced to leave her Croatian home, a village near Split, after two years of active service as a combatant and after the murder of five members of her family by the Germans who 'took revenge' once her 'exploits' came to their attention. When she joined the Partisan unit Barich was 'trained in the use of hand grenades and became an expert left-handed thrower. She knew that 72 Germans had been killed by her grenades, and the remainder were victims of her sabotage work.' Barich described the precarious life of the Partisans and the privations they suffered. She had once gone without food for seven days: 'their usual food was raw horseflesh and edible grass, as they dared not make fires'. The reporter also told the story of the bayoneting of members of her family, including her 6-year-old brother, because they refused to give her up. The president of the refugees' committee 'said that the women...proved great fighters and he could not find words to describe their bravery'.[101]

Perhaps we should conclude that Anka Barich's resistance story, along with many others, must be subjected to the obligatory demythologization process which would reveal that it reflected the experiences of a minority of Croatian women. However, as we saw above in the example of the recent debates about the 'myth' of Polish resistance, other factors must come into play in such a revisionist enterprise. Most historians agree that there was no 'fascist revolution' in Yugoslavia and that the appeal of the collaborationist regimes was limited to begin with and marginal over time. Further, as Payne has pointed out, the NDH was less lethal as time went on. We also have the hard evidence of an enormous movement of female resisters (including hundreds of thousands of adherents to the Anti-Fascist Front of Women) whose anti-fascist and anti-collaborationist preferences were clear from the way they behaved and in what they did, not just in the way they 'felt' or in passive resignation and retreat into the home.[102] In any other context such evidence alone would lead to a serious modification of the understanding of collaboration. This has yet to occur in Yugoslavia. Instead, there has been a renewed focus on collaboration and the alleged role of women in promoting fascist values. This is in keeping with trends elsewhere, as the pendulum has swung away from the notion of women as victims of the racial state, for example, towards the view that women were as culpable as men for the crimes of the Third Reich and its collaborators and satellites. Thus while the Ustaše's mobilizing potential from the point of view of women appears to have been limited and the capillary associations specifically targeting women did not enjoy the same success as their parallel structures in Italy and Germany,[103] historians revisiting the subject argue that Pavelić's popularity among Croatian women was greater than has been hitherto suggested.[104] The persistence of the binary divide in Yugoslav historiography, pitting collaboration against resistance, remains one of the greatest barriers to our understanding of the war and the ways in which it shaped Yugoslav identities.[105]

Our onlookers saw in the action of women resisters the elements of a new Yugoslav revolution. We might thus be tempted to argue that the 'Yugoslav synthesis' or the 'Yugoslav consensus' as explored by some contemporary writers had had more success in the Kingdom than our evidence in Chapter 3 implies.[106] However, studies of women's sociability in the interwar years, the experience they brought to the war, tend to support the arguments of historians like Charles Jelavich, whose work on interwar textbooks reveals there was no coherent Yugoslav project in the schools and that the constituent peoples produced their own curricula for local students.[107] Serbian women's groups might have used the words 'national' and 'Yugoslav' interchangeably in their correspondence, but their preoccupations were Serbian rather than 'Yugoslav'. Liturgies and services for the Serbian war dead, raising memorials to the casualties of the First World War and assisting war orphans and the families of fallen soldiers were among the primary concerns of Serbian women's groups in the Kingdom. According to Carol Lilly, these activities were linked with others sponsored by the Serbian Orthodox Church.[108] Lilly also says that because they were so attached to the Karađorđević dynasty, Serbian women's groups embraced the king's integral Yugoslavism, but this could also have indicated that for them embracing the idea of 'three tribes, one nation' simply meant that the 'Yugoslav nation' was in fact Serbian. From the outset Croatian women were not attracted to the 'Yugoslav' women's organizations whose headquarters were in Belgrade. These bodies were dominated by Serbian women and Serbian women's priorities, notably in their twinning of wartime sacrifice and national renewal. A Croat journalist who attended the first congress of the National Women's Union of Serbs, Croats and Slovenes in 1919 returned to Zagreb disappointed. Noting its domination by Serbs and the narrowly Serbian objectives of the newly established 'Yugoslav' association, she called into question its relevance to Croatian women's groups.[109] Evidently local variables, such as life in one's community and social and religious networks, had an important role to play in women's associational life and, it could be argued, a potentially greater influence on women's activism in the war than an overarching woman-centred Yugoslavism that barely existed in the interwar years. Other factors therefore came into play in women's decision to reject collaboration.

Women's involvement in Yugoslav resistance was celebrated after 1945 but perhaps also partially hidden in a period when the Party's struggles to maintain order prevailed. The purging of the old structures of state and the collaborationists (widely defined), communist implantation and economic reconstruction took precedence. As was the case in France, very few women were recognized for their contribution to resistance. In Yugoslavia women honoured as National Heroes were not representative of the two million women in the anti-fascist movement and tended to be young educated Party members rather than peasants. The first wave of writing on women in the resistance emphasized the Yugoslav revolution's liberating impulse, arguing that women had participated in the struggle against the fascists and were reaping the benefits.[110] It was during the war itself that women's role in the resistance was interpreted in this way. For example, in April 1944 *The Contemporary Review* reported that 'The great fight for freedom has achieved one final victory already. It has burst the chains that bound women in Yugoslavia.'[111] Subsequently historians disputed this inflated claim. The fact that the apparently revolutionary activism of women resisters did not lead directly to their social advancement or complete equality seemed to detract from the singularity of their achievements in the war. This 'failure' also diminished the general appreciation of what women's activism in the war revealed about ordinary people's responses to the moral dilemmas with which they were confronted. The problem for historians is that the heroic image of the combatant woman, the romantic and romanticized *partizanka*, which, paradoxically, could easily be distorted, impressed itself on the European imagination, often to the exclusion of the more prosaic aspects of dissent in daily life. The danger of the trivializing of all resistance, and that of women in particular, is that we are left with a stereotypical and undernourished view of resistance as primarily a military activity. Such appraisals, at the time and subsequently, could not take account of the diversity of resistance experiences. They also failed to take into account the social, political and cultural preconditions necessary for successful resistance and the values brought to bear in the choice to refuse collaboration. Moreover, an overemphasis on the 'warrior element' of resistance led to false assumptions about collaboration. We have seen that in France such a dichotomous analytical framework led to a transformation: the nation of resisters became the nation of collaborators. In Yugoslavia the transmogrification was much more condensed in time, with early onset amnesia allowing for the partial view of collaboration as nationally predetermined, and resistance as purely politically or 'Yugoslav-inspired', to dominate unchallenged for decades.

The relative superficiality of our appreciation of the phenomenon of women's resistance relates to the obsession in Yugoslav historiography with the national question. All other questions seem to be secondary or insignificant in the light of the contest between a predetermined, reactionary and 'particularist' national or nationalist inclination and the progressive 'Yugoslav revolution'. Arguing over which nationality was the numerically strongest in the Yugoslav resistance, rather than what, if anything, the national background of resisters signified in their choice to resist, is a debate of limited interest and derives from the narrow pre-war interpretation of Yugoslavia's problems as primarily 'national'. Anti-communist and anti-Croat propaganda did not give proper acknowledgement to the role of anti-collaborationist women in the war. Mitchell generalized from her own narrow experience and prejudices and was dismissive of the stories of women's resistance. A photographer, she had done location work in the interwar years and she decided to stay in the region, settling on the Croatian coast where she remained through to the outbreak of the war. When she became aware of reports of resistance activities, she asked to be sworn into the Chetnik movement. She moved to Belgrade but remained inactive and her life as a Chetnik was short-lived. She was taken prisoner, deported to a German camp and then freed. Mitchell, the 'American Chetnik', was not unlike the women who had come before her and provided aid on the Balkan front during the First World War. As we have seen, she became one of Mihailović's greatest defenders in the United States and referred often to his heroism in the First World War. But Mitchell, who saw no action herself, made a mockery of the conference of Anti-Fascist Front of Women, adding that the paper produced by women resisters was 'non-existent, like the organisations of which it is supposed to be the organ'.[112] Croat collaborators promoted their own fiction and called all Partisan activity Serbian and communist-inspired, in an attempt to diminish the significance of Croatian initiatives in the resistance struggle. Anti-Partisan propaganda also depicted women combatants as unwomanly and, often, immoral. Soviet women combatants were similarly perceived in German reports on the 'unnatural' female soldiers within the enemy's ranks.[113] On such foundations it would prove impossible for the first generation of postwar historians to get a sense of the life of ordinary men and women in wartime Yugoslavia and impossible to understand how and why people refused to submit in the course of their daily lives.

A study of the resistance enterprise of women sheds light on the extent of the penetration of fascist ideas or, in our case, the imperviousness of many sectors of the population to those ideas. Daily-life studies have the potential to show us another way of perceiving nonconformity and dissent as well as collaboration. (The particular case of Croatian resistance and collaboration, for example, can be illuminating on the question of the impact of the Ustaše on daily life and the limited extent of receptivity over time to their ideals.) Further, resistance studies alert us to the fact that nonconformism and dissent were broad-based and wide-ranging in Yugoslavia. Even the most cursory comparison with resistance in other countries suggests the story of women's activism in Yugoslavia has only been half-told. Its relative neglect by historians of the war is puzzling and the failure to integrate the subject more fully into a social and political history of the war even more so. A partial explanation may be found in the preponderance of military themes in resistance history. Even though the majority of female resisters were not soldiers, women's involvement in the armed struggle has quite simply reinforced the masculine stereotype of guerrilla fighters in Yugoslavia. Elsewhere, in France for example, a gendered interpretation of resistance has amplified the story of refusal, dissent and nonconformism as well as non-military resistance. Women's engagement in the war in Yugoslavia tells the story of widespread refusal to accept the norms of the 'Quislingovitches'. It is uncontested that women's participation in the resistance was one of the keys to its success. In itself this phenomenon attracted comment at the time and it is worthy of still more detailed attention than it has received in the historiography. In the context of our narrative it is significant because it highlights the obsession of historians and outsiders with the overarching national question and with narrow interpretations of the significance and nature of all Yugoslav resistance. Resistance was meaningful only in so far as it could be marshalled to the Allied goal of total victory in a total war and secure stability in postwar Yugoslavia. This perspective had an impact on process (the writing of wartime history) and policy (the intertwining of the memory of war and the received wisdom about the war on attitudes towards Yugoslavia) until the country's final collapse.

Layered Memories and New Creation Myths

We have seen that much of the Chetniks' appeal lay in the ongoing impact of the memory of the First World War. Sir Nevile Henderson wrote to *The Times* in 1941 praising the actions of the Serbs who had effected the coup. He said that these men were the real heirs of the legacy of King Aleksandar, 'Liberator and Martyr', and had done what 'their great King...would have wished his people to do'. Henderson nostalgically recalled the life and work of Aleksandar, adding: 'No one knows better than the Yugoslav from tragic experience the full horrors and sufferings of war. Yet no people – and here I speak from experience, for I also served in Serbia during the last War – possess in a higher degree the qualities of love of freedom, courage and endurance, honour and loyalty than the Yugoslavs.'[114] American and English magazines evoked memories of the First World War in their articles on Serbia and Yugoslavia. There was not much to distinguish between pro-Serb propaganda in 1914–18 and in the period 1941–3, that is, while Mihailović remained in favour. The Serbs had earned their 'place of honour' in the First World War but their heroism and self-sacrifice in March 1941 were 'even greater'.[115] They had lost a third of their population between 1914 and 1918 in the fighting and through 'disease, hunger and exposure'. They 'suffered more than any of the other Allies' then, and now the Serbs were 'again the greatest sufferers'.[116]

Mitchell, who came from a military family, similarly evoked the Serbs' experience of the First World War. She spent some months in prison with other women including Flora Sandes who, as we know, fought with the Serbs in the First World War, was decorated for her bravery and revered for her loyalty.[117] When the tide was turning against the Chetniks, Mitchell was especially outspoken and wrote in July 1943: 'In the last war Serbia was the first country in Europe to throw off the German invader; history is likely to repeat itself.' Mihailović, she continued, 'has kept hope and faith in an Allied democratic victory burning in the heart of the Balkans. He will be as important in building the peace as in finishing the war....The fortress of Europe has a key and its name is Mihailovich.' If anyone doubted her, they had only to recall that Mihailović had fought 'in practically every battle on the Salonika Front' and returned highly decorated.[118] It was Mihailović who went to Marseilles and who had laid the wreath at the monument to the soldiers of the French

Orient Army in a gesture of solidarity and in the king's name after Aleksandar's funeral.[119] Former allies were invited to recall their shared history, as reported in the English Catholic magazine, *The Month*, in 1944: it would have been tragic if the 'cradle of war' between 1914 and 1918 became 'the grave of our high hopes of what is to follow this second world war'.[120] In London, the French and the Yugoslavs had a high regard for each other and de Gaulle awarded Mihailović the *Croix de Guerre* as an act of solidarity.[121] The Allies had to find a way of securing Yugoslavia's future without betraying the memory of the First World War.

Some elements of Yugoslavia's foundation narrative that had appealed to outsiders in 1918 and in the interwar period no longer applied in the Second World War. Others, including the belief that the successor state reunited, after a long and heart-wrenching separation, people who constituted a single race, had become embarrassing and had to be discarded. The memory of war set back the process of nation-building in the Kingdom, but outsiders continued to evoke it and conflated the shared experience of the two world wars as if it formed a continuous thread linking generations across Europe. They did this because it was necessary to win the war and to remain loyal to one's friends. Allies in the First World War by and large had remained allies in the Second World War, and the fact that they were witnessing another 'Yugoslav revolution' comforted outsiders. The revolutionary potential of the Partisans, if problematic ideologically for the liberal democracies, was conveniently rationalized as the latest variant of the people's will in the new Yugoslavia. In any case, it would have been difficult to condemn Tito's communism when the Soviet Union was the member of the Grand Alliance responsible for the greatest victories of the war and for advancing further towards Berlin than any other European power could have done, even with the help of the United States. In addition, the sheer incompetence and impotence of the government-in-exile and its declining influence over time, made outsiders more responsive to the voices of Yugoslav leaders other than Serbs. In 1943, Radica wrote in *The Nation* that the peoples of Yugoslavia, betrayed 'for centuries' by their leaders and by foreign powers 'which have exploited them for their own imperialist ambitions', were 'finally approaching political and social liberation'. They were 'conscious of the end of one world and the beginning of a new'; the 'poor and ill-equipped Balkan masses' were in control and 'fighting valiantly': 'No one will be able to use them as a tool. They are forging their own destiny.'[122]

The interwar catch cry, 'the Balkan States for the Balkan peoples', encapsulated that sentiment.[123]

There remained the question of the makeup of the new Yugoslavia. It was not simply the nature of the state that had to change but the understanding of the Yugoslav ideal itself. Yugoslavism could still mean different things to different people, but there was less room for significant deviation from the general principle that while a degree of national equality was essential, an overemphasis on differences between the South Slavs threatened stability. Outsiders remarked often that the vast majority of Yugoslavs wanted the Yugoslav state restored but that Croats wanted a 'free Croatia in a free Yugoslavia', Macedonians wanted a 'free Macedonia in a free Yugoslavia', and so forth. Most Yugoslavs were ready to 'forego' aspects of their own nationality for a common one because Yugoslavism was 'not incompatible' with specific nationalisms.[124] However, it was beginning to look as if the Serbs, whose Chetniks were entirely Serbian and who had 'foregone' nothing by way of national privileges in the old Yugoslavia, would lose some of those advantages in the newly imagined and constructed state. All this was very different from the view of Yugoslavia as Serbia enlarged or a reward for the Serbs for their special suffering and sacrifice in the First World War. Nonetheless it did not imply a complete about-face either. In his glowing 1942 review of West's *Black Lamb and Grey Falcon* referred to above, Namier wrote: 'Each of the component Yugoslav countries is difficult to place anywhere except in a united Yugoslavia; yet it is equally difficult to solder their aggregate into one.'[125] His use of the verbs 'to place' and 'to solder' testify to the persistence of the attitude that the Yugoslav peoples had to be 'placed' and 'soldered' in order to meet a goal that might or might not have related to their precise needs or wants. We can see with hindsight that the Serbs' disillusionment with Yugoslavia grew from the fact that they believed that they would have to (and did) 'forego' a great deal in the projected federal and apparently nationally egalitarian Partisan agenda. The new Yugoslavism would mark a backward step for the Serbian nation and its territorial expansion since the nineteenth century.

One of our newly ascendant Yugoslavs abroad, Adamic, wrote in 1943 that the future would belong to the Partisans and the 'indigenous and spontaneous' Liberation Front 'if the great powers permitted the Serbian, Croatian, and Slovenian people to decide for themselves'.[126] Adamic continued in this vein when he wrote in 1944 that the victory of the Partisans would finally conclude the story of Yugoslav unification: 'Yugoslavia came into existence at the demand of historic forces which had appeared more than a century earlier.'[127] Radica had flagged this position in September 1943 when he wrote in *The Nation* that for the most part Croats were not supporting the Ustaše. He evoked the ideals of Radić, which acted as a counterweight to the false promises of Ustaša ruralism: the 'peasant philosophy of the Croatian people seeks the rebirth of a Yugoslav commonwealth based on democratic federalism'. Men and women all over Croatia, he continued, were fighting, and 'the rebellious spirit of the people has never bowed to the Italian or German invader'. The next month Radica built on this argument, writing that the interior was 'flaming with revolutionary fervor'. Partisans 'surged down the coast from Gorica to Split'. All nations had come together in one 'movement of liberation', with its promise of freedom, democracy, the 'full recognition of national rights' and 'no radical changes' in social structure.[128] Adamic described the Partisan army as one 'composed of Communists and many shades of non-communists ... analogous to a crude, hastily constructed raft built of logs, planks, and debris that floated about in the rising flood-waters of the people's resistance'.[129]

In one of his early demonstrations of support for the Yugoslavs (in this case for those who had effected the 1941 coup d'état in Belgrade), Churchill, whose own son was to serve in Yugoslavia, called on Yugoslavs to fight on as traditional defenders of democracy. The example he drew on in his description of these traditional 'defenders of democracy' was the sixteenth-century Croat peasant uprising under the leadership of Matija Gubec. Tito, who was born near the original field of this uprising, said that the story was inspirational to him from his earliest years, as did Pavelić. The memory of Gubec, like that of other iconic national figures elsewhere – Joan of Arc in France, for example – could be manipulated to serve both sides in the war. Churchill may well have understood that he would have been ill-advised to have drawn on the example of the interwar Yugoslav government in this call to arms in the defence of democracy, but it is significant that he wanted to make his position historically justifiable.[130] It is also significant that the Allies had no intention of ensuring democratic institutions were established in postwar Yugoslavia, nor did they particularly care whether they would be. The crusade for democracy which had led to the death of millions of people in the First World War and which was one of the founding tenets of the successor states had no lasting impact. Nor would the crusade for freedom and democracy in the Second World War resonate for the majority of Europeans after 1945. No one was prepared to admit that, however, and our outsiders were more than happy to bury their heads in the sand when necessary. In early 1944 the *Contemporary Review* described 'government by the Partisans' in the liberated territories and noted the emphasis on democracy and education, on the 'organisation and unity of the masses against the Fascist intruders'.[131] According to Adamic, the war and revolution in Yugoslavia were 'the climax' of the upheavals 'which began in the eighteenth century' in various parts of the world, including America. The liberation front was an 'instrument of hope' and its slogan 'Death to Fascism! Liberty to the people!' was 'politically perfect' and a 'complete programme'.[132] Radica, in 1944, described the Partisans as the strongest fighting force in the Balkans. The growth of resistance was evidence of 'the revolutionary character' of the war and the extent of the rejection of the old regime.[133] The views of Radica and Adamic carried weight because they conformed to America's postwar vision for Yugoslavia. Towards the end of the war it became clear that there would be two spheres in Europe and it was then that the United States 'gave notice' of its intention to withdraw its forces and allow the Soviet Union to become 'the unchallenged arbiter of Europe'.[134] Even though it was out of the question that Americans should have a physical presence in the region, stability and a strong negotiating position were highly desirable.

The territorial integrity of Yugoslavia and the recourse to old, albeit modified, nostrums about the birth of the state were important considerations in the shift in policy that ensured Tito's was the dominant Yugoslav voice in negotiations regarding postwar Yugoslavia. Outsiders began to reject the Serbs' blanket attack on Croats not because they did not believe that the Serbs had suffered but because the Serbs' accusations were sweeping, because they overstated their case, because they had ulterior motives and because it was impolitic to focus at that point on just one collaborationist group. Most importantly, their attitude would not help to win the war or resolve the national question. Outsiders recognized Tito's as the most effective anti-fascist force. For this reason he was more appealing to them than the Serbian old guard and they believed his stance in the war (if not his communist project for the country's future) was more representative of Croatian opinion than was Pavelić's.[135] The most important task for the 'Big United Nations' was 'to achieve and maintain postwar unity' in Yugoslavia.[136] The history people brought to the war, the way the war was fought, the rise of Tito and the Partisans, the dominance of the Soviet Union in the 'liberation' of Hitler's Europe, the place of Yugoslavia in the postwar world and the spectre of a divided Europe after 1945: all of these factors affected the way the country made the transition to peace. A new set of variables applied in international attitudes towards the state, but these could never dispel all the old myths and the view of Yugoslavia as a necessity was stronger than ever. Whereas after the First World War the state was the prize for 'tribes' seeking 're-unification', in 1945 it was seen as the means of containing violence and extreme behaviours which, in fact, the 'prize' had spawned. This paradox was not in the forefront of the international negotiators' minds. As the extent of the human catastrophe of the war and genocide began to sink in, the Yugoslavs' fate was not a priority. Nonetheless, if there was not the same naïve idealism we observed after 1918, there was a sense of hope that the future would be better if for no other reason than it could not really get much worse.

5 'A society almost free': Tito's Yugoslavia

In Tito's Yugoslavia the government's main challenge was containing the difference between the rhetoric of the state's *raison d'être* and the Yugoslav ideal, and the reality of the people's lived experience. In this sense, the second Yugoslavia strongly resembled the first. This chapter brings together a number of the strands of our story. We will observe some continuities in perceptions of the first and second Yugoslavia and the general outside acceptance of the mechanics of government. There was also continuity in the role of Yugoslavia in international politics, as alliances largely remained intact through from one world war to another. The parallels between King Aleksandar and Tito, notably their standing resulting from their involvement in wartime struggles and victories, are also significant. Transgressions such as abandoning or withholding democratic rights did not diminish their reputations. Outsiders continued to rationalize that Yugoslav democracy was dispensable. The context of the Cold War made the partition of Europe seem permanent and was not conducive to deep reflection on the future of its unfree citizens. It was not entirely satisfactory that the 'necessary' Yugoslav state was also a communist dictatorship, but justifying it came easily enough in the wake of total war.

There was an even greater concord between the internal forces for order and outside supporters of the Yugoslav state after 1945 than there had been in 1918. Paradoxically, that convergence weakened the state, and the greater the outsiders' commitment to strengthening Yugoslavia the greater the divergence between what it claimed to do and what it achieved. Over time it became clear that Tito would be no more successful than Aleksandar at effecting a Yugoslav synthesis. Notionally the intention was to strengthen the whole 'Yugoslav nation' by promoting diversity and ensuring all nationalities were respected equally through 'the federative idea'; but the lack of basic freedoms and continuing domination from the centre made this goal impossible to realize. In fact there were surprisingly few self-identifying Yugoslavs. In 1978, two years before Tito died, one American commentator wrote: 'the "melting pot" may work in the New World but it does not function in Yugoslavia'. He added that to many it would 'seem strange' that there were 'practically no Yugoslavs' in Yugoslavia, only 273,000 out of a population of 20.5 million, according to the 1971 census.[1]

The temptation is strong to explain Yugoslavia's history in a teleological fashion, as if the inherent difficulties faced by both the Kingdom and communist Yugoslavia doomed them to failure. As I have already suggested, many of Yugoslavia's chroniclers in the 1990s sought to explain its collapse from the perspective of the state's 'fatal flaws'. There are some moments in the history of Yugoslavia since 1945 that, retrospectively, seem to indicate its fall was inevitable. However, prior to the years when the reform movement in the Soviet Union gained momentum, there was nothing to suggest that the international community would have tolerated Yugoslavia's fragmentation or that the centrifugal republican forces had the will or capacity to effect any irreversible changes. What had weakened the country in the period 1920–41 would weaken it again after 1945. Its main problems included the failure to take full account of the state's inherent political and national contradictions, its hypocrisy and its elites' abuse of power. These concerns were not mere 'teething problems' or 'bourgeois distractions' but fundamental to people's well-being on a daily basis and to their sense of attachment to the state and its administrative structures. The dogged belief, inside and out and against all evidence to the contrary, that the communist dictatorship marked the end of Serb hegemony and that all would be well as a result did not allow for a critical evaluation of the past or the present.

An enormous array of books on Tito's Yugoslavia provides information on the political, economic and diplomatic history of the period and it would be pointless to duplicate that body of work here. So, in a sense, our travels through the communist state will be impressionistic, mirroring contemporaneous responses to its development.

This will help us understand why the problems that seem so obvious to us in retrospect were not obvious to post-1945 commentators or to their intellectual heirs in the 1980s and 1990s. Tito was perceived to be the only person who had been able to defuse nationalist tensions in Yugoslavia and impose a more equitable federal structure after 1945. He would win the propaganda war on several fronts as workers' self-management and then market socialism heralded a new communist reality. Yugoslav communism, or Titoism, promised citizens a third way between the ravages of the *laissez-faire* economy and Soviet-style state capitalism. Workers in Yugoslavia would be managing themselves and managing their enterprises, thus creating more humane social relationships. It was very affirming after the destruction of the Second World War and in a 'bipolar' Europe. Further, Yugoslavia came to assume the reputation of a one-party communist dictatorship that was more liberal than other European communist states without being aligned either to the West or to the East. All of this was to occur under the paternal gaze of Tito, a man whose capacity to attract positive international attention was unparalleled among communists at the time. To understand the aura that surrounded Tito we must revisit the early postwar years and take stock of the atmosphere in a truncated continent emerging self-consciously from the ravages of total war and the anti-fascist struggle.

Yugoslavia in the Shadow of European Fascism

When the Federal People's Republic of Yugoslavia was established in 1945 it appeared as if another South Slav revolution had taken place, one that would bring the ideal of a coherent and cohesive Yugoslav identity closer to realization. The new state constituted six socialist republics (Croatia, Bosnia-Herzegovina, Macedonia, Montenegro, Serbia and Slovenia) and two autonomous provinces (Vojvodina and Kosovo-Metohija). Internationally, Yugoslavia had few serious detractors and much support. The military struggle against fascism may have come to an end but the political struggle was far from over, wrote Stoyan Pribićević, son of the interwar Serbian politician Svetozar Pribićević.[2] Yugoslavia was not totalitarian, not even 'Tito-talitarian'. But all the fascists had not disappeared, and for the Central European and Balkan 'antifascist democracies' the battle continued.[3] For them and many other Europeans, fascism was the greatest evil of the century and, as such, it was necessary to ensure that its defeat was comprehensive. Pribićević wrote of the 'explosion' of Yugoslavia onto the international scene after 1945, not as something caused by the communists but as 'an inexorable, spontaneous process'. People had flocked to the Partisans because they were rejecting the old parties and cliques. Some of the pre-war politicians had not been tainted by collaboration, but none was strong enough to do what the Partisans had done.[4] Most importantly, this revolution would not prove to be 'a mask for Serbian predominance' because the 'unitarianism' of the new state was based 'on the unity of "working people"'.[5]

In the late 1940s, as it became clear that Tito would not permit Yugoslavia to be governed from Moscow, Frank Gervasi reported in *The New Republic* that it was the country's 'war-born homogeneity' that would give him the power he needed in his battle against the Kremlin.[6] Tito would prove more independent than leaders in the satellite states because, as the *Contemporary Review* noted, nowhere else was there a 'genuine revolt of a Communist proletariat or a natural revolution of any kind as there unquestionably was in Yugoslavia'.[7] Significantly, and in contradistinction to the Soviet Union's 1936 constitution, on which the 1946 Yugoslav constitution was in effect modelled, there was to be no 'leading nation' in the new Yugoslavia. All the rhetoric emphasized emphatically the equality of the constituent nationalities and the rights of minorities in the federation. Pribićević was not alone when he spoke of the 'Federalist Revolution': federalism would be the cornerstone of the new democracy.[8] How this would sit with the notion of 'war-born homogeneity' and the Yugoslav revolution, however, remained an unresolved problem, as it had done after 1918.

In this final chapter, the outside observers seem more responsive or reactive to the internal machinations of Yugoslav politics than their predecessors. There was also eventually a greater sense of stability deriving from the acceptance of what seemed to be the permanent division of Europe and the belief that Yugoslavia was better off than countries in the Soviet sphere. External support still remained essential for the state's survival and development. After the break with Stalin in 1948, Yugoslavia's continued existence depended upon aid received from the West. The projection of Tito as the personification of Yugoslavia saw the transition of the notion of 'Yugoslavia as necessity' into 'Tito as necessity', understandable at the time but detrimental in the long run. It led, again, to the identification of the Yugoslav ideal buttressed by a 'strong man' and dictatorship, as had been the case in the Kingdom under Aleksandar. The foundational narrative of the second Yugoslavia was as important and influential as that of the first and equally confusing, as war memories, layered one on top of the other, legitimized a regime whose surfeit of legends and constant diet of hyperbole would dull the critical faculties of most onlookers.

Tito was a leading light in the early meetings of communists from Central and Eastern Europe. This was the background to reports from visitors to Yugoslavia in the late 1940s. The state was 'omniscient and omnipotent' and people were glad to be able to leave it once their work was done, but the repression was acceptable to the Yugoslavs who had 'never known freedom'.[9] An optimistic tone also characterized bulletins on Yugoslavia at this time. A nation, reborn, was 'emerging from a wilderness'.[10] After travelling to Belgrade and interviewing Tito in 1948, George Bilainkin (1903–81), who had been a correspondent in Prague, Belgrade and the Soviet Union, wrote in the *Contemporary Review*: 'The vivacity of the young people of new Yugoslavia at work, at play, in the streets, has to be seen to be credited. ... There is among them no trace of Spenglerism or even Toynbeeism, and their leader remains Tito.'[11] Bilainkin expressed some concerns over Mihailović's execution but also accepted that things could not have proceeded any differently. After his first postwar visit to the country in 1946, Bilainkin noted that the Yugoslavs had never enjoyed living under a democracy, implying that they could not be expected to miss what they had never known. High-ranking Yugoslavs had assured Bilainkin of this. In any case, the 'test of the new regime' would be its economic rather than its political policies, because the latter had less of an impact on 'the Yugoslav peoples, who have rarely if ever known political freedom in the way we conceive it'. The secret to success would be to keep the 'degree of compulsion...to a minimum'.[12] Less piously, Gervasi had noted that there was a 'democratic, equable [*sic*] distribution of misery'.[13]

The nature of the war and its outcome shaped outsiders' attitudes towards Yugoslavia, as was the case in 1918. The split between those who thought Mihailović rather than Tito should have been the preferred leader of the Yugoslav resistance and the recipient of Allied aid divided Yugoslavists as they had not been divided after the First World War, but the impact of this division was not felt for some time. Mihailović's champions, of whom there were many on both sides of the Atlantic, included anti-communist First World War veterans. For them Yugoslavia and Greater Serbia remained interchangeable. Fotich, former Yugoslav Ambassador to the United States, mentioned above in Chapter 4, wrote in 1952 that Tito, 'drunk with his own propaganda' and full of 'the idea of his own importance', behaved rather like a Byzantine emperor. This was in marked contrast to the 'great popular Serbian leader', Mihailović, whom Fotich had defended vigorously during the war and at the time of his capture by the communists.[14] According to his critics, Tito behaved as if he had had no help from the Soviets; indeed he had duped Yugoslavs into thinking he would be their best protection from them. For Serb nationalists and royalists like Fotich, Tito never would (and never could) represent Serbian interests 'as one of our own', even when he broke with the traitorous Soviets who had distorted the true nature of Russia and attacked its Church.[15] Members of the Titoist camp would not tolerate this position. Titoists included a range of new outside voices, including Maclean and Deakin, who had observed Tito and the Partisans first-hand and who had been instrumental in promoting them when it was obvious that the government-in-exile and the Chetniks were no longer dependable. This personal connection was significant. Deakin and Maclean would write about their wartime experiences.[16] Deakin, as the first president of the new Oxford College, St Antony's, a graduate college dedicated especially to the social sciences and international relations, and Maclean, in the House of Commons, continued to influence a generation of students and politicians on attitudes and policy towards Yugoslavia. At the time of Mihailović's trial, Maclean spoke out publicly against those concerned by international 'abandonment' of the Serb leader, explaining precisely why the Allies had stopped assisting the Chetniks.[17] After the war Maclean remained close to Tito, often visiting Yugoslavia and sojourning in a villa on the picturesque Croatian island of Korčula.

The United States and the Soviet Union were more powerful than Britain after 1945. British academics were still shaping the intellectual landscape on subjects concerning Yugoslavia but their American counterparts were now playing a similar role to that of men like Seton-Watson in the first half of the century. The lines between the work of advisers on foreign policy and American academics specializing in Yugoslav studies were often blurred. For example, Hamilton Fish Armstrong, a Princeton graduate whose work we have encountered above, became the editor of *Foreign Affairs* in 1922 and remained in this position until 1972. Under his direction the journal's reputation and influence extended beyond the confines of academia.

Recipient of two Serbian decorations (in 1918 and 1919), Armstrong had visited Aleksandar, whose dictatorship he would defend. The Yugoslav king, wrote Armstrong, 'reared on principles of individual and national freedom', had 'nothing in common with dictatorial demagogues of postwar Europe who grimace or shriek'. According to Armstrong, Aleksandar's only choice was to bring an end to the period of 'dangerous uncertainty' with 'necessary reorganisation'.[18] That regard for Balkan strongmen remained an undercurrent in his later appraisal of Tito. (His book, *Tito and Goliath*, was published in 1951.) Armstrong had a lifelong interest in American foreign policy and in Yugoslavia. He had been attached to the State Department during the Second World War and served on the Council on Foreign Relations for much of his working life. He managed several Serbian and Yugoslav philanthropic organizations and corresponded with and published articles by prominent 'Yugoslavists'. The example of Armstrong illustrates well the overlap between 'process' and 'policy' in the work of Yugoslav experts in the United States after 1945. Both the Soviet Union and the United States provided Yugoslavia with the material and moral support it needed at different times, but American money sustained communist Yugoslavia. Tito was not always ready to admit to this dependence on the capitalist West.

The formation of a 'breakaway' British-based Yugoslav association, the Emergency Yugoslav Committee, symbolized the division between Yugoslavists that emerged during the war. Some of the founders of the original Yugoslav Association, including Seton-Watson, threw in their lot with the new generation, the Titoists. No longer was it possible for an association like the Serbian Relief Fund to be seen to stand for a commitment to all South Slavs and the Yugoslav ideal, as it had done in the First World War. Like many academics of standing, Seton-Watson had been involved in various aspects of intelligence work which, in his case, and to his chagrin, according to his sons, amounted to little more than compiling reports, a task he found dull and frustrating. It was entirely different from the influence he exerted in the First World War and in the interwar years. His sons suggested this was because in the first decades of the century, as policy towards Central and south-eastern Europe was in its infancy, experts like their father wielded confident authority in policy formation.[19] Interestingly, in the United States groups like the Serbian National Federation and the Serbian National Defense Council were active during the war and, like the Serbian Relief Fund in the First World War, presented themselves as the voice of Yugoslavia, indicating that the problems of the South Slav racial synthesis remained unresolved in some quarters.[20] For their part, Yugoslavia's leaders were conscious of the new balance of power. They came to recognize that their independence relied upon the goodwill of the arbiters of the new international order and did not want to be seen to be overly reliant on either of the 'blocs'.

External Yugoslav experts, trained by the generation of international historians who had been actively engaged in the events they discussed, remained unshakeable on key questions about the state and its leadership. First, the territorial integrity and 'necessity' of Yugoslavia were more important than ever, given the perceptions of the imperialistic inclinations of the Soviet Union. Second, Tito was deserving of his place as head of a one-party dictatorship. He was deemed deserving because he had fought the enemy single-mindedly, because he oversaw the emergence of a new Yugoslavia, because he respected and maintained the peace and because he seemed to have support from the people. All of this resembled closely the reasons for the easy ascendancy of the Karađorđevićs in the Kingdom after 1918, the belief in the triumph of the 'revolutionary synthesis' and the continuing support for Aleksandar after he proclaimed the dictatorship in 1929. There was one significant departure: most believed that Tito would not be the head of a Serbian-dominated clique. The Yugoslav specialists, working in fields ranging from sociology, the political sciences and diplomatic history to economics and industrial relations, established elaborate formulas explaining why the innovative 'socialist reality' Tito had introduced in Yugoslavia would eventually transform the country. However, as it was with the interwar generation of outside observers, the new men largely skirted around the issue of the absence of civic freedoms and the abuse of human rights. They were also fixated on the national question. There was cause for optimism, therefore, as the Montenegrins, Macedonians, Albanians and Muslims enjoyed national recognition regardless of the fact that their desire for self-actualization in the communist state created resentments elsewhere, especially in the Serbian republic.

It had not gone completely unnoticed that the wartime propaganda promised something entirely different from a communist revolution. The Partisans had not preached 'the pure doctrine of Marx' and they had won 'half their political battles in Eastern Europe' by maintaining their support for 'all the ideals of national emancipation and liberal parliamentary democracy'.[21] Apparently when asked whether he had some concerns regarding the possibility of a communist takeover in Yugoslavia, Churchill had responded that as he would not be living there, he had none. The primary concern was winning the war and fostering harmonious relations between Yugoslavs to that end. In spite of all the destruction and suffering during the war and in its aftermath, 'Brotherhood and Unity', the slogan of the regime, appeared to have greater general application than ever before. The belief that Tito alone was capable of keeping a lid on the national tensions prevailed. Joseph Frankel (1913–89), lecturer at the University of Aberdeen and later Professor of Politics at the University of Southampton, published widely on international affairs and foreign policy. In 1954 he noted that the First World War had not forged the same bonds as the war of National Liberation, the 'crucible in which real Yugoslav unity was formed'. Ex-Partisans in the prime of their lives formed an elite and veterans' organizations, together with the party and the army, represented 'powerful cementing factors'.[22]

There would be casualties in the new state-building exercise in the period of intense communist socialization in the early post-war period. For example, some remarked that the peasants would bear the greatest costs of the social transformation. The West and Marxists, one 1948 article averred, despised peasants – 'ignorant and reactionary, and incapable of thinking freely' – and thus did not hesitate to exploit them. The new system was a retrograde step for those peasants who had 'known better' than what was offered to them. Self-determination and self-government were appropriately broached in discussions on the future of 'Asiatic peoples' but not, it seemed, for the peasant of Danubian Europe: 'whole countries' had been 'written off from the community of nations and pushed behind an iron curtain'. The highly organized and democratic peasant movements and parties of interwar Europe had been erased from memory. The author of this article predicted (correctly) that collectivization would not work if there were no distinction between the range of peasant traditions across the region. The richness of the sociability contained within communal and economic life was one of the defining characteristics of rural culture and politics. The communists did not understand this. For them it was simply a question of land redistribution or erasing distinctions between the better and worse off, and they did not realize that there was a cohesion and independence to peasant culture that would resist strategies or policies that treated them as one and unvariegated.[23] Melissa Bokovoy has argued that peasant resistance to agrarian policy in the period of communist implantation in Tito's Yugoslavia was so effective that it led to a retreat and change in direction. She has suggested that it was here, in the countryside, where they believed they had already won their definitive political victory during the war, that the communists experienced the first of their major political setbacks. It would prove difficult, if not impossible, for them to gain the upper hand in this sphere again.[24]

Double standards, so evident to us now in the ruminations of our interwar observers of Yugoslav affairs, also underscored post-1945 perceptions of the state's political foundations. According to *The Times*, the success of Tito's National Front candidates in the elections for the Federal Parliament in 1945 was a 'foregone conclusion'. There were no opposition candidates and there were no ballot papers. There were voting balls and two boxes at each booth. Voters could endorse the official candidates by dropping the ball in one box or they could choose not to endorse them by dropping the ball in the second box. Voters put their hands in both boxes and as the balls dropped noiselessly out of their hands there was allegedly a degree of secrecy to the procedure. Yet this elaborate charade was peripheral because 'the issue is not between parties in the usual sense of the word. It is not even between Communists and non-Communists. It is a clear-cut fight between the old and the new.' There were considerable disincentives to vote against the National Front candidates. But at the same time the article noted the 'regime is highly sensitive to the suggestion that the elections will be rigged'. The authorities, from 'Marshal Tito downwards', insisted that their 'notion of democracy is genuine, even if not of the Westminster variety, in that they stand for social and economic equality among the peoples of Yugoslavia'.[25] The election had proven a 'festive occasion', as one report on voting day in a Macedonian village attested: 'The polling booths this morning were decked with flowers and bunting. Amusing scenes occurred when old women, whose ideas of sex equality are of the haziest, came in to vote for the first time in their lives.' In one booth 70 miles from Belgrade, the village committee was up all night checking the rubber voting balls. However, the *Times* correspondent was cautious, noting that although it seemed everything had been carried out 'in complete order and without intimidation', it 'should be added that, in the eyes of the partisans and their supporters, the election is the seal of their victory, and very great moral pressure exists therefore on the electorate to vote for their candidates'.[26] These were typical of the observations in early reporting on Tito's Yugoslavia.

The Balkanist paradigm was exploited by the communists themselves as they justified their monopoly over the decision-making processes. Where the Balkanist perception of the 'backward' Slavs originally played into the hands of outsiders who either overlooked or justified the unjustifiable, it became a convenient device for Yugoslav leaders. We recall that Aleksandar had 'no choice' but to silence the rowdy separatists-cum-terrorists. For his part, Tito had to take 'firm control' in order to bring all of Yugoslavia into the twentieth century through modernization and thereby put an end to nationalist-inspired violence with economic progress. The constant references to Yugoslavia's underdevelopment, followed by paternalistic remarks on the good (but not excellent) rate of progress, reflected well on the communists, who approached the problem of ruling 'realistically'. Tito had embraced the idea of Yugoslavia's backwardness, noting that the path ahead was long and difficult. There would have to be heavy sacrifices for the rewards to be rich. Socialism could not be achieved overnight; success could not be measured objectively in terms of Western progress and civil liberties, for these were as unevenly distributed in bourgeois societies as they were in socialist societies. As long as they were on the correct path, the end would justify the means. Discussions on 'Yugoslavia and the West' noted that the Yugoslavs understood that they had 'not yet resolved the problem of freedom'. What was most important from the West's perspective was that Tito's communism, which he would never give up, was not for export.[27] Dr Vladimir Velebit, a former Partisan, confidant of Maclean and one of the early postwar ambassadors to the United Kingdom, wrote that democracy was a word used loosely, often interpreted in 'contradictory ways' and with widely divergent meanings. Yugoslavs, he continued, did not reject 'entirely' the liberal conception of democracy, but the only people against his countrymen's 'democratic dictatorship' were 'the dispossessed remnants of the Yugoslav bourgeoisie' who wanted 'to restore their rule and the financial privileges they have lost'. The 'element of compulsion' would diminish as the resistance from 'reactionary forces' diminished.[28]

As one of the acclaimed European champions of the anti-fascist struggle, and the architect of the liberation and reconstruction of Yugoslavia, Tito was larger than life. First a favourite of the Soviets and then the great hope of the West, both American capitalists and, eventually, Europe's New Left, he was able to draw on the prestige he had accumulated as the leader of what was generally described as a successful and militarily daring resistance movement. This was indisputably the case, regardless of what his Soviet critics were going to say about Yugoslav resistance after the split. Bilainkin, who had met Tito on at least four occasions, wrote in 1948 that for the great war leader the transition from soldier to statesman was smooth because of his 'magnificent' story of resistance, which would 'surely live in the annals of warfare'. The Partisans' work covered all manner of activities, from printing bulletins to making bullets, and Tito was not above the most prosaic of tasks. He had drive and, touchingly, an 'inordinate tenderness toward Tiger, his big Alsatian at my feet'.[29] According to one representative 1951 observation, Tito enjoyed a high regard because he fought in the war. Most of the other European communist leaders had been in Moscow and re-entered their countries 'through the back door' and 'in the rear of the Soviet Army without whose help they would have been unable to return'. It was for this reason that there was no danger of Titoism spreading westwards. Tito was unique because his 'fighting past', combined with the party discipline, 'steeled in the trenches', and his 'justifiable pride' enabled him to tower over others who had simply urged their compatriots to fight from afar 'from comfortable radio studios'.[30] Knowing how he was perceived and confident in his authority, Tito could map out an independent path for Yugoslav socialism.

Tito Turns His Back on Stalin: The 'Battle of the Marshals'[31]

Tito's break with Stalin would mar for a time his reputation among fellow-travellers in the Soviet sphere and Western Stalinists, but it marked a high point in his popularity in Yugoslavia and among non-communists in the West. At the time of the split many Yugoslavs feared a Soviet invasion and believed that in the event of such an invasion only Tito could protect the country. Tito did not exactly strike down 'Goliath', but stood up to him. Communists in the East and West saw Tito as a traitor and heretic until such time as they, too, found themselves at odds with Stalinism or its heirs. After differences with the Soviet Union led to its expulsion from the Cominform in 1948, Yugoslavia's reputation soared as the country that had chosen a more moderate and acceptable brand of communism: it had chosen 'the Yugoslav way'.

Yugoslavia was expelled from the Cominform, ostensibly for its deviation from Marxist-Leninist orthodoxy, but in fact because Stalin could not control Tito. Stalin feared that Tito would prove a negative influence on other communist leaders and decided to make an example of him, but his gesture backfired. No one in the Soviet sphere of influence had the capacity to do what Tito did in 1948. This was partly because Tito had no powerful wartime rivals. The resistance struggle was planned and waged by Tito and his followers, seemingly without much guidance or support from Moscow until late in the piece, that is at the time of the liberation of Belgrade in October 1944. Moreover, there were no prominent Yugoslavs in Moscow and no Yugoslav Moscow-trained agents to install once the war was over.[32] That did not stop critics of the regime from describing Tito and the Yugoslav leadership as Moscow's lackeys and accusing the former Partisans of claiming Chetnik victories as their own. The Yugoslavs' pride in their achievements in the war also led Stalin to criticize them. The Soviet leader noted that one of the Yugoslavs' chief errors was their overestimation of their own prowess in the war and their undervaluing of the assistance afforded by the Soviet Union in their liberation. The Yugoslav Partisans, said Stalin, 'certainly do not suffer from modesty [and they] have deafened everyone by their exaggerated boastfulness'.[33] (Interestingly, this did not differ greatly from what the anti-communist Serb, Fotich, had had to say about Tito.) Provocative acts on the Soviets' part included a period of name-calling. Tito was variously a bandit, traitor, greedy ape, chattering parrot, deserter, coward, comedian and insolent dwarf. For its part Belgrade spoke of the Russian octopus and one of Tito's closest comrades in the war, Moša Pijade, concluded simply that Moscow had 'ceased to be guided by the principles of international communism'.[34] There was also a fear of invasion, and the concentration of Soviet troops on Yugoslavia's borders with Hungary, Romania and Bulgaria led to many incidents between 1948 and 1950. The following (1950) observation succinctly makes a point that many others made: it was unlikely the Soviets would invade Yugoslavia because they realized Tito was a force to be reckoned with and because the West would not likely tolerate the Red Army advancing as far as the shores of the Adriatic, where it had 'never yet set foot'.[35] (Similarly, in the nineteenth century no one had wanted the Russians to move too far westwards and make the eastern Mediterranean 'a Russian lake'.[36]) Still many within and without feared that Stalin would not endure Tito's spirited refusal to conform.

A degree of intensity and earnestness characterized the debates regarding the ideology and practice of Marxism that came in the wake of the Tito–Stalin split. Tito and Yugoslavia were inspirational for some, renegades for others. In 1951 communists in Paris shunned the Polish émigré Czesław Miłosz (1911–2004) on the publication of his indictment of Stalinism, *The Captive Mind*. Similarly, hardline Western Stalinists had no time for Titoist deviationism and most communists (apart from some Italians) distanced themselves from the Yugoslav leader. In the immediate aftermath of the expulsion, Tito experienced almost complete isolation.[37] This had serious economic consequences. The Soviets stopped sending aid and sought to cut Yugoslavia off from potential trading partners in the East through the Council for Mutual Economic Assistance (Comecon) established in January 1949. In other quarters there was a seismic shift in perception when Tito began to criticize the Soviet Union: his was a heroic and courageous stance. Banac notes that many believed (wrongly) that the critique of Stalin and the Soviets indicated that Yugoslav communism leaned naturally towards pluralism, a diluted and transient version of which was really only an unintentional consequence of the 'search for a new ideology' after 1948.[38]

Overall, there was not much philosophical difference between the Partisans as a group before and after the split with Stalin or between the tactics of Tito and those of Stalin. Just under 5000 Yugoslav communists who remained loyal to the Soviet Union, so-called Cominformists, emigrated. Banac tells us they had not formed a movement and as such there was minimal political disruption.[39] There were disproportionately more Montenegrin and Serbian Cominformists but there is no profile of a typical Cominformist. Different factors came into play for different individuals from different republics including, for Serbs, the Chetnik background of some Cominformists. The Croatian communist Andrija Hebrang, who had been out of favour since the war years on account of his alleged Croatian nationalist proclivities, was accused of treachery for supporting the Soviets. He was incarcerated and died under suspicious circumstances while in prison. However, other Croats were 'loyal' because of the fear of Soviet encroachments (or invasion) and the belief that 'Titoist centralism' would preserve Croatian identity and better serve their interests, regardless of the fact that Belgrade remained the capital.[40] The actions of the State Security Administration (*Uprava državne bezbednosti*, UDBa) or secret police, under the Serb Aleksandar Ranković (1909–83), led to at least

16,000 (mostly arbitrary) arrests of party members and the incarceration, psychological harassment and political 're-education' of 2572 people in various camps across the country, the most brutal of which was on the island of Goli Otok. Thousands more were arrested or under surveillance.[41]

There was a certain audacity in the Yugoslavs' stance against the Soviets and they were made to suffer for it in the short term, when they lost much needed Soviet financial assistance. Possibly the long-term effect of the split was the slow erosion of the fabric of communist hegemony in Yugoslavia and the rise of alternative and mutually exclusive tales of wartime resistance and commitment to postwar communist reconstruction, as depicted in the films of Emir Kusturica, for example.[42] In any case, Moscow misjudged the situation, believing the potential for rallying Yugoslav fifth columnists against Tito to be greater than it was. It could be argued that Tito's refusal to submit to Stalin politicized more people than had the war itself, convincing them of their need for strong leadership. This was the high point of Yugoslav unity. There had never been such unanimous support for the Yugoslav state. However, if this was Yugoslavia's moment, it was going to be relatively short-lived, given it was largely a product of the threat and fear of invasion so soon after the devastation of the Second World War.

Milovan Djilas (1911–95), minister without portfolio, who was later to turn against his fellow Yugoslav communists with his critique of the 'new class' of oppressors, was in the front line of the attack on Stalin, whom he, like Tito, had formerly revered. One of the leading four communists in postwar Yugoslavia, Djilas was scathing in his critique of Stalinist corruption and bureaucratization. He was one of the architects of Yugoslavia's new communism, predicated on the need to forge a more 'democratic' and less hierarchical future for its peoples. Speaking in London in 1951 on Yugoslavia's expulsion from the Cominform, Djilas observed it was not 'a Communist family squabble'. What was at stake was 'the struggle of a nation for its independence and free internal development, in opposition to those who long ago abandoned both Communism and democracy'.[43]

For some outsiders, in this 'red dog fight' the real enemy was not communism but Soviet imperialism. And this was why many, including Dean Acheson, American Secretary of State (1949–53), favoured a 'no strings policy of aid' to the Yugoslavs. There was much to admire in Tito's regime. It respected private property, it was anti-imperialist and it aimed for 'social democracy'. According to *The New Republic*, by coming to the rescue of the Yugoslavs the message Americans would be sending to the Soviets was that they believed a strong Yugoslavia would thwart Soviet aggression.[44] While he was, admittedly, 'an offspring of Stalinism', Tito was redeemable, the *Nineteenth Century and After* suggested, because he was a 'patriot' and not imperialistic. Thus his 'inborn Yugoslav patriotism' survived Russification (but not Stalinization) when he was in Moscow at the time of the purges. Tito's independence infuriated his mentors and led them to denounce him as one who had already sold out to the British and the United States during the war.[45]

Djilas, during his address in London, revisited the question of the Yugoslavs' liberation, noting that if they had been as dependent on the Soviets as the latter claimed, then the Yugoslav communists would not have been able to hold the country together when the Russians set out to undermine them. Soviet foreign policy, he continued, was but an extension of its internal policy: repressive, exploitative, imperialistic and non-democratic.[46] To outsiders Yugoslav communists seemed to have the capacity to distance themselves from the Soviets and to avoid the communist superpower's 'errors'. Wartime rhetoric about the future Yugoslav state often noted that Tito sought to avoid the mistakes of interwar Yugoslavia. The image of him attempting to avoid those of the Soviet Union struck a chord as well. Interestingly, the 'error' of Serbian hegemony persisted in all of the key institutions of state, most obviously the army, as did the recourse to political control through authoritarian centralism and dictatorship.

Some have argued, then and since, that there was nothing particularly ideological about the Tito–Stalin confrontation, that it was based on divergent interests and that ideology for Tito came into play only after the event, to justify it retrospectively. Titoism, in this context, was not a political philosophy but the product of political pragmatism and historical circumstances.[47] According to this reasoning, Tito was more reactive than ideologically precocious or original. His responses to international events were primarily motivated by the desire to boost the country's (and thereby his own) prestige rather than to forge innovative socialist pathways for the Yugoslav peoples. The only way he could aggrandize himself was by refusing to succumb to Stalin's threats. The fact remains that his refusal to succumb in those early years, an achievement in itself, reflected an independent strain unique among European communists at the time. Whether his belief in a 'special' Yugoslav socialism or Titoism was a cause or consequence of the split is of little import to our argument. There had been ample evidence of Tito's defiance before 1948. During the war he had been less malleable than the Soviets would have liked and disregarded their directives on a number of occasions. Tito's response to the Greek Civil War (1946–9) alienated him from the Soviets, who did not want to antagonize their former allies so soon after the war by supporting the Greek communists.[48] The Soviets were further irritated by Yugoslavia's attitude on the question of Trieste, a territorial dispute with Italy which was not settled until 1957, well after Stalin's death. Stalin was also concerned that the close relations between Yugoslavia and Bulgaria would result in a rival centre of power in the form of a renewed Balkan Federation. Generally, retrospective criticisms of Tito do not take into account the atmosphere of hostility in which he acted and the attendant risks. Stalin was vexed by the Tito's stand and there could be no reconciliation between the Soviet Union and Yugoslavia while Stalin was alive.

Yugoslavia's supporters spanned the political spectrum, as the country retained its strong identification with progressivism and anti-Stalinism. While in these early postwar years there was not much to separate Tito from Stalin, in terms of both ideology and methods, the Yugoslav leader nevertheless came to be seen not simply as the acceptable face of the postwar communist ascendancy but as an adaptable theorist. Belgrade rivalled Moscow as 'the Mecca' for the West's Left, as one 1957 account noted.[49] Tito had silenced potential and actual opponents in preparation for the task of rebuilding the country after the devastation of the war. The fact that half of Europe seemed to be controlled by Moscow generated fear among Yugoslavs and Western Europeans and an ongoing commitment to containing, if not toppling, Soviet imperialism. A strong, nonaligned Yugoslav state became a central component of the West's strategy for the duration of the Cold War. The basic calculation of outsiders, Americans included, was that an independent communist Yugoslavia was preferable to a Kremlin-dominated Yugoslavia. This understanding of the strategic significance of the country was also informed by perceptions of the changing relations between the Soviet Union and Yugoslavia with the result that once the former disappeared, there would be less direct interest in the latter.

The New Communism: Ideology in Action

After the split Yugoslavia seemed also to be turning away from Soviet-style government and propaganda. The failed experiments with collectivization and the economic difficulties associated with the attempts at forging a new social (communist) reality led to a certain ideological relaxation or redirection. In contrast to the 1946 constitution, that of 1953 departed from the Soviet model and Yugoslavia emerged stronger from the Eastern bloc isolation imposed after 1948. The principles of Titoism were self-management, federalism and non-alignment.[50] Features of the new socialism, as espoused by the Yugoslavs, included a strong emphasis on decentralization, some degree of workers' autonomy in decision-making in local enterprises and accommodations with elements of the market economy. Tito's claim that he would embrace an 'enlightened' communism attracted praise from outsiders. The Western love affair with Yugoslavia continued and intensified as revelations about the horrors of Stalinism made it difficult for all but the most fanatical of Europe's Left to idealize the Soviet Union and favour it over Yugoslavia.

When the Communist Party of Yugoslavia was renamed the League of Communists of Yugoslavia at the Sixth Congress of the Communist Party in November 1952, some asked whether the new label marked a cosmetic change or indicated that Yugoslavia was reconfiguring traditional communist structures. From literature on Yugoslavia dating from the 1950s we can note that postwar optimism was founded on the belief that Yugoslavia, in its ideal sense, was coming closer to fruition and that its leadership was learning from past mistakes. The lesson gleaned from recent history was that the essential factor underlying the Kingdom's crises and its collapse in 1941 was not dictatorship but national inequality: the regime would founder and fail if it did not take enough care to eliminate inequalities among its peoples. It was a delicate balance. Decentralization was potentially good for local democracy but, if the centre gave up its various controls, there could be a loss of direction, with progress impeded.

Yugoslav communism generated considerable academic interest across many disciplines. Leading Yugoslavs took the opportunity to publish in English, as had various individuals in the interwar years. Velebit, for example, wrote in 1954 that an undue focus on 'so-called civic rights' and 'individual freedom', topics so engaging to the West, obscured the great progress that had been made already.

Critics would do better to note that while there was still much to do, Yugoslavs were continuing 'to advance on their way to a classless society'. It was not the 'so-called civic rights', but the economic freedoms, the freedom to work and maintain one's family, that were the true 'test of democracy'.[51] Fred Warner Neal (1915–96), an American academic and commentator on Yugoslav affairs, contributed to this discussion. Neal had spent time as Chief of Foreign Research on Eastern Europe for the Department of State. He was sometimes affectionately referred to as 'Fred the Red' because of his constancy towards Yugoslavia even when its relations with the United States were strained. In 1987 he was the recipient of one of Yugoslavia's highest honours, the Decoration of the Yugoslav Flag with Golden Wreath.[52] Neal wrote in 1957 that the Yugoslav communists identified and avoided the worst evil, bureaucratism. Workers' councils in particular would counter bureaucratism.[53] Evaluations of political life under dictatorships were too simplistic, explained the high-ranking former Partisan, Edvard Kardelj, in an article in *Foreign Affairs* in 1956. Dictatorships could be reactionary or progressive, while democracies could undermine freedom. By focusing on individuals (rather than the state), the regime would foster new democratic forms of social life. It was fatuous, he continued, to differentiate between one-party and multi-party systems, as if the former were by default less democratic than the latter: Yugoslavs were heading towards a 'non-party Socialist democracy'.[54] Tito had said in his report to the National Assembly in 1950 that

the transfer of factories and mines...to management by workers' collectives will prevent the infectious disease known as bureaucracy becoming endemic in our economy. This disease is carried with incredible ease and rapidity from bourgeois society and it is dangerous in the transitional period, because like a squid with a thousand tentacles, it holds back and hampers the correct process and the speed of development.[55]

National equality and individual equality went hand in hand, but without economic advances there could be no equality. In 1957 it seemed obvious to outsiders that Tito had deliberately 'chosen to govern through incentives rather than by the big stick', even though the incentives had been 'inadequate'.[56] Ideally, the Yugoslavs would avoid the bureaucratism of the Soviets and allow for greater opportunities for personal development and the successful socialization of communist principles. Workers' self-management would give real power to the producers and allow for political participation at the lowest level of social and economic interaction. Self-management would remain one of the most praised hallmarks of Yugoslav communism for outside observers right up until the 1990s.

Yugoslavia remained a one-party state. No one could deny that this was the primary determinant of political and social life. In addition, the secret police, or UDBa, and the military intelligence (*Kontra-obavještajna služba*, KOS) were effective and feared. Ranković ran the UDBa ruthlessly. He had been a leading Partisan and was fiercely centralist. In spite of this, Neal could write that 1952 had marked the 'high point of enthusiasm for democracy among the Yugoslav Communist leaders' and a high point of relations with the West, as witnessed in the deliberations of the Sixth Party Congress.[57] However, the pre-eminent role of party members in politics, administration, government and the army resulted in too many overlaps, or what today we might describe as conflicts of interest. From 1954 onwards Djilas periodically drew attention to this anomaly. There were various attempts at broadening the base of Party support and the Socialist Alliance went some way to achieving that. Workers and women were more visible in its ranks, while the percentage of peasants was declining. A number of capillary associations also acted as ideological 'transmission belts' among veterans, young people, women, journalists, writers and artists. In his address to the Sixth Party Congress Tito reported favourably on the fact that each year 650 Party courses were organized for military personnel, that people had attended a total of one million political lectures and 700,000 discussion groups in the new Yugoslavia.[58]

The main strength attributed to Tito, always, was his capacity to contain national extremism; if this problem was seen to be addressed then most other criticisms of the regime could be accommodated by Yugoslav observers. As we have seen, many believed that the national question was under control, or, in Tito's words, 'regulated'. The war had brought Yugoslavs together and Tito's federalism had succeeded as a containment device. In part Tito was able to speak of such 'regularization' of the national question because of the flight, repression and mass killings of 'nationalists' and alleged collaborators in the purges at war's end and in part because of the power of the secret service and the army, one of the main legitimizing institutions of the state. In 1954 Frankel stressed the importance of the relatively smooth transition signalling the end of national enmities after 1945. He wrote that while some of the 'old antagonisms' were 'still latent', a 'major outbreak is inconceivable under the present regime'. There was also the stated commitment to national diversity. Communist propaganda projected this diversity as a strength rather than a weakness, especially in the potential it afforded for equalizing the distribution of wealth and raising the overall standard of living. Visiting Slovenia's Academy of Fine Arts in 1948, Tito had said:

> The solution [to the problem of the nationalities] is the expression of our revolution. ... We have formally disunited in order to unite better in reality. ... [T]he rights of the great and the small nationalities are recognised on equal footing. There is no more with us the hegemony of one nation over another. And this is exactly what makes us firm and monolithic.[59]

Expanding on this theme nine years later, in 1957, Frankel noted that Tito put forward a multinational Politburo in opposition to 'Great-Serbian oppression', but still counselled caution on the Croatian question as young people were not immune to the 'jingoist virus'.[60]

The detailed discussion of the interplay between nationalism and communism in the new state underscored the need for continued watchfulness. In 1955 Frankel had scrutinized closely the Yugoslav concept of federalism and concluded that this was really a quasi-federal state. In fact the 'real power' resided in the 'strictly centralized machinery of the Communist party' which remained 'outside the constitutional framework'. Workers, not nations, were paramount in the new state and the intention was to support associations that transcended national boundaries and which would make the republics 'redundant', as an all-embracing Yugoslav identity emerged.[61] When previously Frankel had discussed this vision in more detail, he noted that the communists would not make the same mistake as Aleksandar by 'enforcing an artificial concept of Yugoslav unity which does not yet exist'.[62] The view was long-term and resembled closely the idea dear to all Yugoslavists in the interwar years, that national homogeneity was not only desirable but still possible. There was a degree of semantic manipulation on this topic, with emphasis on the people's 'unity' rather than their 'integration' and 'localisms' being accommodated 'within a stronger all-embracing Yugoslav patriotism'.[63] The rationalization of the state continued apace. All of its constituent nationalities had better prospects in Yugoslavia than elsewhere. For Slovenes it was a simple case of growth and 'life' in Yugoslavia, or national extinction outside its borders.[64] The Slovenes may have had some misgivings about their ongoing association with regions more 'backward' than their own, but they also enjoyed certain advantages. Theirs was an ethnically homogeneous population and among the most powerful individuals close to Tito were two Slovenes: his wartime companion, Edvard Kardelj (1910–79) and Boris Kidrič (1912–53).[65]

In the early 1960s Neal wrote that while the nationalities question had not been solved, for the 'first time' in its history 'fratricidal conflict is not a danger' to Yugoslavia. He related this to the improvement in living standards, implying that economic hardship exacerbated national rivalries.[66] One could not always predict a political response to events in Yugoslavia based on national background, as Banac has shown for the Cominformists, about whom it is difficult to generalize nationally. Croats, for example, might be found on either side. Similarly, Slovenes could be pro-Moscow so long as the Soviets supported their territorial claims against Italy, then unambivalent Titoists because they thought the Partisans were more likely to protect their interests. There were, however, continuities between the interwar hegemony of Serbs, and their identification with Cominformism.[67] Later this would become more apparent in the reluctance of leading Serb communists like Ranković to embrace reformism and in their espousal of narrow centralism. The concept of 'national communism' proved attractive to the architects of the United States' foreign policy, even though the definition of this phenomenon was unclear as it applied to Yugoslavia. According to Lorraine Lees the Americans believed in the capacity of national communism, as opposed to the desire for democratic rights, to keep Soviet imperialism in check. (The example of Hungary in 1956, however, revealed that Secretary of State John Foster Dulles's 'liberation policy' was primarily for 'domestic consumption' and not supported by 'operational content'.[68]) In states like Czechoslovakia and Yugoslavia, the shelf life of national communism was difficult to predict. The dogged disregard in the United States (and elsewhere) for the fact that Yugoslavia had no 'national core' to bind disparate groups shows two things about perceptions of Yugoslavia after 1945. First, that much of the early pre-1918 Yugoslavist rhetoric on race and nation had survived, strengthened by the calamitous experience of the Second World War, and second, that observers had little idea of, or interest in, what was happening in Yugoslavia outside

Belgrade.[69] It was also plain that there was near complete outside acceptance of the permanence of the existing order.

Open Dissent I: A Communism Like Any Other

Another of the continuities between the Kingdom and communist Yugoslavia was the persistence of opposition and the severe treatment of nonconformists. Bokovoy alerts us to the fact that the rural landscape was an important (possibly the first) site of successful opposition activism, with the peasants' rejection of the communists' agrarian 'reforms'.[70] The international onlookers' interpretation of the dissident voices is important. We will note that, largely, calls for reform fell on deaf ears, within and without. The greater the threat to stability, the less responsive were outsiders to the dissidents. To Tito, the original deviationist, fell the task of containing further mutations. Tito had many weapons in this battle to retain ideological and political control including, as we have seen, the backing of the secret police, the army and international opinion. However, his control could not be total.

Just five years after the split with Stalin one of the founding fathers of communist Yugoslavia, Djilas, directed a scathing critique at its core beliefs and institutions. The first serious attack from within communist ranks, as opposed to the more predictable critiques by the anti-communists, who had been easily eliminated immediately after the war, came not from Stalinist Cominformists, but from a Yugoslav hardliner who had championed and helped fashion the new state. It had also been the case in the Kingdom that some of the most influential lobbyists for South Slav union almost immediately rejected the form the new state took and were estranged from the political process. Djilas attracted more sympathetic attention internationally than did dissenters under the Kingdom. Perhaps the critique from one of Tito's closest colleagues was all the more potent because other voices had already been silenced or intimidated into submission. The prospect of endlessly mutating heresies was, possibly, the inevitable cost of choosing an alternative socialist path. Tito had promised democracy but, as we have seen, his concept of democracy eschewed 'bourgeois' political freedom or the 'false democracy of rights' for a direct and true, that is to say economic, democracy. The reality was that Yugoslavs had limited rights and could be imprisoned, often without trial, if they did not conform politically.[71]

There were accepted bounds within which social, cultural, political, academic and national discourse could take place. Depending on the source of the critique, the leadership might respond favourably to criticism and push for further reforms, as occurred in the 1960s, or it might close ranks and repel liberalizing tendencies. Predictably, the first generation of post-1945 dissidents, coming from outside the Partisan fraternity, was crushed in the name of the allegedly still incomplete battle against fascism. It was relatively straightforward to liquidate anti-communists (actual, supposed and potential) in the atmosphere of fear and retribution just after war's end. When dissidence emanated from within the ranks of the communist vanguard, it was more challenging.

Those who focus on the immediate precursors of the final collapse of communist Yugoslavia, including, in particular, its economic difficulties, and the latent 'rabid' nationalism, would do well to revisit the nature of the critique directed against it from within and from an early juncture. After having defended Yugoslavia against Stalin, Djilas rebelled against the regime he had risked his life establishing, and whose theoretical underpinnings he had helped mould. His vigorous stance against Stalinism eventually led to his disillusionment with communism itself. Djilas's own path away from Yugoslav communist dictatorship began in 1953 with the publication in the chief organ of the state, *Borba*, of a series of articles critical of the careerism and inertia in the party. The problem with the system was that it did not lead to 'true' (democratic) socialism. Rather it was hegemonic, bureaucratic and stifled individual creativity. (The system was also inhumane towards opponents, as Djilas had discovered on an official visit to Goli Otok.) An article about Djilas in *Foreign Affairs* appearing in 1955 noted that he had identified one of the 'chief enemies' of the system, 'bureaucratic despotism', evident in the party's monopoly of power. For all the talk of the differences between the Soviets and the Yugoslavs, so long as there were no free elections, the systems were basically the same.[72] Another national figure, Vladimir Dedijer, came to Djilas's defence.[73] Both were expelled from the party and faced trial, but their sentences were suspended.[74]

Tito's response to Djilas was initially relatively indulgent. According to a January 1954 article in *The Times*, Tito himself had also pledged to 'wage war against centralism and bureaucracy', which he condemned as Stalinism, and hoped to reach a stage of 'pure' communism. Djilas's comments were, however, not timely and many of his colleagues stood to lose their 'power, prestige and privilege', if his suggestions had been acted upon. The British paper juxtaposed Djilas's 'visionary enthusiasm' against Tito's 'more practical caution'.[75] Then, early the following year (1955), *The Times* noted Tito was growing less patient both with the voices of opposition and outside commentaries on them. In India 'from his ship in the Bay of Bengal', he said that the amount of international coverage of the Djilas episode 'represented "inadmissible" interference'.[76] It was not long before Tito asserted his authority and ostracized Djilas and Dedijer. Djilas was guilty of succumbing to 'reformist opportunism' and his position derived from an attachment to 'bourgeois democracy'.[77] In any case, the celebration in 1954 of the tenth anniversary of the establishment of the secret police had been the regime's pointed rebuttal to potential opposition and a reminder that, like the regime it had succeeded, communist Yugoslavia would not tolerate serious criticism for long.

Djilas did not withdraw his comments and he remained a critic of the regime. He observed the same exploitation and inertia in his own party as that he had abhorred in the Soviet bureaucracy. Those whom he blamed for erring from the path towards socialism were members of his infamously labelled new class, described in his book, first published abroad in 1957. The new class, benefiting from bureaucratism and repression, comprised non-productive members of the communist administrative elite. Unlike other emergent classes in history, the bourgeoisie most notably, this new class had not produced the revolution but existed because of it. The new class had no attachment to the ideals of democratic socialism because materialism and careerism, not ideology, were its motivations. Djilas wrote: 'When the new class leaves the historical scene – and this must happen – there will be less sorrow over its passing than there was for any other class before it. Smothering everything except what suited its ego, it has condemned itself to failure and shameful ruin.'[78] He wrote that theft of 'social property' and exploitation were rife and endemic to communist systems. He described the 'tyranny over the mind' which subjected people to half-truths, censorship and the false consciousness of 'socialist realism', which really stood for 'ideological monopolism'.[79] Djilas called for the immediate 'withering away' of the party and a return to the ideals of democratic socialism. Following St Augustine, Tito said that such a withering away was something they all looked forward to, but not quite yet. The socialist state was too fragile to accommodate this self-criticism.

The vanguard protecting the collective Partisan memory could not abide such an attack. In effect, Partisans constituted a large section of this new class and it was far too soon after the war for their reputation and credibility to be scrutinized under such a harsh light.[80] In France, while not all accounts of the war were triumphalist, routine dismissal of resistance as a 'myth' did not begin until the early 1970s. Further, relations with the Soviet Union impacted on Tito's domestic policy.

In 1950 the Soviet Union had not approved Yugoslavia's election to the Security Council and not long afterwards Djilas was in London railing against Soviet repression and expansionism. However, soon after the death of Stalin in 1953 relations between Yugoslavia and the Soviet Union began to improve. The economic blockade against Yugoslavia was lifted in 1954 and in 1955 Khrushchev and Bulganin were in Belgrade with the intention of healing the rift. Tito's return visit the following year was another symbolic gesture indicating rapprochement was possible. A period of mutual respect, support and rededication to the principles of international communism followed. The renewed friendship survived the Hungarian crisis of 1956 and the invasion of Czechoslovakia 12 years later. Both Yugoslavia and the Soviet Union, brothers in arms in the Grand Alliance, sought stability. They benefited from an international climate that also valued stability. The West recognized and rewarded their sacrifice in war and made clear that it had little interest in the domestic politics of either state.

In addition, outsiders and insiders were too steeped in a particular view of the problems of Yugoslav history as being national, rather than political and social, or even cultural, to be able to accept a critique of the regime that took as its starting point problems arising from corruption, nepotism, the absence of rights and the abandonment of even an aspiration towards democratic processes. An article in *The New Statesman* in 1957 noted that Djilas's 'wild denunciations', constituting a 'new treachery' and deriving from 'an accumulation of personal bitterness', were unfortunate given that conditions were better in Yugoslavia than elsewhere in the Soviet bloc.[81] Tito's old comrade-in-arms, Pijade, described Djilas's observations on the double standards of communists, their greed, snobbery and loose morals as 'political pornography'.[82] As he was turning away from communism, Djilas's writings provided little hope for others who felt an allegiance towards the state and who still retained an optimistic belief in Yugoslavia's socialist future.

Djilas continued to write and register his dissent from the communist leadership and remained one of the best-known dissident figures in postwar Yugoslav history. This was at some personal cost. In 1955 he had to give up his villa, one of the privileges reserved for prominent members of the new class, and on and off he was interned in the late 1950s and the early to mid-1960s. However, he remained, as one observer put it, 'literarily active' throughout his long life. Djilas outlived Tito by 15 years and witnessed the beginning of the final break-up of the state. As we will see, the comparative leniency of the treatment of the likes of a Djilas is in stark contrast to the treatment of some others who dared to voice their disapproval of aspects of Tito's regime. Significantly, Yugoslavia's enthusiastic supporters outside the country did not seem to have been especially put out by Djilas's critique. They did not simply continue to tolerate the regime; they lionized it and chose to trivialize or ignore its inconsistencies, ideological incoherence and repressive policies.

Ideological Indeterminacy

The Yugoslav model of modernizing developmental socialism had wide appeal. Yet there was also a generalized sense of resignation. This was the best that could be expected under the circumstances, and of necessity progress would be slow.[83] It was an odd combination of ideological fervour and realism. The argument that it was progressive and better than the alternatives had been the country's justification through its entire history, but the sentiment was more pronounced after 1945. In fact, no alternative was acceptable to the outside world because Yugoslavia had never stopped being seen as a necessity. The appeal of this 'modernizing model' of state-building recalled the appeal of the idea of the new state as the crowning edifice of a progressive Yugoslav national movement in the early twentieth century. By contrast, historians have generally rejected the argument that Fascist Italy was a modernizing dictatorship.[84] At a stretch, historians might accept that the attempt of the fascist regime to mobilize women, for example, had politicized some women and exposed them to novel experiences, which constituted modernization by default in certain circumstances. It is clear, however, that Italian fascism was ultimately reactionary and demeaning to women.[85] Communist Yugoslavia was also demeaning to almost all of its citizens and policed them closely. The idea that a communist dictatorship could be modernizing (and thus acceptable) and that, on ideological grounds, a fascist regime could not, is just one more example of the double standard as it applied to interpretations of Yugoslavia in history.

In 1967, ten years after the first English publication of *The New Class*, Anthony Sylvester wrote in *Survey* that most Yugoslavs had no idea of Djilas or of the leaders of the Praxis movement, which gathered under its mantle philosophers seeking to find a balance between the theory and practice of Marxism in the modern state. These philosophers published their journal, *Praxis*, from Zagreb and its English-language version attracted an international following. Sylvester believed that the localized political and ideological ferment occasioned by debates among philosophers and social scientists was 'incomprehensible' to the majority of people, who were simply interested in maintaining a quality of life that enabled them to sun themselves on the coast during their annual leave. One had only to visit the beaches of Croatia to get a sense of the standard of living in Yugoslavia and the fact that this was, indeed, a workers' paradise. Moreover, he continued, Yugoslavs were free to emigrate and such freedom of movement was unknown in other communist countries. Then, without any trace of irony, he compared Yugoslavia favourably with Albania, possibly the most insular and repressive of all the communist states. His fulsome descriptions of life in Yugoslavia and his underlying Balkanist perspective highlight the strands of continuity between travellers' accounts of the South Slavs across several generations and the seepage between the popular and the academic in political assessments of the state of a country that was 'almost free'.[86]

For all the talk of 'Brotherhood and Unity', Serb centralism was never far from the surface. This was in part because Serbs had come to dominate most key institutions, much as they had in the Kingdom, irrespective of the rhetoric about national equality. Ranković, a leader among the anti-reformists, had considerable power and a loyal following of like-minded Serbs. His ejection from the inner sanctum in 1966 for an unbending commitment to centralism and intransigence on matters such as the devolution of power to the republics spoke of Tito's commitment to republican integrity and the victory of reformism over conservatism. Ranković's ousting was a hopeful sign to outsiders, indicating that it was still possible for the League of Communists in Yugoslavia 'to lead society without governing it', as had been reported the previous year.[87] Such reasoning provided yet another opportunity to ignore the regime's contradictions and problems.

The policy of non-alignment and coexistence, in opposition to that of continuous international revolution and imperialism, also had a broad appeal in the era of decolonization and communist containment. In fact, Yugoslavia could not do much practically to foster international peace and harmony, but leadership of the non-aligned nations brought Tito a certain stature on the global stage. At the time Yugoslavia's position on non-alignment highlighted the disparity between its promotion of self-determination for colonized peoples and its failure in practice to acknowledge fully the rights of all the national groups within its own borders. In the light of this anomaly, the improved treatment and recognition of Macedonians, Muslims and Albanians were important concessions. Under Ranković, however, the UDBa monitored the Albanians closely and they were routinely terrorized by local police.[88] Further, he had blocked the Macedonians' desire to establish an autocephalous Church. By forcing Ranković out of power and allowing the Macedonians to establish their own Church, Tito hoped to show his commitment to federalism.[89] Declaring the Muslims a constituent nationality in 1969 would prove still more controversial as various groups, including the Macedonians, stood to lose a proportion of their ethnic and regional majorities to the new Muslim nation. This policy was criticized as pragmatic posturing, lip-service to equality on the part of a man more inclined towards maintaining power than promoting a strong sense of Yugoslavism. However, Yugoslavism was still regarded by many as centralist or unitarist rather than federalist. That is why concessions to the republics and the minorities were seen as leading to decline and ruin rather than an extension of local sovereignty. We saw above that Tito had said that Yugoslavs had 'formally disunited in order to unite better in reality'. Yet devolution seemed to highlight the growing gap between perceptions of an overarching Yugoslav identity and (particularist) republican national interests. For some historians this marks the beginning of the end of the compatibility of multiple 'Yugoslav' identities, despite the rhetoric and gestures of Tito suggesting the opposite.

As the rift between the Soviet Union and Yugoslavia had proved temporary Tito was to take advantage of straddling both 'worlds'. The Cold War provided the atmosphere for Tito's success. Initially the withdrawal of Soviet aid and the blockade led to serious shortages and deprivation in many places across the country. In the long term it strengthened Tito's position as he turned westwards for assistance. American aid, which was generous, unconditional and constant, would keep Tito 'afloat' and give him the freedom largely to do as he wished. The United States never really expected Tito to make any political concessions in return for the lifeline it provided.[90] In 1952 Fotich, noting the help the United States offered to alleviate the Yugoslavs' suffering, wrote that Tito wanted 'everything' but gave back nothing.[91] What was important to the United States was the sense of reassurance that came with the belief that the Yugoslavs would remain impervious to the Soviets if they had sufficient moral and material support from the West. Yugoslavia went on to enjoy a level of economic buoyancy that set it apart from the Soviet bloc countries. Such was the capacity of the Yugoslav communists to adapt to their 'in-between position' that, by the 1960s, many observers were arguing that Yugoslavia had done better than any of the communist states and that this had to be because 'the correlation between communist theory and practice ... is high'.[92] The country's economic development was applauded and the standard of living and the availability of consumer goods in the richer republics were generally used as a gauge of 'progress'. Rapid economic growth concealed Yugoslavia's dependence on foreign loans and aid packages and its reliance on the permanent or temporary departure of hundreds of thousands of unemployed workers to join Europe's *Gastarbeiters* (guest workers). Those who left in this exodus included industrial labourers as well as highly skilled multilingual professional people, and their departure had a negative impact demographically, socially and economically.

In fact economic difficulties, both in terms of the unevenness of the development between republics and the dependency on outside aid, were never far from the surface. In 1950 per capita incomes in Slovenia were three times higher than in Kosovo and five times higher in 1960.[93] By 1970 'a million Yugoslavs were working abroad, mostly in West Germany'.[94] This, together with the relaxation of emigration laws, further masked the country's inability to provide its workers with gainful employment. Of those leaving Croatia, where departures were highest and the birth rate the lowest, 50 per cent were under the age of 30 and 63 per cent were men.[95] One can only marvel at Tito's endless capacity to attract more foreign loans, even when there was no evidence that the state would or could pay anything back. By the end of 1976 the World Bank had lent Yugoslavia

$US1,500 million and it was able to secure more loans (totalling $US112 million) from the Bank in 1977 and 1979.[96] No hard economic decisions ever had to be made. Even when inflation was at its worst, the full effects of the dire economic situation were not felt equally by Yugoslavs. This would contribute to nostalgia for the communist regime, once it was gone.

Over time the theoretical innovation for which Yugoslav communism was renowned, workers' self-management, became one of its hollowest jokes and its greatest contradiction. In his address to the Jubilee Session of the Anti-Fascist Council of the National Liberation of Yugoslavia in 1968, Tito spoke of the 'innovative' and 'unique' system 'fostering...initiative and greater incentive for the solution of the crucial problems of production and income distribution' and conceiving of the 'working man...as a free and independent creator in a self-managing society'.[97] In reality, the system was unsustainable. Among other problems was the fact that self-managed workers were paying themselves more than 'their' companies were earning.[98] Nor could the promise of producers owning and organizing their enterprises be fulfilled when the party made all the important decisions and when no social, cultural or economic unit could have a viable life outside the reach of the controlling centralized structures. Obvious to us now, these contradictions were buried beneath ideological posturing, one of the least disputed aspects of Yugoslav political life.

We have seen that the international edition of *Praxis* received contributions from Left intellectuals all over the world. Seemingly audacious and critical of the established socialist norms, the views of the Praxis group, dubbed the 'heresy within a heresy',[99] addressed the theoretical foundations of the Marxist state in a framework that today seems barely credible. It is apparent that the members' stature at the time was out of proportion to their intellectual endeavour. Most of them faded into oblivion and their publications, like the primers of self-management, have not stood the test of time. The Praxis group had grown out of discussions among a new generation of Marxist thinkers. They argued that socialist theory could go down another path from that advocated by Lenin and Stalin. The problem was that the first generation of twentieth-century Left-wing radicals, the *fin-de-siècle* revolutionaries, had not known the work of the young Marx. New insights were to be found in Marx's early writings, where the problems of the relationship between theory and practice were treated in an altogether more humane and

flexible manner than one would have surmised from the later, dogmatic writings of twentieth-century communists, or indeed from the
actions of the revolutionary communist vanguard. The new Marxist
ideologues of Yugoslavia and their European counterparts argued
that nothing was fixed and that a theory established in isolation,
without due reference to practice, life itself, was a theory without
vigour and without meaning. Alienation resulted not simply from
stultifying work, but from the void that came as theory and practice, one's potential and one's actual existence, drifted wider and
wider apart. Alienation also arose from the complacency that came
with uncritical acceptance of the ruling ideologues and when form
was more important than content. While the finer points of the
philosophical foundation of the Praxis group may now leave us
underwhelmed, this movement was a sign to outsiders on the Left
in particular that Yugoslavia retained a certain vitality and an intellectual and ideological viability. As long as this was the case, support, moral and material, was guaranteed, especially from those
outsiders whose infatuation with communist Yugoslavia resembled
that of their predecessors with the Kingdom.

Praxis's impact was fleeting and the group eventually lost official support. Its followers' belief in a system, which, they said, 'did
not believe in itself', could not protect the theoreticians of the new
socialist order or protect the order itself. They were especially critical of the 'liberal' (deemed nationalist) communists in the republics,
notably Croatia. The funds for publication of the journal were with-
drawn in 1974 and the Praxis summer schools on the idyllic island
of Korčula, where the thinkers in residence wrestled with the challenges of socialism within a short walk of the sparkling waters of the
Adriatic, came to an end. Belgrade philosopher Mihailo Marković
who, interestingly, was to became one of Slobodan Milošević's
advisers, wrote in 1975 in his retrospective appraisal of the Praxis
Group:

> For a brief time, until 1947, the only interpretation of Marxism
> that was available was 'dialectical materialism' in the form elab-
> orated by Soviet philosophers. But very soon, even before the
> conflict with Stalinism in 1948, the most gifted students of phil-
> osophy in the universities of Belgrade and Zagreb began to doubt
> whether what they found in the fourth chapter of the *History of
> the Communist Party of the Soviet Union (Bolsheviks)* was really the
> last word in revolutionary philosophy. It sounded superficial,

simplified, and dogmatic, and it altogether lacked any criticism of the existing forms of socialist society.[100]

Nor did the last word in revolutionary philosophy emanate from Praxis. The group was not equipped to furnish the rising generation with a workable formula for negotiating a path between arcane jargon and the prosaic tasks faced daily by men and women struggling to make ends meet.

It was a delicate balancing act trying to reconcile workers' self-management and local autonomies with a centralist communist regime and a one-party dictatorship. Eminent Harvard professor and expert on Soviet affairs, Adam Ulam (1922–2000), was thus moved to write in 1973 that Titoism was not a philosophy of politics but a response to changing circumstances and pressures as they arose. It was a 'synthesis of communism and Yugoslav nationalism', but the modicum of liberalism and tolerance thrown into the mix, he argued, did not equate to an ideology. Rather, Tito had to find a balance between ideology, expediency, self-interest and maintaining peaceful relations within and without.[101] One of the main sources of international optimism over Tito throughout the period of his rule was the comparison with countries where the abuse of human rights was more aggressive, or at least more visible, and consumer goods less abundant. Clearly, the people making these comparisons were not as bold as our nineteenth-century travellers and did not venture down the paths 'untouched by Macadam', of which there were still many in Tito's Yugoslavia.

In the early 1960s, even when key men like Kardelj and Ranković were in their prime, succession planning was a concern as people started imagining Yugoslavia after Tito and speculating on the problems that would follow his death.[102] There were no obvious successors groomed to take control during the transition and beyond. It was apparent to some in the late 1970s that little had been done to prepare for the vacuum that his passing would leave, and many would have agreed with the assertion that the statement 'L'état, c'est moi!' was more true for him than for any other communist leader.[103] This observation from a 1978 article in *Current History* titled, aptly, 'Yugoslavia and Tito: The Long Farewell', related not simply to the extent of his control but to the very existence of the state. The author of the article described Yugoslavia's nationality problem as a potential 'time bomb' built into the system, adding it was surprising that there had not been more inter-ethnic disputes.[104] One could not conceive of Yugoslavia without Tito. As his death seemed imminent, some of the earlier generalizations about the state, the 'extreme' nationalist tendencies of one of its constituent nationalities and the need for a firm hand gained a new momentum, along with an anti-nationalist discourse that was steeped in the anachronistic language of the fighting Partisan generation.

Open Dissent II: Generational Change

The generational revolt of the 1960s left its mark in Yugoslavia as it did elsewhere. The regime quelled student unrest in Belgrade in 1968 and violently suppressed the social and political ferment in Croatia which became known as the Croatian Spring (1970–1). We now know that what seemed like a passing moment in the history of the postwar world, exemplified by the people's revolt in Prague in 1968, spoke of a deeper malaise in the communist bloc. While there had been dissident voices previously, it is to this unresolved turmoil of the 1960s that we can trace the short-term precursors to the disintegration of Yugoslavia.

Djilas, as we have seen, was the best known figure in the first wave of dissent after the split with Stalin and the isolation of the Cominformists. Once Yugoslavia had begun to establish its independence and its own style of 'socialist social relationships', anomalies in the system became apparent. Most of the critics of the regime would have argued that theirs was a Yugoslav-friendly approach. They sought to resolve the problems they identified, without questioning the integrity of the state. In retrospect we can see that the cumulative effect of the successive ideological 'debates' was that they weakened the state. This was not because the people involved were cynical and sought to undermine the state by stealth, but because it was only a matter of time before the debates would challenge most of Yugoslavia's founding principles, whether they dated from 1918 or 1945. Furthermore, the range of the criticisms highlighted that the opposition voices were disparate and, eventually, incompatible and that this would make it harder for them to find common ground within a Yugoslav state, whether federal or centralist.

The incident that sparked the direct action of the Belgrade students in 1968 involved the barring of a large proportion of the student body from admission to an oversubscribed concert. The ensuing demonstrations were indicative of a deeper dissatisfaction among students, many of whom were facing the choice between long-term unemployment and emigration. Thus, as it was in the Kingdom, the relatively optimistic appraisals of Yugoslavia's 'unique' (in this case 'liberal communist') experiment did not match the lived experience of Yugoslavs. The student demonstrations articulated the sense of alienation identified by Djilas, but in a distinctive fusion of the language of 1960s youth culture and socialist doctrine. The movement did not capture the full support of the workers (but nor were they hostile) and the unrest did not reverberate much further afield in the first instance. Tito was an acute observer of trends elsewhere and addressed the problem in his inimitable paternalistic fashion.[105] He appeared on television and embraced the students' criticisms as legitimate. He acknowledged and took responsibility for the ruling authorities' sins, made his *mea culpa*, defused the situation and survived the crisis. Unlike de Gaulle, who lost the battle to win over the rising generation and whose flagging fortunes in the last years of his political career he had observed closely, Tito could still count on a degree of cross-generational support. However, it had not been easy to keep abreast of the changes occurring at home and abroad or to retain his progressive image.

Tito had not condoned the Soviet invasion of Hungary in 1956 but nor had he condemned it. We saw that Yugoslavia's situation vis-à-vis the Soviet Union was in the delicate stages of rapprochement at that time and Tito found himself in a difficult situation. Even though he had felt an affinity with the Hungarian reform movement, Tito had virtually given his consent to Khrushchev to intervene and failed to anticipate the extent of the unrest and the attention it would attract. As the movement gained momentum and evolved into an anti-communist campaign, Tito was less supportive but he faced a dilemma. He wanted to be seen in the best light by both blocs. Further, he had provided the Hungarian revolution's leaders with asylum in the Yugoslav embassy in Budapest, which made his position even more precarious. Eventually he publicly described Soviet intervention in Hungary as a 'necessary evil', even though he was angered by the Soviets' deception and their execution of the leaders of the revolution, including Imre Nagy, after their departure from the safety of the Yugoslav embassy.[106] Events during the Prague Spring of 1968 troubled Tito more.[107] According to the so-called 'Brezhnev doctrine', a socialist state was obliged to intervene in another socialist state if socialism itself was threatened, and this was potentially menacing to the independent-minded Tito. While he was critical of the Soviet invasion, he refrained from supporting the Czech reformers outright. He intimated that the Prague Spring had possibly gone too far and that all reformers had to have limitations built into their expectation for change. This attitude was indicative of his belief that there was a need for greater ideological control from the centre, as his stand against unrest in Croatia attests.

Tito's measured response to the Belgrade students' unrest contrasted with his reaction to the Croatian Spring just two years later. The background to the Croatian Spring was the 1967 'Declaration on the Status and Name of the Croatian Standard Language'. The Novi Sad agreement of 1954 had effectively denied the existence of the Croatian language. The publication in 1967 of the first volumes of a national dictionary that failed to take note of the specificity of Croatian variants and called them examples of a 'local dialect' roused the indignation of Croats across the political spectrum. Croat communists, intellectuals, writers and politicians signed the Declaration. They called for the recognition of Croatian as a separate language. While this action was the centrepiece of what became the Croatian Spring, the movement stood for more than a *cri de cœur* for Croatian linguistic integrity. It was a call for social and democratic reform. Nonetheless, in appraisals of the Croatian Spring, the Declaration was one of the main factors to be drawn out, as it was representative of the 'national parochialism' whence all other (puffed up) complaints, economic, social, cultural and political, were said to have derived.

The Croatian reform movement had its roots in the governmental changes of the mid-1960s, opposed by Ranković, that precipitated further decentralization. The organ of the Croatian Spring, *Hrvatski tjednik* (*Croatian Weekly*), canvassed many debates dealing with Croatia's place within Yugoslavia and the republic's economic grievances. One serious concern was the lack of funds available for investment in infrastructure including hospitals, highways and bridges. Other concerns were the social and cultural cost of short- and long-term emigration, the failure to recognize the Croatian literary language and the concentration of power and decision making in Belgrade. There was also dissatisfaction with the lack of administrative accountability and with corruption within state and party structures. The Croats' critique of the system was dismissed by their opponents as a right-wing separatist provocation. The Croatian Spring had to be defined in essentialist terms, as a 'nationalist backlash', because of the ideological legacy of the pre-war period and because most of the historiography on extremism in Yugoslavia focused on the example of the 'restless' Croats in the Kingdom and on the collaboration of the Independent State of Croatia. Croats themselves unwittingly accepted the polarities after the war as their 'Ustaša complex', discussed in Chapter 4, reveals. Yet however chastened Croats had come to feel as a result of the heavy burden of the 'Ustaša complex', there was a generalized sense of frustration with the depiction of the leaders of the mass protest movement as infected by the nationalist contagion. The fact that activists of sound and proven Left credentials, like the eminent writer Miroslav Krleža (1893–1981), were associated with the movement seemed to be of little significance. The editors of *Hrvatski tjednik* often drew attention to the way in which their views were being misrepresented by their critics and labelled pejoratively as 'separatist' and 'revisionist' at best, and Ustaša-inspired at worst. The paper's columnists made clear that they advocated not 'separatism' but greater local authority and greater central accountability. Furthermore, their call for the recognition of the Croatian language would have constituted a reasonable demand in any other context, and the state's refusal to afford it seemed an intolerable injustice. As Krleža stated simply in 1971: 'Ever since I began writing I have written in Croatian, just as all Serbian writers write in Serbian.'[108] Yugoslavists within and without failed to understand that the Croatian Spring was a symptom of deeper frustrations articulated by Croat communist elites and by the time they did, it was too late.

International observers as well as the government saw the unrest in Croatia, unlike that in Belgrade, as a threat and as unrelated to problems of state or the international protest movement. Rather it had to be a product of something 'outside history', Croatian nationalism and separatism. This theme returned in the 1990s, when critics of the movements for democracy and then independence in Slovenia and Croatia were to deny those movements' relationship to the international context, the collapse of communism, and deem them nationalistic and economically driven. The Croatian Spring illustrated once again the 'endemic flaw' of the Croats that the 'nation-state' needed to crush, or at least control. It did not alert outsiders to the possibility that the imposition of a communist dictatorship in a time of social and generational transition would result in systemic failure. Instead, it confirmed to them that greater liberalization produced a reaction from the politically 'backward' nationalists who, unused to freedom, expressed it only with recourse to tribal symbols and who thus jeopardized Yugoslav harmony.[109]

Tito was to become less generously disposed towards the Croat reformers in the course of the year. His solution was to wrench power from the hands of the 'republican oligarchies' that had nurtured regressive republican nationalism and that had to be 'stamped out'.[110] The Belgrade students, still recognizably 'Yugoslav', did not attract the same negative comment. Repression of the Croatian movement in December 1971, on the other hand, led to the purging of the Croatian communist leadership and expulsions from the party. There were also mass arrests. Croat communists and student leaders and activists received long prison sentences. (Some of them, including the future President of Croatia, Dr Franjo Tuđman, were prominent in the democratic movement in the late 1980s and the 1990s.) The harassment did not end with the suppression of the movement but continued through to the late 1970s and early 1980s.[111] Without commenting negatively on the violence with which the Croatian Spring had been put down or the severity of the sentences received by Croat communists, Ulam, writing in 1973, commended Tito on his ability to alleviate national conflicts. Ulam's chief concern was the 'resurgence of Croatian nationalism' which 'once more put in question the synthesis of communism and Yugoslav nationalism' as achieved by Tito.[112] Ulam was not alone. Some recalled Engels's view of Croats as 'a people of almost nomadic barbarism'. Others revisited Seton-Watson's descriptions of the Croats as 'agin the government' or 'obstructionist' by nature and history, and of Croatia as a 'revisionist nation' with the habit of mounting opposition for opposition's sake.[113] Interestingly, the Soviets were so impressed with Tito after the suppression of the Croatian Spring that they decorated him with the Order of Lenin.[114]

In this context it seems reasonable to suggest that Tito was more responsive to developments in the East than the West. Brezhnev had offered military support to Tito to contain the Croats and while he politely refused, his disregard for the sovereignty of the Croatian republic showed that he was more than willing to resort to force to contain perceived threats to the system. The 1970s witnessed an intensification of central controls with greater overlaps between the institutions controlling public life.[115] The proportion of officers in the Central Committee was increasing and in 1977 over 98 per cent of officers and 90 per cent of NCOs were party members.[116] Although Tito and Kardelj said that the military and political authorities were not going to resort to the 'administrative measures' (incarceration) of less enlightened times, clearly they did.[117] Human rights 'fetishists' continued to be the object of disdain.[118] Tito wanted to restore enthusiasm for international communism, as his many friendly meetings with Brezhnev would attest. The Yugoslav leader became more, not less, ideologically dogmatic after the threats of liberalization outside and inside the country, and in due course he would no longer be seen as the leader of an alternative and more moderate communist movement. However, this was not evident to our Yugoslav enthusiasts for at least another two decades.

The fact remained that one's interpretation of the nationalist hydra did rather depend on the group in question and what might be called its 'pre-history'. For example, in his 1981 retrospective appraisal of the beginnings of the unravelling of the total authority of the state and party, Djilas (a Montenegrin) wrote of the impact of Serb 'liberals', Slovene 'technocrats' and, predictably, Croat 'nationalists'.[119] Given what we know about the framing of the national question in the interwar period, there is nothing surprising about this classification. Just as in the 1930s dictatorship had been 'necessary' to control the Croats and protect the state so, too, it was necessary now. The extreme centralists pointed their finger at Croatian 'separatists' in order to stifle the liberalizing tendencies within Croatian communist circles and to impress upon the world that the Yugoslav state was not made more precarious by dictatorship, but by the pre-existing nationalist evil. The consequences of the response to the Croatian Spring would begin to be felt after Tito's death.

The disturbances in Belgrade and then in Croatia did not put outsiders on guard against the accepted stereotypical view of the merits of Yugoslav socialism and the evils of Croatian nationalism, but confirmed them. Indeed, in some cases an almost wilful disregard for the contradictions in the system the Yugoslav state enshrined led to a renewed fervour for the 'Yugoslav way'. Even a few years before Tito's death, outsiders could still look on in wonder at the Yugoslav model of 'socialist social relations'. This was evident in an adaptation of workers' participation and self-management in late 1970s Australia. The Premier of the state of South Australia, Donald Dunstan (1967–8, 1970–9), visited Yugoslavia in 1976 while on an overseas study tour. He observed models of worker participation and industrial democracy, which he praised publicly in a prestigious national event, the Chifley Memorial Lecture, that same year.[120] In 1978 the city of Adelaide hosted an international conference on industrial democracy. Sessions were conducted by two Belgrade academics and a local union official. The union representative spoke of his government-funded study tour to Europe and said: 'The highlight of my overseas tour, without doubt, was the eight weeks spent in Yugoslavia. I sincerely believe that the socialist self-management system as practised in Yugoslavia opens up new horizons for human, cultural, political and socio-economic relationships.' He had been apprehensive about the trip but soon realized his 'apprehensions…were unfounded': 'I take the opportunity to dispel some of the slanders, lies and misconceptions being promulgated by some people in Australia about Yugoslavia.'[121] The South Australian premier attempted to institute workers' participation and industrial democracy throughout the public sector. The state of mind represented by this Australian politician and other uncritical observers of the Yugoslav economy and workplace relations indicates, in part, why there was no basis for an appropriate response to the crisis Yugoslavia faced just over a decade after this antipodean tribute to workers' self-management.

Internal criticisms of the Yugoslav system were routinely dismissed as 'nationally inspired'. This obsession with nationalist deviationism cleared the way for still more inflated analyses of Yugoslav 'successes' and militated against pluralism. It also ensured the old argument, that there was nothing wrong with Yugoslavia, but that its people were troublesome, could never subside. Thus, in the 1970s, acclamation of Tito was thunderously loud, as the slogan 'After Tito – Tito!' attested. Supporters were still in the majority. Tito, the most Stalinist of all his peers had, in 1945, appeared 'a most improbable candidate for heresy'.[122] However, to his credit in the eyes of outside observers he had risen to the occasion and proved an adaptable head of state. At the time the political and intellectual climate internationally could not have tolerated a more critical stance. Academic culture was stamped by 'anti-fascism' or, in some cases, Marxism, which might mean any number of things, from a theoretical underpinning to one's work to a loose association with Leftist politics. Regardless, in this intellectual context, for outsiders a Croat-inspired protest movement could bring nothing but nationalist ferment. The contradictory view of Croatian politics as representing the best (Yugoslav) and the worst (national separatist) of the Balkan postwar experiment was possible while a strong Croat leader like Tito remained in power and while there was still cross-national support for the state. Eventually key national groups began openly to articulate mutually exclusive alternatives of the Yugoslav state. Serbian national resurgence, generally drawing on a deep animosity towards 'the Croat' Tito, could not accommodate the reactions it engendered among non-Serbs. Slovenes, then Croats, sought greater devolution, confederalism, autonomy and, finally, independence. It became plain that multiple local, republican and Yugoslav identities could no longer coexist.

The perception of dissidents as either redeemable (political) or irredeemable (national) had a negative bearing on the capacity of like-minded individuals to come together in cross-national or cross-republic associational movements. The constant references to their allegedly 'separatist' and 'fascist' proclivities led to exasperation on the part of many Croats, including those communists associated with the Croatian Spring. This, coupled with a blanket and persistent condemnation of all Croatian social and political activism as Ustaša-inspired, led to an intellectual paralysis in the response to Yugoslavia's problems. The state of the international historiography of fascism, still in its 'primitive' stage, was such that nationalism and fascism might be used interchangeably in certain contexts. This was relevant, especially where dissidence was coupled with a wartime record that left itself open to distortion. Such distortions, we have seen, also related to the state of the historiography of the Second World War. The long-term effect of this situation was that no structured opposition based on shared aspirations or a civic sense of what it meant to be Yugoslav could emerge. Intellectuals might be cut off from wider interlocking social networks and either hibernated or, if they were more career-minded, chose the path of labouring as indentured servants of the state, inventing new and ever more vacuously elaborate explanations and justifications of the system and its 'progressive' core. The hibernators may have been without particular power or influence, but they did not believe in the regime's false promises.[123] The salient characteristic of all Yugoslav hibernators, regardless of their background, was the absence of strong attachment and loyalty to Yugoslavia, however defined. Its most passionate defenders were those who stood to gain from it, and the number of people who fell into that category diminished over the years.

When there was no strong personality at the helm, the tensions that had remained unresolved would appear in a new, post-communist, guise. The impulse for social and democratic reform would be articulated in republican and then national terms since it had become obvious that the 1945 promise of a new 'Yugoslav homogeneity' was unlikely ever to be realized. There was no common language of civic identity that could be drawn upon to delay the sequence of events in Yugoslavia after Tito's death. To the outside world Yugoslavia had seemed to make great strides, having shunned the most obvious trappings of the totalitarian state. However, this 'liberal' strain of communism did not spring from a deep humanitarian impulse or respect for individual rights but from the fact that the regime accepted there were limitations to what it was capable of achieving. Paradoxically, the seemingly liberal tendencies of Yugoslav communism made those who opposed it seem disagreeable, even disturbing, both in the context of the Cold War and as Soviet and Central and Eastern European communism imploded. While many had praised Yugoslavia for the concurrence there of 'theory and practice', it was in fact the vast chasm between theory and practice, and the failure of outsiders to recognize that chasm and its consequences, that led to the state's unravelling.

Conclusion

Yugoslavia was constructed, promoted and sustained by a combination of international and transnational forces. Nothing remotely resembling the state as it had been imagined either in 1918 or 1945 ever existed. Just as Europe's history is much more than a history of nations and nation-states,[1] so too is Yugoslavia's history much more than the history of a state in isolation. Yugoslavia was never outside the strategic and diplomatic orbit of European and global politics. In this book I have exposed the hollowness of the exceptionalist approach to Yugoslav history. Exceptionalism focuses not simply on Yugoslavia's difference from European historical trends but on its fundamental incompatibility with them and its allegedly unique experience of particular phenomena, such as nationalism, and events, such as the Second World War. Throughout I have emphasized the role of outsiders in the construction of Yugoslavia and how their perceptions of its various political and national actors influenced perceptions of the state as a whole. From the outset Yugoslavia was deemed a necessary state, one that would promote peace and stability in the region dubbed the 'powder keg' of Europe. Over time, the Yugoslavs themselves began to take greater prominence in the construction of this history, as was evident in the Second World War. Even though the international context remained of primary significance in defining the state through to the last stages of its existence, by the late 1980s and early 1990s the Yugoslavs took centre stage. Some were to make the most of the propitious climate, notably the collapse of the Soviet Union and the end of the Cold War, to assert their desire for self-determination. They faced international hostility and the lingering feeling that fundamentally primitive South Slavs driven by tribal nationalisms were incapable of stable self-government. However, within a very short period of time the Yugoslav ideal lost its allure and outsiders came to the conclusion that the state was no longer 'necessary'.

Summing Up

Chapter 1 traced the imagining and inventing of Yugoslavia in accounts of the region and its populations by an array of travellers, academics and journalists whose adventures took them to 'Savage Europe'. We observed the process whereby the outsiders identified an integrated South Slav race and nation and carved out a virtual space for its state well before its 'national revolution' of 1918. Theirs was an understandable impulse, given the race discourse of the times, the place of the nation-state in the liberal conception of the modern world, the mounting hostility towards the Habsburgs and the Ottomans and the role of the Balkans in the Great Powers' search for equilibrium on the Continent. As early as the 1860s, we find examples of the observation that 'nature' and historical forces had deemed Belgrade the most fitting capital of a South Slav state. Many politicians in Britain remained pragmatically tied to the Ottoman presence in the region, while also accepting Austrian expansion eastwards because they sought, above all, to curb Russian imperialism. Eventually a permanent shift in European alliances led to the rapprochement between old rivals, Russia, France and Britain. The idea of dismantling the Central European and Ottoman empires and replacing them with nation-states became more and more appealing. The concept of a Yugoslav state gained greater momentum when Western Europeans believed the German octopus, hidden from view by the nationalistically haphazard Austro-Hungarian Empire, was stealthily spreading its tentacles towards Baghdad.

In Chapter 2 we saw that the First World War was interpreted as corroborating what prominent commentators on European affairs had believed for several decades: that the Serbs were indeed the natural leaders of the South Slavs. Their appeal lay in their military prowess evident as they freed themselves from Ottoman rule and expanded their territory twofold in the Balkan Wars. The First World War provided the occasion for the triumph of the national ideal in the Balkans. Lobbying to this end among the British and French was enormously successful because it built on a set of established ideas about the South Slavs and their history. However, late nineteenth- and early twentieth-century views about nations and nationalities were not based on firm principles but subject to modification. Much depended on the circumstances, on the perceived viability of the states in question and the consequences of their existence for the balance of power, not just in the region but globally. This was never more true than at the Paris Peace Conference with the 'uneven' application of Wilson's Fourteen Points. At the time of Yugoslavia's final demise in the 1990s commentators argued that it had failed as a state because it was 'artificial', hastily conceived and without deep resonance among the very people said to have propelled a South Slav national revolution. On one level this is a plausible explanation, but it is also inadequate because it does not take into account the great moral investment by transnational forces in the creation of this state and others like it, including the double-barrelled nation, Czechoslovakia. I have shown that the national revolution was, indeed, hastily conceived but it was endorsed as the culmination of the centuries-long indigenous quest for the independence of an integrated race. The legacy of generations of publicists on the subject and the exigencies of war made this possible. In the wake of the collapse of empires a reconfiguration of European borders was imperative as a means to fill a political vacuum, to contain the spread of communism in the wake of the Bolshevik revolution and to provide stability and a balance of power. The architects of the New Europe believed there was nothing ad hoc about the way in which the new borders were drawn and that they were merely facilitating an inevitable process whereby 'Gallant Serbia' was transformed into Yugoslavia.

In Chapter 3 I argued that the character of the state determined the nature of the problems it faced. The inherent contradiction was that while the Yugoslav nation was said to be centuries old, successive governments could not establish a viable and inclusive Yugoslav identity, ethnic or civic. I have shown that this contradiction was not a cause for concern among our observers and for historians subsequently because they did not take full account of the role of the state as one of the primary agents of nation-building. The way in which ruling elites interpreted what it meant to be Yugoslav affected how they governed. How Yugoslavia was governed and the way in which Yugoslavs were treated as subjects, citizens or 'uncitizens' in turn affected the country's evolution, and the extent to which Yugoslav identity would be contested. Oblivious to this key point, observers were thus able to speak of 'perennial' problems emanating from Croatian quarters because Croats were 'historically' (thereby nationally) disinclined towards consensus and naturally obstructionist. Political behaviour and developments within the Kingdom were applauded as pro-Yugoslav or deplored as anti-Yugoslav, regardless of the fact that 'Yugoslavs' like King Aleksandar established a brutal dictatorship and opposition politicians like Radić did not contemplate the destruction of the state and were committed democrats. As I have stated, Yugoslavia made its malcontents, and outsiders who took the Yugoslav 'nation-state' as a preordained given were incapable of recognizing this fact.

The architects of the New Europe did not realize that old axes of transnational influence would not disappear with the stroke of a pen. For example, Habsburgian group identities could not be eclipsed for all the centre's attempts to do so. The point here is not so much that cultural affiliations predating the establishment of the new state were stronger than any Yugoslav identity, but that the coexistence of the old with the new 'national reality' became uneasy and then impossible. This was because in the centralist Kingdom Yugoslavism came to be identified with the dominant Serbian cultural and political institutions. There were persistent problems of civic identity in the hybrid state, which led to the immediate legitimation of a hierarchy of Yugoslavs and Yugoslavisms, the preferred and the out of favour, and to what we might refer to a little unfashionably as the Whig interpretation of South Slav history.

The idea of Yugoslavia as the product of a long struggle against oppression and then 'the war to end all wars', as well as the necessary precondition of peace in Europe, dominated interwar discussions about the state. The critical factors shaping the history of the Kingdom were the notion that Yugoslavia was Serbia's prize for its loyalty in the First World War, the false perception of the Yugoslav race and nation as an integral whole, the memory of war, and the inability of the government to provide stability or adequate representation for all its constituents. The outsiders' response to the shooting of Croat politicians in the Belgrade parliament in 1928 and their easy acceptance of the dictatorship and police state in 1929 reveal the extent of their attachment to the idea of the state, regardless of its nature. The assassination of King Aleksandar in October 1934 did not lead them to question this attachment but strengthened their commitment to an overarching Yugoslavism. Outsiders were also convinced that certain South Slavs were sabotaging that ideal.

The memory of war dominated perceptions of Yugoslavia, as demonstrated by French veterans, bearing witness to the indestructibility of ties forged in battle, making their way as pilgrims to the sites of commemoration on the Balkan front. Not all outsiders agreed with the dominant views of the Yugoslav state expressed by key individuals like Seton-Watson and his colleagues. The latter were vexed by the opinions of some of their opponents and, indeed, tried to silence them. The debates of the time show why certain views came to prevail and why some dissident Yugoslav voices could not sway international opinion. Edith Durham became Seton-Watson's *bête noire*. He criticized her vigorously, yet some of Durham's observations and predictions, for example on the fate of Albanians within Yugoslavia, proved more illuminating and insightful than anything Seton-Watson had to say on the subject. By silencing and ridiculing her he silenced and ridiculed those whose problems genuinely concerned her.

Chapter 4 showed that the Second World War, like the First World War, was a pivotal moment in Yugoslav history and had an impact on the way Yugoslavism was understood. However, the understanding of the Yugoslavs' experience of the war was partial and remained so for decades. During the period 1941–5 tensions evident in interwar Yugoslavia played themselves out in the context of a total war of unprecedented destruction and violence. Traditionally historians have examined the war in Yugoslavia in isolation and as exceptional, a practice which, I have argued, relies on an essentialist and dichotomous reading of the Yugoslavs' behaviour at this time. Josip Županov has written that historians often focus on the difference between the 'unkempt Dinaric showman, the imaginative torturer and killer' and the technocrat, or 'Maidanek killer'. He goes on to say that these 'culturological differences' are meant to illuminate the difference between crimes 'carried out on industrial principles and those on the principle of home economy', concluding that 'on the whole the differences should not be overplayed'.[2] On that score Županov notes the negative effect on historical understanding over time of the 'two value orientation' which allowed only for absolute good and absolute evil in the reconstruction of the anti-fascist struggle in Yugoslavia.[3] As we have seen, Davies discusses this premise with regard to the disjointed historiography of the Second World War generally and of the Grand Alliance in particular. Without the background of the interwar period and without the context of the international historiography of fascism, national socialism, collaboration and resistance, the war in Yugoslavia makes no sense. Normalizing this history and Europeanizing the historiography of the war in Yugoslavia has been a primary goal in this book, as it is the only way we can begin to move beyond the stereotypes of unparalleled barbarism in the Balkan theatres of war. It is also the only way we can discover the Yugoslav people and begin to understand the true impact of the war in their history and in memory. The Ustaša movement, in large part the product of the marginalization of Croatian opposition in the Kingdom, was not a mass movement and failed to capture the imagination of a cross-section of Croatian nationalists in the 1930s. In 1941, however, Croats who would not have backed Pavelić previously may well have been prepared to give him a hearing. Experience had shown them that the old regime had little to recommend it. Until the nature of the Independent State of Croatia became apparent, there was no reason to believe it would be any worse than the Kingdom. Similarly, the behaviour of the government-in-exile, Mihailović and his Chetniks has much to teach us about the Kingdom and the way in which nationalist Serbs perceived Yugoslavism.

Identifying the ethically tolerable options for action available to different Yugoslav people in the war helps us to understand that total war and occupation, not communist ideology, shaped or made possible the second 'Yugoslav revolution'. People were saying 'no' to collaboration and fascism, as the example of women resisters testified, rather than 'yes' to a communist revolution. Tito was the hero of Yugoslav resistance. For many he was the hero of European resistance. Those upholding the revised (and ultimately preferred) Yugoslav model inside the country were the Partisans who were able to appeal to a broad cross-section of people with their new Yugoslav vision of a federal state of equal nations. Yugoslavia was still seen as a necessity ensuring stability in the region, regardless of the fact that it was to be a Stalinist dictatorship run by former guerrilla fighters. Without a coherent integrated national or civic identity, however, the new Yugoslavia was recognized politically and patriotically primarily on its anti-fascist credentials which meant, in reality, as a communist state.

Chapter 5 established that communism was imposed from above and that the period of implantation was ruthless and far from democratic, even in the limited sense the Partisans had promised it would be. Yugoslavia's socialist experiment was none the less very appealing in a bipolar world, especially after its expulsion from the Cominform. Tito's was a new communism, one that promised true self-actualization through workers' self-management. To its devotees, Yugoslavia's socialist experiment was not dogmatic, as its eventual openness to market socialism testified, and it was no more than necessarily oppressive. Although it was not ideal, it was the best option for all concerned, as a strong Yugoslav state was also the wedge against Soviet expansion westwards. Yugoslavia made the best of the atmosphere of the Cold War. Tito's independence and non-alignment appeared most attractive when tensions between East and West were at their height. Further, Tito was seen to have 'rescued' his people from the Balkan fury that the war had unleashed and to have suppressed nationalist yearnings, extreme and distasteful as they were, to secure stability in 'the chief danger spot' in Europe. Tito himself, like many communists, freely used the Balkanist paradigm to justify his methods as the Yugoslavs travelled down the path to 'modernity'. How far that 'danger spot' had been of the Balkan populations' making and how far it was the product of Yugoslavia's creation and development and the abuse of power by its leaders was never seriously considered. Nor was the extent to which outsiders and the ruling elites manipulated perceptions of 'danger spots', to whom they were in fact dangerous and why.

After 1945 Yugoslavia, as an ideal, again came to mean different (but still broadly compatible) things. To hundreds of thousands of travellers it was a sunny holiday spot. Tourists flocked to the Croatian coast for their cheap and pleasant 'getaway'. If politics was ever a concern for such visitors, it was only in so far as they could note that Yugoslavia was not nearly as grey as other communist states. Tito had great drawing power. A star-studded cast, including Richard Burton and Elizabeth Taylor, joined him on his island retreat in the Adriatic and drove in his convertible Cadillac. Indeed, Burton was cast as Tito in the 1973 film *Sutjeska*, commemorating the Fifth Partisan Offensive. Yet another new wave of writing on Yugoslavia, disconcertingly similar to the travellers' and academics' accounts that feature in Chapter 1, appeared. Its refrain was that the Yugoslavs were a breed of people who had experienced a terrible civil war and whom Tito had saved from their own worst instincts. While inside the country economic and political developments led to greater differentiation between Yugoslavs, from the outside there was immense moral and material investment in the country with more attempts to project a homogeneous nation. Even though our observers were less likely to evoke the image of a single

Yugoslav race, the slogan of the new Yugoslavia, 'Brotherhood and Unity', seemed to capture the new optimism and the international rededication to the integrated state. This was despite the growing evidence of maldistribution of national wealth and the fact that the country was dependent on a seemingly endless source of aid from the United States.

The memory of war was as important in the life of communist Yugoslavia as it had been in the Kingdom. There was an overwhelming official identification with a reading of the war which privileged the actions of the dominant (masculine) voices of the wartime generation, and this had damaging repercussions over time. As was the case in the 1920s and 1930s, the potentially integrative narrative fusing the themes of war, nation and identity came to be associated with a system of rule that cynically undermined its foundational myths and that was unrepresentative and dismissive of individual and collective rights and freedoms. The dogged refusal to accept that Yugoslavia was becoming a dysfunctional state was understandable in an atmosphere in which international diplomacy celebrated and rewarded hypocrisy. Careerism and corruption led to disengagement and alienation in Yugoslavia on a scale unforeseen by the regime ideologues. They could not satisfy the materialistic generation they had, in fact, created. Youth surveys conducted between 1956 and 1963 showed that the rising generation was not interested in politics but in finding gainful employment, even if it meant leaving their homeland. More importantly, young people were less interested in committing themselves to a public life of service than in fulfilling their personal ambitions.[4] Questionnaires directed at youth might well have produced similar results elsewhere, but these responses are also a little surprising, given this survey was conducted at a time of international optimism for Yugoslavia and youth empowerment and idealism. If the answer to all the pressing questions posed by an alienated rising generation of Yugoslavs was to be found in a rereading of the 'young Marx', as the Praxis philosophers averred, then there was little hope for the regime. Yet few could entertain such a thought.

The belief that Yugoslavs inhabited a political space outside normal European experience persisted through to the end of Tito's life and beyond. Two years before his passing one could still read comments like this in Anglophone magazines: 'Admittedly by western standards the Titoist system, as it has developed over the last three decades, is in essential aspects authoritarian. ... By western standards, of course, it is not a satisfactory situation. There is however the question whether western standards can or should be applied at all to Yugoslavia.'[5] Others rationalized that the Yugoslavs did not aspire to greater pluralism, noting that 'the number of political parties is irrelevant to thought divergence'.[6] On Tito's death in 1980 his old wartime companion and friend, Fitzroy Maclean, wrote:

> Though Yugoslavia possesses a single-party system, this does not mean that there is not a lively and continuing public debate on a wide range of subjects between genuinely conflicting interests, the interests, that is, of different regions and different sections of the community and economy, all requiring to be satisfied before a consensus can be arrived at. It is not parliamentary democracy, as the West understands it, but in its own way it works.[7]

This comment from one of the greatest champions of communist Yugoslavia, which sounds patronizing and even a little preposterous today, was representative. It was uttered long after the idealism that dominated the immediate post-war period had subsided. Maclean's comment reflected the attitude of powerful outsiders who watched on as Yugoslavia's rulers kept the country in an almost permanently (politically) infantile and economically ruinous state, rendering it incapable of carrying its citizens peacefully through the great European upheaval of the 1980s and 1990s.

The End of the Illusion

It is necessary to go beyond the usual suspects (nationalism, religion and economic failure) to establish the causes of Yugoslavia's collapse. We are told that the legendary Yugoslav 'consensus', by which Tito was able to govern, was shattered by a minority of nationalist extremists taking advantage of economic crisis. They then manipulated an unsuspecting citizenry. Consensus is a word much abused in studies of political participation in modern dictatorships. Joining a party for the sake of one's career did not translate either into good party members or produce motivated, ideologically well-formed professionals. Numerous studies of the effects of quasi-compulsory party membership in Fascist Italy note that the extent of depoliticization was in direct proportion to the increased rate of party membership. Mass membership may have led to conformism, but it did not lead to fascistization on a mass scale.[8] The fact that the ruling party became the only social reality had to have a political impact while Mussolini's regime lasted, but that impact did not endure or out-live the regime, as the easy discarding of the Duce in 1943 was to demonstrate. Similarly, in Tito's Yugoslavia, party membership was not a marker of civic engagement but (understandable) self-interest. According to one 1973 observation of Yugoslav life and letters, with the 'crackdown' that followed the Croatian Spring, Tito complained that the intellectuals and professors had corrupted young people with anarcho-liberal ideas. Moreover, not enough Marxists were emerging from the system and those who did were poorly trained. Tito deplored the fact that insufficient attention was devoted to 'the classics of Marxism' across the educational institutions. This article went on to note (eight years after the author's fulsome account of the new socialism and Yugoslavia's future prospects) how much more difficult it was going to be for Tito as a new generation, left cold by the endless retelling of the 'Partisan epic', was coming of age.[9] The absence of serious reflection on the nature of 'citizenship' and civil society, identified simply as an ill-defined fetish of the West and its bourgeois distractions, is instructive. The 'Yugoslav way' was neither transcendent nor humanist, but as crassly materialistic as any capitalist society without the bourgeois 'fetishisms' of political rights and freedoms as sweeteners. The degree and rate of disaffec-tion from the regime after 1945 would not have been as obvious as the disillusionment in the early years of the Kingdom but this did not constitute 'consensus'; people did not 'choose' the Yugoslav way. That does not mean Tito was not popular or that people did not find his Yugoslavia a refuge and a relief. In the absence of alterna-tives his Yugoslavia became the new 'necessity' and the only social reality first, for want of tolerable options then by force and, finally, by desultory habit.

Signs of the elusive Yugoslav 'consensus' therefore rely on a loose understanding of the word. They call to mind the way in which it has been used to describe how people negotiated their daily lives in Fascist Italy and Nazi Germany. There it signified the absence of open opposition or active resistance. Balancing consent and coer-cion is never a simple matter in the study of social life under dic-tatorships. The problem is, however, that the very words 'consent' and 'consensus' suggest a choice has been made freely. Further, as the Yugoslav regime had limited resources to draw on in its search for consensus around common values predating 1945, the ground on which that manufactured consensus depended grew shaky. Some have tried to identify what precisely constituted political or civic life prior to the 1980s, noting that nationalism or religion (or both) drowned out the cross-national voices of reason which sought to identify a Yugoslav citizenry.[10] However, there is little evidence to suggest that a strong Yugoslav civic identity was any more likely to emerge in the 1980s than previously or that either nationalism or religion blocked the expression of such an identity. There is even less evidence to support the theory that either nationalism or religion, or a brew comprising both, were strong enough to fragment consensus had it, indeed, existed.[11] The absence of a people's revolt against dictatorship does not by default signify consensus or the emergence of what historians of communist regimes have called participatory dictatorships. Scholars have established that there were many ways, other than open dissent (of which there was a great deal in Yugoslavia in any case), by which disaffection from a totalitarian regime or one-party dictatorship might be articulated. The corrosive effects over time of such deliberate daily refusal to submit must not be underestimated.

Everyone feared the death of Tito would precipitate unrest and all were relieved that in the short term it did not. However, his passing marked the end of the nexus between personality politics and the Yugoslav ideal. It also marked the symbolic passing of the Partisan generation and the rapid process of the demythologization of the resistance ideal and the anti-fascist struggle. What legitimacy the state had enjoyed disappeared with Tito. Economic problems, of which there were many, in themselves could not have brought down the system. System failure at a time of economic crisis is the result of the abandonment of the government by elites or of their removal by revolutionary forces, for example. Economic crisis challenges all states and can lead to administrative instability, social upheaval and uncertainty. But other factors must be present for such a crisis to result in the overthrow of a government or the total collapse of a system. The Depression provided the background and the context of the collapse of the Weimar Republic, although the nature and consequences of that collapse were not and could not be determined by the economy alone. Nor was it the case that economic failure alone precipitated the collapse of Yugoslavia. In a sense the catchcry 'After Tito – Tito!' expressed the wishful thinking of outsiders as much as it informed that of the Yugoslavs who had coined it. It was not altogether different from the view expressed after Aleksandar's death in 1934 that the only solution to the problems the country faced was to continue the work of the dead king and to 'preserve his Yugoslavia'. The assassination of Aleksandar had led to national mourning as his body was transported by rail through the country from the coast to Belgrade. It gave outsiders the sign they needed that all would be well: tragedy had brought about unity. There was also an outpouring of grief when Tito died. His funeral, like Aleksandar's, was a call to international solidarity behind the Yugoslav ideal. Both leaders had had to resort to unsavoury politics for a higher good. Their respective war records attested to the fact that at heart they were capable and dependable and under them dictatorship was therefore acceptable, especially if it meant they would keep in check the centrifugal nationalisms and Soviet imperialism, while preserving the territorial integrity of the state. In 1980 fulsome tributes praised Tito and his political career, much like the tributes to Aleksandar in 1934. Each of these men represented the limited and partial aspirations outsiders held for a Yugoslavia where the level of progress, however defined, was not to be measured against the same benchmarks as those of other European countries. Tito was the last leader of the country with the power to evoke and defend an internationally tolerable version of the Yugoslav ideal. Without him the state struggled while the political repression, economic mismanagement and national inequalities stood out. A revisionist account of Tito's leadership emerged in the 1980s. In due course he would be identified as one of the chief architects of Yugoslavia's demise. The anti-Tito bandwagon was capacious at that stage. The notion that Tito was responsible for 'fragmenting' what was once whole presupposes a coherency to Yugoslavism which could be destroyed at will by ill-intentioned individuals. This was never the case, but it was a powerful idea.

In the end there seemed to be less enthusiasm for the Yugoslav ideal than resignation and, finally, indifference. In the mid-1980s not one-twentieth of the population declared itself 'Yugoslav' and in Bosnia-Herzegovina, where the population was more mixed than elsewhere and one might have expected a higher proportion of people to identify themselves as 'Yugoslav', as few as 5.5 per cent of the population (mainly urban elites) did so. That said, it is curious Tito should be held accountable because he did not groom another strongman or group of men to take his place. To blame Tito for not securing a smooth path for an equally controlling successor or not democratizing Yugoslavia is to blame him for doing precisely the job outsiders propped him up to do, to keep a ramshackle system going by whatever means. As we have seen, there was never any expectation that he should be held accountable for anything else.

The interwar period attracted renewed interest among nationalist writers and intellectuals in Serbia in the 1980s when they revisited the themes of their suffering in the twentieth century. There was also a special focus on the First World War and its aftermath. Novelists often began their family sagas with the martyrdom of Serbs in the Second World War but the memory of the First World War was revived in their elaboration of the pedigree of sacrifice and suffering.[12] Interestingly, it was also in the 1980s that a number of memorials to the British women who had provided humanitarian aid in the First World War were renovated and rededicated.[13] In 1989 the classic work by Laffan mentioned in Chapter 2, *The Guardians of the Gate*, was reissued in the United States. Based on lectures Laffan had delivered while serving in Salonika and first published in 1918, the book traces the history of the Serbs in the nineteenth century and then describes their trials in the First World War. It concludes with a resounding call for loyalty on the part of the British. The dust-jacket of the 1989 edition explains that the book, out of print for many years, is a classic work on an important but misunderstood nation and recommends it to 'anyone interested in a historical perspective on a great and heroic people'. The timing and stated intention of this new edition are of particular interest. Equally significant is the fact that it was translated into Serbian and published in Belgrade in 1994.[14] The persistent resonance of the cyclical narrative of decline and resurgence played an important role in the violent disintegration of the country. In the official history of the First World War the projected Yugoslav synthesis could be seen by Serbs as denying aspects of their personal and collective history because it had attempted (unsuccessfully) to universalize them. Further, Serb nationalist intellectuals and politicians believed that the state that bore Tito's unmistakable imprint no longer represented their interests. An early indication of this sentiment was the public display of emotion in Belgrade on the death of Ranković in 1983. (We saw in Chapter 5 that Ranković had been the head of the secret police and was ousted in 1966.) His funeral occasioned a demonstration of some 100,000 people protesting against Serbia's 'inferior position' in Yugoslavia.[15] Now seemed the time for Serbs to take back their past. Serbs believed their sacrifices in the struggle against the infidel, for the 'liberation' of other South Slavs and then in the establishment of both Yugoslavias, went unrecognized in a homogenized history of the region. Yugoslavia was no longer their reward but their burden, and Serbian identity could not coexist with a Yugoslav identity that did not take full account of their unique history of anguish and struggle.

The upsurge in Serbian nationalism that combined in a powerful ideology of racism, 'preservation psychosis', a selective reading of the Serbian and South Slav past and pseudo-intellectualism precipitated the collapse of Yugoslavia.[16] This was in part because it was so out of step with the currents of late twentieth-century European history and the fundamental principles which marked the reformism of Mikhail Gorbachev's Soviet Union. In this wider context Yugoslavism was looking less progressive and less necessary as a containment device. The Serbs' vision of 'all Serbs in one state' as the solution to their 'national question' led to an upsurge in their agitation and hostility under the leadership of Slobodan Milošević.[17] Nationalist Serbs accused most other Yugoslavs of negating Serbian culture and identity at best, and of possessing genocidal intentions at worst. Claims and counter-claims by Kosovars and Serbs of policies of ethnic exclusion culminated in the latter alleging the Kosovars were having large families in order deliberately to squeeze Serbs out of their 'historic' and 'spiritual' home. Sixty years previously Edith Durham had predicted conflict between the Serbs and the Albanians who would not be forcibly 'Slavized', and she was proven correct.

Further, the 'pre-emptive' theories casting Croats as a 'genocidal nation', as proclaimed in 1986 by the Serb historian Vasilije Krestić, averred that the crimes of the Ustaše were not atypical but inherent to the Croatian psyche, as exemplified by the tyranny of Ustašism's successor, Croatian communism.[18] Thus, over time, an inversion had taken place. The Croats, considered first restless, then irredeemably nationalist and, finally, 'fanatically' separatist because of their seeming obsession with Serbian centralist hegemony, had become the oppressors. This inversion was effected through their identification with a Yugoslav ideal or synthesis which allegedly denied elements of Serbia's 'Yugoslav' history. However broadly the Allies had seemed to attribute the sufferings South Slavs endured in the First World War, it was never the case that all could share equally in the glory and the collective bereavement. In the Second World War, British servicemen who fought alongside Croat Partisans and who fell and were buried on Croatian soil were exhumed and reinterred after the war in the Commonwealth War Graves established in Belgrade and Niš.[19] This bureaucratic act symbolically disenfranchised further those who had not been conceded a place in the international fraternity of veterans after 1918 and who could never redeem themselves, not even by their 'exemplary' behaviour and allegiance in subsequent wars. After 1945 it was evident to observers that 'Even the staunchest Croatian nationalists cannot entertain the traditional ideas of a separate statehood without remembering the compromising history of Pavelić's "independence" and without realizing that, as a separate state, Croatia would not be economically viable.'[20] In the 1980s their Communist past along with Ustašism was the Croats' encumbrance, as the memory of war and post-war repression merged into a generalized critique of the flawed nation. Only now it was Serbia's economic viability that came into play. (We recall that economic viability had been one of the earliest rationalizations for the South Slav synthesis and for the rejection of the proliferation of small states in the region in the nineteenth century.) The Slovenes were mostly spared this kind of scrutiny and their secession was, mercifully, relatively painless. An altogether different fate awaited the Republics of Croatia and Bosnia-Herzegovina.

Yugoslavia failed twice as an integrated state. Apart from the Party or League of Communists and the army, which were the repressive organs of a corrupt and self-serving ruling elite, all-Yugoslav cross-republican institutions fell well short of attracting lasting interest. The idea of Yugoslavia had died well before the state finally disappeared. How was it possible for the rulers of that rump of Yugoslavia in 1992 to retain the name without an acute sense of the absurdity of the situation? That the Serbs and Montenegrins clung to 'Yugoslavia' was more than ironic. It was an indication of the way in which the state, from beginning to end, was perceived by the majority of Serbs and most outsiders even when they threw their lot in with Tito's federalism. Competing views about the state and the form it should take coexisted throughout its history, at times more happily than at others, without seriously threatening Yugoslavia's place as a fixture on the European landscape. This coexistence was possible because of the international situation. The collapse of communism changed everything, not because the Yugoslavs' potential to democratize excited outsiders but because it marked a tumultuous turning point in the balance of power on the Continent.

The fall of the Soviet Union and the communist 'alliance' in Central and Eastern Europe was the necessary precondition for people to begin to imagine a world without Yugoslavia. It became more and more difficult to ignore the internal voices that demanded political freedom and equality. It was no longer possible to continue to label all oppositionists national extremists. This was because the Serbs, once deemed the historic protectors of the Yugoslav flame, were evidently more nationalistically extreme than the non-Serbs. Initially few outsiders cared to contemplate the ramifications of such a transformation and when they did, it was not with any enthusiasm or optimism. The persistence of the Balkanist framework (now less obvious in one of its newer and more acceptable guises, relativism or moral equivalence) and the impact of the layered memories of the world wars on the collective consciousness of insiders and outsiders were at the root of the delayed response to the crisis in Yugoslavia. At the same time, while the fall of the Berlin Wall had been a thrilling moment in the history of the twentieth century, once the euphoria had subsided it was clear that a reunited Germany became the bogey the 'Teutonic' empire had been for our Western outsiders prior to 1914. This context in part explains the unpreparedness of Yugoslav 'experts' in the face of the state's terminal crisis and their inability to offer appropriate explanations for what was occurring. They reasoned that the democratic revolution could not be embraced by peoples who had never known or valued individual rights and freedoms and so the Yugoslav unrest was of a different order from that experienced in states where national integrity was not in question, such as Hungary, for example. Nor was Czechoslovakia's Velvet Revolution of 1989, which led to the peaceful establishment of two republics in 1993, relevant to the much more 'complex' and 'intractable' Yugoslav situation.

A Cold War mentality prevailed in those crucial early months prior to the Serbian-initiated attack on Slovenia and Croatia in 1991. If democratization led to a surge in what George Bush Senior was to refer to as 'suicidal nationalisms', then it was unacceptable and counterproductive. Interestingly, his argument was almost exactly the same as the nineteenth-century position that rejected seemingly minor independence movements that threatened to spawn 'destructive anarchy'.[21] So, where the Central Intelligence Agency had predicted the violent break-up of Yugoslavia some eighteen months prior to the collapse, political leaders in the United States had neither the will nor the experience to apply serious statecraft to address the problems Yugoslavia faced. Further, old friendships and alliances still had the capacity to shape international relations. France was willing to tolerate and support dictatorship in an otherwise 'friendly' country in the 1930s when its interests were at stake, and when the friendship or bond (in our case the wartime bond between Serbs and the French established on the Balkan front) was strong enough. It was willing to do so again in the 1990s as it 'followed Britain into spinelessness', much as it had done just over fifty years previously.[22] It could be argued therefore that the Slovenes and Croats, recognizing this inflexibility, perhaps even subconsciously, made the decision to pull out of the federation when they did because they knew there would never be a better or, indeed, an acceptable time, either from the point of view of the international community or the Serbs, to democratize Yugoslavia and to make it more nationally and ethnically equitable. The fact that in 1991 when the Croatian city of Vukovar fell to the Serbs after relentless bombing by the so-called Yugoslav People's Army, a street was named Puniša Račić, after Radić's assassin, seemed to bear this out.

In the first instance, the Wars of Yugoslav Succession were often described as 'fratricidal' because this suited the outsiders' view that Yugoslavia's collapse was an internal matter or dispute between 'Yugoslavs' and (minority) 'anti-Yugoslavs' and unrelated to the European revolution. Outsiders therefore initially brandished the Yugoslav ideal as something that had been realized and was now in danger of being dashed or shattered because of the actions of a handful of people of bad faith. Exponents of the 'if only' school of Yugoslav historical interpretation perpetuated this (mythical) version of events. They mourned the loss of something, never really asking themselves if it had actually ever existed, and sought reasons for this apparent loss in the events and policies immediately preceding the wars of the 1990s. Susan Woodward served as senior adviser to the top United Nations official in Yugoslavia and special representative of Secretary General, Boutros Boutros-Ghali, and counselled a 'hands off' policy. She spoke out vehemently against 'taking sides'.[23] Curiously, Woodward did not consider the policy of supporting unrepresentative 'Yugoslavs' who had seized almost all of the country's weaponry and preventing certain parties from purchasing arms while their attackers had such a huge material advantage that they sold weapons outside the region in order to bolster their war economy, to be 'taking sides'.[24] One of Woodward's core arguments was that if enough energy had been put into bolstering and strengthening Yugoslavia then the allegedly marginal and extreme forces working to destroy its integrity would have been overwhelmed by the majority of Yugoslav people who, in fact, she wrote, hoped and worked for the preservation of the state. Yet it was the case that huge amounts of money and aid of all kinds had already gone into keeping the Yugoslavs afloat since 1945. The efforts of the United States and international financial institutions to maintain Yugoslavia had not led to significant change or improvements across a period of over forty years. What did Woodward think might tip the balance in favour of stability and 'progress' as the country was disintegrating? It was a disingenuous position and sustainable only until the evidence of ethnic cleansing and other war crimes demanded a more rational response.

Ethnic cleansing as it occurred on several occasions during the Wars of Yugoslav Succession entailed, for example, the systematic eradication by Serbs of Bosnian Muslims and Kosovars from designated areas by various means including massacres, rape and forced migration. Civilians queuing for food or water became targets for Serb snipers during the four-year siege of Sarajevo. The discovery of the genocide Serbs committed against the Muslims in Srebrenica in 1995 shocked all international onlookers and it would be fair to say that for most of them the Yugoslav ideal died at that point. What made matters worse was that the peacekeepers had sat at table and negotiated with the perpetrators of the crime, known murderers and proponents of ethnic cleansing. The United Nations representatives facilitated the handover of at least 6700 Muslim men of military age to their certain death. These men were taken off in groups, killed within a few days and buried in mass graves.[25] The United Nations later admitted that its men on the ground made a gross 'miscalculation' and had 'misjudged' the situation.[26] It was this admission that showed how badly things were being managed. It marked a definitive turning point in the history of the idea of Yugoslavia. That the international peacekeepers regarded 'safe havens' or ethnically distinct areas of jurisdiction as an appropriate solution to the difficulties facing non-Serbs in Bosnia-Herzegovina indicates how poorly prepared was the United Nations to frame a suitable response. One of the reasons the international community tolerated ethnic cleansing up to that point was the perception of problems there as 'unsolvable' because of the nature of the people in question. Like Seton-Watson, many believed the salad could not be 'unmixed'. After 1945 there was also the perceived problem of an 'endemic' cult of ethnic violence. Then the relativist position that all the Yugoslavs were 'as bad as each other' or 'equally to blame' for war crimes became the greatest impediment to a balanced analysis of events.[27]

International security institutions expressly designed to deal with such crises failed. They failed because the governments that wielded the most power within these organizations, and which advocated non-intervention, used them as instruments of their foreign policy.[28] In the case of Britain and France, the motive was to oppose German initiatives, not because they feared for the well-being of Yugoslavs but because, after the collapse of the Soviet Union, they were worried that Germany was becoming a rival in a reintegrating Europe. To take Germany's lead was tantamount to accepting a shift eastwards in the centre of European power. Furthermore, the idea that Serbs would respond to international pressure to withdraw if they knew the stakes were high enough was never properly considered in the 1990s.[29] Instead, everything was negotiable because there was in the West 'a high tolerance for the worst atrocities in Europe since the Nazi era' which, according to one author, Milošević quickly discerned.[30]

There was also a fear that the new 'imbalances' of power on the Continent might engulf it in a general war. That is why, for those who were unsympathetic to the cause of the Slovenes, Croats and Bosnians in the first instance, Germany's position, its 'premature' recognition of the breakaway republics, was not acceptable whereas Russia's stand was. The Russians supported and defended the Serbs because they believed the whole world had 'ganged up on Serbia' and 'Russia alone' came to its aid. The Chairman of the Russian Parliament's Foreign Affairs Commission 'denounced the "myth" of concentration camps on the territory of Yugoslavia', claiming 'they were like "poor quality sports camps" serving free food that was "perfectly decent by contemporary Moscow standards"'. In the absence of political will in a powerful country like the United States 'to take responsibility for the management of political change in post-Soviet Europe', some believed that 'the immense democratic and pacific possibilities of 1989' were going to be squandered.[31]

It was finally clear that the majority of non-Serbs had no desire to remain in a Yugoslav state and that the South Slavs had no common sense of identity. This was not so much because their histories were different or because distinct nations and peoples came into the new state with their long and self-contained histories intact, but because in Yugoslavia history was made fungible and deliberately marshalled to justify the unjustifiable. Moreover, the lived experience of Yugoslavs from the state's very inception led to disparate and ultimately incompatible views on its future. The final collapse was a shock and a disappointment to Yugoslavists and had tragic consequences for Yugoslavs. Perhaps one of the greatest difficulties in dealing with the history of these events is that it was dominated by the writings of people who had something to lose by the break-up of Yugoslavia. Victor Meier, who was a Balkan correspondent for 30 years, completed a doctoral thesis on 'The New Yugoslav Economic System' which, he writes, seemed 'meaningful and relevant' in the 1950s. He never regarded Yugoslavia as an 'artificial creation' but, once 'the state formation became unrealistic and politically unsustainable, it became necessary to draw the appropriate conclusions'.[32] It also became necessary to take into account the views of Yugoslavs. Not everyone was as unsentimental and sanguine as Meier. The fact that others were less willing to question their assumptions and received wisdom about Yugoslavia had disastrous repercussions, as Brendan Simms has shown so forcefully and disturbingly.[33]

Another New Europe

Yugo-nostalgia is an inappropriate vehicle for studying the history and demise of the Yugoslav ideal. It is also dangerous. It is ahistorical and romanticizes an imagined past, creates new myths, perpetuates and recasts old ones and inhibits an open engagement with conflicting historical narratives. In 2002 an Australian woman, Anna Funder, wrote a book on the German Democratic Republic, exploring the corrosive impact of the secret police, the Stasi, and its pathological watchfulness on people's ordinary lives.[34] Often anodyne acts were infused with a political significance simply because of the context in which they were observed. It is an uncomfortable and confronting story for those who were involved with the Stasi, as well as their victims. Many Germans would probably prefer not to have to remember the accommodations they made daily to survive, or the loss of personal integrity when they acted as informants with agents of the ruling ideology for little reward, passing on banal details about those upon whom they spied. It is well known that reminiscences of those who lived through the Third Reich, while insightful and full of anecdotal interest to outsiders, are also less likely to contain information about the inroads of National Socialism into daily life and how it influenced personal values.[35] This partial amnesia is an example of the unconscious desire to reject the notion that National Socialism contaminated the private sphere in the same way that it contaminated the public sphere. It could be said that Tito's

Yugoslavia awaits its Anna Funder. That is a story the people who stood to lose from the collapse of the regime are unlikely to tell, or want to tell, as dispassionately as those who did not. By the late 1980s Yugoslavia was no longer viable. This was not because Tito had squandered a golden opportunity, but because the state had no obvious or admirable reason to exist. Western observers may well have wanted the aspirations of the republics to be compatible and to merge, but they finally recognized that they could neither will this nor impose it. Almost a hundred years of campaigning on behalf of an ultimately elusive Yugoslav ideal had finally taught them that. The constituent tribes could not be 'soldered' in the way that many had hoped in the interwar years and Namier still advocated in 1942. When Yugoslavia would no longer seem a necessity in the global context, and once powerful outsiders had less interest in its territorial integrity, then the will of the internal actors who wanted change prevailed.

A huge amount has been written about the destruction of Yugoslavia, much of it by people who lived through it. Professional Yugoslavists had a difficult time of it and only rarely did individuals like Meier announce without much fuss that there were new sets of variables to consider and that these warranted a change of opinion. Mark Mazower has written that the 'almost universal failure to predict the collapse of communism drove a large nail in the coffin of Western political science'. Academics as well as policy makers and commentators on international affairs were taken by surprise. Just months before the collapse they were writing their prognoses on the continued stability of the Soviet Union. Mazower adds that to 'recall such prognoses is not to mock their authors, who were after all entirely in sympathy with the outlook of their times', but 'to recapture some essential elements of what happened in 1989 itself'.[36] Historians, according to Mazower, have only begun to scratch the surface of the complex and puzzling history of the fall of communism. I would add that they also have much to discover about the history of one of the states in which so much of the enthusiasm of the epoch was invested and in which the ideological polarizations of twentieth-century Europe played themselves out in miniature. The wave of nostalgia for the old regimes, following the revolutions of 1989, blurred people's vision of the recent past. It led many to treat communism rather as though it constituted a lifestyle choice. It was a 'choice' among any number of options, or if one were just slightly more critically disposed, it had been a regrettable reality about which no one could do anything. The violence that accompanied the demise of the second Yugoslavia would be attributed to everything except the nature of the state itself.

As it became evident that the shattering experience of the First World War had devastated a generation and brought to an end a certain conception of European alliances, ushering in an era of 'nation-states', people began to speak of a New Europe. The New Europe would be full of hope and idealism. However, there remained a fear of war, and in order to prevent it compromises had to be made and alliances struck to ensure peace and stability. Thus while people spoke of the death of the old diplomacy, they unwittingly ensured its survival for almost the entire century. Another shattering war further eroded hope and idealism. For a second time people witnessed the birth of a New Europe. It was rather greyer than its predecessor and a temporary victim of the ideological struggle between East and West. The devastation wrought gave way to an overt pragmatism. Naked calculation underpinned international relations in what became the bipolar world. Eventually it would be subsumed by an immobilizing relativism. Again, compromise was the order of the day, and while few would have argued that this was an entirely satisfactory state of affairs, at the same time Cold War 'warriors' were not especially committed to bringing about change. Eventually, however, the European voices that had been silenced or marginalized in the global politics of the Cold War made themselves heard and communist regimes fell, one after another. At first the Yugoslavs were denied their place in this democratic revolution because theirs was labelled a national rather than a political struggle. In due course Yugoslav communism also collapsed and the nature of its collapse reflected the nature of the regime. The fall of Yugoslavia signalled an end but it also signalled a beginning. Yugoslavia's history was enmeshed within a broader narrative and cannot be separated from it. A greater understanding of that fact is not a cause for pessimism or alarm, but should be accepted as part of a process that helps make visible and understandable the various actors who played a part in constructing Yugoslavia and the historical context in which they did so.

Chronology

This chronology aims to complement rather than duplicate material covered in the book and thus focuses particularly on the state's internal political history and events leading to the destruction of Yugoslavia.

*c.*500–600	Appearance of people, generally known by the common name 'Slavs', in Byzantine Illyricum.
1371–1526	Ottoman conquest of Macedonia (1371), Serbia (1389–1453), Bosnia (1453), Herzegovina and Montenegro (1488), Slavonia and parts of Dalmatia (1526).
1804–15	Serbian wars of liberation from Ottoman Empire. Serbia becomes the first *de facto* (but not *de jure*) independent South Slav country. Remains a principality until 1882, when it became a kingdom.
1809–13	Illyrian provinces created by Napoleon from Slovenian and Croatian territories formerly under Austrian rule.
1844	*Начертаније* (*Načertanije*, The Draft). Foreign policy plan of Ilija Garašanin, adviser to Serbian Prince Miloš Obrenović, to include South Slav lands into expanded Serbia.
1875–8	Uprising of the Christian population against Turkish rule in Bosnia.
1878 (13 June–13 July)	Congress of Berlin. Serbia and Montenegro become independent; Bosnia occupied by Austria-Hungary.
1888 (16 December)	Aleksandar Karađorđević born in Cetinje, Montenegro.
1892	Josip Broz (Tito) born in Kumrovec, Croatia.
1903 (11 June)	Coup in Belgrade, resulting in change of dynasty. (King Aleksandar Obrenović and Queen Draga assassinated and the following year Petar Karađorđević crowned Petar I.)

1908 (6 October)	Bosnia annexed by Austria-Hungary.
1912 (8 October–3 December)	First Balkan War.
1913 (16 June–31 July)	Second Balkan War.
1914 (28 June)	Gavrilo Princip assassinates Archduke Franz Ferdinand and his wife, Sophie Chotek (Duchess of Hohenberg), in Sarajevo.
1914 (28 July)	Austria-Hungary attacks Serbia.
1914 (16–19 August)	Battle of Cer. Austrian defeat by Serbian army.
1914 (16 November–15 December)	Battle of Kolubara. Austrian defeat by Serbian army.
1914 (22 November)	Yugoslav Committee established in Florence, but not publicly announced until 30 April 1915.
1914 (7 December)	Serbian government issues Niš Declaration calling for the unification of South Slavs into a single state as a Serbian war aim.
1915 (October through to winter)	Coordinated attack by Austro-Hungarian and Bulgarian Armies commanded by Field Marshal Mackensen results in fall of Serbia and retreat of its army.
1916 (September)	Macedonian (Salonika) Front established by Entente powers.
1916 (18 December)	Declaration in Paris by Yugoslav Committee emphasizing Serbs, Slovenes and Croats as leading nations in future South Slav state.
1917 (20 July)	Corfu Declaration between Serbian government in exile and Yugoslav Committee signed by Serbian Prime Minister, Nikola Pašić, and the Croat, Ante Trumbić, for the Yugoslav Committee.
1918 (15–29 September)	Allied army comprising Greek, French, Serb, British and Italian troops under Commander Franchet d'Espéray breaks out on Salonika front and knocks out Bulgaria from the war, recovering Macedonia and Serbia from the Central Powers.
1918 (5–6 October)	National Council of Slovenes, Serbs and Croats formed in Zagreb.
1918 (11 November)	End of First World War.
1918 (1 December)	Regent Aleksandar proclaims Kingdom of Serbs, Croats and Slovenes. Act of unification passed by National Council two days later.
1919 (21–23 April)	Social Democratic and Communist parties unite to form the Socialist Workers' Party of Yugoslavia in Belgrade.

1920 (20–25 June)	Socialist Workers' Party renamed Communist Party of Yugoslavia.
1920 (28 November)	First elections. Delegates' representation includes (Serb) Democrats (92), (Serb) Radicals (91), Communists (58) and Croat Republican Peasant Party (50) out of 419 overall.
1921 (21 January)	Radicals and Democrats form new government in alliance with Yugoslav Muslim Organization. Pašić becomes prime minister.
1921 (28 June)	Vidovdan Constitution passed with 161 representatives (Croat parties and the Communists) boycotting the proceedings.
1921 (August)	Croat Republican Peasant Party, Croatian Union and Croatian Party of Right form Croatian bloc under leadership of Stjepan Radić.
1921 (2 August)	Communist Party banned after attempted assassination of the Regent, Aleksandar, and the assassination of the Minister of the Interior.
1921 (16 August)	King Petar I dies.
1921 (6 November)	Aleksandar crowned King Aleksandar I.
1922 (28 April)	The government divides state into 33 centrally controlled districts (*oblasti*).
1923 (18 March)	New elections. Gains for Radicals (108) and Croat Republican Peasant Party (70) and serious losses for Democrats (51).
1925 (18 July)	Stjepan Radić, leader of Croat Peasant Party, agrees to work within the system and join a coalition with the Radicals. In turn he gains concessions from the king regarding control of administrative decisions affecting Croatia.
1926 (10 December)	Death of Pašić.
1927 (11 November)	The Serb centralist-turned-federalist, Svetozar Pribićević, and his Independent Democratic Party form a coalition with Radić's Peasant Party and embrace an anti-centralist agenda.
1928 (28 June)	Montenegrin deputy Puniša Račić shoots five – and kills two – Croat deputies in Belgrade parliament (*Skupština*). Radić wounded.
1928 (1 August)	King appoints Slovene, Monsignor Korošec, as prime minister, Independent–Peasant coalition (now led by Vladko Maček) withdraws from Assembly and rejects Constitution.
1928 (8 August)	Radić dies.
1929 (6 January)	Royal dictatorship of Aleksandar I. Retired general, Petar Živković, appointed prime minister.
1929 (3 October)	The king proclaims Kingdom of Yugoslavia. Country divided into nine administrative districts (*Banovine*).

1931 (3 September)	Aleskandar I proclaims new constitution that gives him significant power both in appointing members of new upper house and influencing legislation.
1932 (7 November)	Independent–Peasant coalition issues 'Zagreb manifesto' calling for Croatian autonomy and opposing the king.
1934 (9 October)	Aleksandar I assassinated in Marseilles. Three-man regency led by Aleksandar's cousin, Prince Pavle (Paul) Karađorđević, appointed.
1937 (July)	Tito becomes general secretary of Communist Party, at that time an illegal organization.
1938 (11 December)	Elections resulting in gains for Croat Peasant Party and a major setback for Yugoslav Radical Union of Prime Minister Stojadinović whom the Regent, Paul, replaces with Dragiša Cvetković.
1939 (26 August)	Agreement (*Sporazum*) between Prime Minister Cvetković and Maček, resulting in creation of Croatian *Banovina* that foreshadows significant autonomy for Croats. Maček becomes deputy prime minister.
1941 (25 March)	Yugoslavia signs Tripartite Pact.
1941 (27 March)	Military coup and large demonstrations in Belgrade against signing of Tripartite Pact. Petar II proclaimed of age. Military government of General Dušan Simović established.
1941 (6 April)	Germany invades Yugoslavia despite new government's adherence to Tripartite Pact.
1941 (10 April)	Proclamation of Independent State of Croatia led by Dr Ante Pavelić.
1941 (17 April)	Royal Yugoslav Army capitulates. King Petar II and government go into exile in Athens, later moving to London.
1941 (12–13 May)	Formation of Yugoslav Royal Army in the Fatherland (Chetniks) led by Colonel Dragoljub (Draža) Mihailović on Ravna Gora.
1941 (19 September)	Meeting of Mihailović and Tito establishing short-lived co-operation of Chetniks and Partisans.
1942 (11 January)	Mihailović appointed Commander in Chief of the army and Minister of War by Yugoslav government-in-exile.
1942 (26–27 November)	First meeting of Antifascist Council of the People's Liberation of Yugoslavia (AVNOJ) meets in Bihać.
1943 (29–30 November)	Second session of AVNOJ in Jajce. AVNOJ declares itself the government of Democratic Federative Yugoslavia, prohibits Petar II from

	returning, and proclaims new Yugoslavia as federated state.
1944 (1 June)	Petar II names Croat, Ivan Šubašić, prime minister-in-exile. Šubašić takes over from Mihailović as Minister of Defence but Mihailović remains commander of the army.
1944 (16 June)	Tito and Šubašić sign first agreement on the island of Vis with a view to forming joint government.
1944 (12 August)	Tito meets Churchill.
1944 (29 August)	Petar II dissolves Royal Army in Yugoslavia, and orders Chetniks to join Partisans.
1944 (21 September)	Tito leaves for Moscow to meet Stalin and they agree upon joint operations involving Partisans and the Red Army in Yugoslavia.
1944 (1 November)	Second agreement of Šubašić and Tito. AVNOJ named supreme legislative body.
1945 (7 March)	Provisional government with Tito as prime minister.
1945 (15 June)	War in Yugoslavia ends.
1945 (29 November)	Federal People's Republic of Yugoslavia (FPRY) proclaimed by Constituent Assembly in Belgrade. Monarchy abolished and king and dynasty deprived of all rights.
1946 (31 January)	Constitution of FPRY promulgated. State established as federation of 6 republics, Slovenia, Croatia, Bosnia-Herzegovina, Serbia, Montenegro and Macedonia, and 2 autonomous provinces, Vojvodina and Kosovo-Metohija (both as a parts of Serbia). Constitution based on 1936 constitution of the USSR.
1946 (19 April)	USA formally recognizes new Yugoslav regime.
1946 (10 June/15 July)	Trial of Mihailović (captured 13 March) and 23 other people. Mihailović executed on 18 July together with nine other officers.
1946 (11 October)	Monsignor Alojzije Stepinac (1898–1960), Archbishop of Zagreb (1937–60), Cardinal from 1952, found guilty of treason and war crimes and sentenced to 16 years in prison. Served 5 years. In 1951 released from prison to house arrest, where he remained until his death.
1946 (1 December)	Nationalization of 80 per cent of industry, as well as all mines, transport, banking and wholesale trade. Agrarian reform initiated and estates over 45 hectares expropriated.
1948 (April)	Full nationalization of industry.
1948 (28 June)	Yugoslav Communist party expelled from the Cominform in Bucharest for its independent foreign policy in the Balkans.

1949 (28 September)	Soviet Union, followed by other socialist states, breaks off the treaty of friendship with Yugoslavia.
1950 (27 June)	Basic Law on the Management of State Economic Enterprises and Higher Economic Associations by the Working Collectives (self-management of workers) enacted in the Assembly.
1951 (6 January)	USA and Yugoslavia sign agreement on aid to Yugoslavia.
1951 (14 November)	USA and Yugoslavia sign agreement on US military assistance.
1952 (2–7 November)	Sixth Congress of the Communist Party. Party changes name to the League of Communists of Yugoslavia (LCY).
1953 (13 January)	Parliament adopts amendments to 1946 constitution that enact decentralization. Federal Executive Council formed (government) and Assembly restructured into two houses: Federal Council and the Council of Producers. Tito made president of the republic for life.
1953 (5 March)	Stalin dies and tensions with the USSR ease.
1953 (29 March)	Members of peasant cooperatives allowed to return to individual farming after failure of collective farming.
1953 (October)	President of Assembly and member of Central Committee of the LCY, Milovan Djilas, begins to publish series of articles in the Belgrade government daily, *Borba*, attacking bureaucratization of the party and demands further democratization.
1954 (16–17 January)	Third plenum of LCY meets at Brijuni and leadership denounces Djilas, who is stripped of his positions and offices.
1954 (1 October)	Yugoslavia and USSR sign trade agreement ending six years of trade war.
1954 (December)	Novi Sad Agreement between Serbian and Croatian Cultural organizations (*Matica srpska* and *Matica hrvatska*). Creation of single language, Serbo-Croatian and/or Croato-Serbian.
1955 (January)	Djilas sentenced to 18 months in gaol but sentence suspended. In December 1956 Djilas sentenced to three years' prison after denouncing Soviet intervention in Hungary and criticizing Yugoslav foreign policy in an interview with the French press agency, France-Presse. Further sentences (in 1956 and 1962) follow.
1955 (26 May)	Soviet leaders Nikita Khrushchev and Nikolai Bulganin arrive in Belgrade to apologize for conflict between USSR and Yugoslavia.

1955 (2 June)	Belgrade Declaration signed by Tito and Bulganin recognizes Yugoslavia's separate path to socialism.
1956 (19 July)	Brijuni declaration between Gamal Abdal Nasser of Egypt, Jawaharlal Nehru of India and Tito paves way for establishment of Non-Aligned Movement, together with Bandung Conference of April 1955.
1956	Tito declares Soviet invasion of Hungary necessary to prevent counter-revolution.
1961 (6 October)	First conference of non-aligned states in Belgrade.
1963 (7 April)	New constitution promulgated. State renamed the Socialist Federated Republic of Yugoslavia (SFRY). LCY proclaimed governing (as opposed to leading) power in the state.
1965 (25 July)	Federal Assembly introduces economic reform programme, allowing much greater degree of market freedom for republics and increased decentralization. Reforms opposed by Vice-President Aleksandar Ranković and a mainly Serb centralizing faction ('the unitarists').
1966 (1 July)	Fourth Plenum on island of Brijuni. Ranković removed from his posts (vice-president of republic and head of security service).
1967 (17 March)	Declaration on the Status and Name of the Croatian Standard Language signed by a number of Croatian cultural organizations and intellectuals calling for annulment of the Novi Sad Agreement of 1954. Declaration asserts right of Croatian language to separate existence from Serbian.
1967 (19 July)	Macedonian Orthodox Church declared autocephalous, though it is not formally recognized by some Orthodox churches, including the Serbian Church.
1968 (3–12 June)	Violent student demonstrations in Belgrade. Students demand better conditions, but also end of social inequality. Students calmed after Tito himself promises to address their grievances.
1968 (21 August)	Tito critical of Soviet invasion of Czechoslovakia.
1968 (27–29 November)	Riots in Kosovo-Metohija. Demonstrators demand that Kosovo be accorded the status of a republic and be allowed to secede from SFRY. Riots quelled with force, followed by party purge and numerous arrests.
1968 (26 December)	Assembly passed amendments to the constitution giving significant autonomy to provinces of Vojvodina and Kosovo.

	Kosovo-Metohija renamed Socialist Autonomous Province of Kosovo.
1969 (9–11 January)	League of Communists of Bosnia-Herzegovina at Fifth Congress recognizes Muslims (considered either Croats or Serbs after 1945) as separate national group.
1970 (15–17 January)	Tenth Meeting of Central Committee of League of Communists of Croatia in Zagreb. Informal beginnings of the 'Croatian Spring' or 'Mass movement'.
1971 (23 November–3 December)	Students strike at the University of Zagreb demanding end of economic exploitation of Croatia and better conditions.
1971 (1–2 December)	Twenty-sixth session of Executive Bureau of LCY in Karađorđevo. Tito dismisses leaders of the Croatian Spring for reasons of 'nationalism' and 'counter-revolution'.
1974 (21 February)	New constitution promulgated, independent position of republics strengthened and autonomous provinces become constitutive elements of the federation. New consensus-based decision-making process introduced, economic decentralization strengthened and more pronounced role for the army.
1975 (May)	Tenth Congress of the LCY endorses further centralization of the party.
1980 (4 May)	Tito dies in Ljubljana after series of illnesses. Presidency becomes collective head of state with eight voting members representing republics and provinces and president of the LCY as a non-voting member. Presidents of Presidency regularly rotated after one-year term.
1981 (11 March)	Outbreak of anti-Yugoslav demonstrations in Kosovo. Demonstrators demand republican status for Kosovo and equality of Albanians with other constituent nationalities of Yugoslavia.
1981 (2 April)	SFRY Presidency declares state of emergency and deploys federal police and army to Kosovo resulting in around 1000 casualties. The province is temporarily pacified.
1984 (8–19 February)	14th Olympic Winter Games held in Sarajevo.
1986 (April–May)	Slobodan Milošević becomes leader of LC of Serbia.
1986 (24 September)	Memorandum of Serbian Academy of Sciences and Arts (SANU) released to public. This was a draft document claiming to address the grievances of the Serbs regarding their position in the federation. It called for the revision of the 1974 constitution and the restoration of the

'sovereignty' of the Serbs in areas where they
were in the minority.

1987 (24–25 April) Milošević visits Kosovo and gives full
support to complaints of Serbs in Kosovo
against alleged resurgence of Albanian
nationalism.

1987 (23–24 September) Eighth Session of Central Committee of LC
of Serbia. Milošević becomes undisputed
leader in Serbia.

1988 (9 July) Serbs and Montenegrins travel to Vojvodina to
demonstrate for a reduction in its autonomy,
marking the beginning of 'anti-bureaucratic
revolution' staged by Milošević. The 'anti-
bureaucratic revolution' spreads, with further
demonstrations.

1988 (July–October) Demonstrations in Titograd, Priština and
Novi Sad by Serbs calling for an end to the
autonomous status of Vojvodina and Kosovo.

1988 (19 November) 1,000,000 people attend a rally of 'Brotherhood
and Unity' in Belgrade.

1989 (10–11 January) Montenegrin leadership forced to resign after
massive demonstrations in Titograd.

1989 (24 February) Amendments to Serbian constitution
stripping Kosovo and Vojvodina of their
veto power over future constitutional
changes in Serbia.

1989 Mass gathering of almost 1,000,000 people in
(28 February–1 March) Belgrade demanding settlement of situation in
Kosovo.

1989 (28 June) Celebration of the 600th anniversary of the
Battle of Kosovo attracts 1,000,000 Serbs at
Gazimestan on the site of the battlefield itself.
Milošević delivers speech emphasizing Serbian
unity and 'Serbian defence of European values'.
First mention of possible 'armed battles' in the
future.

1990 (1–2 February) Severe clashes between police and Albanian
demonstrators in Kosovo.

1990 (8 April) Free elections in Slovenia. Opposition wins
majority in parliament. The communist Milan
Kučan elected president.

1990 (22 April) General elections in Croatia. Croatian
Democratic Union (HDZ) wins majority;
Dr Franjo Tuđman becomes president of Croatia.

1990 (5 July) Serbian Parliament dissolves Parliament of
Kosovo.

1990 (17 August) Clashes between Croatian police and Serbs
in Kninska Krajina. Serbs set up barricades –
Balvan revolucija (the 'trunk revolution').

1990 (November)	Elections in Macedonia and Bosnia-Herzegovina bring victory to nationalists.
1990 (9 December)	Elections in Serbia and Montenegro. Milošević wins in Serbia, as does his ally Momir Bulatović in Montenegro.
1990 (21 December)	Declaration of Serbian Autonomous District of Krajina (SAO Krajina) in Croatia.
1990 (23 December)	Plebiscite in Slovenia results in 88 per cent voting in favour of independence.
1991 (19 May)	Referendum in Croatia results in 94 per cent of voters opting for independence.
1991 (25–26 June)	Slovenia and Croatia declare independence. SAO Krajina cuts links with Croatia.
1991 (27 June–7 July)	Federal army attacks Slovenia on authorization of Prime Minister Ante Marković, but fails to achieve military success. EC representatives negotiate moratorium on independence of Slovenia and Croatia.
1991 (7 September)	Referendum in Macedonia leads to vote of 74 per cent in favour of independence.
1991 (24–25 October)	Parliament of Serbian people in Bosnia-Herzegovina constituted, followed by referendum of Serbs where 90 per cent of those who vote decide to remain in Yugoslavia.
1991 (18 November)	Yugoslav army takes Croatian city of Vukovar after three months of siege. Croats in Bosnia-Herzegovina proclaim Croatian Community of Herzeg-Bosnia.
1991 (19 December)	SAO Krajina declared Republic of Serbian Krajina (RSK).
1991 (23 December)	Germany recognizes independence of Slovenia and Croatia.
1992 (15 January)	UK, Austria and Belgium recognize independence of Slovenia and Croatia.
1992 (1 March)	Referendum on independence of Bosnia-Herzegovina. With a turnout of 64 per cent, 99.4 per cent of those who vote support independence. Referendum in Montenegro results in 96 per cent support for the formation of a common state with Serbia.
1992 (6 April)	EC Ministerial Council recommends recognition of Bosnia-Herzegovina. USA recognizes Slovenia, Croatia and Bosnia-Herzegovina. Parliament of Serbs in Bosnia declares independence of Serbian Republic of Bosnia-Herzegovina (from 12 August, Republika Srpska, RS).
1992 (27/28 April)	Federal Republic of Yugoslavia established, comprising Serbia and Montenegro. Formal dissolution of SFRY.

1992 (22 May)	Slovenia, Croatia and Bosnia-Herzegovina admitted to UN.
1995 (12–22 July)	Srebrenica massacre of 6700–8000 Bosniak men by Serb forces following Serbian takeover of UN protected enclave.
1995 (4–9 August)	Operation Storm (*Oluja*) conducted by the Croatian army leads to recapture of Kninska Krajina, destruction of the military forces of Serbs in Croatia and the end of RSK except for the remnant in eastern Slavonia.
1995 (30 August–20 September)	Operation Deliberate Force conducted by NATO against RS in Bosnia after shelling of market in Sarajevo. This leads to start of peace negotiations that result in Dayton peace accord.
1999 (24 March–11 June)	NATO bombing campaign against Yugoslavia after it refuses to sign Rambouillet Accords and continues fighting in Kosovo. Campaign ends with Serbian withdrawal and NATO, later UN, occupation and administration of Kosovo.
2001 (31 March)	Milošević arrested by Serbian authorities for corruption charges. On 28 June, Milošević extradited to International Criminal Tribunal for Former Yugoslavia in the Hague.
2003 (4 February)	Parliament of Yugoslavia declared State Union of Serbia and Montenegro as a loose confederation of Serbia and Montenegro. End of Yugoslavia.
2006 (21 May)	Referendum on independence of Montenegro with 0.5 per cent over the required 55 per cent voting in favour.
2006 (3 June)	Parliament of Montenegro declares independence.
2008 (March)	Kosovo declares independence.

Prime Ministers and Presidents

Prime Ministers, 1919–41

Name	Term begins	Term ends	Party
Nikola Pašić	01/12/1918	22/12/1918	(Serbian) People's Radical Party
Stojan Protić	22/12/1918	16/08/1919	People's Radical Party
Ljubomir Davidović	16/08/1919	19/02/1920	(Serbian) Democratic Party
Stojan Protić	19/02/1920	16/05/1920	People's Radical Party
Milenko Vesnić	16/05/1920	01/01/1921	People's Radical Party
Nikola Pašić	01/01/1921	28/07/1924	People's Radical Party
Ljubomir Davidović	28/07/1924	06/11/1924	Democratic Party
Nikola Pašić	06/11/1924	08/04/1926	People's Radical Party
Nikola Uzunović	08/04/1926	17/04/1927	People's Radical Party
Velimir Vukičević	17/04/1927	28/07/1928	People's Radical Party
Anton Korošec	28/07/1928	07/01/1929 (resigns 30/12/1928)	Slovene People's Party
Petar Živković	07/01/1929	04/04/1932	Yugoslav Radical Peasant Democracy
Vojislav Marinković	04/04/1932	03/07/1932	Yugoslav Radical Peasant Democracy
Milan Srškić	03/07/1932	27/01/1934	Yugoslav Radical Peasant Democracy
Nikola Uzunović	27/01/1934	22/12/1934	Yugoslav Radical Peasant Democracy (becomes Yugoslav National Party)
Bogoljub Jevtić	22/12/1934	24/06/1935	Yugoslav National Party/Yugoslav Radical Union
Milan Stojadinović	24/06/1935	05/02/1939	Yugoslav Radical Union
Dragiša Cvetković	05/02/1939	27/03/1941	Yugoslav Radical Union

Prime Ministers of Royal Government-in-Exile (London, Cairo) and Provisional Government within Yugoslavia (Josip Broz only)

Name	Term beginning	Term ending	Party
Dušan Simović	27/03/1941	12/01/1942	non-party(military)
Slobodan Jovanović	12/01/1942	26/06/1943	non-party
Miloš Trifunović	26/06/1943	10/08/1943	(Serbian) People's Radical Party
Božidar Purić	10/08/1943	08/07/1944	non-party
Ivan Šubašić	08/07/1944	30/01/1945	Croat Peasant Party
Drago Marušić	30/01/1945	07/03/1945	non-party
Josip Broz (Tito)	07/03/1945	29/11/1945	Communist Party

Prime Ministers and Presidents of the Federal Executive Council (after 1953)

Name	Term beginning	Term ending	Nationality	Republic/ province of birth
Josip Broz (Tito, prime minister)	29/11/1945	14/01/1953	Croat	Croatia
Tito (president of FEC)	14/01/1953	29/06/1963	Croat	Croatia
Petar Stambolić	29/06/1963	16/05/1967	Serb	Serbia
Mika Špiljak	16/05/1967	18/05/1969	Croat	Croatia
Mitja Ribičič	18/05/1969	30/07/1971	Slovene	Slovenia
Džemal Bijedić	30/07/1971	18/01/1977	Bosnian Muslim	Bosnia-Herzegovina
Veselin Đuranović	18/01/1977	16/05/1982	Montenegrin	Montenegro

Presidents of the Presidium of the Communist Party/League of Communists

Name	Term beginning	Term ending	Nationality	Republic/ province of birth
Josip Broz (Tito)	23/10/1937	04/05/1980	Croat	Croatia
Branko Mikulić (acting for Tito)	19/10/1978	23/10/1979	Croat	Bosnia-Herzegovina
Stevan Doronjski (acting for Tito until 04/05/1980)	23/10/1979	20/10/1980	Serb	Vojvodina

Chairmen of the Presidency (all members of the Communist Party except Stjepan Mesić, who was a member of the Croatian Democratic Union)

Name	Term beginning	Term ending	Nationality	Republic/ province of birth
Lazar Koliševski	04/05/1980	15/05/1980	Macedonian	Macedonia
Cvijetin Mijatović	15/05/1980	15/05/1981	Serb	Bosnia-Herzegovina
Sergej Kraigher	15/05/1981	15/05/1982	Slovene	Slovenia
Petar Stambolić	15/05/1982	15/05/1983	Serb	Serbia
Mika Špiljak	15/05/1983	15/05/1984	Croat	Croatia
Veselin Đuranović	15/05/1984	15/05/1985	Montenegrin	Montenegro
Radovan Vlajković	15/05/1985	15/05/1986	Serb	Vojvodina
Sinan Hasani	15/05/1986	15/05/1987	Albanian	Kosovo
Lazar Mojsov	15/05/1987	15/05/1988	Macedonian	Macedonia
Raif Dizdarević	15/05/1988	15/05/1989	Bosnian Muslim	Bosnia-Herzegovina
Janez Drnovšek	15/05/1989	15/05/1990	Slovene	Slovenia
Borisav Jović	15/05/1990	15/05/1991	Serb	Serbia
VACANT	15/05/1991	30/06/1991		
Stjepan Mesić	30/06/1991	03/10/1991 (formally resigned 05/12/1991)	Croat	Croatia

Presidents of the Federal Executive Council (Prime Ministers)

Name	Term beginning	Term ending	Nationality	Republic/ province of birth
Veselin Đuranović	18/01/1977	16/05/1982	Montenegrin	Montenegro
Milka Planinc	16/05/1982	15/05/1986	Croat	Croatia
Branko Mikulić	15/05/1986	16/03/1989	Croat	Bosnia-Herzegovina
Ante Marković	16/03/1989	20/12/1991	Croat	Bosnia-Herzegovina

Presidents of the Presidium of the Communist Party/League of Communists

Name	Term beginning	Term ending	Nationality	Republic/ province of birth
Stevan Doronjski (acting for Tito until 04/05/1980)	23/10/1979	20/10/1980	Serb	Vojvodina
Lazar Mojsov	20/10/1980	20/10/1981	Macedonian	Macedonia
Dušan Dragosavac	20/10/1981	29/06/1982	Serb	Croatia
Mitja Ribičič	29/06/1982	30/06/1983	Slovene	Slovenia
Dragoslav Marković	30/06/1983	26/06/1984	Serb	Serbia
Ali Šukrija	26/06/1984	25/06/1985	Albanian	Kosovo
Vidoje Žarković	25/06/1985	28/06/1986	Montenegrin	Montenegro
Milanko Renovica	28/06/1986	30/06/1987	Serb	Bosnia-Herzegovina
Boško Krunić	30/06/1987	30/06/1988	Serb	Vojvodina
Stipe Šuvar	30/06/1988	17/05/1989	Croat	Croatia
Milan Pančevski	17/05/1989	17/05/1990	Macedonian	Macedonia

Notes

Introduction

1. See for example Sabrina Petra Ramet, *The Three Yugoslavias: State Building and Legitimation 1918–2005* (Washington, DC and Bloomington, 2006); Leslie Benson, *Yugoslavia: A Concise History* (Basingstoke, 2004); Ann Lane, *Yugoslavia: When Ideals Collide* (Basingstoke, 2004); John Allcock, *Explaining Yugoslavia* (London, 2000); and John R. Lampe, *Yugoslavia as History: Twice there was a Country* (Cambridge, 1996). All of these books contain useful bibliographies. See also Sabrina Petra Ramet, *Thinking about Yugoslavia: Scholarly Debates about the Yugoslav Breakup and the Wars in Bosnia and Kosovo* (Cambridge, 2005) for a synthesis of different approaches to the final collapse of the state.
2. Glenda Sluga, 'The Nation and the Comparative Imagination' and Deborah Cohen and Maura O'Connor, 'Introduction: Comparative History, Cross-national History, Transnational History – Definitions', in Deborah Cohen and Maura O'Connor (eds), *Comparison and History: Europe in Cross-National Perspective* (New York and London, 2004), pp. 103–14 (106) and pp. ix–xxiv (xviii).
3. Allcock, *Explaining Yugoslavia*, p. 211.
4. Sluga, 'The Nation and the Comparative Imagination', p. 111.
5. See Dubravka Ugrešić, *The Culture of Lies: Antipolitical Essays*, trans. Celia Hawkesworth (London, 1996). Ugrešić, having been accused of Yugo-nostalgia, believes it a term of abuse applied by 'nationalists' to critics (like herself) of the post-communist regime in Croatia.
6. Chris Lorenz, 'Comparative Historiography: Problems and Perspectives', Forum on Comparative Historiography, *History and Theory*, 38 (1999), pp. 25–39 (34).
7. I have taken this phrase from Mark Almond's *Europe's Backyard War: The War in the Balkans* (London, 1994). He has quoted Dr Radovan Karadžić, indicted war criminal and so-called 'Butcher of Bosnia', on the title page: 'The proposition "Bosnia is Europe's backyard" is more than stupid – it stinks of neo-imperialist arrogance.'

274

8. See Sanjeev Khagram and Peggy Levitt, 'Constructing Transnational Studies', in Sanjeev Khagram and Peggy Levitt (eds), *The Transnational Studies Reader: Intersections and Innovations* (New York and Abingdon, 2008), pp. 1–18.
9. Patricia Clavin, 'Defining Transnationalism', *Contemporary European History*, 14 (2005), pp. 421–39 (423).
10. Ibid., p. 424.
11. Denisa Kostovicova and Natalija Basic, 'Conference Report. Transnationalism in the Balkans: The Emergence, Nature and Impact of Cross-national Linkages on an Enlarged and Enlarging Europe, 26–27 November 2004', *Contemporary European History*, 14 (2005), pp. 583–90 (590).
12. Here I am referring to a comparative history project – the publication of a textbook for use in schools in the region – facilitated by the History Department of the Central European University. See www.hist.ceu.hu/?q=node/27.
13. Philipp Ther, 'Beyond the Nation: The Relational Basis of a Comparative History of Germany and Europe', *Central European History*, 36 (2003), pp. 45–73 (65, 67).
14. Maria Todorova, *Imagining the Balkans* (New York and Oxford, 1997).
15. See Jasna Dragović-Soso, *'Saviours of the Nation', Serbia's Intellectual Opposition and the Revival of Nationalism* (London, 2002); Marko Attila Hoare, 'Whose is the Partisan Movement? Serbs, Croats and the Legacy of a Shared Resistance', *Journal of Slavic Military Studies*, 15 (2002), pp. 24–41; Wolfgang Hoepken, 'War, Memory and Education in a Fragmented Society: The Case of Yugoslavia', *East European Politics and Societies*, 13 (1999), pp. 190–227; and Wolfgang Höpken, 'History Education and Yugoslav (Dis-) Integration', in Melissa Bokovoy, Jill Irvine and Carol Lilly (eds), *State–Society Relations in Yugoslavia, 1945–1992* (New York, 1997), pp. 79–104.
16. Andrew Baruch Wachtel treats this theme in a cultural context in *Making a Nation, Breaking a Nation: Literature and Cultural Politics in Yugoslavia* (Stanford, 1998). I have discussed this idea in Vesna Drapac, 'The Memory of War and the History of the First Yugoslavia', *War and Society*, 23 (2005), pp. 23–41.
17. In Chapter 3 we will see that recent work on commemorative practices in Serbia in the interwar years is illuminating on this point.
18. Ugrešić, *The Culture of Lies*, pp. 234–5.
19. Ida Blom, 'Gender and Nation in International Comparison', in Ida Blom, Karen Hagemann and Catherine Hall (eds), *Gendered Nations: Nationalisms and Gender Order in the Long Nineteenth Century* (Oxford and New York, 2000), pp. 3–26 (14–17).
20. Ther, 'Beyond the Nation', p. 47.
21. See Hugh and Christopher Seton-Watson, *The Making of a New Europe: R.W. Seton-Watson and the Last Years of Austria-Hungary* (London, 1981); Ljubo Boban *et al.* (eds), *R.W. Seton-Watson i Jugoslaveni: Korespondencija 1906–1941*, 2 vols (Zagreb, 1976); and 'Tributes to R.W. Seton-Watson: A Symposium', *Slavonic and East European Review*, 30 (1952), pp. 331–63.

22. For an introduction to Edith Durham and her work see John Hodgson, 'Edith Durham, Traveller and Publicist' and June Hill, 'Mary Edith Durham as a Collector', in John B. Allcock and Antonia Young (eds), *Black Lambs and Grey Falcons: Women Travellers in the Balkans* (Bradford, 1991), pp. 8–28, 30–4; Jane Robinson, *Wayward Women: A Guide to Women Travellers* (Oxford, 1990), pp. 260–1; and Dea Birkett, *Spinsters Abroad: Victorian Lady Explorers* (London, 1991) pp. 288–91 and *passim*. See also the entry for Durham by Harry Hodgkinson in H.C.G. Matthew and Brian Harrison (eds), *Oxford Dictionary of National Biography* (Oxford and New York, 2004), Vol. 17, p. 399.

23. Cohen and O'Connor, 'Introduction', p. xv.

24. See Norman Davies, *Europe: A History* (London, 1997), pp. 39–42; 'Misunderstood Victory', in *Europe East and West* (London, 2006), pp. 240–8; and *Europe at War, 1939–1945: No Simple Victory* (London, 2006), pp. 11–16.

25. See for example D'Ann Campbell, 'Women in Combat: the World War II Experience in the United States, Great Britain, Germany, and the Soviet Union', *Journal of Military History*, 57 (1993), pp. 301–23; and Roger D. Markwick, '"A Sacred Duty": the Red Army Women Veterans Remembering the Great Fatherland War, 1941–1945', *Australian Journal of Politics and History*, 54 (2008), pp. 403–20.

26. Susan R. Grayzel, 'Across Battle Fronts: Gender and the Comparative Cultural History of Modern European War', in Cohen and O'Connor, *Comparison and History*, pp. 71–84 (71, 78, 81–2).

27. See for example Robert Gellately, *Backing Hitler: Consent and Coercion in Nazi Germany* (Oxford, 2003); Elizabeth Harvey, *Women and the Nazi East: Agents and Witnesses of Germanization* (New Haven, CT and London, 2003); Vandana Joshi, *Gender and Power in the Third Reich: Female Denouncers and the Gestapo 1933–1945* (Basingstoke, 2003); and Klaus-Michael Mallmann and Gerhard Paul, 'Omniscient, Omnipotent, Omnipresent? Gestapo, Society and Resistance', in *Nazism and German Society, 1933–1945*, ed. David F. Crew (London and New York, 1994), pp. 166–96.

28. Susan Pedersen, 'Comparative History and Women's History: Explaining Convergence and Divergence', in Cohen and O'Connor, *Comparison and History*, pp. 85–102 (94). See also Mary Fulbrook (ed.), *National Histories and European Histories* (London, 1993).

29. Pedersen, 'Comparative History and Women's History', p. 97.

30. Todorova, *Imagining the Balkans*, pp. 10–12. See also Milica Bakić-Hayden, 'Nesting Orientalisms: The Case of the Former Yugoslavia', *Slavic Review*, 54 (1995), pp. 917–31.

31. Ther, 'Beyond the Nation', p. 71.

32. Clavin notes that transnational encounters are often retrospectively described as 'consistently progressive and co-operative' in 'Defining Transnationalism', p. 424.

33. Jürgen Kocka, 'Comparison and Beyond', *History and Theory*, 42 (2003), pp. 39–44 (44).

34. Ramet, *The Three Yugoslavias*.

1 Imagining Savage Europe and Inventing Yugoslavia: 1850–1914

1. H.N. Hutchinson, J.W. Gregory and R. Lydekker, *The Living Races of Mankind: A Popular Illustrated Account of the Customs, Habits, Pursuits, Feasts and Ceremonies of the Races of Mankind Throughout the World*, 2 vols (London, n.d. [1902]), Vol. 2, pp. 444, 446, 454.
2. Todorova, *Imagining the Balkans*, p. 169.
3. Andrew Hammond, 'The Uses of Balkanism: Representation and Power in British Travel Writing, 1850–1914', *Slavonic and East European Review*, 82 (2004), pp. 601–24.
4. Todorova, *Imagining the Balkans*, pp. 95, 97.
5. See for example Larry Wolff, *Inventing Eastern Europe: The Map of Civilization on the Mind of the Enlightenment* (Stanford, 1994); Barbara W. Maggs, 'Three Phases of Primitivism in Portraits of Eighteenth-Century Croatia', *Slavonic and East European Review*, 67 (1989), pp. 546–63; Stevan K. Pavlowitch, 'Early Nineteenth-Century Serbia in the Eyes of British Travelers', *Slavic Review*, 21 (1962), pp. 322–9; and Barbara Jelavich, 'The British Traveller in the Balkans: The Abuses of Ottoman Administration in the Slavonic Provinces', *Slavonic Review*, 33 (1955), pp. 396–413.
6. John Pemble, *The Mediterranean Passion: Victorians and Edwardians in the South* (Oxford, 1988).
7. Humphry Sandwith, 'A Trip into Bosnia', *Fraser's Magazine* (Dec. 1873), pp. 698–713 (701).
8. Harry de Windt, *Through Savage Europe* (London and Glasgow, 1907).
9. Geoffrey Drage, 'The Balkan Main Current', *Edinburgh Review* (Jan. 1913), pp. 197–216 (198).
10. See Dorothy Anderson, *Miss Irby and Her Friends* (London, 1966) and *The Balkan Volunteers* (London, 1968). See also Robinson, *Wayward Women*; Birkett, *Spinsters Abroad*; and Allcock and Young, *Black Lambs and Grey Falcons*. Anderson describes the volunteers' networks, describing that Florence Nightingale monitored Irby's work and provided advice and encouragement at different times.
11. G[eorgina] M[uir] Mackenzie and A[deline] P[aulina] Irby, *The Turks, the Greeks and the Slavons: Travels in the Slavonic Provinces of Turkey-in-Europe* (London, 1867), p. 663.
12. Some notable examples include Gardner Wilkinson, *Dalmatia and Montenegro with a Journey to Mostar in Herzegovina* (London, 1848); A.A. Paton, *Highlands and Islands of the Adriatic*, 2 vols (London, 1849); Viscountess Strangford, *The Eastern Shores of the Adriatic in 1863 with a visit to Montenegro* (London, 1864); Arthur J. Evans, *Through Bosnia and the Herzegovina on Foot during the Insurrection* (London, 1876) and *Illyrian Letters addressed to the 'Manchester Guardian' during the year 1877* (London, 1878); E.A. Freeman, *Sketches from the Subject and Neighbour Lands of Venice* (London, 1881); T.G. Jackson, *Dalmatia, the Quarnero and Istria with Cettigne in Montenegro and the Island of Grado*, 3 vols (Oxford, 1887); Robert Munro, *Rambles and*

Studies in Bosnia-Herzegovina and Dalmatia (Edinburgh and London, 1900); and John Booth, *Trouble in the Balkans* (London, 1905).

13. Todorova, *Imagining the Balkans*; and Vesna Goldsworthy, *Inventing Ruritania: The Imperialism of the Imagination* (New Haven and London, 1998).

14. Todorova, *Imagining the Balkans*. See especially Ch. 4, 'Patterns of Perception until 1900'.

15. For a critique of Britain's position see Georgina Muir Mackenzie, 'Montenegro, the Herzegovine, and the Slavonic Populations of Turkey', *MacMillan's Magazine* (Aug. 1862), pp. 345–52.

16. Henry Vignoles, 'A Ride through Bosnia', *Fraser's Magazine* (Nov. 1875), pp. 549–65 (558).

17. E.L. Mijatovics, 'Panslavism: Its Rise and Decline', *Fortnightly Review* (July 1873), pp. 94–112 (109, 110, 112).

18. Lepel Griffin, 'The Present State of the Eastern Question', *Fortnightly Review* (Jan. 1874), pp. 21–42 (33).

19. Robert Gildea, *Barricades and Borders: Europe 1800–1914* (Oxford, 1987), pp. 237, 239.

20. See for example Edmond Fitzmaurice, 'Hungary and Croatia', *MacMillan's Magazine* (May 1877), pp. 34–42 (42).

21. Henry Reeve, 'Bosnia and Bulgaria', *Edinburgh Review* (Oct. 1876), pp. 535–72 (559, 571). In this review article Reeve drew on the works of several authors, including Arthur Evans.

22. W.E. Gladstone, *Bulgarian Horrors and the Question of the East* (New York and Montreal, 1876), p. 29.

23. A number of organizations supported the Orthodox rebels. These included the Serbian Hospital Fund, the Eastern War Sick and Wounded Fund, the Bulgarian Relief Fund, the Bosnian and Herzegovinian Fugitives and Orphan Relief Fund, the Serbian Red Cross, the Bulgarian Peasant Relief Fund, the Manchester and Salford Bulgarian Relief Committee and the Serbian Distress Relief Fund. There were also appeals for the English Hospital in Belgrade. Some agencies offered aid to all victims whether or not they were Christian. See Anderson, *The Balkan Volunteers*.

24. R.W. Seton-Watson, J. Dover Wilson, Alfred E. Zimmern and Arthur Greenwood, *The War and Democracy* (London, 1914). From Seton-Watson's library, bequeathed to his Oxford college, New College, we can also note that he was familiar with much of the literature to which I refer here. For a comprehensive survey of his early work see H. and C. Seton-Watson, *The Making of a New Europe*.

25. E.A. Freeman, 'The Election and the Eastern Question', *Contemporary Review* (June 1880), pp. 956–76 (960).

26. Ibid., p. 966.

27. D.C. Lathbury, 'The European Concert', *Fortnightly Review* (Aug. 1880), pp. 200–9 (202, 209).

28. Arthur Evans, 'The Austrian Counter-revolution in the Balkans', *Fortnightly Review* (Apr. 1880), pp. 491–524 (491).

29. Ibid., pp. 491–2, 493.

30. Ibid., p. 498.

31. E.A. Freeman, 'The Position of the Austrian Power in South-Eastern Europe', *Contemporary Review* (May 1882), pp. 727–48 (727).

32. Interestingly, this was the view of a core group of radicals who, during the First World War, lobbied against the dissolution of the Dual Monarchy on the grounds that peace would not be assured were it to be replaced by smaller multinational states claiming to be nation-states.

33. Dalmatia was under Austrian jurisdiction whereas Croatia-Slavonia was in the Hungarian sphere.

34. G. Campbell, 'Home Rule in Several Countries', *Fortnightly Review* (May 1880), pp. 644–55 (646, 652, 654).

35. See Maura O'Connor, *The Romance of Italy and the English Political Imagination* (New York, 1998), pp. 149ff.

36. Evans, 'The Austrian Counter-revolution in the Balkans', pp. 494, 501.

37. Ibid., p. 495.

38. Freeman, 'The Position of the Austrian Power in South-Eastern Europe', p. 736.

39. Ibid., p. 744.

40. W.J. Stillman, 'Austro-Hungary', *Fortnightly Review* (June 1880), pp. 785–800 (786). Stillman was the American consul in Rome between 1861 and 1865 and correspondent for *The Times* between 1876 and 1898. His publications included *The Uprising in Herzegovina*. See *Who was Who in America 1897–1942* (Chicago, 1962 [1943]), p. 1157.

41. Evans, 'The Austrian Counter-revolution in the Balkans', p. 496.

42. Olga Novikoff, 'The Crisis in Serbia', *Contemporary Review* (Feb. 1882), pp. 290–307 (306). Anderson describes Novikoff as a 'glamorous Russian' who hosted a small salon in Claridges and corresponded with Gladstone. She expressed strong opinions against the Turks, to the embarrassment of the Russian Embassy, and the Turcophile press denounced her as a Turcophobe. See Anderson, *Miss Irby and Her Friends*, p. 135.

43. Evans, 'The Austrian Counter-revolution in the Balkans', p. 505.

44. See for example M.E. Grant-Duff, 'British Interests in the East', *Nineteenth Century* (Apr. 1880), pp. 658–76.

45. Frederic Harrison identified the problems associated with analyses of the Eastern Question that drew primarily on the injustices Christians suffered under Ottoman rule by pointing out that they suffered equally under 'fanatical' Christian rulers elsewhere. Britain had to take factors other than religion into account when deciding whether to intervene in disputes on the Continent. 'Cross and Crescent', *Fortnightly Review* (Dec. 1876), pp. 709–30. See also Henry Reeve, 'Turkey and Russia', *Edinburgh Review* (Jan. 1877), pp. 262–98 for a critique of British attacks on Muslims.

46. The Society of Jesus, founded in the sixteenth century, was instrumental in bringing about reforms within the Church in response to the Reformation. Jesuits undertook missionary work and were great founders of centres of learning. They were, according to their constitution, at the disposal of the Pope. In the eighteenth century Jesuits

faced opposition within the Church and were expelled from France, Portugal and Spain. The order was protected and continued working in Central Europe, which explains our observers' obsessively disparaging remarks regarding the links between the Habsburgs and the Jesuits. Of particular note, for example, was the fact that 'Francis Joseph himself was a pupil of the Jesuits'. See L.S. Amery, 'The Internal Crisis in Austria-Hungary', *Edinburgh Review* (July 1898), pp. 1–36 (13).

47. For example George Bowen, 'Montenegro', *Edinburgh Review* (Apr. 1859), pp. 461–85 (484–5).

48. Anderson, *The Balkan Volunteers*, p. 21.

49. Julie Wheelwright, *Amazons and Military Maids: Women who Dressed as Men in the Pursuit of Life, Liberty and Happiness* (London, 1989), pp. 41, 169.

50. Stevan K. Pavlowitch, 'À Propos de l'Église serbe: considérations d'un historien orthodoxe sur le malheur d'être une agence, un monument ou un revêtement', *Bulletin: Association Internationale d'Études Sud-Est Européen*, 30 (2000), pp. 163–71.

51. Evans, *Through Bosnia and the Herzegovina on Foot,* pp. xlff.

52. Evans, 'The Austrian Counter-revolution in the Balkans', p. 505.

53. Amery, 'The Internal Crisis in Austria-Hungary', p. 13.

54. See for example Harry Hanak, *Great Britain and Austria-Hungary during the First World War: A Study in the Formation of Public Opinion* (London, 1962), pp. 35, 122–3.

55. Stillman, 'Austro-Hungary', pp. 798, 799.

56. Ibid., pp. 799–800.

57. Ibid., p. 800.

58. Novikoff, 'The Crisis in Serbia', pp. 292–3, 299, 304, 306–7.

59. Bowen, 'Montenegro', p. 78. See also Mackenzie, 'Montenegro, the Herzegovine, and the Slavonic Populations of Turkey'; and Malcolm MacColl, 'Some Current Fallacies about Turks, Bulgarians, and Russians', *Nineteenth Century* (Dec. 1877), pp. 831–42. MacColl's article bemoans the abandonment of Christians to the 'Mussulmans'.

60. Mackenzie, 'Montenegro, the Herzegovine, and the Slavonic Populations of Turkey', p. 351.

61. [Georgina Muir Mackenzie and Adeline P. Irby], *Notes on the Slavonic Countries in Austria and Turkey in Europe*, ed. with a preface by Humphry Sandwith (Edinburgh and London, 1865), p. 51.

62. Evans, *Through Bosnia and the Herzegovina on Foot*, pp. 119, 183, 184.

63. Mackenzie and Irby, *The Turks, the Greeks and the Slavons*, pp. 631–2, 661, 663.

64. For example the 1849 notion that there existed 'no great cordiality' between 'Latins' and the Orthodox and that 'each charges the other with destructive heresy' remained deeply embedded in views about the South Slavs until the country's final demise. See Alexander Charles Fraser, 'Dalmatia and Montenegro', *Blackwood's Magazine* (Feb. 1849), pp. 202–18 (211). However, outside champions of the Yugoslav ideal also often underplayed the potential for discord on cultural or religious grounds, especially in the first half of the twentieth century.

65. Edith Durham, *The Burden of the Balkans* (London, 1905).
66. Evans, 'The Austrian Counter-revolution in the Balkans', pp. 515–16.
67. Freeman, 'The Position of the Austrian Power in South-Eastern Europe', pp. 745, 748.
68. Georgina Muir Mackenzie, 'Exodus of Mussulmans from Servia', *MacMillan's Magazine* (June 1863), pp. 87–96 (91).
69. Quoted in A.J.P. Taylor, *The Trouble Makers: Dissent over Foreign Policy 1792–1939* (London, 1957), p. 76.
70. Edward A. Freeman, 'The Southern Slaves', in *Historical Essays* (London and New York, 1892), pp. 384–433 (401). The article first appeared in the *British Quarterly Review* in July 1877.
71. Freeman, 'The Election and the Eastern Question', p. 974.
72. Edwin Pears, 'A Programme of Reforms for Turkey', *Nineteenth Century* (June 1880), pp. 1020–39 (1021, 1022, 1025).
73. Ibid., pp. 1028–9.
74. M.E. Grant-Duff, 'British Interests in the East', *Nineteenth Century* (Apr. 1880), pp. 658–76 (664–8).
75. E.N. Bennett, 'The Turkish Point of View', *Edinburgh Review* (Apr. 1913), pp. 278–96 (279, 290–1).
76. A. Patterson, 'From Agram to Zara', *Fortnightly Review*, Part I (Apr. 1872), pp. 359–86 and Part II (May 1872), pp. 509–32. See Part I, pp. 378–9, 381 and Part II, p. 513.
77. Mackenzie and Irby, *Notes on the Slavonic Countries*, pp. 40–1.
78. Edward Willoughby, 'Notes on the Slavonian Races', *Fraser's Magazine* (Sept. 1877), pp. 368–74 (373).
79. A principality from the fourteenth century and occupied by the Ottomans for two periods, Montenegro proved a difficult opponent and impossible to dominate completely, in part because of its mountainous terrain. In 1799 the Sultan acknowledged Montenegro's autonomy. Developments through the nineteenth century included partial political modernization and formal independence in 1858 following a war against the Ottomans, though it was not until 1905 that its last ruler, Prince (then King) Nicholas I, gave Montenegro a constitution. In 1910 Montenegro became a Kingdom and, as a result of the Balkan Wars and its support for the Serbs, it enjoyed considerable territorial expansion prior to the First World War. While Montenegro again went to war in support of the Serbs in 1914, it succumbed in 1915 and Nicholas I left for France. The Austrian army occupied Montenegro from 1916 and in November 1918 the assembly deposed the king (who died in exile in 1921) and voted to join Serbia, which led to Montenegro's inclusion in the Kingdom of Serbs, Croats and Slovenes.
80. Mackenzie, 'Montenegro, the Herzegovine, and the Slavonic Populations of Turkey', p. 352.
81. A meeting of clan leaders decided the treacherous clan members who had converted to Islam were to be killed in order to enable the true believers to withstand the Turkish threat more effectively. *Mountain Wreath* speculates on the dilemma facing Bishop Danilo, who had to reconcile his religious beliefs with a policy of murder and fratricide. See Wachtel, *Making a Nation, Breaking a Nation*, pp. 101ff, 142ff.

82. Alfred Lord Tennyson, 'Montenegro', *Nineteenth Century* (May 1877), p. 359.
83. W.E. Gladstone, 'Montenegro: A Sketch', *Nineteenth Century* (May 1877), pp. 360–79 (360).
84. Ibid., pp. 363, 371.
85. Ibid., pp. 365, 371.
86. Ibid., pp. 378–9.
87. Ibid., pp. 375–6.
88. Ibid., p. 361.
89. Frederic Boase, *Modern English Biography* (London, 1965 [1901]), 3, pp. 406–7.
90. Humphry Sandwith, 'Preface', in Mackenzie and Irby, *Notes on the Slavonic Countries*, p. 16.
91. See for example Vincent Caillard, 'The Bulgarian Imbroglio', *Fortnightly Review* (Nov. 1885), pp. 840–51.
92. A.A. Paton, *Researches on the Danube and the Adriatic: Or Contributions to the Modern History of Hungary and Transylvania, Dalmatia and Croatia, Servia and Bulgaria*, 2 vols (London, 1862 [1861]), 2, pp. 123–4.
93. See for example Edmond Fitzmaurice, 'Hungary and Croatia', *MacMillan's Magazine* (May 1877), pp. 34–42. Fitzmaurice wrote that because of the repressive nature of Hungarian rule in Croatia the 'political tendencies of the Croatian population are to gravitate towards their Serbian brethren' (41). See also Robert Seton-Watson, *Absolutism in Croatia* (London, 1912), one of a number of pieces by Seton-Watson critical of Hungary.
94. Evans, Letter VIII, 'Through the Lika', *Illyrian Letters*, p. 66; and Evans, *Through Bosnia and the Herzegovina on Foot*, p. 37.
95. *Who was Who, 1916–1928* (London, 1929), p. 525.
96. H.H. Howarth, 'The Spread of the Slaves. Part I: The Croats', *Journal of the Anthropological Institute*, 7 (1878), pp. 324–41 (341).
97. Freeman, 'The Southern Slaves', p. 417.
98. Mackenzie and Irby, *The Turks, the Greeks and the Slavons*, p. 143.
99. Mackenzie and Irby, *Notes on the Slavonic Countries*, p. 32.
100. Griffin, 'The Present State of the Eastern Question', pp. 22–5.
101. Stillman, 'Austro-Hungary', p. 791.
102. Mackenzie and Irby, *Notes on the Slavonic Countries*, p. 38. The authors were quoting from an article published in the *Revue des Deux Mondes* in 1864.
103. De Windt, *Through Savage Europe*, p. 129.
104. Novikoff, 'The Crisis in Serbia', pp. 306–7. Novikoff was discussing the ideas of Emile de Laveleye, whom she described as Austria's 'admirer and eulogist'.
105. Mackenzie and Irby considered different multinational conglomerates to deal with the South Slav question and noted that the Serbs did not find them amenable because they wanted to be free of the 'foreign yoke': 'Peoples are not to be governed, they are to govern themselves.' Mackenzie and Irby, *The Turks, the Greeks and the Slavons*, pp. 586–7, 590.
106. Francis W. Hirst, 'A Dissolving Empire', *Fortnightly Review* (July 1898), pp. 56–71 (56, 71).

107. See Robert Wolfson, *Years of Change: European History 1890–1945* (London, 1992), pp. 201–3.

108. Willoughby, 'Notes on the Slavonian Races', p. 373. Dušan, born in 1307, was the greatest leader up to that point and revered as such in spite of his having been implicated in the murder of his father. See Tim Judah, *The Serbs: History, Myth and the Destruction of Yugoslavia* (New Haven and London, 2000), Ch. 2.

109. Caillard, 'The Bulgarian Imbroglio', p. 846.

110. Evans, 'The Austrian Counter-revolution in the Balkans', pp. 495, 516.

111. Ibid., pp. 515, 518.

112. Ibid., p. 517.

113. Ibid., pp. 521, 522, 524.

114. Count Lützow, 'Austria at the End of the Century', *Nineteenth Century* (Dec. 1899), pp. 1008–19 (1019).

115. Francis Gribble, 'Servia Irredenta', *Edinburgh Review* (July 1914), pp. 41–59 (52).

116. Mackenzie and Irby, *Notes on the Slavonic Countries*, pp. 53, 54–6.

117. Sandwith, 'A Trip into Bosnia', pp. 712, 713.

118. Evans, *Through Bosnia and the Herzegovina on Foot*, p. 434.

119. Freeman, 'The Election and the Eastern Question', p. 973.

120. Freeman, 'The Position of the Austrian Power in South-Eastern Europe', pp. 743–4.

121. Ibid., p. 748; and Freeman, 'The Southern Slaves', pp. 389, 419–20. 'The Southern Slaves' was first published prior to Austria's occupation of Bosnia-Herzegovina, but Freeman added these comments in a note when it appeared in his book of essays.

122. Anon., 'European Reconstruction and British Policy', *Edinburgh Review* (Jan. 1913), pp. 217–37 (226–8).

123. Reeve, 'Bosnia and Bulgaria', pp. 537, 552.

124. Agnes M. Clerke, 'Albania and Scanderbeg', *Edinburgh Review* (Oct. 1881), pp. 325–56 (354).

125. Ibid., pp. 354, 355.

126. This was the case before Bulgaria entered the First World War in 1915, for example. Both the Entente and the Central Powers would try to secure Bulgaria's military support with the promise of territorial gains in Macedonia.

127. See Drage, 'The Balkan Maincurrent', p. 204; and Anon., 'European Reconstruction and British Policy'.

128. See *Who was Who, 1941–1950* (London, 1967), pp. 470–1.

129. Gribble, 'Servia Irredenta', p. 41.

130. Ibid., p. 52. See also anon., 'European Reconstruction and British Policy', p. 227.

131. Gribble, 'Servia Irredenta', p. 52.

2 The Expansion of Gallant Serbia into Yugoslavia: 1914–1920

1. R.W. Seton-Watson, 'Austria-Hungary and the Southern Slavs', in Seton-Watson *et al.*, *The War and Democracy*, pp. 121–61 (159–60).

2. R.W. Seton-Watson, 'The Issues of the War', in Seton-Watson *et al.*, *The War and Democracy*, pp. 237–98 (262).

3. H. and C. Seton-Watson, *The Making of a New Europe*, pp. 142, 153–4.

4. The term *Mlada Bosna* did not come into general use until after the war. *Mlada Bosna* was not a structured movement with a highly evolved programme of action or a coherent ideology. Rather it was a collective term for a range of groups that were generally anti-Habsburg and loosely 'Yugoslav' in aspiration. However, the groups' close links with Serbian nationalist agitation have always been difficult for Yugoslav propagandists to explain adequately because of the desire to project it as a multinational movement. See Wayne S. Vucinich, 'Mlada Bosna and the First World War', in Robert A. Kann, Bela K. Kiraly and Paula S. Fichtner (eds), *The Habsburg Empire in World War I: Essays on the Intellectual, Military, Political and Economic Aspects of the Habsburg War Effort* (New York, 1977), pp. 45–70.

5. Vladimir Dedijer, prominent Partisan and 'regime historian', stated plainly that '[t]he Archduke was killed by the joint action of the secret revolutionary societies of Bosnia and Belgrade', regardless of the fact that Colonel Dragutin Dimitrijević (Apis), one of the leaders of the Black Hand, withdrew support for the plot days before the Archduke's visit. See his 'Sarajevo Fifty Years After', *Foreign Affairs*, 42 (1964), pp. 569–84 (584). In 1917 Apis, along with a number of other members of the military known to be associated with the Black Hand and who were implicated in the 1903 assassinations, were tried and executed for allegedly conspiring to assassinate the prince regent, Aleksandar Karađorđević. The Salonika trials drew much attention and criticism from Serbia's allies. There were clearly irregularities of process and this concerned our outside observers at the time. Historians suggest different reasons for Aleksandar and Prime Minister Pašić's determination to initiate the trials. Some suggest that they felt that elements in the military, and the Black Hand conspirators in particular, who acted as a rival power base, needed to be brought more closely under the control of the government or eliminated. Further, as Apis and his associates were also implicated in the Sarajevo assassinations, their demise would have facilitated the (unrealistic) goal of securing a separate peace with Austria-Hungary, which was fleetingly thought to be a possibility by the Serbs. See James Joll, *The Origins of the First World War* (London and New York, 1992), p. 89; Lampe, *Yugoslavia as History*, p. 102; and Ivo Banac, *The National Question in Yugoslavia: Origins, History, Politics* (Ithaca and London, 1984) p. 133.

6. See for example Imanuel Geiss, 'Origins of the First World War', in H.W. Koch (ed.), *The Origins of the First World War: Great Power Rivalry and German War Aims*, 2nd edn (Basingstoke, 1984), pp. 46–85 (82).

7. Sir Valentine Chirol, *Serbia and the Serbs*, Oxford Pamphlets No. 13 (London, 1914), pp. 14–17.

8. *La Serbie*, 29 Oct. 1916, in *La Serbie et L'Europe (1914–1918). Exposé de la Politique Serbe par des Publicistes Serbes* (Geneva, 1919), p. 29.

9. Ibid., p. 30. See also *La Serbie*, 21 Jan., 18 Feb., 25 Feb. 1917, in *La Serbie et L'Europe*, pp. 30–6.

10. *La Serbie*, 20 July 1917, in *La Serbie et L'Europe*, pp. 38–43 (42).
11. See Samuel R. Williamson, Jr, *Austria-Hungary and the Origins of the First World War* (Basingstoke, 1991), pp. 186–9; and Ruth Henig, *The Origins of the First World War*, 2nd edn (London and New York, 1993), p. 22.
12. The ultimatum set out a number of conditions, 'including the suppression of anti-Austrian propaganda in Serbia, the dissolution of the Serbian nationalist association *Narodna Odbrana*, the purging of officers and officials who were guilty of propaganda against Austria, the arrest of named officers suspected of aiding and abetting the conspirators who murdered the Archduke and the tightening up of controls on the Serbian-Austrian-Hungarian border'. Further, the ultimatum demanded Austrian participation in the inquiry into the assassination plot. Joll, *The Origins of the First World War*, p. 12.
13. Letter quoted in H. and C. Seton-Watson, *The Making of a New Europe*, pp. 101–2; original emphasis. Henry Wickham Steed, head of the foreign department and later (1919) editor of *The Times*, was R.W. Seton-Watson's close friend and co-lobbyist for the successor states. John St Loe Strachey (1860–1927) was the editor of the *Spectator*. Seton-Watson's reference to the need to 'save' Zagreb's Diet is an early indication of an inherent contradiction and a certain ambivalence in his approach to Yugoslavism.
14. Chirol, *Serbia and the Serbs*, pp. 3, 8, 12.
15. F.F. Urquhart, *The Eastern Question* (Oxford Pamphlets No. 15, London, 1914), pp. 12, 17.
16. *Report of the International Commission to Inquire into the Causes and Conduct of the Balkan Wars*, produced by the Carnegie Endowment for International Peace (Washington, DC, 1914).
17. G.M. Trevelyan, 'Serbia Revisited', *Contemporary Review* (Mar. 1915), pp. 273–83 (282–3).
18. R.W. Seton-Watson, 'Serbia's Need and Britain's Danger', *Contemporary Review* (Nov. 1915), pp. 576–81 (579).
19. Williamson, *Austria-Hungary and the Origins of the First World War*.
20. Vladimir Dedijer was among the leading proponents of this school of thought in post-1945 Yugoslavia. See for example Vladimir Dedijer, Ivan Božić, Sima Ćirković and Milorad Ekmečić (eds), *History of Yugoslavia*, trans. Kordija Kveder (New York, 1974).
21. See Ch. 34, 'The Assassination in Sarajevo and the Outbreak of World War I', in ibid., pp. 467–74 (469). Dedijer wrote this chapter.
22. R.W. Seton-Watson, 'Panslavism', *Contemporary Review* (Oct. 1916), pp. 419–29 (427).
23. The first English edition appeared in 1959 and Andrić was awarded the Nobel Prize in 1961.
24. Hamilton Fish Armstrong, 'Confessions of the Assassin Whose Deed Led to the World War', *Current History* (Aug. 1927), pp. 699–707 (699).
25. See Rudolf Jeřábek, 'The Eastern Front 1914–1918', in Mark Cornwall (ed.), *The Last Years of Austria-Hungary: Essays in Political and Military History* (Exeter, 1990), pp. 101–16.

26. Chirol, *Serbia and the Serbs*, p. 18.

27. Adolphe Smith, 'Zadrougas: the Strength of Serbia', *Contemporary Review* (Apr. 1915), pp. 515–20 (520).

28. *In Darkest Europe: Austria-Hungary's Effort to Exterminate her Jugoslav Subjects* (London, 1917), pp. 4, 7.

29. Gordon Gordon-Smith was a war correspondent and the author of *Through the Serbian Campaign: The Great Retreat of the Serbian Army* (London, 1916); *From Serbia to Jugoslavia: Serbia's Victories, Reverses and Final Triumph* (New York and London, 1920); and numerous articles. In the interwar years he was an attaché of the Royal Jugoslav Legation.

30. Gordon Gordon-Smith, 'The War Won on the Eastern Front', *Current History* (Aug. 1921), pp. 826–32 (828, 830).

31. Keith Robbins, *The First World War* (Oxford, 1985), p. 152.

32. Anti-fascist diplomat and statesman Carlo Sforza argued in the late 1930s that many Italians genuinely supported the cause of South Slavdom in opposition to Austria, their common enemy. However, it was generally felt that the poet Gabriele D'Annunzio was more representative of Italian opinion when in 1919 he seized and occupied the Croatian coastal city, Rijeka (known to Italians as Fiume) with a band of his nationalist supporters, departing only when the liberal Italian government finally acceded to international pressure to recall him. See Count Carlo Sforza, 'Italy and the Jugoslav Idea: Past and Present', *Foreign Affairs*, 16 (1938), pp. 323–38. Sforza wrote that Mazzini was one of the earliest 'prophets of political independence for the South Slavs' (p. 323).

33. The flurry of activity on this question is evident in Ljubo Boban *et al.* (eds), *R.W. Seton-Watson i Jugoslaveni: Korespondencija 1906–1941*, 1: 1906–1918, pp. 212ff.

34. For a detailed examination of the territorial claims of the various groups in question and the attempts at resolving this problem, see H. and C. Seton-Watson, *The Making of a New Europe*, pp. 125–41.

35. Philip J. Green, 'Balkan Front, 1916', in Spencer C. Tucker (ed.), *The European Powers in the First World War: An Encyclopedia* (New York and London, 1996), pp. 102–4.

36. *La Serbie*, 8 Oct. 1916, in *La Serbie et L'Europe*, pp. 104–10 (107).

37. 'Americano' [Emily Simmonds], 'Fighting for Serbia', *Cornhill Magazine* (Aug. 1918), pp. 153–66 (154). Often the point is made that the French were much less interested in the South Slav project for unification than the Czechoslovak cause. Pamphlet literature produced during the war suggests a deeper French attachment to the Yugoslavs' (or Serbs') cause and mutual admiration between the French and the Serbs. *La Grande Serbie*, the 1915 book by Ernest Denis, professor at the Sorbonne and founder of the Institut d'Études Slaves, described Serbia as 'the most Francophile country in the world'. See Jacques Bariety, 'La France et la naissance du "Royaume des Serbes, Croates et Slovènes" 1914–1919', *Revue d'Europe Centrale*, 2 (1994), pp. 1–12 (4–5).

38. Jeřábek, 'The Eastern Front 1914–1918', pp. 111ff.

39. Robbins, *The First World War*, pp. 72, 80.

40. Claire Hirschfield, 'In Search of Mrs Ryder: British Women in Serbia during the Great War', *East European Quarterly*, 20 (1987), pp. 387–407 (390). By the end of 1915, approximately 600 British women, including 60 doctors, had served in Serbia and Macedonia. See Monica Krippner, 'British Medical Women in Serbia during the First World War', in Allcock and Young, *Black Lambs and Grey Falcons*, pp. 65–81 (70).

41. The Serbian Relief Fund was functioning by September 1914. It was established by R.W. Seton-Watson and a select group of his influential acquaintances. The Fund and other related bodies were very successful in raising awareness in Britain for Serbia and its war aims and in providing humanitarian aid for Serbian victims of the war. The Queen was its patron and other supporters included Lord Curzon, Sir Arthur Evans and the Archbishop of Canterbury. See Krippner, 'British Medical Women in Serbia during the First World War', p. 66; H. and C. Seton-Watson, *The Making of a New Europe*, p. 106; and Hanak, *Great Britain and Austria-Hungary during the First World War*, pp. 64–75.

42. Krippner, 'British Medical Women in Serbia during the First World War', p. 69.

43. M.A. St Clair Stobart, 'With the Serbian Army in Retreat', *Contemporary Review* (Apr. 1916), pp. 437–47 (437). See also Krippner, 'British Medical Women in Serbia during the First World War', p. 71.

44. Stobart, 'With the Serbian Army in Retreat', p. 441.

45. Ibid., pp. 445, 446, 447.

46. Quoted in Julie Wheelwright, 'Flora Sandes – Military Maid', *History Today*, 39 (Mar. 1989), pp. 42–8 (44).

47. Ibid., pp. 45, 47.

48. Ibid., p. 48. See also Julie Wheelwright, 'Captain Flora Sandes: a Case Study in the Social Construction of Gender in a Serbian Context', in Allcock and Young, *Black Lambs and Grey Falcons*, pp. 82–9; and *Amazons and Military Maids*. Below we will see how the memory of such activism could divide Yugoslavists.

49. Wheelwright, *Amazons and Military Maids*, pp. 40–1, 108, 170.

50. Alec Waugh, *The Lipton Story: A Centennial Biography* (London, 1951), pp. 184–5.

51. See Krippner, 'British Medical Women in Serbia during the First World War'.

52. Stobart, 'With the Serbian Army in Retreat', p. 438.

53. Lady Paget, *With our Serbian Allies* (London, 1915), p. 43.

54. Kathleen E. Royds, 'With the Serbians in Corsica', *Contemporary Review* (Jan. 1918), pp. 40–50 (50).

55. Krippner, 'British Medical Women in Serbia during the First World War', pp. 67, 70, 76, 78.

56. I. Emslie Hutton, *With a Woman's Unit in Serbia, Salonika and Sebastopol* (London, 1928), pp. 104, 110–11. Dr Hutton worked with the Scottish Women's Hospitals.

57. Isobel Ross, *Little Grey Partridge: The Diary of Isobel Ross, Serbia 1916–1917*, ed. and intro. Jess Dixon (Aberdeen, 1988).

58. Janet Lee, 'A Nurse and Soldier: Gender, Class and National Identity in the First World War Adventures of Grace McDougall and Flora Sandes', *Women's History Review*, 15 (2006), pp. 83–103 (95).

59. Lee writes of her two case studies that 'even though their war record demonstrates an inadvertent feminism that fought for the rights of women to enter and succeed in the most masculine of public spaces, their intentions were patriotic and never intended to disrupt the status quo'. There is more to be learnt from their experiences than the extent to which 'they made the case for women's presence on the battlefield', as important as that may be. See Lee, 'A Nurse and Soldier', p. 100. For a discussion of these broader themes see Joan Beaumont, 'Whatever Happened to Patriotic Women, 1914–1918?', *Australian Historical Studies*, 31 (2000), pp. 273–86.

60. *The Serbian (Jugoslav) National War Aims.* Inaugural Meeting at the Mansion House, London on July 25th 1918 (London, 1918), p. 3.

61. Letter from R.W. Seton-Watson to Milenko Vesnić, 17 July 1916. The use of the word 'Yugoslav' is almost tokenistic here. In a letter to Jovan Cvijić the previous day Seton-Watson wrote that in its deliberations on the donations for Serbian students in Switzerland, the Committee had not used the word 'Yugoslav' and that it was not at all necessary to make distinctions between the 'several categories' of Yugoslavs. Aid was to be distributed strictly according to need and without distinction (that is, not according to any 'categories'), although Seton-Watson did not elaborate on how this was to be guaranteed given the circumstances. Boban *et al.* (eds), *R.W. Seton-Watson i Jugoslaveni*, 1, pp. 269–71. See also R.W. Seton-Watson, *Serbia, Yesterday, Today, and Tomorrow: A School Address* (London, n.d. [1916]).

62. See Branimir Anzulovic, *Heavenly Serbia: From Myth to Genocide* (London, 1999) Chs 2 and 6; and Hanak, *Great Britain and Austria-Hungary during the First World War*, pp. 75–8.

63. Dedijer *et al.*, *A History of Yugoslavia*, Ch. 35, 'The Collapse of the Austro-Hungarian Offensive of 1914', pp. 474–83 (483). Dedijer wrote this chapter.

64. *La Serbie*, 19 Aug. 1917, 14 Sept., 21 Oct., 4 Nov. 1918, in *La Serbie et L'Europe*, pp. 65–74.

65. In the Niš Declaration the Serbs stated their aim was to unite the South Slavs in a single state. It was designed to appeal to Habsburg South Slavs, and though there was no mention of 'Great Serbia' in the Declaration, an underlying premise was, clearly, Serbian expansion in the event of an Entente victory. See Lampe, *Yugoslavia as History*, pp. 100–1; and Banac, *The National Question in Yugoslavia*, pp. 114–18.

66. Lane, *Yugoslavia: When Ideals Collide*, pp. 32–3.

67. Gordon Gordon-Smith, 'Jugoslavia's Attitude toward Bulgaria', *Current History* (Apr. 1922), pp. 131–2 (132).

68. H[inko] Hinkovitch, *Les Croates sous le Joug Magyar* (Paris, 1915), p. 38. Hinković was a member of the Croatian *Sabor* and a member of the Yugoslav Committee. He was close to Seton-Watson and inclined towards the unitarist view of the racial integrity of the Yugoslavs rather than the federalist view of a union of distinct nations as espoused by Supilo, for example.

69. *The Southern Slavs: Land and People*, Southern Slav Library II (London, 1916), pp. 3, 4, 6–7.
70. Nevill Forbes, *The Southern Slavs* (Oxford Pamphlets, London, 1914–15), pp. 6, 16, 17.
71. *La Serbie*, 29 June 1918, in *La Serbie et l'Europe*, pp. 79–81 (81).
72. Hinkovitch, *Les Croates sous le Joug Magyar*.
73. *La Serbie*, 15 Oct. 1916, in *La Serbie et L'Europe*, pp. 75–7 (75, 76).
74. See Banac, *The National Question in Yugoslavia*.
75. Janko Pleterski, 'The Southern Slav Question 1908–1918', in Cornwall (ed.), *The Last Years of Austria-Hungary*, pp. 77–100 (94–7).
76. Stevan K. Pavlowitch, *Yugoslavia* (London, 1971), pp. 50–1.
77. Pleterski, 'The Southern Slav Question 1908–1918', p. 83.
78. Forbes, *The Southern Slavs*, pp. 5, 6.
79. Trevelyan, 'Serbia Revisited', p. 273. He first travelled to Serbia during the Second Balkan War in 1913.
80. *The Serbian (Jugoslav) National War Aims*, p. 7; emphasis added.
81. R.G.D. Laffan, *The Guardians of the Gate: Historical Lectures on the Serbs* (Oxford, 1918).
82. Dedijer *et al.*, 'The Last Days of Austria Hungary', pp. 497–8.
83. Gordon-Smith, 'Jugoslavia's Attitude toward Bulgaria', p. 132.
84. Dedijer *et al.*, 'The Last Days of Austria-Hungary', pp. 496–501.
85. *Le Programme yougoslave* (Paris, 1916), p. 12. This is from the memorandum mentioned above which was first drafted in English by R.W. Seton-Watson as a response to the Treaty of London.
86. Auguste Gauvain, *La Question yougoslave* (Paris, 1918), p. 81.
87. Harrison, 'Cross and Crescent', p. 712.
88. R.W. Seton-Watson, 'Austria-Hungary and the Federal Solution', *Contemporary Review* (Mar. 1918), pp. 257–64 (257–8, 260).
89. Quoted in K. R. Stadler, 'The Disintegration of the Austrian Empire', *Journal of Contemporary History*, 3–4 (1968), pp. 177–90 (182).
90. See Magda Adam, *The Versailles System and Central Europe* (Aldershot, 2004).
91. Harold Nicolson, 'Peacemaking 1919 – A Critique', in Ivo J. Lederer (ed.), *The Versailles Settlement: Was it Foredoomed to Failure?* (Boston, 1960), pp. 17–23 (22–3).
92. See Todorova, *Imagining the Balkans*, pp. 32–3.

3 A State in Search of a Nation: the Kingdom, 1920–1940

1. Christian Axboe Nielsen has provided a unique insight into the failure of the Yugoslav project under Aleksandar's dictatorship in his doctoral thesis, which draws on a range of hitherto underused sources, including police records. He shows how people at the local level negotiated and ultimately repelled the centripetal and homogenizing policies that signified an unacceptable intrusion into their private lives and the negation of local group identities. Neilsen's study is a welcome departure from the top-down focus of most works on the period. See his 'One State, One Nation, One King: The Dictatorship of King Aleksandar and his Yugoslav Project, 1929–1935', PhD thesis, Columbia University, 2002.

2. See R.W. Seton-Watson, *The Historian as a Political Force in Central Europe* (London, 1922). This was Seton-Watson's inaugural lecture as Professor of Central European History at the University of London. See also Seton-Watson, *A Plea for the Study of Contemporary History*, Creighton Lecture, 1928, reprinted from *History*, 14 (1929). He wrote (p. 17):

> a close study of recent history is an essential corollary of the new international peace movement which centres round the League of Nations, and on which the avoidance of fresh upheavals must so largely depend. I am not so foolish as to plead for the enlistment of historians as mere propagandists of this or that campaign of pacifism or disarmament; but it is self-evident that they have a very special function to perform in promoting that scientific study of recent times which is one of the essential foundations on which a new world and a new mentality must be constructed.

3. Some of the following material draws on Drapac, 'The Memory of War and the History of the First Yugoslavia'.
4. These are Jay Winter's words, quoted in Peter Fritszche, 'The Case of Modern Memory', *Journal of Modern History*, 73 (2001), pp. 87–117 (105). See also Antoine Prost, 'Monuments to the Dead', in Pierre Nora (ed.), *Realms of Memory; The Construction of the French Past*, 2, trans. Arthur Goldhammer (New York, 1997), pp. 307–30; and J. M. Winter, *Sites of Memory, Sites of Mourning: The Great War in European Cultural History* (Cambridge, 1995).
5. See François Grumel-Jacquignon, *La Yougoslavie dans la stratégie française de l'Entre-deux-Guerres (1918–1935): Aux origines du mythe serbe en France* (Bern, 1999); and Ann Lane, 'Yugoslavia: The Search for a Nation-state', in Seamus Dunn and T.G. Fraser (eds), *Europe and Ethnicity: The First World War and Contemporary Ethnic Conflict* (London and New York, 1996), pp. 30–46 (34).
6. Seton-Watson, 'The Issues of the War', p. 262; and Gordon-Smith, *From Serbia to Jugoslavia* are just two of countless examples of this kind of propaganda appearing in various books and magazines on both sides of the Atlantic.
7. 'A Croat View of the Jugoslav Crisis', *Slavonic Review*, 7 (1929), pp. 304–10 (307).
8. Gordon-Smith, 'Jugoslavia's Attitude toward Bulgaria', p. 132.
9. Wachtel, *Making a Nation, Breaking a Nation*, pp. 112–15. See also Melissa Bokovoy, 'Kosovo Maiden(s): Serbian Women Commemorate the Wars of National Liberation, 1912–1918', in Nancy M. Wingfield and Maria Bucur (eds), *Gender and War in Twentieth Century Eastern Europe* (Bloomington and Indianapolis, 2006), pp. 157–70; and Melissa Bokovoy, 'Scattered Graves, Ordered Cemeteries: Commemorating Serbia's Wars of National Liberation, 1912–1918', in Maria Bucur and Nancy M. Wingfield (eds), *Staging the Past: the Politics of Commemoration in Habsburg Central Europe, 1848 to the Present* (West Lafayette, IN, 2001), pp. 236–54.

10. See for example Mark Cornwall, 'Mémoires de la Grande Guerre dans les Pays Tchèques, 1918–1928', in *Démobilisations Culturelles après la Grande Guerre*, special issue of *14–18 Aujourd'hui, Today, Heute*, 5 (2002), pp. 88–101.

11. Jan-Werner Müller, 'Introduction: The Power of Memory, the Memory of Power and the Power over Memory', in Jan-Werner Müller (ed.), *Memory and Power in Post-War Europe: Studies in the Presence of the Past* (Cambridge, 2002), pp. 1–38 (2). See Winter, *Sites of Memory*; Paul Fussell, *The Great War and Modern Memory* (London, Oxford and New York, 1977 [1975]); and George L. Mosse, *Fallen Soldiers: Reshaping the Memory of the World Wars* (New York and Oxford, 1990). Winter and Fussell offer different interpretations of the cultural impact of the memory of war, while Mosse makes more connections between memory and politics in interwar Germany.

12. This is now changing. See Wingfield and Bucur (eds), *Gender and War in Twentieth Century Eastern Europe*, and Bucur and Wingfield (eds), *Staging the Past*.

13. Some of these themes are broached in a European context in Keith Wilson (ed.), *Forging the Collective Memory: Government and International Historians through Two World Wars* (Providence and Oxford, 1996) and in Dunn and Fraser (eds), *Europe and Ethnicity*. *Forging* also explores the relationship between commissioned histories and national politics.

14. Müller, 'Introduction', pp. 1–38 (2–3, 28–30). Studies of the impact of the memory of war on Yugoslav history since 1945 are more numerous and focus especially on the Partisan generation. See for example Ilana R. Bet-El, 'Unimagined Communities: the Power of Memory and the Conflict in the Former Yugoslavia', in Müller, *Memory and Power*, pp. 206–22; Hoepken, 'War, Memory and Education in a Fragmented Society; Höpken, 'History Education and Yugoslav (Dis-) Integration'; and Robin Okey, 'The Legacy of Massacre: The "Jasenovac Myth" and the Breakdown of Communist Yugoslavia', in Mark Levene and Penny Roberts (eds), *The Massacre in History* (New York and Oxford, 1999), pp. 263–82.

15. See Drapac, 'The Memory of War and the History of the First Yugoslavia'; and Müller, 'Introduction', where he discusses the convergence of 'memory' and 'money' and of culture and self-interest in European affairs after 1945. What he argues is applicable to interwar Yugoslavia.

16. 'En Serbie: Les funérailles du roi Pierre', *L'Illustration*, 3 Sept. 1921, p. 199. Two pages of photographs accompanied this article. See pp. 200–1. Aleksandar was in Paris at the time and unable to attend his father's funeral owing to illness.

17. 'Pierre Ier de Serbie', *L'Illustration*, 20 Aug. 1921, p. 164.

18. 'En Serbie: Les funérailles du roi Pierre'.

19. 'Au Mausolée de Topola', *L'Illustration*, 10 Sept. 1921, p. 215.

20. 'En Serbie: Les funérailles du roi Pierre'.

21. Ibid.

22. 'Pierre Ier de Serbie'.

23. 'Une manifestation d'amitié serbe', *L'Illustration*, 4 Aug. 1923, p. 110.
24. Mislav Gabelica, 'Žrtve sukoba na Jelačićevom trgu 5. prosinca 1918', *Časopis za suvremenu povijest*, 37 (2005), pp. 467–77. See also Bogdan Krizman, *Hrvatska u prvom svjestkom ratu: Hrvatsko-srpksi politički odnosi* (Zagreb, 1989), pp. 361ff.
25. See Banac, *The National Question in Yugoslavia*, pp. 403–4.
26. Dr Ivan Schvegel (late member of the Jugoslav parliament, Belgrade), 'Jugoslavia's Constitutional Problems', *Current History* (July 1921), pp. 624–6 (624).
27. 'The Jugoslav Constitution', trans. Howard Webster Wolfe and Arthur Irving Andrews, *Current History* (Feb. 1922), pp. 832–47 (832).
28. Constantine Stephanove, 'Drifting toward a Jugoslav Federation', *Current History* (Mar. 1922), pp. 930–7 (936).
29. Ludwell Denny, 'Pacifist Revolution in Croatia', *Current History* (Nov. 1922), pp. 255–9 (258).
30. David Mitrany, 'The Unmaking of Jugoslavia', *The New Republic* (28 Jan. 1925), pp. 253–5 (255).
31. Dejan Djokić, *Elusive Compromise: A History of Interwar Yugoslavia* (London, 2007). See also his '(Dis)Integrating Yugoslavia: King Aleksandar and Interwar Yugoslavism', in *Yugoslavism: Histories of a Failed Idea 1918–1992*, ed. Dejan Djokić (London, 2003), pp. 136–56.
32. Benson, *Yugoslavia*, pp. 34–6.
33. Franjo Šuklje, 'Centralism and Autonomy in Jugoslavia', *Slavonic Review*, 2 (1923–4), pp. 328–35 (330).
34. Mitrany, 'The Unmaking of Jugoslavia', p. 253.
35. See Bokovoy, 'Scattered Graves, Ordered Cemeteries', p. 251; Maria Bucur and Nancy M. Wingfield, 'Introduction', in Bucur and Wingfield (eds), *Staging the Past*, p. 7; Bokovoy, 'Kosovo Maiden(s)'.
36. See for example C. Douglas Booth, 'The Political Situation in South-Eastern Europe, I: Hungary and Jugoslavia', *Journal of the Royal Institute of International Affairs*, 8 (1929), pp. 318–43. This article was based on a paper read on 11 June 1929 and I refer to it in more detail below.
37. 'A Croat View of the Jugoslav Crisis', p. 309.
38. Benson, *Yugoslavia*, pp. 38–9.
39. Ibid., p. 39.
40. Mitrany, 'The Unmaking of Jugoslavia', p. 254. See also Bosiljka Janjatovic, 'Karađorđevićevska centralizacija i položaj Hrvtaske u Kraljevstvu (Kraljevini) SHS', *Časopis za suvremenu povijest*, 27 (1995), pp. 55–76. Her numbers are 3000 and 4700 votes for Serb and Croat members, respectively (62).
41. Vucinich continues:

    In the subsequent period, from January 1929 to March 1941, there were 15 different cabinets of whose ministers three-fifths (73) of the total were Serbs. ... In all 39 cabinets, the minister of Army and Navy was always a Serb general on the active list. Again, of the 165 generals in 1938 only two were Croats and two Slovenes; all others were Serbs. (Quoted in Barbara Jelavich, *History of the Balkans: Twentieth Century*, Cambridge, 1983, p. 152)

42. Quoted in ibid., p. 153.
43. Between 1920 and 1925 the Peasant Party was officially known as the Croat Republican Peasant Party.
44. See Mark Biondich, *Stjepan Radić, the Croat Peasant Party, and the Politics of Mass Mobilization, 1904–1928* (Toronto, 2000).
45. Denny, 'Pacifist Revolution in Croatia', p. 256.
46. Hamilton Fish Armstrong, 'Pashitch [*sic*], the Last of the Balkan Pashas', *Current History* (July 1927), pp. 611–17 (613). The same photograph was reproduced several times in *Current History*.
47. V.A. Drignakovitch (Ex-attaché of the Serbian Delegation to the Peace Conference in Paris), 'Pashitch [*sic*], Creator of Modern Yugoslavia', *Current History* (Aug. 1926), pp. 735–9 (735, 738).
48. Armstrong, 'Pashitch, the Last of the Balkan Pashas', pp. 611, 614, 617.
49. 'The Balkans and Emancipated Central Europe', *Current History* (May 1921), pp. 516–18 (517); and Zvonimir Kulundžić (ed.), *Stjepan Radić: Politički spisi* (Zagreb, 1971), pp. 404–9, 550–4.
50. He was referring to the fact that Croatia-Slavonia fell within the Hungarian sphere under the Dual Monarchy.
51. Stephanove, 'Drifting toward a Jugoslav Federation', pp. 934–5.
52. Ibid. See also Biondich, *Stjepan Radić*, pp. 183–6.
53. Denny, 'Pacifist Revolution in Croatia', pp. 256, 258.
54. Ibid., p. 259
55. Biondich, *Stjepan Radić*, p. 196.
56. Šuklje, 'Centralism and Autonomy in Jugoslavia', p. 332.
57. Ibid., p. 335.
58. Biondich, *Stjepan Radić*, pp. 239ff.
59. Booth, 'The Political Situation in South-Eastern Europe', pp. 328, 330, 332–3.
60. R.W. Seton-Watson, 'Jugoslavia and Croatia', *Journal of the Royal Institute of International Affairs*, 8 (1929), pp. 117–33 (119, 120, 124, 125). (Based on a paper read on 29 January 1929.) Privately Seton-Watson also expressed his aggravation with the dispute between Serbs and Croats. See for example Seton-Watson to Ivo Lupis-Vukić, 30 Sept. 1928, in Boban *et al.* (eds), *R.W. Seton-Watson i Jugoslaveni*, 2, pp. 176–7.
61. Frederic Ogg, 'The Death of Stefan Raditch', *Current History* (Sept. 1928), p. 1047.
62. See for example Aleksandar Pavković, *The Fragmentation of Yugoslavia: Nationalism and War in the Balkans* (Basingstoke and New York, 2000), pp. 28–9.
63. Eric Dorn Brose, *A History of Europe in the Twentieth Century* (New York and Oxford, 2005), pp. 153–4.
64. Frederic Ogg, 'The Political Crisis in Yugoslavia', *Current History* (Oct. 1928), pp. 157–9 (158).
65. Frederic Ogg, 'Political Murders in Yugoslavia', *Current History* (Aug. 1928), pp. 872–3 (872, 873).
66. 'A Croat View of the Jugoslav Crisis', p. 310.
67. Ibid., p. 307.
68. Račić was captured, 'retried' and executed by the Partisans in 1944.
69. 'Une grande revue militaire en Serbie: Un peuple qui ressuscite', *L'Illustration*, 20 Oct. 1928, pp. 454–5.

70. See for example *Appeal of the Croatian Academicians to the World of Civilisation. How the Croatian savant Professor of University [sic], Dr Milan Sufflay, was murdered by the Serbian Royal Dictatorship*, produced by the Croatian University Clubs Association (Zagreb, 1931).

71. 'Yugoslavia. Despotism of Dictatorship in the Name of "National Unity"', *Danubian Review*, 1 (Aug. 1934), pp. 43–4.

72. For example Pierre Bernus, 'La Crise Yougoslave', *La Revue de Paris*, 36 (Jan.–Feb. 1929), pp. 530–55 (533). See also Seton-Watson, 'Jugoslavia and Croatia', pp. 124–5. During the discussion after the lecture the Chairman, Sir Alban Young, said Radić was 'an impossible and incalculable person', pp. 129–30. Hamilton Fish Armstrong follows a similar line in 'After the Assassination of King Alexander', *Foreign Affairs*, 13 (1934–5), pp. 204–25 (210–11).

73. Brose, *A History of Europe in the Twentieth Century*, p. 154.

74. 'Le Pèlerinage des poilus d'Orient aux tombes de leurs camarades de Macédoine et de Serbie', *L'Illustration*, 19 Oct. 1929, pp. 432–5.

75. The coverage of this 'pilgrimage' was extensive and amply illustrated. Ibid.; also 2 Nov. 1929, pp. 490–6 and 16 Nov. 1929, pp. 563–8.

76. 'Le Pèlerinage', *L'Illustration*, 19 Oct. 1929, p. 432.

77. Ibid.

78. Ibid.

79. 'Le Pèlerinage', *L'Illustration*, 2 Nov. 1929, pp. 491, 492.

80. Ibid., p. 492.

81. Ibid.

82. Ibid., p. 495.

83. Ibid., p. 495.

84. Ibid., p. 496.

85. 'La Commémoration de l'Illyrie Napoléonienne', *L'Illustration*, 26 Oct. 1929, pp. 460–1.

86. Nevile Henderson, *Water under the Bridges* (London, 1945), pp. 67–8. This memoir was published posthumously.

87. See entries on 'Sir Nevile Meyrick Henderson' by O. G. Sargent in the *Dictionary of National Biography, 1941–1950*, pp. 376–8 and by Peter Neville in the *Oxford Dictionary of National Biography*, 26, pp. 329–32. See also Peter Neville, *Appeasing Hitler: The Diplomacy of Sir Nevile Henderson, 1937–1939* (Basingstoke and New York, 2000).

88. Patricia Meehan, *The Unnecessary War: Whitehall and the German Resistance to Hitler* (London, 1992), p. 23.

89. Ibid., p. 6.

90. Neville, *Appeasing Hitler*, pp. 14, 23, 25 and 'Sir Nevile Meyrick Henderson', p. 330.

91. Henderson, *Water under the Bridges*, p. 180.

92. Ibid., p. 190.

93. Ibid.

94. Ibid., pp. 171, 181.

95. Svetozar Pribičević (1875–1936) was a Serb politician and among the chief architects and promoters of the centralist state and its

constitution. He was the Kingdom's first Minister of the Interior and one of Radić's most bitter opponents, but he renounced his centralism and in 1927 formed a coalition with the Peasant Party. He was critical of the dictatorship and after a period of internment, left the Kingdom in 1931 and died in exile. During the Second World War his son, Stoyan, ended up in the United States and lobbied in support of Tito's Partisans.

96. Seton-Watson had planned most of the lecture, which was published in the Institute's journal, together with the discussion that followed, towards the end of 1928. He was understandably cautious in his appraisal of the newly established dictatorship. Seton-Watson, 'Jugoslavia and Croatia', pp. 125–6, 127.
97. Ibid., pp. 122–3, 128.
98. Ibid., pp. 118, 119, 128.
99. Evans had grown disillusioned with the failure of democracy in Yugoslavia. Though he was 'disgusted at the royal dictatorship', he 'never doubted for a moment that Jugoslavia would survive the assaults of her enemies'. In 1932, on his first visit to the region after 50 years, he 'steadfastly avoided' Belgrade because he could not abide its 'Pan-Serb atmosphere'. R.W Seton-Watson, 'Arthur Evans', *Slavonic and East European Review*, 24 (1946), pp. 47–55 (55).
100. All of these comments were recorded in Seton-Watson, 'Jugoslavia and Croatia', pp. 129–33.
101. Henderson to Seton-Watson, 19 June and 25 Aug. 1930. In Boban *et al.* (eds), *R.W. Seton-Watson i Jugoslaveni*, 2, pp. 201–2, 204–5.
102. These are standard themes in reports from Belgrade. See *Britanci o Kraljevini Jugoslaviji: godišnji izveštaj Britanskog poslanstva u Beogradu 1921–1938*, 2 vols, ed. Živko Avramovski (Zagreb, 1986).
103. Seton-Watson to Milan Ćurčin, 1 Feb. and 15 Mar. 1931. In Boban *et al.* (eds), *R.W. Seton-Watson i Jugoslaveni*, 2, pp. 211–13.
104. R.W. Seton-Watson, 'The Background to the Jugoslav Dictatorship', reprinted from the *Slavonic Review*, 10 (1931), pp. 1–14; 'The Yugoslav Dictatorship'. An address given at Chatham House on 3 December 1931, *International Affairs*, 11 (1932), pp. 22–39; and 'The Jugoslav Dictatorship', *Contemporary Review* (Jan. 1932), pp. 23–31.
105. Seton-Watson, 'The Yugoslav Dictatorship', p. 25.
106. Ibid.
107. Seton-Watson, 'The Jugoslav Dictatorship', pp. 24–5.
108. Seton-Watson, 'The Yugoslav Dictatorship', pp. 25, 27.
109. Seton-Watson, 'The Background to the Jugoslav Dictatorship', pp. 10, 14.
110. Ibid., pp. 10–11.
111. Seton-Watson, 'The Jugoslav Dictatorship', p. 30.
112. Ibid.
113. Seton-Watson, 'The Yugoslav Dictatorship', p. 25; 'The Jugoslav Dictatorship', p. 24.
114. Seton-Watson, 'The Background to the Jugoslav Dictatorship', pp. 5, 7.
115. Ibid., p. 7.

116. Seton-Watson, 'The Jugoslav Dictatorship', p. 24.
117. Ibid., p. 31.
118. Seton-Watson, 'The Yugoslav Dictatorship', p. 34.
119. Ilija Jukić to Seton-Watson, 23 Apr. 1933 and Svetozar Pribičević to Seton-Watson, 13 July 1933, in Boban *et al.* (eds), *Seton-Watson i Jugoslaveni*, 2, pp. 279–80, 285–6.
120. Henderson to Seton-Watson, 19 Apr. 1934 in ibid., pp. 293–4. Henderson was to remain inflexible on this point.
121. See Robinson, *Wayward Women*; Birkett, *Spinsters Abroad*; and Allcock and Young (eds), *Black Lambs and Grey Falcons*. We saw in Chapters 1 and 2 that the impact of this work was significant in that it brought much needed assistance and publicized widely the plight of local inhabitants. However, the relationship between these networks and policy either at the time or subsequently has yet to be explored fully.
122. John Hodgson, 'Edith Durham, Traveller and Publicist', pp. 26–7. According to Hodgson, Durham's name was included in later editions. The 1982 Penguin edition of West's *Black Lamb and Grey Falcon* does not contain Durham's name in this passage but does refer to her within the same context and again, disparagingly, in another related paragraph, p. 20.
123. Arthur Evans to Seton-Watson, 28 and 31 Dec. 1916, in Boban *et al.* (eds), *Seton-Watson i Jugoslaveni*, 1, pp. 285–6.
124. See Introduction, n.22 for works relating to Durham.
125. Rebecca West, *Black Lamb and Grey Falcon*, pp. 20–1. West's caricature of Durham may be countered by Barbara Pym's sympathetic description of one of the characters, Edith Liversidge, in her 1950 novel, *Some Tame Gazelle*. Liversidge is not modelled on Durham but on a member of Pym's circle. Drawn from Pym's first-hand experiences with researchers at the International African Institute, Liversidge, an intrepid traveller, having had many adventures, has returned home. She is happily, or perhaps resignedly, ensconced in village life. Liversidge is often described by other villagers as 'splendid'. She had done 'some relief work after the 1914 war among refugees in the Balkans. Work of rather an unpleasant nature too, something to do with sanitation.' Pym's agreeable description of Liversidge predated by many years the heightened awareness among academics of the legacy and great historical resource contained within the writings of women like Durham. See Hazel Holt, *A Lot to Ask: A Life of Barbara Pym* (London, 1990), p. 54; and Barbara Pym, *Some Tame Gazelle* (London, 1981), p. 13.
126. Seton-Watson to Jovan M. Jovanović, 17 Nov. 1924 in Boban *et al.* (eds), *Seton-Watson i Jugoslaveni*, 2, pp. 120–1.
127. Seton-Watson to William Miller, 17 Feb. 1925 in ibid., pp. 126–8 (127).
128. Seton-Watson to Svetozar Pribićević, 14 Jan. 1933 in ibid., pp. 262–3 (263).
129. Seton-Watson reviewing Edith Durham, *The Serajevo* [sic] *Crime* (London, 1925), *Slavonic Review*, 4 (1925), pp. 513–20 (520).

130. R.W. Seton-Watson, *Sarajevo: A Study of the Origins of the Great War* (London, 1926).
131. In Seton-Watson, 'Jugoslavia and Croatia', p. 130.
132. Seton-Watson, 'The Yugoslav Dictatorship', pp. 35, 38–9.
133. In Seton-Watson, 'Jugoslavia and Croatia', pp. 130, 131.
134. Durham Papers, Royal Anthropological Institute, London. MS51, 'Political Manuscripts including Serajevo Crime' and MS55, 'Balkan Politics'.
135. Seton-Watson to Durham, 12 Feb. 1929. Copy in Seton-Watson Papers, School of Slavonic and East European Studies (SSEES).
136. Durham to Seton-Watson, n.d. [Feb. 1929]. Seton-Watson Papers, SSEES, Correspondence, SEW 17/6/9.
137. Durham to Seton-Watson, 23 Feb. 1920. Seton-Watson Papers, SSEES.
138. Grumel-Jacquignon, *La Yougoslavie*, pp. 463–4.
139. *Le Temps*, 9 Oct. 1934.
140. Wachtel, *Making a Nation, Breaking a Nation*, pp. 47–8. Discussing the epic literature evoking Kosovo and 'Serbian historical consciousness in general', Wachtel notes that 'time tends to collapse, with the interval between events of the Battle of Kosovo and the present (whenever that may be) reduced almost to nothing'.
141. See for example *Le Temps*, 12 and 15 Oct. 1934.
142. *Je suis partout*, 13 Oct. 1934.
143. Marshal Franchet d'Esperey, 'Alexandre 1er, mon compagnon d'armes', *Revue des deux Mondes* (15 Dec. 1934), pp. 765–92 (790–1).
144. See for example 'Les Journées funèbres de Belgrade', *L'Illustration*, 27 Oct. 1934, p. 301; and 'Les Relations séculaires entre la France et la Yougoslavie', *L'Illustration*, 10 Nov. 1934, p. 354. The 27 October issue of the magazine paid tribute to Raymond Poincaré and included an image of Aleksandar meeting with the French president during the war.
145. *Le Temps* (including the summary of a report in *Le Petit Parisien*), 11 Oct. 1934.
146. See *L'Illustration*, 15 Dec.1934, p. 557.
147. 'L'Homage à la mémoire du roi Alexandre à l'Arc de Triomphe, au soir du 10 Novembre', *L'Illustration*, 17 Nov. 1934, p. 403.
148. For example *Obzor*, 22 Nov. 1934.
149. 'Le Pèlerinage des Poilus d'Orient au tombeau du Roi Alexandre', *L'Illustration*, 12 Jan. 1935, p. 34.
150. Grumel-Jacquignon, *La Yougoslavie*, pp. 487–536.
151. Ibid., pp. 470–1, 482. See also Miro Kovač, *La France, la création du royaume "yougoslave" et la question croate, 1914–1929* (Bern, 2001).
152. 'Il y a cinq ans Alexandre de Serbie violait la constitution', *L'Humanité*, 8 Jan. 1934. Reproduced in Grumel-Jacquignon, *La Yougoslavie*, p. 482.
153. Coverage summarized in *Le Temps*, 11 Oct. 1934.
154. Grumel-Jacquignon, *La Yougoslavie*, pp. 589–602.
155. 'Les Journées funèbres de Belgrade', *L'Illustration*, 27 Oct. 1934, pp. 301–2.

156. *Le Temps*, 18 Oct. 1934.
157. Charles Loiseau, 'Après la mort du Roi', *La Revue universelle*, 59 (15 Nov. 1934), pp. 401–14 (407).
158. *Le Temps*, 18 Oct. 1934.
159. Edouard E. Plantagenet, *Les Crimes d'ORIM, organisation terroriste* (Paris, [n.d.]), p. 29.
160. *Le Temps*, 11 Oct. 1934. See also *Le Temps*, 14 and 15 Oct. 1934.
161. R.W. Seton-Watson, 'King Alexander's Assassination: Its Background and Effects', address given at Chatham House, 30 Oct. 1934, reprinted from *International Affairs*, 14 (Jan–Feb. 1935), pp. 20–47 (41).
162. Ibid., p. 35.
163. Quoted in, for example Armstrong, 'After the Assassination of King Alexander', p. 225 and Seton-Watson, 'King Alexander's Assassination', p. 40.
164. 'Yugoslavia's New Regime', *Current History* (Sept. 1935), pp. 660–1 (661).
165. Edith Durham, reported in Seton-Watson, 'King Alexander's Assassination', p. 43. A number of other speakers drew attention to the obvious discontentment and discrimination suffered by those denied the right to 'national expression' in the Kingdom.
166. Sir Edward Boyle, reported in Seton-Watson, 'King Alexander's Assassination', p. 42.
167. Seton-Watson, 'King Alexander's Assassination', p. 46.
168. Lane, *Yugoslavia*, pp. 65–6.
169. *Chips: The Diaries of Sir Henry Channon*, ed. Robert Rhodes James (Harmondsworth, 1987). Channon provides fascinating insights into the formal and informal aspects of British diplomacy in Yugoslavia.
170. Wolfson, *Years of Change*, p. 200.
171. Stephen J. Lee, *The European Dictatorships 1918–1945* (London and New York, 1992), p. 281.
172. Crampton goes on to say that 'this was not entirely disadvantageous', given the instability. R.J. Crampton, *Eastern Europe in the Twentieth Century* (London and New York, 1994), pp. 139ff.
173. R.W. Seton-Watson, 'Jugoslavia and the Croat Problem', *Slavonic Review*, 16 (1937), pp. 102–12 (108).

4 'The future lies with the federative idea': War and Dissolution, 1941–1945

1. Tito was a member of the outlawed Communist Party and spent many years underground organizing disparate Yugoslav communist forces across Europe in liaison with Moscow. Born into a large family in 1892 in the Croatian village of Kumrovec, near Zagreb, Tito fought with the Austro-Hungarian forces in the First World War and was wounded and captured in 1915 on the Eastern front. He spent time in a prisoner of war camp, learnt Russian, read widely, observed some Bolshevik insurgency from close quarters in St Petersburg, married a Russian woman,

and returned to his home in 1920. Tito was a determined and diligent student of the communist revolutionary struggle and between 1928 and 1934 spent about five and a half years in prison for his political and trade union activities. He periodically lived in France and the Soviet Union where, unlike many other Yugoslav communists, he survived Stalin's purges. Tito became General Secretary of the Yugoslav Communist Party and was to be known by various pseudonyms (including Walter, Georgijević, Comrade Rudi and so forth). Even though there is some difference in opinion regarding the date when Tito was made General Secretary, most agree it was in 1937 but some say it was as late as 1940, he was effectively leading the party during that period. In the 1930s the Party spoke overtly of its battle against 'great Serbian imperialism' and it aimed to attract women and young people. Under Tito's leadership party membership grew from 1500 to about 8000 by April 1941. See for example Phyllis Auty, *Tito: A Biography* (Harmondsworth, 1974); Stevan K. Pavlowitch, *Tito: Yugoslavia's Great Dictator. A Reassessment* (London, 1992); and Neil Barnett, *Tito* (London, 2006). See also Vladimir Dedijer, *With Tito through the War: Partisan Diary 1941–1944* (London, 1951); and *Tito Speaks: His Self-Portrait and Struggle with Stalin* (London, 1953).

2. Ute Frevert, 'Europeanising Germany's Twentieth Century', *History and Memory*, 17 (2005), pp. 87–116 (107–9).

3. Stanley Payne writes that the Independent State of Croatia was responsible for proportionately the greatest number of deaths of any Balkan dictatorship or European regime 'save that of Hitler'. He adds that this did 'not stem from any purely Croatian or Yugoslav origins but was inspired by the example and patronage of the Third Reich'. See Stanley Payne, 'The NDH in Comparative Perspective', *Totalitarian Movements and Political Religions*, 7 (2006), pp. 409–16 (412). (This is a special issue devoted to the Independent State of Croatia and edited by Sabrina Petra Ramet.)

4. Davies, *Europe at War 1939–1945*, p. 15.

5. The Katyn massacres involved the shooting of approximately 14,000 Polish officers taken prisoner by the Soviets who occupied eastern Poland after the signing of the Nazi-Soviet Pact. Stalin ordered this massacre but denied any involvement in the atrocity blaming instead the Germans. In 1991 the Russian government under Boris Yeltsin admitted that Stalin was responsible for the executions.

6. In 1946 it was agreed that 1,706,000 Yugoslavs had perished in the years 1941–5. Some suggested the total was even higher and closer to 2 million. Serb propagandists claimed that the total number of Serbian victims of the NDH alone was in excess of 700,000. While some Yugoslav academics and politicians privately acknowledged that the official figure for the total number of deaths was inflated by hundreds of thousands, it was generally understood that it was to remain 'fixed', with no deviation tolerated. Croat and Serb historians and demographers eventually came to similar totals (to within a few thousand) on the statistics for wartime deaths from all causes, including the victims of racial and political persecution. It is now commonly accepted that between 1,014,000 and 1,027,000 victims comprise the total population

losses in Yugoslavia between 1941 and 1945, including 80,000 who died abroad. See Vladimir Žerjavić, *Population Losses in Yugoslavia, 1941–1945*, trans. Lidija Šimunić Mesić (Zagreb, 1997); and Bogoljub Kočović, *Žrtve Drugog Svetskog Rata u Jugoslaviji* (London, 1985). See also Ramet, *Three Yugoslavias*, pp. 160–2.

7. Richard Bessel, 'Introduction', in Richard Bessel (ed.), *Life in the Third Reich* (Oxford and New York, 1987), pp. xi–xix (xii).

8. 'The President (Roosevelt) to the King of Yugoslavia (Petar II), April 8, 1941', in S. Shepard Jones and Denys P. Myers (eds), *Documents on American Foreign Relations*, 3, July 1940–June 1941 (Boston, 1941), p. 330.

9. 'The Government of the United Kingdom to the Government of Yugoslavia, April 6 1941', in ibid., p. 330.

10. George Glasgow, 'Jugoslavia and the Balkan Campaign', *Contemporary Review* (May 1941), pp. 507–18 (510, 518).

11. Henry Baerlein, 'Italians in Yugoslav Country', *Nineteenth Century and After* (Oct. 1941), pp. 245–8 (245).

12. Membership of the government-in-exile included several ministers who had followed the king and his family first to Greece and then to London. The government formed by General Simović after the coup was made up of 22 ministers, representing most political parties, 15 of whom left the country. (Maček decided not to leave.) The London cabinet was streamlined but nonetheless remained divided and ineffectual. The young and inexperienced king did not inspire confidence among the Allies even though his godfather, George VI, tried to influence him to be more statesmanlike. Further, Petar was unable to project himself as the representative of all South Slavs, as the government's dependence on Mihailović was to demonstrate. For a sympathetic account of the London Yugoslavs see Stevan K. Pavlowitch, 'Out of Context – The Yugoslav Government in London 1941–1945', *Journal of Contemporary History*, 16 (1981), pp. 89–118 (91–3).

13. Office of Strategic Services (OSS), Research and Analysis Branch (RAB), 1563, 'The Yugoslav Partisan Movement', 26 Nov. 1943, in Paul Kesaris (ed.), *Germany and Its Occupied Territories during World War Two: Office of Strategic Services Intelligence and Research Reports* (Washington, DC, 1977). Microfilm, reel 22, 'USSR and Yugoslavia'. The OSS was established in 1942 to deal with intelligence, subversion and research.

14. OSS, RAB, 1396, 'Yugoslavia – Government-in-Exile', in ibid.

15. Bogdan Raditsa [*sic*], 'The Spirit of Kossovo', review of Louis Adamic's *My Native Land* in *The New Republic* (Nov. 1943), pp. 692–4.

16. OSS, RAB, 'Survey of Yugoslavia, General Historical Background – Political', in *Germany and Its Occupied Territories*.

17. R.H. Markham, 'Yugoslavia Yields', *The Nation* (15 Mar. 1941), pp. 289–91 (290).

18. Ibid., pp. 289, 290.

19. Nicholas Mirkovich, 'Jugoslavia's Choice', *Foreign Affairs*, 20 (1941–2), pp. 131–51 (149).

20. Ibid., p. 147.
21. See for example Djokić, *Elusive Compromise.*
22. For a general introduction to debates about the nature and definitions of fascism see Stanley Payne, *A History of Fascism 1919–1945* (London, 1995); and Roger Griffin, *International Fascism: Theories, Causes and the New Consensus* (London, 1998).
23. Pavelić, a lawyer, was a deputy and the leader of the Croatian Party of Right. Frustrated by the discrimination faced by Croats and their inferior status in the Kingdom, he came to the position that Croatian identity could not survive unless Croats had their own state. On the establishment of the dictatorship in 1929 he left the country and founded the Ustaša movement in 1931. Ustaša sympathizers also lived in exile in Hungary. After the assassination of King Aleksandar Mussolini refused to extradite members of the Ustaša to France to face trial for their involvement in the plot to kill the king. See James J. Sadkovich, 'Italian Support for Croatian Separatism: 1927–1937', PhD thesis, University of Wisconsin, Madison (1982).
24. Mar. 1935 report on the Croatian question quoted in ibid., pp. 603, 604. See also pp. 41ff, 236, 281.
25. Payne, 'The NDH in Comparative Perspective', pp. 409–16.
26. Walter Manoschek, *"Serbien ist judenfrei". Militärische Besatzungspolitik und Judenvernichtung in Serbien 1941/42* (Munich, 1993). See also Benson, *Yugoslavia*, pp. 77–9.
27. See Ivo Goldstein, 'Ante Pavelić: Charisma and National Mission in Wartime Croatia', in Antonio Costa Pinto, Roger Eatwell and Stein Ugelvik Larsen (eds), *Charisma and Fascism in Interwar Europe* (London and New York, 2007), pp. 87–96.
28. There have been different views on the ideological coherence of the NDH. Some have placed the Ustaša phenomenon within an essentialist Balkanist paradigm describing it as an irrational outburst of ultranationalist religiously-inspired violence at a time of systemic collapse and foreign invasion. Others have sought to establish the roots of the Ustaša movement in the works of (unsuspecting) Croat thinkers and writers of the nineteenth and early twentieth century in order to establish its ideological pedigree. (These positions may be understood as extreme (and crude) variants of the divisions existing between historians who focus on the immediate circumstances of the fascist and national socialist seizure of power and those who focus on the long view.) The positions I have outlined can also converge in the strand of writing, evident since the 1930s, that confers on the Ustaše an ideological consistency which draws on an apparently endemic or historical Croatian proclivity towards extreme nationalism and violence. For example, compare Rory Yeomans, 'Cults of Death and Fantasies of Annihilation: The Croatian Ustasha Movement in Power, 1941–1945', *Central Europe*, 3 (2005), pp. 121–42 and 'Militant Women, Warrior Men and Revolutionary Personae: The New Ustasha Man and Woman in the Independent State of Croatia, 1941–1945', *Slavonic and East European Review*, 83 (2005), pp. 685–732 with Hervé Laurière, *Assassins au nom de Dieu* (Paris, 1951). These works either draw largely

on speeches and propaganda materials produced by the regime with little reference to their actual reception or the selective use of documents (including some predating the regime) to explain events with which they have no established connection. See also Rory Yeomans, 'Of "Yugoslav Barbarians" and Croatian Gentlemen Scholars: Nationalist Ideology and Racial Anthropology in Interwar Yugoslavia', in Marius Turda and Paul J. Weindling (eds), *"Blood and Homeland": Eugenics and Racial Nationalism in Central and Southeast Europe, 1900–1940*, (Budapest and New York, 2007), pp. 83–122. Yeomans's chapter ends with the following question: 'Could it be that an eccentric group of nineteenth-century gentleman scholars inspired a movement of Croatian barbarians?' (p. 117). It is only recently that historians have begun (tentatively) to question the exceptionalist approach to the study of Pavelić and the NDH.

29. See Michael R. Marrus and Robert O. Paxton, *Vichy France and the Jews* (New York, 1981), pp. 249–52. See also Sabrina Petra Ramet, 'The NDH – An Introduction', *Totalitarian Movements and Political Religions*, 7 (2006), pp. 399–408 (402); and Ramet, *Three Yugoslavias*, pp. 131–3.

30. François and Renée Bédarida, 'La Persécution des Juifs', in Jean-Pierre Azéma and François Bédarida (eds), *La France des années noires*, 2 vols (Paris, 1993), 2, pp. 129–58 (158); Asher Cohen, *Persécutions et sauvetages: Juifs et Français sous l'Occupation et sous Vichy* (Paris, 1993); and Renée Poznanski, *Être juif en France pendant la Seconde Guerre Mondiale* (Paris, 1994). See also Milan Ristović, 'Yugoslav Jews fleeing the Holocaust, 1941–1945', in John K. Roth and Elisabeth Maxwell (eds), *Remembering for the Future: the Holocaust in an Age of Genocides*, 3 vols. (New York, 2001), 1, pp. 512–26; and Ivo Goldstein *et al.* (eds), *Anti-Semitism, Holocaust, Anti-Fascism*, trans. Nikolina Jovanović (Zagreb, 1997).

31. Payne, 'The NDH in Comparative Perspective', pp. 412, 414.

32. Some members supported the Ustaše, though this was not the position of the party's leadership.

33. Mira Kolar-Dimitrijević, 'Povijest gradnje spomenika kralju Tomislavu u Zagrebu 1924 do 1947 godine', *Povijesni prilozi*, 16 (1997), pp. 243–307.

34. Marko Samardžija, *Hrvatski jezik, pravopis i jezična politika u NDH* (Zagreb, 2008).

35. *Pjesmarica za pučke škole* (Zagreb,1942).

36. *Hrvatska umjetnost* (Zagreb, 1943). Yeomans ascribes fascist themes and styles to the work of some popular artists in the NDH in 'Militant Women'. See Dubravko Jelčić, 'Kulturni život u Nezavisnoj Državi Hrvatskoj', *Časopis za suvremenu povijest*, 27 (1995), pp. 521–6 for a discussion of some of these questions.

37. R.H. Markham uses the word 'Quislingovitches' in 'Yugoslavia Yields', p. 290.

38. See Jonathan E. Gumz, '*Wehrmacht* Perceptions of Mass Violence in Croatia, 1941–1942', *Historical Journal*, 44 (2001), pp. 1015–38 and 'German Counterinsurgency Policy in Independent Croatia, 1941–1944', *Historian*, 61 (1998), pp. 33–50.

39. See for example Joanna Burke, *The Second World War: A People's History* (Oxford, 2001). Burke writes that the NDH was 'particularly brutal', that the Ustaše killed 'enthusiastically', and present 'an extreme example, *even* amongst Croatian Catholics'. On top of this, she adds that the resistance in Yugoslavia was extremely complicated (p.105; emphasis added).

40. See Wingfield and Bucur (eds), *Gender and War in Twentieth-Century Eastern Europe*.

41. The Editor, 'Yugoslavia', *Nineteenth Century and After* (Jan. 1944), pp. 1–13 (4).

42. Robert Lee Wolff, 'Mihailovich: A Post-Mortem', *Atlantic Monthly* (Oct. 1946), pp. 43–9 (46). Wolff concluded that it would be wrong to eulogize Mihailović as a 'martyr in the cause of democracy' (p. 49) and was critical of the exaggerated reports in the American press about the Chetniks' successes.

43. See for example John Plamenatz, *The Case of General Mihailović* (London, 1944) for a vigorous defence of Mihailović and a critique of Allied support for Tito.

44. He also singles out the Romanian regime of Ion Antonescu. Payne, 'The NDH in Comparative Perspective', p. 413.

45. John E. Pollard, reviewing Margherita Marchione, *Pope Pius XII: Architect for Peace* (Mahwah, NJ, 2000) in *Catholic Historical Review*, 86 (2000), pp. 703–4 (704).

46. Vesna Drapac, *War and Religion: Catholics in the Churches of Occupied Paris* (Washington, DC, 1998). See especially Ch. 1, 'Interpretations'.

47. See Michael Phayer, *The Catholic Church and the Holocaust, 1930–1945* (Bloomington and Indianapolis, 2000); and *Pius XII, the Holocaust, and the Cold War* (Bloomington and Indianapolis, 2008).

48. Jure Krišto, *Sukob simbola: Politika, vjere i ideologije u Nezavisnoj Državi Hrvatskoj* (Zagreb, 2001). See also Stella Alexander, *The Triple Myth: A Life of Archbishop Alojzije Stepinac* (Boulder, 1987); and Ramet, 'The NDH – An Introduction', p. 402.

49. Briefly, the debate between intentionalists and functionalists grew out of different views on the point at which the Final Solution became 'final'. Intentionalists argued that Hitler's genocidal intent was present from the outset and prior to the seizure of power. Others, without denying the extreme anti-Semitism of the Nazi regime and its persecutions in the 1930s, and without minimizing the centrality of Hitler's anti-Semitism, believed the idea of the Final Solution evolved over time and was only possible in a state of total war. The functionalist approach also considers the impact of indoctrination over time and posits that agents of the ideology, collectively and individually, assumed responsibility for the success of the extermination programme, for example, by 'working towards the Führer' and 'anticipating' his will. The controversy between intentionalists and functionalists has become less engaging. It stimulated important discussions about various aspects of life under the Nazi dictatorship, the nature of the dictatorship and the nature of National Socialism. Michael Burleigh and Wolfgang Wippermann, for example, demonstrated the centrality of racialism and eugenics in Nazi

social policy and the consequences of this policy for a range of people, including 'Aryan' and Jewish women in *The Racial State: Germany 1933–1945* (Cambridge, 1991). See Ian Kershaw, *The Nazi Dictatorship: Problems and Perspectives in Interpretation* (London, 4th edn, 2000) for a summary of the historiographical debates surrounding the nature and evolution of the National Socialist regime.

50. Mark Biondich, 'Religion and Nation in Wartime Croatia: Reflections on the Ustaša Policy of Forced Religious Conversions, 1941–1942', *Slavonic and East European Review*, 83 (2005), pp. 71–116.

51. See for example the Catholic underground resistance papers, *Cahiers du Témoignage Chrétien*, XV–XVI, 'Les voiles se déchirent' (Lyons, Aug. 1943 and Paris, Dec. 1943), pp. 26–7; and *Courrier Français du Témoignage Chrétien*, 4 (Oct. 1943), p. 6.

52. Jozo Tomasevich, *War and Revolution in Yugoslavia, 1941–1945*, 2 vols (Stanford, 1975 and 2001), 2, p. 522.

53. Jure Krišto, 'Hrvatsko katoličanstvo i ideološko formiranje Stjepana Radića (1893–1914)', *Časopis za suvremenu povijest*, 23 (1991), pp. 129–65; and Biondich, *Stjepan Radić*, Ch. 2.

54. Catholic Action was especially promoted by Pius XI. It called for the participation of the laity in the life and work of the Church. Catholic Action generally involved specialized and highly organized groups – students, young workers, professionals, agricultural communities, men and women alike – embarking on specific tasks with the goal of spiritual renewal in their immediate locality or interest group. The aims of Catholic Action were to be strictly religious in an age of heightened statism and secularism. In Fascist Italy Catholic Action was under attack and vigorously defended in Pius XI's 1931 encyclical, *Non abbiamo bisogno*, which rejected the totalitarian claims of the fascist state.

55. The encyclicals, *Mit brennender Sorge* and *Divini Redemptoris*, were issued in March 1937.

56. This did not mean that individual Catholics were not political or that the Church was above manipulation by various groups for political ends. Some believe that the Archbishop of Sarajevo, Ivan Šarić, became a member of the Ustaše in 1934 and that the Bishop of Banja Luka, Josip Garić, may also have joined. Sabrina P. Ramet, *Nihil Obstat: Religion, Politics, and Social Change in East-Central Europe and Russia* (Durham, NC and London, 1998), p. 156.

57. Robert D. Kaplan, *Balkan Ghosts: A Journey Through History* (New York, 1993). He states that 'Nazism, for instance, can claim Balkan origins' (p. xxiii).

58. Stephen Clissold served with the Military Mission to Yugoslavia during the Second World War and later at the British Embassy in Belgrade. He went on to become a prominent commentator on Yugoslav affairs.

59. For a critique of this position see Pierre Laborie, *L'Opinion française sous Vichy* (Paris, 1990); and John Sweets, *Choices in Vichy France: The French under Nazi Occupation* (New York, 1986). See also Robert Gildea, *Marianne in Chains: In Search of the German Occupation, 1940–1945* (London, 2002); and Julian Jackson, *France: The Dark Years 1940–1944* (Oxford, 2001).

60. This was the conclusion I drew in my close study of Parisian Catholics and their associational life in the parishes during the occupation. Jacques Semelin explores the theme of 'civilian resistance' in a comparative context in his *Unarmed against Hitler: Civilian Resistance in Europe 1939–1943*, trans. Suzan Husserl-Kapit (Westport, CT and London, 1993). See also Anna Bravo, 'Armed and Unarmed: Struggles without Weapons in Europe and Italy', *Journal of Modern Italian Studies*, 10 (2005), pp. 468–84.

61. The Editor, 'Mihailovitch', *Nineteenth Century and After* (Aug. 1943) pp. 49–66 (50).

62. Klaus-Peter Friedrich, 'Collaboration in a "Land without a Quisling": Patterns of Cooperation with the Nazi German Occupation Regime in Poland during World War II', *Slavic Review*, 64 (2005), pp. 711–46; and John Connelly, 'Why the Poles Collaborated so Little – And why that is no Reason for Nationalist Hubris', *Slavic Review*, 64 (2005), pp. 771–81.

63. Mark Wheeler writes that the Yugoslavs were searching for 'tolerable alternatives' at this time in 'Pariahs to Partisans to Power: the Communist Party of Yugoslavia', in Tony Judt (ed.), *Resistance and Revolution in Mediterranean Europe 1939–1948* (London and New York, 1989), pp. 110–56 (125).

64. John Murray, 'Yugoslavia Today: Problems and Tragedies', *The Month*, 180 (1944), pp. 255–66 (264).

65. Mirkovich, 'Jugoslavia's Choice', p. 151.

66. Lewis B. Namier, reviewing Rebecca West, *Black Lamb Grey Falcon* in 'Yugoslavia', *Nineteenth Century and After* (July 1942), pp. 15–22 (21).

67. The Editor, 'Mihailovitch', p. 49.

68. From the Spanish paper *Arriba!* (1 June 1943), quoted by Murray in 'Yugoslavia Today', p. 261.

69. Zivko Topalovič [*sic*], 'Memorandum on Yugoslavia', *Nineteenth Century and After* (Sept. 1944), pp. 137–44 (139–41).

70. F. A Voigt, 'The Liberation of Yugoslavia', *Nineteenth Century and After* (Apr. 1945), pp. 145–51 (150).

71. OSS, RAB, 1396, 'Yugoslavia – Government-in-Exile', in *Germany and Its Occupied Territories*.

72. OSS, RAB, 998, 'Survey of Yugoslav Relief Agencies', 12 Aug. 1943, in ibid.

73. Quoted in Ivo Banac, 'Historiography of the Countries of Eastern Europe: Yugoslavia', *American Historical Review*, 97 (1992), pp. 1084–104 (1086).

74. Raditsa [*sic*], 'The Spirit of Kossovo', pp. 692, 693.

75. Bogdan Raditsa [*sic*], 'Tito's Partisans', *The Nation* (2 Oct. 1943), pp. 380–2 (381).

76. H. and C. Seton-Watson, *The Making of a New Europe*, p. 432.

77. C.F. Melville, 'The Yugoslav Revolt', *Fortnightly Review* (Jan. 1942), pp. 30–7 (36).

78. See Wheeler, 'Pariahs to Partisans to Power: the Communist Party of Yugoslavia'. See also Jozo Tomasevich, 'Yugoslavia during the Second World War', in Wayne S. Vucinich (ed.), *Contemporary Yugoslavia: Twenty Years of Socialist Experiment* (Berkeley and Los Angeles, 1969), pp. 59–118; and *War and Revolution in Yugoslavia, 1941–1945*, 2 vols.

79. The Editor, 'Yugoslavia', p. 3.
80. Ruth Mitchell, 'General Mihailovich: The Story of a Frame-Up', *American Mercury* (July 1943), pp. 25–34 (27, 28, 29).
81. Leon Dennen, 'The Riddle of Yugoslavia', *American Mercury* (Feb. 1944), pp. 194–202 (196, 199). Dennen was responding to Adamic's *My Native Land* (New York, 1943). See also Lorraine M. Lees, *Yugoslav Americans and National Security during World War II* (Urbana and Chicago, 2007).
82. Louis Adamic, 'The Liberation Front in Yugoslavia', *The Nation* (30 Oct. 1943), pp. 500–2 (500, 501).
83. See for example, Mitchell, 'General Mihailovich: The Story of a Frame-Up', p. 26.
84. William Miller, 'Yugoslavia' (Literary Supplement), *Contemporary Review* (Mar. 1943), pp. 191–2.
85. This is confirmed by Lees in *Yugoslav Americans*. While many criticized Fotich, some believed working through him was preferable to dealing with less experienced Yugoslavs, even if they were seemingly more representative. Lees also makes the point that the Americans were more concerned with establishing diplomatic relationships and practices that would see them through to the postwar period than influencing policy regarding the war in Yugoslavia.
86. See for example OSS, RAB, 1396, 'Yugoslavia – Government-in-Exile', in *Germany and Its Occupied Territories*. This was a common theme.
87. OSS, RAB, 1563, 'The Yugoslav Partisan Movement', Nov. 1943, in ibid.
88. Auty, *Tito*, pp. 264–5.
89. Tomasevich, *War and Revolution in Yugoslavia, 1941–1945*, 1, p. 471. Of the 1200 Yugoslavs who had fought with the Loyalists in the Spanish Civil War, about one-half died and one-quarter returned to play an important role in the Partisan leadership. See also Tomasevich, 'Yugoslavia during the Second World War', p. 84.
90. OSS, RAB, 1563, 'The Yugoslav Partisan Movement', Nov. 1943, and 'Biographical Records', in *Germany and Its Occupied Territories*.
91. OSS, RAB, 1563, 'The Yugoslav Partisan Movement', Nov. 1943, in ibid.
92. Ibid.
93. Ibid.
94. Ivo Banac, *With Stalin against Tito: Cominformist Splits in Yugoslav Communism* (Ithaca and London, 1988), pp. 83–4, 92–3.
95. See for example National Archives of Australia, A989, 'Yugoslav Patriotic Funds for Yugoslav Forces and Refugees, 1943–4'.
96. See Ivan Čižmić, *Hrvati u životu Sjedinjenih američkih država* (Zagreb, 1982); and Lees, *Yugoslav Americans*.
97. Ralph Bates, 'Mihailovich and the Partisans', *The Nation* (28 Nov. 1942), pp. 577–8 (578).
98. Wolff, 'Mihailovich: A Post-Mortem', p. 45.
99. Murray, 'Yugoslavia Today', p. 264. On this occasion Murray was quoting from a Stockholm paper.
100. Elma Dangerfield, 'The Fighting Women of Yugoslavia', *Nineteenth Century and After* (Mar. 1943), pp. 130–2 (130).

101. 'Women Fighters of Yugoslavia', *The Times*, 21 Jan. 1944, p. 3.

102. For an overview of women in the resistance see Barbara Jancar-Webster, *Women and Revolution in Yugoslavia, 1941–1945* (Denver, 1990); Barbara Jancar, 'Yugoslavia: War of Resistance', in Nancy Loring Goldman (ed.), *Female Soldiers – Combatants or Non-combatants? Historical and Contemporary Perspectives* (Westport, CT and London, 1982), pp. 85–105; and 'Women in the Yugoslav National Liberation Movement: an Overview', *Studies in Comparative Communism*, 14 (1981), pp. 143–64. See also Mary Elizabeth Reed, 'Croatian Women in the Yugoslav Partisan Resistance 1941–1945', PhD thesis, University of California Berkeley (1980).

103. See Melissa Bokovoy, 'Croatia', in Kevin Passmore (ed.), *Women, Gender and Fascism in Europe, 1919–1945* (Manchester, 2003), pp. 111–23.

104. See Yeomans, 'Militant Women, Warrior Men and Revolutionary Personae'.

105. Elsewhere I have speculated on the relationship between the history of daily life and women's resistance in a comparative context. See Vesna Drapac, 'Women, Resistance and the Politics of Daily Life in Hitler's Europe: The Case of Yugoslavia in a Comparative Perspective', *Aspasia*, 3 (2009), pp. 55–78.

106. See Wachtel, *Making a Nation, Breaking a Nation*; and Djokić, *Elusive Compromise*.

107. Charles Jelavich, 'South Slav Education: Was there Yugoslavism?', in Norman M. Naimark and Holly Case (eds), *Yugoslavia and Its Historians: Understanding the Balkan Wars of the 1990s* (Stanford, 2003), pp. 93–115.

108. See Carol S. Lilly and Melissa Bokovoy, 'Serbia, Croatia and Yugoslavia' and Carol S. Lilly, 'Serbia', in Passmore (ed.), *Women, Gender and Fascism in Europe*, pp. 91–110 (104). See also Bokovoy, 'Kosovo Maiden(s)'; and 'Scattered Graves, Ordered Cemeteries'.

109. Bokovoy, 'Croatia', pp. 111–23 (111).

110. Olga Kovačić, *Women of Yugoslavia* (Belgrade, 1947).

111. Alfred Joachim Fischer, 'Free Yugoslavia', *Contemporary Review* (Apr. 1944), pp. 234–8 (237).

112. Mitchell, 'General Mihailovich: The Story of a Frame-Up', p. 33.

113. Campbell, 'Women in Combat: the World War II Experience in the United States, Great Britain, Germany, and the Soviet Union'; and Markwick, ' "A Sacred Duty": the Red Army Women Veterans Remembering the Great Fatherland War, 1941–1945'. See also Kenneth Slepyan, *Stalin's Guerrillas: Soviet Partisans in World War II* (Lawrence, KS, 2006).

114. Nevile Henderson to *The Times*, 7 Apr. 1941, p. 5.

115. Lewis Namier, 'Yugoslavia', *Nineteenth Century and After* (July 1942), p. 17.

116. The Editor, 'Mihailovitch', p. 50.

117. Mary Van Rensselaer Thayer, 'Ruth Mitchell: American Chetnik', *American Mercury* (Jan. 1943), pp. 16–23 (20, 21).

118. Mitchell, 'General Mihailovich: The Story of a Frame-Up', pp. 27, 34.

119. *L'Illustration*, 15 Dec. 1934, p. 532.
120. Murray, 'Yugoslavia Today', p. 266.
121. *The Complete War Memoirs of Charles de Gaulle*, trans. Jonathan Griffin and Richard Howard (New York, 1998), pp. 532–3.
122. Raditsa [*sic*], 'Tito's Partisans', p. 382.
123. Robert Machray, 'The Balkans and the War', *Contemporary Review* (Aug. 1940), pp. 138–45 (138). This was written prior to the German invasion of the Soviet Union and encapsulated the general concern for the vulnerability of the region to German and Russian imperialism.
124. OSS, RAB, 'Survey of Yugoslavia, General Historical Background – Political', in *Germany and Its Occupied Territories*.
125. Namier, 'Yugoslavia', p. 21.
126. Adamic, 'The Liberation Front in Yugoslavia', p. 500.
127. Louis Adamic, 'Yugoslavia and the Big United Nations: 1941–1943', *Slavonic and East European Review*, 22 (1944), pp. 1–15 (2).
128. Bogdan Raditsa, 'Fascism in the Balkans', *The Nation* (4 Sept. 1943), pp. 267–9 (268, 269); and 'Tito's Partisans', p. 380.
129. Adamic, 'Yugoslavia and the Big United Nations: 1941–1943', p. 8.
130. Churchill's broadcast, 13 Apr. 1941, in Murray, 'Yugoslavia Today, p. 259.
131. Fischer, 'Free Yugoslavia', p. 236.
132. Adamic, 'The Liberation Front in Yugoslavia', pp. 500, 501.
133. Bogdan Raditsa, 'Russia in the Balkans', *The Nation* (15 Apr. 1944), pp. 440–2 (440).
134. Davies, *Europe at War 1939–1945*, p. 194.
135. OSS, RAB, 1396, 'Yugoslavia – Government-in-Exile', in *Germany and Its Occupied Territories*.
136. Adamic, 'Yugoslavia and the Big United Nations: 1941–1943', p. 15.

5 'A society almost free': Tito's Yugoslavia

1. Thomas F. Magner, 'Yugoslavia and Tito: The Long Farewell', *Current History* (Apr. 1978), pp. 154–8, 182 (154).
2. See Chapter 3, n.95.
3. Stoyan Pribichevich, 'Yugoslavia in the Balkans and Central Europe', Address given at Chatham House on 17 May 1945, *International Affairs*, 21 (1945), pp. 448–58 (448–9).
4. Ibid., p. 451.
5. Joseph Frankel, 'Federalism in Yugoslavia', *American Political Science Review*, 49 (1955), pp. 416–30 (430).
6. Frank Gervasi, 'Tito's Revolution is Unique', *The New Republic* (12 Dec. 1949), pp. 12–15 (14).
7. G.E.R. Gedye, 'Tito Versus Stalin', *Contemporary Review* (Jan. 1950), pp. 1–5 (1).
8. Pribichevich, 'Yugoslavia in the Balkans and Central Europe', p. 454.
9. Gervasi, 'Tito's Revolution is Unique', p. 15.
10. Ibid., p. 12.

11. George Bilainkin, 'Marshal Tito', *Contemporary Review* (Sept. 1948), pp. 147–50 (150). Bilainkin wrote a book about his travels in Yugoslavia after the war and a biography of Tito in 1949.
12. George Bilainkin, 'Impressions of Yugoslavia', *Contemporary Review* (Feb. 1946), pp. 76–80 (79). See also Alex N. Dragnich, 'Yugoslavia's New Constitution', *Current History* (May 1946), pp. 420–3 (423).
13. Gervasi, 'Tito's Revolution is Unique', p. 15.
14. Constantin Fotitch, 'Tito and the Western Democracies', *Journal of Central European Affairs*, 11 (1952), pp. 353–71 (354).
15. Ibid., p. 369.
16. See for example F.W.D. Deakin, *The Embattled Mountain* (New York, 1971); Fitzroy Maclean, *Eastern Approaches* (London, 1949); and *Disputed Barricade: The Life and Times of Josip Broz-Tito, Marshal of Jugoslavia* (London, 1957).
17. Brigadier F.H.R. Maclean MP, 'Tito and Mihailović', *The Times*, 11 June 1946, p. 5.
18. Armstrong, 'After the Assassination of King Alexander', p. 209.
19. H. and C. Seton-Watson, *The Making of a New Europe*, pp. 428ff.
20. See Lees, *Yugoslav Americans*.
21. Anton Logoreci, 'Albania and Yugoslavia', *Contemporary Review* (June 1950), pp. 360–4 (360).
22. J. Frankel, 'Communism and the National Question in Yugoslavia', *Journal of Central European Affairs*, 15 (1954), pp. 49–65 (64).
23. Dr Juraj Krnjević, 'Peasant Movements in Eastern Europe', *Contemporary Review* (Aug. 1948), pp. 111–14 (112).
24. Melissa K. Bokovoy, *Peasants and Communists: Politics and Ideology in the Yugoslav Countryside, 1941–1953* (Pittsburgh, 1998).
25. 'Elections in Yugoslavia', *The Times*, 9 Nov. 1945, p. 4.
26. 'Yugoslavia at the Polls', *The Times*, 12 Nov. 1945, p. 4.
27. K. Zilliacus, 'Yugoslavia and the West', *Contemporary Review* (July 1950), pp. 6–11 (11).
28. Dr Vladimir Velebit, 'Yugoslavia on her way towards a Socialist Democracy', address delivered at Chatham House, 26 Nov. 1953, *International Affairs*, 30 (1954), pp. 156–65 (156, 158–9).
29. Bilainkin, 'Marshal Tito', p. 150.
30. Josef Korbel, 'Titoism: An Evaluation', *Journal of Central European Affairs*, 11 (1951), pp. 1–9 (6).
31. This is the subtitle of Jan Yindrich's *Tito v. Stalin* (London, 1950).
32. Korbel, 'Titoism: An Evaluation', pp. 6–7.
33. Quoted in ibid., p. 6.
34. Quoted in Gedye, 'Tito Versus Stalin', p. 2.
35. Ibid., p. 5.
36. Harrison, 'Cross and Crescent', p. 727.
37. Banac, *With Stalin*, pp. 135ff.
38. Ibid., pp. 254–7.
39. Ibid., pp. 219ff.
40. Ibid., pp. 183–4. See pp. 196–9 for information on Macedonian responses and fears of Serbian supremacy. It was alleged that Hebrang had committed suicide on Goli Otok.

41. See Lampe, *Yugoslavia as History*, pp. 248–9; and Ramet, *Three Yugoslavias*, pp. 178–9.
42. See for example *When Father Was Away on Business* (1985) and *Underground* (1995).
43. Milovan Djilas, 'Yugoslav–Soviet Relations', address delivered at Chatham House, 30 Jan. 1951, *International Affairs*, 27 (1951), pp. 167–75 (172).
44. Frank Gervasi, 'The Defense of the Tito Regime', *The New Republic* (19 Dec. 1949), pp. 15–16.
45. Ruth Fischer, 'Tito and Trotsky', *Nineteenth Century and After* (Mar. 1950), pp. 158–73 (166, 168).
46. Djilas, 'Yugoslav–Soviet Relations', pp. 167–8, 174–5.
47. Adam Ulam, 'Tito, Titoism', in C.D. Kernig (ed.), *Marxism, Communism and Western Society. A Comparative Encyclopedia*, 8 (New York, 1973), pp.181–8; Banac, *With Stalin*, p. 129.
48. By 1948 there were 8000 Greek communist refugees in Yugoslavia. Banac, *With Stalin*, p. 35.
49. Robert Byrnes, 'Heresy in Yugoslavia', *Current History* (July 1957), pp. 16–21 (19).
50. Ulam, 'Tito, Titoism'.
51. Velebit, 'Yugoslavia on Her Way towards a Socialist Democracy', pp. 162, 163, 165.
52. Neal had studied in America and Europe. He was a correspondent for the *Wall Street Journal* and went on to teach at the Universities of California, Los Angeles and Colorado. He wrote a number of books, including one on Tito's break with Stalin (which was published in 1958) and another on Yugoslavia's 'new communism' in 1962.
53. Fred Warner Neal, 'The Communist Party of Yugoslavia', *American Political Science Review*, 51 (1957), pp. 88–111 (90).
54. Edvard Kardelj, 'Evolution in Yugoslavia', *Foreign Affairs*, 34 (1956), pp. 580–602 (593).
55. 'On Workers' Management in Economic Enterprises, Belgrade, 26 June 1950, Report to the National Assembly', in Henry M. Christman (ed.), *The Essential Tito* (New York, 1970), p. 84.
56. Barbara Castle, 'Yugoslavia after Djilas', *New Statesman*, 54 (10 Aug. 1957), pp. 165–6 (166).
57. Neal, 'The Communist Party of Yugoslavia', p. 91.
58. Ibid., pp. 100, 102.
59. Quoted in Frankel, 'Communism and the National Question in Yugoslavia', p. 55.
60. Ibid., pp. 54, 60.
61. Frankel, 'Federalism in Yugoslavia', pp. 423, 424, 430.
62. Frankel, 'Communism and the National Question in Yugoslavia', p. 64; emphasis added.
63. Ibid., p. 65.
64. Ibid., p. 60.
65. Kardelj was Minister for Foreign Affairs (1948–53), Vice-President of the Federal Executive Council after 1963, president of the *Skupština* (1963–7), and a member of the Presidency of the Socialist Federated

Republic of Yugoslavia at the time of his death. Kidrić was prime minister of Slovenia (1945–6) and had an important role in economic planning at the federal level.

66. Fred Warner Neal, 'Titoism in Flux', *Current History* (May 1963), pp. 294–8, 309–10 (295).

67. Banac, *With Stalin*, pp. 175–6.

68. Johanna Granville, 'Hungary, 1956: The Yugoslav Connection', *Europe–Asia Studies*, 50 (1998), pp. 493–517.

69. See Lorraine Lees, *Keeping Tito Afloat: The United States, Yugoslavia and the Cold War* (University Park PA, 1997) for a discussion of the United States' perception of and hopes for 'national communisms'.

70. See Bokovoy, *Peasants and Communists*.

71. According to an article about the release from prison of dissident academic Mihajlo Mihajlov in *Index on Censorship*, 7 (1978), p. 56, 'Yugoslavia: Ready to Return', the state officially admitted to there being 500 political prisoners. Mihajlov suggested that there were at least twice as many. (On his release from prison in 1978 Mihajlov left for the United States, where he worked for 20 years.) The subject of the number of political prisoners is one few historians address directly and, if they do, it is in a truncated fashion or with regard to specific flashpoints such as the split with the Soviet Union. There are writers who argue that political repression did not exist under Yugoslav communism and that it is a myth promulgated by post-communist nationalists. See for example Ugrešić, *The Culture of Lies*. Ugrešić's book is a classic exposition of the (internal) Balkanist perspective.

72. Thomas Taylor Hammond, 'The Djilas Affair and Jugoslav Communism', *Foreign Affairs*, 33 (1955), pp. 298–315.

73. See Chapter 2, n.5 for information on Dedijer.

74. Neal, 'The Communist Party of Yugoslavia', pp. 108–10.

75. 'Too Orthodox', *The Times*, 12 Jan. 1954, p. 7.

76. 'Interest not Interference', *The Times*, 26 Jan. 1955, p. 9.

77. Neal, 'The Communist Party of Yugoslavia', pp. 105ff.

78. Milovan Djilas, *The New Class* (New York, 1957), p. 69.

79. Ibid., pp. 140–1.

80. There were some who thought Djilas did not go far enough in his critique and that he was self-interested. Others were sceptical because Djilas did not acknowledge the part he himself had played in the violent implantation of communist rule. See for example Slobodan M. Draskovich, 'The Case of Milovan Djilas', *Modern Age: A Conservative Review*, 2 (1958), pp. 152–63.

81. Castle, 'Yugoslavia after Djilas', p. 166.

82. Hammond, 'The Djilas Affair and Jugoslav Communism', p. 309.

83. Jill Irvine outlines this and other interpretations in 'Introduction: State-Society relations in Yugoslavia, 1945–1992', in Bokovoy, Irvine and Lilly (eds), *State–Society Relations in Yugoslavia*, pp. 1–24.

84. See for example Roland Sarti, 'Modernisation in Italy: Traditional or Revolutionary?', *American Historical Review*, 75 (1970), pp. 1029–45. See also A. James Gregor, 'Fascism and Modernisation: Some Addenda', *World Politics*, 26 (1974), pp. 370–84; and *Italian Fascism*

and Developmental Dictatorship (Princeton, 1979). The broader question of the relationship between fascism, national socialism and modernity and/or modernization still generates debate, as Roger Griffin's *Modernism and Fascism: The Sense of a Beginning under Mussolini and Hitler* (Basingstoke, 2007) attests.

85. See for example Perry Willson, 'Italy', in Passmore (ed.), *Women, Gender and Fascism in Europe*, pp. 11–32; and Victoria De Grazia, *How Fascism Ruled Women: Italy 1933–1945* (Berkeley, 1992).
86. Anthony Sylvester, 'Intellectual Ferment in Yugoslavia', *Survey*, 62 (1967), pp. 121–8 and 'Revisionists and Stalinists in the Balkans', *A Monthly Review of East European Affairs*, 16 (1967), pp. 2–8. The '*Life* World Library' survey of the Balkans first published in 1963 contains a chapter on Yugoslavia entitled 'A Society Almost Free'. See Edmund Stillman *et al.*, *The Balkans* (Nederland, NV, 1966).
87. Alvin Z. Rubinstein, 'Yugoslavia's Opening Society', *Current History* (Mar. 1965), pp. 149–53, 179 (153). Rubinstein was a Professor of Political Science at the University of Pennsylvania and the author of a number of books, including works on Soviet and Yugoslav foreign policy. He was also one of *Current History*'s contributing editors.
88. Ramet, *Three Yugoslavias*, pp. 294–5.
89. The Archbishopric of Ohrid, founded in 1958, was under the jurisdiction of the Serbian Orthodox Church until 1967, when the Macedonian Church was established.
90. Lees, *Keeping Tito Afloat*. Lees discusses in detail the evolution of United States policy towards Yugoslavia after 1945.
91. Fotitch, 'Tito and the Western Democracies', p. 364.
92. Fred Warner Neal, 'Titoist Theory and Titoist Practice', *Journal of International Affairs*, 15 (1961), pp. 115–24 (124).
93. Lane, *Yugoslavia*, p. 127
94. Benson, *Yugoslavia*, p. 114.
95. Lane, *Yugoslavia*, pp. 139–40.
96. Ibid., p. 146.
97. 'Address to the Jubilee Session of the Anti-Fascist Council of the National Liberation of Yugoslavia – the Twenty-Fifth Anniversary of the New Yugoslavia, Jajce 30 November 1968', in Christman (ed.), *The Essential Tito*, pp. 184, 186–7.
98. See for example Ljubo Sirc, *The Yugoslav Economy under Self-Management* (London and Basingstoke, 1979). Sirc was a Slovenian Partisan and academic. He was arrested for anti-government activities and escaped to Italy in 1955, after which he made his way to the United Kingdom. Sirc became a lecturer in economics at the Universities of St Andrews and Glasgow.
99. Dennis Reinhartz reviewing Gerson Sher, *Praxis: Marxist Criticism and Dissent in Socialist Yugoslavia* (1977) in *Slavic Review*, 38 (1979), p. 524.
100. Mihailo Marković, 'The Praxis Group' (1975), in Gale Stokes (ed.), *From Stalinism to Pluralism: A Documentary History of Eastern Europe since 1945* (New York and Oxford, 1996), pp. 116–21 (116).
101. Ulam, 'Tito, Titoism'.

102. Abraham Rothberg, 'Yugoslavia: After the Partisan Generation', *Yale Review*, 53 (1963–4), pp. 221–32.
103. Magner, 'Yugoslavia and Tito: The Long Farewell', p.157.
104. Ibid., pp. 155–6.
105. See Lane, *Yugoslavia*, pp. 137–9.
106. Granville, 'Hungary, 1956: The Yugoslav Connection'; and Barnett, *Tito*, p. 106.
107. See for example, Ljubo Sirc, 'A New Look at Tito's "Non-Alignment"', *Journal of Social and Political Studies*, 3 (1979), pp. 173–80.
108. Miroslav Krleža quoted in Branko Lenski, 'Yugoslav Literature and Politics', *Survey*, 18 (1972), pp. 158–71, 164.
109. See Lane, *Yugoslavia*, pp. 139–42.
110. Alvin Z. Rubinstein, 'Whither Yugoslavia?', *Current History* (May, 1973), pp. 202–6, 228 (204)
111. See Ramet, *Three Yugoslavias*, pp. 307–11.
112. Ulam, 'Tito, Titoism', p. 187.
113. Cynthia W. Frey, 'Yugoslav Nationalisms and the Doctrine of Limited Sovereignty', *Eastern European Quarterly*, 10 (1976), pp. 427–57 (435, 439).
114. Ramet, *Three Yugoslavias*, p. 307.
115. Mihajlo Mihajlov, 'Yugoslavia – the Approaching Storm', *Dissent*, 21 (1974), pp. 370–2.
116. While party membership among the officer corps was traditionally strong these figures marked 'an all-time high'. Lenard J. Cohen, 'Partisans, Professionals, and Proletarians: Elite Change in Yugoslavia', *Canadian Slavonic Papers*, 21 (1979), pp. 446–78 (467).
117. Sirc, 'A New Look at Tito's "Non-Alignment"', p. 177; and Cohen, 'Partisans, Professionals, and Proletarians: Elite Change in Yugoslavia', p. 463.
118. Sirc, 'A New Look at Tito's "Non-Alignment"', pp. 176–7.
119. Milovan Djilas, *Tito: The Story from Inside*, trans. Vasilije Kojić and Richard Hayes (London, 1981), p. 72. Djilas wrote that the most important consideration for Tito was the preservation of personal power.
120. Joseph Benedict (Ben) Chifley was prime minister of Australia between 1945 and 1949. The annual Chifley Memorial Lecture honoured his memory.
121. He was referring to the activities of the anti-communist and anti-Yugoslav Australians of Croatian and Serbian background. The former, in particular, were compared unfavourably with 'Yugoslav' Croats. See Vesna Drapac, 'Perceptions of Post-WWII Croatian Immigrants: The South Australian Case', *Croatian Studies Review*, 3–4 (2005), pp. 27–39.
122. Rubinstein, 'Whither Yugoslavia?', p. 203.
123. See Michael Balfour, *Withstanding Hitler in Germany 1933–45* (London and New York, 1988), pp. 62–3 for a discussion of 'hibernation' as a form of withstanding the inroads of the ruling ideology under a dictatorship or totalitarian regime.

Conclusion

1. Ther, drawing on the work of Mary Fulbrook in 'Beyond the Nation', p. 73.
2. Josip Županov, 'Fascism and anti-Fascism in the Light of a Bipolar Value Orientation', in Goldstein *et al.* (eds), *Anti-Semitism, Holocaust, Anti-Fascism*, pp. 200–11 (210).
3. Ibid., p. 204.
4. Stanislaw Skrzypek, 'The Political, Cultural, and Social Views of Yugoslav Youth', *Public Opinion Quarterly*, 29 (1965), pp. 87–106.
5. Carl Gustave Ströhm, 'Tito, After 30 Years', *Encounter*, 51 (1978), pp. 75–7 (76).
6. Dean A. Frease, 'A Politicisation Paradigm: the Case of Yugoslavia', *Sociological Quarterly*, 16 (1975), pp. 33–47 (46).
7. Fitzroy Maclean, *Josip Broz Tito: A Pictorial Biography* (London, 1980), p. 121.
8. For a summary of this argument see Martin Blinkhorn, *Mussolini and Fascist Italy* (London and New York, 2006), pp. 35–8, 50–5. For a slightly different emphasis see Emilio Gentile, 'Fascism in Power: the Totalitarian Experiment', in Adrian Lyttelton (ed.), *Liberal and Fascist Italy 1900–1945* (Oxford, 2002), pp. 139–74.
9. Rubinstein, 'Whither Yugoslavia?', pp. 205–6, 228.
10. See for example Paul Mojzes, 'The Role of Religious Communities in the Development of Civil Society in Yugoslavia, 1945–1992', in Bokovoy, Irvine and Lilly (eds), *State–Society Relations in Yugoslavia, 1945–1992*, pp. 211–31.
11. One of the popular theories at the time of the Yugoslav Wars of Succession was that 'ethno-religious' conflict destroyed the country. For a discussion of these themes see V.P. Gagnon, Jr, *The Myth of Ethnic War: Serbia and Croatia in the 1990s* (Ithaca and London, 2006); Vjekoslav Perica, *Balkan Idols: Religion and Nationalism in the Yugoslav States* (Oxford, 2002); and Michael A. Sells, *The Bridge Betrayed: Religion and Genocide in Bosnia* (Berkeley and Los Angeles, 1996).
12. Wachtel, *Making a Nation, Breaking a Nation*, pp. 200ff.
13. Krippner, 'The Work of British Medical Women in Serbia', p. 78.
14. See R.G.D. Laffan, *The Serbs: The Guardians of the Gate* (New York, 1989); and Robert Lafan [*sic*], *Čuvari kapije: predavanja o istoriji Srba*, intro. Dušan T. Bataković (Belgrade, 1994).
15. Željan Šuster (ed.), *Historical Dictionary of the Federal Republic of Yugoslavia* (Lanham and London, 1999), p. 257.
16. See for example Dragović-Soso, *"Saviours of the Nation"*; and Nick Miller, 'Postwar Serbian Nationalism and the Limits of Invention', *Contemporary European History*, 13 (2004), pp. 151–69.
17. Reneo Lukic and Allen Lynch, *Europe from the Balkans to the Urals: the Disintegration of Yugoslavia and the Soviet Union* (Oxford, 1996), pp. 187ff.
18. Ivo Goldstein, *Croatia*, trans. Nikolina Jovanović (London, 1999), pp. 200–1. See also Lukic and Lynch, *Europe from the Balkans to the Urals*, pp. 191–2.

19. See 'Commonwealth War Dead in Serbia and Montenegro' and 'Commonwealth War Dead in Croatia', on the Commonwealth War Graves Commission website (www.cwgc.org/).

20. Frankel, 'Communism and the National Question in Yugoslavia', p. 59.

21. Clerke, 'Albania and Scanderbeg', p. 354.

22. See Thomas G. Weiss, 'Collective Spinelessness: U.N. Actions in the Former Yugoslavia' and Stanley Hoffmann, 'Yugoslavia: Implications for Europe and European Institutions', in Richard H. Ullman (ed.), *The World and Yugoslavia's Wars* (New York, 1996), pp. 59–96, 97–121 (116).

23. Susan L. Woodward, *Balkan Tragedy: Chaos and Dissolution after the Cold War* (Washington, DC, 1995).

24. Others noted that prior to its attacks on Slovenia, Croatia and Bosnia-Herzegovina the Yugoslav Army 'disposed of some of the most formidable stockpiles of weapons in Europe'. These had been amassed 'in the event of a Warsaw Pact invasion of Yugoslavia and were of a size and character appropriate to such a mission, with large numbers of tanks, and other armoured vehicles, heavy artillery and combat aircraft'. Before the arms embargo came into force the army 'had purchased an extra 14,000 tons of weaponry from the Middle East'. So well supplied was the army that Serbia was exporting weapons to countries like Somalia 'to pay for hard currency imports like oil'. Various authors quoted in Lukic and Lynch, *Europe from the Balkans to the Urals*, p. 298.

25. Norman Naimark, *Fires of Hatred: Ethnic Cleansing in Twentieth Century Europe* (Cambridge, MA, 2001), p. 163.

26. Ibid., pp. 163–5.

27. I have discussed this in greater detail elsewhere. See Vesna Drapac, 'The End of Yugoslavia', *Contemporary European History*, 10 (2001), pp. 317–31.

28. Weiss, 'Collective Spinelessness'.

29. Richard H. Ullman, 'The Wars in Yugoslavia and the International System after the Cold War', in Richard H. Ullman (ed.), *The World and Yugoslavia's Wars*, pp. 9–41 (31).

30. Weiss, 'Collective Spinelessness', p. 70.

31. Lukic and Lynch, *Europe from the Balkans to the Urals*, p. 402.

32. Viktor Meier, *Yugoslavia: A History of its Demise*, trans. Sabrina Ramet (London and New York, 1999), p. xiii.

33. Brendan Simms, *Unfinest Hour: Britain and the Destruction of Bosnia* (London, 2002).

34. Anna Funder, *Stasiland* (Melbourne, 2002).

35. See Mary Nolan, 'Work, Gender and Everyday Life: Reflections on Continuity, Normality and Agency in Twentieth-Century Germany', in Ian Kershaw and Moshe Lewin (eds), *Stalinism and Nazism: Dictatorships in Comparison* (Cambridge, 1997), pp. 311–42.

36. Mark Mazower, *Dark Continent: Europe's Twentieth Century* (London, 1999), pp. 367–8.

Bibliography

Archives and Collections of Documents

I have consulted a selection of R.W. Seton-Watson's papers held in the School of Slavonic and East European Studies at the University of London and the papers of (Mary) Edith Durham held by the Royal Anthropological Institute. The documents in Ljubo Boban *et al.* (eds), *R.W. Seton-Watson i Jugoslaveni: Korespondencija 1906–1941*, 2 vols (Zagreb and London, 1976) give an indication of the range of Seton-Watson's activities on the Yugoslav question. *La Serbie et L'Europe (1914–1918). Exposé de la Politique Serbe par des Publicistes Serbes* (Geneva, 1919) reproduces a selection of wartime articles from the Swiss-based *La Serbie* and provides insights into the perspective of post-war publicists on the South Slav question in the period 1914–18. *Britanci o Kraljevini Jugoslaviji: godišnji izveštaj Britanskog poslanstva u Beogradu 1921–1938*, 2 vols, ed. Živko Avramovski (Zagreb, 1986) contains reports from the British embassy in Belgrade and is a useful source for the interwar period. Aspects of the American perception of the Yugoslav question during the Second World War may be gleaned from the microfilm collection, *Germany and Its Occupied Territories during World War Two. Office of Strategic Services Intelligence and Research Reports*, ed. Paul Kesaris (Washington, DC, 1977). Microfilm, reel 22, 'USSR and Yugoslavia'.

Magazines and Newspapers

The American Mercury
The Atlantic Monthly
Blackwood's Magazine
The Contemporary Review
Cornhill Magazine
Current History
Danubian Review

The Edinburgh Review
Foreign Affairs
The Fortnightly Review
Fraser's Magazine
L'Humanité
L'Illustration
Je suis partout
MacMillan's Magazine
The Month
The Nation
The New Europe
The New Republic
The New Statesman
The Nineteenth Century [*and After*]
La Revue de Paris
Revue des deux Mondes
Spremnost
Le Temps
The Times

Books and Pamphlets

I have only listed a selection of the books and pamphlets consulted. It is worth noting that many of the general texts and monographs mentioned below contain comprehensive bibliographies for specific topics as well as for the entire period under review. The full reference to all articles cited may be found in the endnotes.

Adam, Magda, *The Versailles System and Central Europe* (Aldershot, 2004).

Alexander, Stella, *The Triple Myth: A Life of Archbishop Alojzije Stepinac* (Boulder, 1987).

Allcock, John B., *Explaining Yugoslavia* (London, 2000).

Allcock, John B., and Antonia Young (eds), *Black Lambs and Grey Falcons: Women Travellers in the Balkans* (Bradford, 1991).

Almond, Mark, *Europe's Backyard War: The War in the Balkans* (London, 1994).

Anderson, Dorothy, *Miss Irby and Her Friends* (London, 1966).

———, *The Balkan Volunteers* (London, 1968).

Anzulovic, Branimir, *Heavenly Serbia: From Myth to Genocide* (London, 1999).

Auty, Phyllis, *Tito: A Biography*, revised edition (Harmondsworth, Middlesex and Baltimore, 1974).

Banac, Ivo, *The National Question in Yugoslavia: Origins, History, Politics* (Ithaca and London, 1984).

———, *With Stalin Against Tito: Cominformist Splits in Yugoslav Communism* (Ithaca and London, 1988).

Barnett, Neil, *Tito* (London, 2006).

Benson, Leslie, *Yugoslavia: A Concise History*, revised and updated edition (Basingstoke and New York, 2004).

Biondich, Mark, *Stjepan Radić, the Croat Peasant Party, and the Politics of Mass Mobilization, 1904–1928* (Toronto, 2000).

Birkett, Dea, *Spinsters Abroad: Victorian Lady Explorers* (London, 1991).

Bjelić, Dušan I. and Savić, Obrad, *Balkan as Metaphor: Between Globalization and Fragmentation* (Cambridge, MA and London, 2002).

Blitz, Brad K. (ed.), *War and Change in the Balkans: Nationalism, Conflict and Cooperation* (Cambridge, 2006).

Blom, Ida, Hagemann, Karen and Hall, Catherine (eds), *Gendered Nations: Nationalisms and Gender Order in the Long Nineteenth Century* (Oxford and New York, 2000).

Bokovoy, Melissa K., *Peasants and Communists: Politics and Ideology in the Yugoslav Countryside, 1941–1953* (Pittsburgh, 1998).

——, Irvine, Jill A. and Lilly, Carol S. (eds), *State–Society Relations in Yugoslavia, 1945–1992* (New York, 1997).

Bucur, Maria and Wingfield, Nancy, M. (eds), *Staging the Past: the Politics of Commemoration in Habsburg Central Europe, 1848 to the Present* (West Lafayette, IN, 2001).

Burke, Joanna, *The Second World War: A People's History* (Oxford, 2001).

Chirol, Sir Valentine, *Serbia and the Serbs* (Oxford Pamphlets 1914, No. 13,).

Christman, Henry M. (ed.), *The Essential Tito* (New York, 1970).

Čižmić, Ivan, *Hrvati u životu Sjedinjenih američkih država* (Zagreb, 1982).

Cohen, Deborah and O'Connor, Maura (eds), *Comparison and History: Europe in Cross-National Perspective* (New York and London, 2004).

Cornwall, Mark (ed.), *The Last Years of Austria-Hungary: Essays in Political and Military History 1908–1918* (Exeter, 1990).

Crampton, R.J., *Eastern Europe in the Twentieth Century* (London and New York, 1994).

Crnobrnja, Mihailo, *The Yugoslav Drama* (London and New York, 2004).

Davies, Norman, *Europe: A History* (London, 1997).

——, *Europe East and West* (London, 2006).

——, *Europe at War 1939–1945: No Simple Victory* (Basingstoke and Oxford, 2007).

Dedijer, Vladimir, Božić, Ivan, Ćirković, Sima and Ekmečić, Milorad (eds), *History of Yugoslavia*, trans. Kordija Kveder (New York, 1974).

de Windt, Harry, *Through Savage Europe* (London and Glasgow, 1907).

Djilas, Milovan, *The New Class* (New York, 1957).

Djokić, Dejan, *Elusive Compromise: A History of Interwar Yugoslavia* (London, 2007).

—— (ed.), *Yugoslavism: Histories of a Failed Idea 1918–1992* (London, 2003).

Dragnich, Alex N., *Serbia, Nikola Pašić, and Yugoslavia* (New Brunswick, NJ, 1974).

Dragović-Soso, Jasna, *"Saviours of the Nation": Serbia's Intellectual Opposition and the Revival of Nationalism* (London, 2002).

Drakulić, Slavenka, *Café Europa: Life after Communism* (London, 1997).

Dunn, Seamus and Fraser, T.G. (eds), *Europe and Ethnicity: World War I and Contemporary Ethnic Conflict* (London and New York, 1996).

Durham, (Mary) Edith, *The Burden of the Balkans* (London, 1905).

——, *Twenty Years of the Balkan Tangle* (London, 1920).

Durham, (Mary) Edith, *The Serajevo* [sic] *Crime* (London, 1925).

Evans, Arthur J. *Through Bosnia and the Herzegovina on Foot during the Insurrection* (London, 1876).

——, *Illyrian Letters addressed to the 'Manchester Guardian' during the year 1877* (London, 1878).

Fehér, Ferenc and Arato, Andrew (eds), *Crisis and Reform in Eastern Europe* (New Brunswick, NJ, 1991).

Fischer, Bernd J. (ed.), *Balkan Strongmen: Dictators and Authoritarian Rulers of Southeast Europe* (London, 2007).

Forbes, Nevill, *The Southern Slavs* (Oxford Pamphlets 1914–15, No. 13).

Freeman, E.A., *Sketches from the Subject and Neighbour Lands of Venice* (London, 1881).

——, *Historical Essays* (London and New York, 1892).

Funder, Anna, *Stasiland* (Melbourne, 2002).

Fussell, Paul, *The Great War and Modern Memory* (London, Oxford and New York 1977 [1975]).

Gagnon, V.P., Jr, *The Myth of Ethnic War: Serbia and Croatia in the 1990s* (Ithaca and London, 2004).

Garde, Paul, *Le Discours balkanique: des mots et des hommes* (Paris, 2004).

Gauvain, Auguste, *La Question yougoslave* (Paris, 1918).

Gladstone, W.E., *Bulgarian Horrors and the Question of the East* (New York and Montreal, 1876).

Goldman, Nancy Loring (ed.), *Female Soldiers – Combatants or Non-combatants? Historical and Contemporary Perspectives* (Westport and London, 1982).

Goldstein, Ivo, *Croatia: A History*, trans. Nikolina Jovanović (London, 1999).

Goldstein, Ivo, *et al.* (eds), *Anti-Semitism, Holocaust, Anti-Fascism*, trans. Nikolina Jovanović (Zagreb, 1997).

Goldsworthy, Vesna, *Inventing Ruritania: The Imperialism of the Imagination* (New Haven and London, 1988).

Grumel-Jacquignon, François, *La Yougoslavie dans la stratégie française de l'Entre-deux-Guerres (1918–1935): Aux origines du mythe serbe en France* (Bern, 1999).

Hanak, Harry, *Great Britain and Austria-Hungary during the First World War: A Study in the Formation of Public Opinion* (London, 1962).

Henderson, Nevile, *Failure of a Mission: Berlin 1937–1939* (London, 1940).

——, *Water under the Bridges* (London, 1945).

Hinkovitch, H[inko], *Les Croates sous le Joug Magyar* (Paris, 1915).

Hoptner, J.B., *Yugoslavia in Crisis 1934–1941* (New York and London, 1962).

Hutchinson, J.W. and Lydekker, Gregory, R., *The Living Races of Mankind: A Popular Illustrated Account of the Customs, Habits, Pursuits, Feasts and Ceremonies of the Races of Mankind Throughout the World*, 2 vols (London, n.d. [1902]).

Hutton, I. Emslie, *With a Woman's Unit in Serbia, Salonika and Sebastopol* (London, 1928).

Jackson, Julian, *France: The Dark Years 1940–1944* (Oxford, 2001).

Jancar-Webster, Barbara, *Women and Revolution in Yugoslavia, 1941–1945* (Denver, 1990).

Jelavich, Barbara, *History of the Balkans*, 2 vols (Cambridge, 1983).

Jezernik, Božidar, *Wild Europe: The Balkans in the Gaze of Western Travellers* (London, 2004).

Joll, James, *The Origins of the First World War* (London and New York, 1992).

Judah, Tim, *The Serbs: History, Myth and the Destruction of Yugoslavia*, 2nd edn (New Haven and London, 2000).

Judt, Tony (ed.), *Resistance and Revolution in Mediterranean Europe 1939–1948* (London and New York, 1989).

Kann, Robert A., Kiraly, Bela K. and Fichtner, Paula S. (eds), *The Habsburg Empire in World War I: Essays on the Intellectual, Military, Political and Economic Aspects of the Habsburg War Effort* (New York, 1977).

Kaplan, Robert D., *Balkan Ghosts: A Journey Through History* (New York, 1993).

Khagram, Sanjeev and Levitt, Peggy (eds), *The Transnational Studies Reader: Intersections and Innovations* (New York and Abingdon, Oxon, 2008).

Koch, H.W. (ed.), *The Origins of the First World War: Great Power Rivalry and German War Aims*, 2nd edn (Basingstoke, 1984).

Kovač, Miro, *La France, la création du royaume "yougoslave" et la question croate, 1914–1929* (Bern, 2001).

Kovačić, Olga, *Women of Yugoslavia* (Belgrade, 1947).

Laffan, R.G.D., *The Guardians of the Gate: Historical Lectures on the Serbs* (Oxford, 1918).

Lampe, John R., *Yugoslavia as History: Twice There Was a Country* (Cambridge and New York, 1996).

Lane, Ann, *Yugoslavia: When Ideals Collide* (Basingstoke and New York, 2004).

Laurière, Hervé, *Assassins au nom de Dieu* (Paris, 1951).

Lees, Lorraine M., *Keeping Tito Afloat: The United States, Yugoslavia, and the Cold War* (University Park, Pennsylvania, 1997).

——, *Yugoslav Americans and National Security during World War II* (Urbana and Chicago, 2007).

Levene, Mark and Roberts, Penny (eds), *The Massacre in History* (New York and Oxford, 1999).

Lukic, Reneo and Lynch, Allen, *Europe from the Balkans to the Urals: The Disintegration of Yugoslavia and the Soviet Union* (Frösunda and Oxford, 1996).

Mackenzie, G[eorgina] M[uir] and Irby, A[deline] P[aulina], *Notes on the Slavonic Countries in Austria and Turkey in Europe*, ed. with a preface by Humphry Sandwith (Edinburgh and London, 1865).

——, *The Turks, the Greeks and the Slavons: Travels in the Slavonic Provinces of Turkey-in-Europe* (London, 1867).

Maclean, Fitzroy, *Eastern Approaches* (London, 1949).

Magaš, Branka, *The Destruction of Yugoslavia: Tracing the Break-Up 1980–92* (London and New York, 1993).

Malcolm, Noel, *Bosnia: A Short History* (London and Basingstoke, 1994).

Manoschek, Walter, *"Serbien ist judenfrei": Militärische Besatzungspolitik und Judenvernichtung in Serbien 1941/42* (Munich, 1993).

Marrus, Michael R. and Paxton, Robert O., *Vichy France and the Jews* (New York, 1981).

Mazower, Mark, *Dark Continent: Europe's Twentieth Century* (London, 1998).

——, *The Balkans* (London, 2000).

Meier, Viktor, *Yugoslavia: A History of its Demise*, trans. Sabrina P. Ramet (London and New York, 1999).

Mosse, George L., *Fallen Soldiers: Reshaping the Memory of the World Wars* (New York and Oxford, 1990).

Müller, Jan-Werner (ed.), *Memory and Power in Post-War Europe: Studies in the Presence of the Past* (Cambridge, 2002).

Naimark, Norman, *Fires of Hatred: Ethnic Cleansing in Twentieth-Century Europe* (Cambridge, MA and London, 2001).

Naimark, Norman and Case, Holly (eds), *Yugoslavia and Its Historians: Understanding the Balkan Wars of the 1990s* (Stanford, 2003).

O'Connor, Maura, *The Romance of Italy and the English Political Imagination* (New York, 1998).

Okey, Robin, *Eastern Europe 1740–1985: Feudalism to Communism*, 2nd edn (Minneapolis, 1986).

Padelford, Norman J., *Peace in the Balkans: The Movement Towards International Organization in the Balkans* (New York, 1935).

Passmore, Kevin, *Women, Gender and Fascism in Europe, 1919–1945* (Manchester, 2003).

Pateman, Carole, *Participation and Democratic Theory* (Cambridge, 1970).

Paton, A.A., *Highlands and Islands of the Adriatic*, 2 vols (London, 1849).

——, *Researches on the Danube and the Adriatic: or Contributions to the Modern History of Hungary and Transylvania, Dalmatia and Croatia, Servia and Bulgaria*, 2 vols (London, 1862 [1861]).

Pavlowitch, Stevan K., *Yugoslavia* (London, 1971).

——, *The Improbable Survivor: Yugoslavia and its Problems, 1918–1988* (Columbus, 1988).

——, *Tito. Yugoslavia's Great Dictator: A Reassessment* (London, 1992).

——, *Hitler's New Disorder: The Second World War in Yugoslavia* (London, 2008).

Pemble, John, *The Mediterranean Passion: Victorians and Edwardians in the South* (Oxford and New York, 1988).

Perica, Vjekoslav, *Balkan Idols: Religion and Nationalism in the Yugoslav States* (Oxford, 2002).

Phayer, Michael, *The Catholic Church and the Holocaust, 1930–1945* (Bloomington and Indianapolis, 2000).

——, *Pius XII, the Holocaust, and the Cold War* (Bloomington and Indianapolis, 2008).

Plamenatz, John, *The Case of General Mihailović* (London, 1944).

Plantagenet, Edouard E., *Les Crimes d'ORIM, organisation terroriste* (Paris, [n.d.]).

Ramet, Sabrina P., *Nationalism and Federalism in Yugoslavia, 1962–1991*, 2nd edn (Bloomington and Indianapolis, 1992).

——, *Balkan Babel: The Disintegration of Yugoslavia from the Death of Tito to Ethnic War*, 2nd edn (Boulder, 1996).

——, *Nihil Obstat: Religion, Politics, and Social Change in East-Central Europe and Russia* (Durham and London, 1998).

——, *Thinking about Yugoslavia: Scholarly Debates about the Yugoslav Breakup and the Wars in Bosnia and Kosovo* (Cambridge and New York, 2005).

——, *The Three Yugoslavias: State-Building and Legitimation, 1918–2005* (Washington, DC, Bloomington and Indianapolis, 2006).

Robbins, Keith, *The First World War* (Oxford, 1985).

Robinson, Jane, *Wayward Women: A Guide to Women Travellers* (Oxford and New York, 1991).

Ross, Isobel, *Little Grey Partridge: the Diary of Isobel Ross, Serbia 1916–1917*, ed. and intro. Jess Dixon (Aberdeen, 1988).

Sells, Michael A., *The Bridge Betrayed: Religion and Genocide in Bosnia* (Berkeley and Los Angeles, 1996).

Semelin, Jacques, *Unarmed against Hitler: Civilian Resistance in Europe 1939–1943*, trans. Suzan Husserl-Kapit (Westport CT and London, 1993).

Seton-Watson, Hugh and Christopher, *The Making of a New Europe: R.W. Seton-Watson and the Last Years of Austria-Hungary* (London, 1981).

Seton-Watson, R.W., *The Southern Slav Question and the Habsburg Monarchy* (London, 1911).

——, *Absolutism in Croatia* (London, 1912).

——, *Serbia, Yesterday, Today, and Tomorrow: A School Address* (London, n.d. [1916]).

——, *The Historian as a Political Force in Central Europe* (London, 1922).

——, *Sarajevo: A Study in the Origins of the Great War* (London, 1926).

——, *A Plea for the Study of Contemporary History*, Creighton Lecture, 1928, reprinted from *History*, 14 (1929).

Seton-Watson, R.W., Wilson, J. Dover, Zimmern, Alfred E. and Greenwood, Arthur, *The War and Democracy* (London, 1914).

Silber, Laura and Little, Allan, *Yugoslavia: Death of a Nation*, revised and updated edition (London, 1997).

Simms, Brendan, *Unfinest Hour: Britain and the Destruction of Bosnia* (London, 2001).

Sirc, Ljubo, *The Yugoslav Economy under Self-Management* (London and Basingstoke, 1979).

Stokes, Gale (ed.), *From Stalinism to Pluralism: A Documentary History of Eastern Europe since 1945* (New York and Oxford, 1996).

Tanner, Marcus, *Croatia: A Nation Forged in War* (New Haven and London, 1997).

Taylor, A J.P., *The Trouble Makers: Dissent over Foreign Policy 1792–1939* (London, 1957).

Todorova, Maria, *Imagining the Balkans* (New York and Oxford, 1997).

Tomasevich, Jozo, *War and Revolution in Yugoslavia, 1941–1945*, 2 vols (Stanford, 1975 and 2001).

Turda, Marius and Weindling, Paul J. (eds), *"Blood and Homeland": Eugenics and Racial Nationalism in Central and Southeast Europe, 1900–1940* (Budapest and New York, 2007).

Ugrešić, Dubravka, *The Culture of Lies: Antipolitical Essays*, trans. Celia Hawkesworth (London, 1996).

Ullman, Richard H. (ed.), *The World and Yugoslavia's Wars* (New York, 1996).

Urquhart, F.F., *The Eastern Question*, Oxford Pamphlets No. 15 (London, 1914).

West, Rebecca, *Black Lamb and Grey Falcon: A Journey through Yugoslavia* (London, 1982 [1941]).

Wheelwright, Julie, *Amazons and Military Maids: Women who Dressed as Men in the Pursuit of Life, Liberty and Happiness* (London, 1989).

Wilkinson, Gardner, *Dalmatia and Montenegro with a Journey to Mostar in Herzegovina* (London, 1848).

Williamson, Samuel R., Jr, *Austria-Hungary and the Origins of the First World War* (Basingstoke and London, 1991).

Wilson, Keith (ed.), *Forging the Collective Memory: Government and International Historians through Two World Wars* (Providence and Oxford, 1996).

Wingfield, Nancy M. and Bucur, Maria (eds), *Gender and War in Twentieth-Century Eastern Europe* (Bloomington and Indianapolis, 2006).

Winter, J.M., *Sites of Memory, Sites of Mourning: The Great War in European Cultural History* (Cambridge, 1995).

Wolff, Larry, *Inventing Eastern Europe: The Map of Civilization on the Mind of the Enlightenment* (Stanford, 1994).

Woodward, Susan L., *Balkan Tragedy: Chaos and Dissolution after the Cold War* (Washington, DC, 1995).

Žerjavić, Vladimir, *Population Losses in Yugoslavia, 1941–1945*, trans. Lidija Šimunić Mesić (Zagreb, 1997).

Theses

Nielsen, Christian Axboe, 'One State, One Nation, One King: The Dictatorship of King Aleksandar and his Yugoslav Project, 1929–1935' (PhD, Columbia University, 2002).

Reed, Mary Elizabeth, 'Croatian Women in the Yugoslav Partisan Resistance 1941–1945' (PhD, University of California Berkeley, 1980).

Sadkovich, James J., 'Italian Support for Croatian Separatism: 1927–1937' (PhD, University of Wisconsin, Madison, 1982).

Index